# THE LIFE AND TIMES
## OF
# SAINT BERNARD

# THE LIFE AND TIMES
## of
# SAINT BERNARD

FR. THÉODORE RATISBONNE

First published in French as *Histoire de Saint Bernard* in 1841.
Translated into English in 1889.
Republished December 8, 2016, Feast of the Immaculate Conception.

Special thanks to J.O.

Paperback ISBN: 978-1-945275-08-1
Hardback ISBN: 978-1-945275-07-4

# Contents

PREFACE TO THE AMERICAN EDITION . . . . . . . i

PREFACE . . . . . . . . . . . . . . . . . . . . . . . . vi

## FIRST PERIOD
### DOMESTIC LIFE OF ST. BERNARD, FROM HIS BIRTH TILL HIS ENTRANCE INTO THE ORDER OF CITEAUX. (1091-1113)

**CHAPTER I**
BIRTH OF ST. BERNARD—FIRST YEARS OF HIS CHILDHOOD—DETAILS REGARDING HIS FAMILY. . . . . . . . . . . . . 3

**CHAPTER II**
EDUCATION OF ST. BERNARD—DOMESTIC MANNERS OF THE MIDDLE AGE. . . . . . . . . . . . . . . . . . . . 8

**CHAPTER III**
BERNARD FINISHES HIS STUDIES AND RETURNS TO FONTAINES- DEATH OF HIS MOTHER—TEMPTATIONS AND CONVERSION. . . . . . . . . . . . . . . . . . . . . . . 13

**CHAPTER IV**
CONVERSION OF ST. BERNARD AND SEVERAL OF HIS FRIENDS. . . . . . . . . . . . . . . . . . . . . . . . . 21

**CHAPTER V**
COMMUNITY LIFE AT CHATILLON—FAREWELL TO THE PATERNAL HOME—CONVERSION OF NIVARD. . . . . . . . 29

# SECOND PERIOD

MONASTIC LIFE OF ST. BERNARD, FROM HIS ENTRANCE INTO THE ORDER OF CITEAUX, TO HIS POLITICAL LIFE, CONNECTED WITH THE SCHISM OF ROME. (1113-1130)

## CHAPTER VI
ORIGIN OF THE ORDER OF CITEAUX—REVELATION CONCERNING ITS FUTURE DESTINY—ARRIVAL OF ST. BERNARD AT THE MONASTERY. . . . . . . . . . . . . 39

## CHAPTER VII
NOVITIATE OF ST. BERNARD—HIS PROFESSION—ENLARGEMENT OF CITEAUX—FOUNDATION OF CLAIRVAUX. . . . 47

## CHAPTER VIII
DEVELOPMENT OF CLAIRVAUX—ILLNESS OF ST. BERNARD—NARRATIVE OF WILLIAM OF ST. THIERRY. . . . . . . . 57

## CHAPTER IX
HISTORY OF ROBERT—LETTER OF ST. BERNARD—FIRST MONASTERY OF THE FILIATION OF CLAIRVAUX—GENERAL CHAPTER OF THE ORDER OF CITEAUX. . . . . . . . . . 66

## CHAPTER X
ANOTHER ILLNESS OF ST. BERNARD—VISION—FRUITS OF HIS RETIREMENT. . . . . . . . . . . . . . . . . . . . . 74

## CHAPTER XI
LABORS OF ST. BERNARD—HIS RELATIONS WITH THE CARTHUSIANS—JOURNEY TO GRENOBLE AND PARIS. . . 82

## CHAPTER XII
SERVICES RENDERED BY CONVENTS—CONVERSION OF HOMBELINE—DEATH OF GAULDRY. . . . . . . . . . . . 87

## CHAPTER XIII
REMARKABLE CONVERSIONS—SUGER, ABBOT OF ST. DENIS —HENRY ARCHBISHOP OF SENS—STEPHEN, BISHOP OF PARIS—DISPUTES OF THE LAST WITH KING LOUIS LE GROS. 92

## CHAPTER XIV
CONTINUATION OF THE FORMER—CONVERSION OF THE DUCHESS OF LORRAINE, OF BEATRICE, OF ERMENGARDE, COUNTESS OF BRETAGNE—THE VIRGIN SOPHIA—PRINCE HENRY OF FRANCE—AMADEUS, PRINCE OF GERMANY... 99

# THIRD PERIOD
## POLITICAL LIFE OF ST. BERNARD.

## CHAPTER XV
WILLIAM DE ST. THIERRY RELATES WHAT PASSED DURING HIS STAY AT CLAIRVAUX—ST. BERNARD'S TREATISE UPON "GRACE AND FREE WILL"—THE SAINT IS CALLED TO THE COUNCIL OF TROYES...................... 111

## CHAPTER XVI
INSTITUTION OF THE TEMPLARS—RETURN OF ST. BERNARD TO CLAIRVAUX—HUMILIATIONS WHICH HE EXPERIENCES— HIS LABORS AND DAILY PREACHING........... 118

## CHAPTER XVII
STATE OF PUBLIC AFFAIRS IN THE TWELFTH CENTURY, (1130-1140) ........................ 128

## CHAPTER XVIII
CONTINUATION OF THE SCHISM AT ROME—ST. BERNARD CAUSES INNOCENT II TO BE RECOGNIZED BY THE PRINCIPAL CHRISTIAN POWERS—THE ANTIPOPE, ANACLETUS, FOUNDS THE KINGDOM OF SICILY..... 138

## CHAPTER XIX
ASSASSINATION OF A MONK—ST. BERNARD PURSUES THE AUTHORS OF THE MURDER—HE RECEIVES A VISIT FROM POPE INNOCENT II AT CLAIRVAUX—HISTORY OF DUKE WILLIAM—COUNCIL OF RHEIMS. . . . . . . . . . . . . 147

## CHAPTER XX
THE EXPEDITION OF LOTHARIUS TO ITALY—ST. BERNARD RESTORES PEACE TO THE ITALIAN REPUBLICS, AND RECONCILES THE FAMILY OF THE HOHENSTAUFFEN WITH LOTHARIUS—COUNCIL OF PISA.. . . . . . . . . . . . . . 158

## CHAPTER XXI
LABORS OF ST. BERNARD IN MILAN—MIRACLES —EFFUSIONS
OF HIS SOUL. . . . . . . . . . . . . . . . . . . . . . 170

## CHAPTER XXII
CONTINUATION OF THE ABODE OF BERNARD IN LOMBARDY—FRESH MIRACLES—DEATH OF ST. STEPHEN, THE FOUNDER OF THE ORDER OF CITEAUX—DEATH OF ST. NORBERT. . . . . . . . . . . . . . . . . . . . . . . 179

## FOURTH PERIOD
SCIENTIFIC LIFE OF ST. BERNARD, FROM HIS DISPUTES WITH THE HERETICS TO THE PREACHING OF THE SECOND CRUSADE. (1140-1145)

## CHAPTER XXIII
RETURN TO CLAIRVAUX—ST. BERNARD'S SPIRIT OF PROPHECY—HE OPPOSES THE ABUSE OF APPEALS—HE EXCITES LOTHARIUS TO A NEW EXPEDITION AGAINST THE SCHISMATICS—HE IS RECALLED TO ITALY.. . . . . . 193

## CHAPTER XXIV
STATE OF AFFAIRS IN HALT—ST. BERNARD AT ROME —CONFERENCE OF SALERNO—END OF THE SCHISM . . 202

## CHAPTER XXV
RETURN FROM ROME TO CLAIRVAUX—FOUNDATION OF
NEW MONASTERIES—DEATH OF ST. BERNARD'S
BROTHER, GERARD—FUNERAL ORATION. . . . . . . . . 210

## CHAPTER XXVI
HAPPY CONSEQUENCES OF THE EXTINCTION OF THE
SCHISM—REPONDERANCE OF THE PAPACY IN ITALY,
GERMANY, AND FRANCE—DISPUTES OF LOUIS VII WITH
THE COUNT OF CHAMPAGNE—MEDIATION OF
ST. BERNARD—VISIT OF ST. MALACHI . . . . . . . . . . 218

## CHAPTER XXVII
PRELIMINARY CONSIDERATIONS—INTELLECTUAL
MOVEMENT OF THE MIDDLE AGE . . . . . . . . . . . . 227

## CHAPTER XXVIII
PETER ABELARD—VIEW OF HIS DOCTRINES, HIS LIFE,
AND MISFORTUNES . . . . . . . . . . . . . . . . . . . 235

# FIFTH PERIOD
### APOSTOLIC LIFE OF ST. BERNARD, FROM THE PREACHING OF THE CRUSADE UNTIL HIS DEATH.
### (1145-1158)

## CHAPTER XXIX
CONTINUATION OF THE PRECEDING CHAPTER—CONTEST
OF ST. BERNARD WITH ABELARD—COUNCIL OF SENS—
CONVERSION AND EDIFYING DEATH OF ABELARD . . . 243

## CHAPTER XXX
APPLICATION OF THE DOCTRINES OF RATIONALISM TO
POLITICS—ARNOLD OF BRESCIA—REVOLUTION AT ROME 251

## CHAPTER XXXI
NEW ANXIETIES OF ST. BERNARD ON ACCOUNT OF
THE ELECTION OF EUGENIUS III—BOOK OF THE
CONSIDERATION . . . . . . . . . . . . . . . . . . . . . 259

## CHAPTER XXXII
CONTINUATION OF THE PRECEDING—GENERAL IDEA OF THE PHILOSOPHY AND MYSTICAL THEOLOGY OF ST. BERNARD . . . . . . . . . . . . . . . . . . . . 269

## CHAPTER XXXIII
A GLANCE AT THE HERESIES OF ST. BERNARD'S TIME . 278

## CHAPTER XXXIV
IDEA OF THE CRUSADES—STATE OF CHRISTIANITY IN THE EAST . . . . . . . . . . . . . . . . . . . . . . . 286

## CHAPTER XXXV
ST. BERNARD IS COMMISSIONED TO PREACH THE CRUSADE—DIFFICULTIES OF THIS MISSION—ASSEMBLY AT VEZELAY. . . . . . . . . . . . . . . . . . . . . 296

## CHAPTER XXXVI
PERSECUTION OF THE JEWS IN GERMANY AT THE TIME OF THE CRUSADE—ST. BERNARD UNDERTAKES THEIR DEFENCE—HIS LETTER TO THE PEOPLE OF GERMANY . . 305

## CHAPTER XXXVII
ST. BERNARD GOES TO GERMANY—HIS INTERVIEW WITH THE EMPEROR, CONRAD III—EXTRAORDINARY MANIFESTATION OF HIS GIFT OF MIRACLES . . . . . . . 315

## CHAPTER XXXVIII
CONTINUATION OF HIS JOURNEY AND HIS MIRACLES— RETURN TO CLAIRVAUX. . . . . . . . . . . . . . . 328

## CHAPTER XXXIX
ASSEMBLY AT ETAMPES—ARRIVAL OF POPE EUGENIUS III IN FRANCE—DEPARTURE OF THE CRUSADERS FOR THE HOLY LAND . . . . . . . . . . . . . . . . . . . . 337

## CHAPTER XL
ST. BERNARD COMBATS THE HERETICS IN LANGUDEOC— HE RECEIVES TWO ILLUSTRIOUS VISITORS AT CLAIRVAUX —THEIR HISTORY—COUNCIL OF RHEIMS . . . . . . . . . 346

## CHAPTER XLI
COUNCIL OF TREVES—EXAMINATION OF THE REVELATIONS OF ST. HILDEGARDE—HISTORY OF THIS PROPHETESS—HER RELATIONS WITH ST. BERNARD—GLANCE AT HER WRITINGS. . . . . . . . . . . . . . . . 356

## CHAPTER XLII
CONTINUATION OF PRECEDING CHAPTER . . . . . . . . 365

## CHAPTER XLIII
VISIT OF POPE EUGENIUS III TO CLAIRVAUX—CHAPTER OF CITEAUX—GREAT CELEBRITY OF ST. BERNARD. . . . 373

## CHAPTER XLIV
DISASTERS OF THE CRUSADE—SORROWS OF ST. BERNARD . . . . . . . . . . . . . . . . . . . . . 380

## CHAPTER XLV
APOLOGY OF ST. BERNARD. . . . . . . . . . . . . . . . 388

## CHAPTER XLVI
DEATH OF THE MOST ILLUSTRIOUS CONTEMPORARIES OF ST. BERNARD—HIS LAST ILLNESS—HIS LAST MIRACLE 397

## CHAPTER XLVII
DEATH OF ST. BERNARD . . . . . . . . . . . . . . . . 405

About the Author . . . . . . . . . . . . . . . . . . . 411

Works of St. Bernard. . . . . . . . . . . . . . . . . 413

# PREFACE TO THE AMERICAN EDITION

It is the remark of a modern historian, that, if we would judge our ancestors with impartiality, we ought not to measure their actions by our ideas and customs, but we should endeavor to bring ourselves back to the age in which they lived, and thus make ourselves acquainted with their institutions, their governments, and their principles of legislation. It has been the custom of too many writers in modern times, in describing what they are pleased to call the dark ages, to invert this order, and, having formed their own idea of institutions, and also of what civilization consists in, they condemn all that is not in accordance with it, never questioning the correctness of their own views, or considering that the state of civilization which they so highly prize, was produced from the chaos which the destruction of the Roman Empire caused in Europe, by the influence of the Church, and by the holy examples and pious teaching of those men whom they have been accustomed to consider as the patrons of ignorance, and as the persons who produced what they have been pleased to call the dark ages. One can scarcely take up any history or modern work treating on these times, but he will find its pages laden with the most absurd charges respecting the ignorance of the ecclesiastics and monks of those days, which, having passed current for centuries, are now looked upon as true, and some of which are so absurd in themselves, that they carry with them their own refutation.

The barbarians, who, issuing from their fastnesses from time to time, laid waste the fair lands of the south, and divided between them the Roman Empire, were altogether strangers to the arts and sciences, and knew no other occupation but the chase or war. The right of the strong to oppress the weak was the only law which they obeyed; conquest was their great and only object of glory. They professed a sovereign contempt for the arts of civilized life, and were not capable of estimating the blessings which a settled polity is calculated to confer. Though the Christian religion, which they embraced, softened by degrees the ferocity of their disposition and the wildness of their habits, it was not until after many centuries that its results were seen; for it was slow and insensible in its progress. And though professing the faith of Christ, they at first preserved their ancient manners, and it was not until generation succeeded generation, that they laid aside their love for war and hunting, and the hatred which they evinced towards those arts and sciences which tend to enlighten the nature of man, and make him cultivate those habits of peace in which alone they flourish. Centuries elapsed before they altogether laid aside that spirit of insubordination and independency which seemed inseparable from their character.

Such was the state of society in Europe in the middle ages. Though the manners and habits of life of the hordes which came forth age after age from their northern hive, tended to efface all the traces of civilization which the declining days of the Roman Empire had shed faintly on the horizon, still, amidst the darkness and mists of ignorance which enveloped society, the faith burnt brightly and shed its hallowed influence around the Church, which was the city set upon the hill, the beacon which gave to all a ray of hope, and excited in their bosoms a profound respect for her doctrines and her ministers; the seductive voice of heresy and its false teachers were not listened to, and infidelity and impiety, with their false prophets, whose teachings tend to sap the foundations of social order and domestic happiness, had not yet raised their hydra heads; for in those ages, which modern civilization calls "dark," God, His Church, and His ministers were everywhere respected. If, in times of disorder, the hand of the warrior was raised against them as well as against others, it arose from the effects of individual passion, and not from contempt for the Church, or for its divine formulas. All seemed impressed with the blessings which the Church, from the riches of her treasury, poured around with a lavish hand. In her monasteries and her schools was centred all the learning of those times. Those precious manuscripts of days gone by were carefully preserved, and copied by diligent transcribers, with a fidelity and a degree of beauty, both of style and illustrations, which modem times may seek to imitate, but which it cannot excel. These holy men, dividing their time between prayer and manual labor and literary employment, pre served society from the ignorance and barbarity which otherwise would have pervaded it. Their holy lives and self-denying labors were bright and shining examples, which all felt bound to reverence, if they were not prepared to follow it. There the monarch came to spend the evening of his days, and though laden with this world's honors and triumphs, he was ready to renounce them all, in order that, by holy living, and in one continual round of never-ending praise, he might be fitted to meet his God; there, too, came the mother, with her little babe, to lay him on the altar, and thus, from his earliest years, dedicate him to the service of God, that thus preserved from the cares and toils of life, and from the tide of corruption which swelled around, he might become a vessel of sanctification and honor, which God had in an especial manner made His own.

Each age seemed to have its wants supplied by the establishment of new religious orders, or by new families of the orders already established, enforcing the discipline and the pious observances of their founders, which length of time had either caused to be forgotten or not to be observed with all the rigor and strictness of their earlier days. Such was the establishment of the monastery of Anianer, in France, in the ninth century; of the foundation of the orders of Cluny, in France, and the Camaldolese, in Italy, in the tenth century; of the order of Chartreux, in the eleventh; of the foundations of the monasteries of Citeaux and Clairvaux, in the twelfth century; and of the establishment of the orders of St. Dominic and St. Francis, in the thirteenth century. Each of these establishments produced a fresh constellation of learned and holy men, whose influence was felt in all parts of society, and maintained, in the midst of ignorance and disorder, the ancient tradition of morals and piety. It was from one of these celebrated houses that the holy man, whose life and times are now for the first time brought before the American public, came forth to perform a distinguished part of the theatre of public affairs in the age in which he lived, and to exercise an influence on ages yet to come, through the holiness and piety which breathes through every line of his writings, and through that tender devotion to the mother of God which so eminently characterized our Saint. It was, indeed, a striking spectacle to behold a holy man come forth from the quietude of his cloister to preach a holy war, which proved, in the results, so beneficial to the common interests of Christianity in Europe as the Crusades have been. No one has stated the happy influence which they produced on the prospects of the Church, and religion in general, in so forcible and eloquent terms, as the Abbé Cambacères, in his panegyric on S. Louis, preached in 1168:

"To transport across the seas rebellious and factious vassals, and thereby render the state calm; to turn against barbarians the fury of untamed lions, who devoured their country, and thereby give peace to the people; to engage their arms against a distant enemy, so that they might not turn them against their king, and thus overturn the throne by these strange wars; to put an end to intestine divisions, was the policy of the Crusades. To combat a ferocious people, who hold as an article of faith the extermination of Christianity, and had caused ravages in Spain, in Portugal, and Germany, and had already commenced them in France; who drew their swords to extinguish Christianity, and might have nearly succeeded in their efforts, if religious had not united the Christian princes of Europe against these rapid conquerors, and by the Crusades delivered Asia and imparted confidence to Europe, proclaims the justice of the Crusades. Let us, then, lay aside our prejudices for a moment, and imagine these holy wars to have been successful, as they might have been, how great would have been the result! Asia would no longer be a prey to barbarians, for the rule of the Gospel would have formed a code to govern its nations and its kingdoms, where now the law of an impostor has established a code of morality which shocks humanity. Europe, Asia, and Africa would have been one great people, the sea would have been free from pirates, commerce would meet with no obstacles, the Christian name would be without enemies, and millions of unfortunate beings, our brethren and fellow countrymen, would not for so many centuries have groaned under the chains of infidels. In thus beholding the world freed from tyranny of the infidel and the Saracen, we would no longer say, 'What folly in these Crusades;' we would rather say, 'What a pity these Crusades have not been revived again.'"

To St. Bernard the family of Ratisbonne owe much. One has written his life; another, through using a prayer composed by him, was converted to Christianity in consequence of the blessed Virgin appearing to him in the Church of St. Andrea delle Fratte, at Rome. It is, indeed, an holy prayer. Let us but make use of it daily, and we shall soon experience its hallowed effects.

"Remember, O most Holy Virgin Mary, that it has never been heard of through all ages, that a sinner had fled to thy protection, had implored thy help, or sought thy intercession, and was unaided by thee. Encouraged by this confidence, I fly unto thee, O Virgin of virgins! O my Mother, I come to thee, sinful and sorrowful! before thee I wait, O Mother of the Lord incarnate! despise not my words, but heed them with mercy, and answer them!"

# PREFACE

The "Life of St. Bernard," by the Abbé Ratisbonne, has already taken its place in the ecclesiastical literature of France. Among its least excellences will be found the strain of pure and natural eloquence in which the narrative is told.

St. Bernard was so eminently the saint of his age, that it would be impossible to write his life without surrounding it with an extensive history of the period in which he lived, and over which he may be truly said to have ruled. The Abbé Ratisbonne has, with this view, very ably and judiciously interwoven with the personal narrative and description of the saint the chief contemporaneous events and characters of the time.

There is, perhaps, in the annals of the Church no more remarkable instance of the power of an individual over the men of his age than in St. Bernard. A solitary religious, in the state of poverty, without office, or rank, or worldly control, or even the ecclesiastical dignities which command the obedience of others, he acquired and wielded a sway over, not his own brethren of the cloister alone, but over people of every character, rank, and state—over the priesthood, over the episcopate, over princes, kingdoms, nations, and pontiffs. The means and appliances for this vast and sustained superiority of the individual over his age were all contained within the four walls of his cell; or, more truly, within the one great heart, inflamed with the love of God; the solitary intelligence, illuminated by the light of faith; and the single will, energetic in itself, and made inflexible by union with the Divine. There seems to have been in this one mind an inexhaustible abundance, variety, and versatility of gifts. Without ever ceasing to be the holy and mortified religious, St. Bernard appears to be the ruling will of his time. He stands forth as pastor, preacher, mystical writer, controversialist, reformer, pacificator, mediator, arbiter, diplomatist, and statesman. He appears in the schools, at the altar, in the preacher's chair, in councils of the Church, in councils of the State, amid the factions of cities, the negotiations of princes, and the contests of antipopes. And whence came this wondrous power of dealing with affairs and with men? Not from the training and schooling of this world, but from the instincts, simplicity, and penetration of a mind profoundly immersed in God, and from a will of which the fervor and singleness of aim were supernatural.

His hand was laid, not upon the mechanism of society, but upon the motive powers which originate and sustain its action. We can hardly conceive St. Bernard invested with the ordinary routine of any official functions, how high so ever they might be; they would have changed the whole idea of his life, and the whole balance and harmony of his character. It is wholesome and timely, in an age like this, when the development of individual character is retarded and kept down by the mechanical forms and movement of modern systems, to lay open and to exhibit what are the true sources of beneficent and controlling power. They are not to be found in the customs and contrivances of social or public institutions, but in the individual, strengthened and elevated by intellectual, and above all, by spiritual culture, through the supernatural grace of the Holy Ghost, the guide and teacher of the Church. Individuals are powerful for good in proportion as they are penetrated and governed by the mind of the mystical body, the one true Church of God, Catholic and Roman, which, from age to age, throughout the world, teaches, judges, and rules in the name and by the presence of Jesus Christ.

The servants of God, in surrendering their individual will and intelligence to the Divine guidance, become, as individuals, perfect and powerful for good. In dying to themselves, they are raised again to another and vaster sphere of life. Out of the one Church, where individuals jealously retain and strive to unfold their personal gifts and influence, they descend in the scale of power; and their greatest works die with them, or survive but a little while, without succession or reproduction. A supernatural principle is necessary to their perfection and their perpetuity, which is to be found alone in the unity of the Church and the mysteries of the altar.

Another reason, also, makes the publication of St. Bernard's life very opportune at this moment.

He stands, with other great and saintly names— such as St. Anselm, St. Francis, St. Bonaventura, St. Peter Damian, and, in these latter days, St. Alphonsus —as a witness to the great spiritual law, that the love of the Virgin Mother of God is not a sentiment or poetry in religion, which may or may not be encouraged by individuals at their will; but that love and veneration, second only to that we pay to her Divine Son, is due to her, by a law which springs from the very substance of the faith.

It is impossible to realize the Incarnation as we ought, and not to love and venerate the Mother of God; it is impossible to love the Son without loving the Mother. In proportion to our love to the Son will be our love to the Mother who bore Him; in so far as we are conformed to the likeness of the Son, we shall love the Mother, who, next to the Eternal Persons, the Father and the Holy Ghost, is the dearest object of the love of the Eternal Son. The love of the Mother of God is the overflow of the love we bear to her Divine Son; it descends from Him to her; and we may measure our love to Him by our love to her. It is impossible to be cold, distant, dry, or reserved towards the Mother of our Redeemer, and to be fervent in our love to Him. Such as we are to Him, such, in due measure, we shall be to her.

Now, of all the writers of the first thousand years of the Church, none is more full of fervent, tender, and adoring love to our Divine Lord, Jesus Christ, than St. Bernard, and none is more conspicuous for ardent love and veneration for the Mother of God. The same burning heart, kindled from heaven, in him is seen beating with love to God in the mystery of the Three Divine Persons—to the Incarnate Word— to her who, though infinitely below her Son, as the creature is below the uncreated, is, yet, immensely above all creatures, human or heavenly, inasmuch as she is the Mother of God.

Again, the name of St. Bernard has been so often invoked by the opponents of the doctrine of the Immaculate Conception, lately defined and declared by the voice of the Church, that it will not be amiss to state what the doctrine of the saint on this point really was.

In the epistle to the canons of the church in Lyons, so often quoted*—or, rather, misquoted—on this subject, St. Bernard maintains as follows:—
1. That the Blessed Virgin Mary was throughout her whole life *without sin*.
2. That she was *without original sin*.
3. That she was *born* without original sin.

It may be further proved—
1. That the doctrine rejected by St. Bernard is a doctrine rejected by the Church at this time—viz., the supposition that the Immaculate Conception of the Blessed Virgin was a peculiarity arising from the order of nature; including her parents, and even her ancestors, within its range.
2. That the doctrine he taught, under the name of the Immaculate Nativity, is, in substance, the doctrine of the Immaculate Conception, as now defined —viz., that the exemption of the Blessed Virgin from original sin was a peculiar and personal privilege, bestowed upon her alone, not by the order of nature, but in the order of grace; not through the mediation of parents, but by the direct operation and infusion of the grace of the Holy Ghost into the soul at the first moment of its existence.

It is remarkable, that this very letter closes with a declaration which reads like a prophecy. He protests that, in all he had written, he submitted himself with entire faith to any judgment which should be afterwards made by the Church, "I reserve," he says, "this point, and all others of the same kind, to the authority and judgment of the Roman Church; and if I have advanced anything contrary to the decision which shall be made by it, I am ready to correct my opinion."†

With what joy would he have hailed the authoritative definition of his own doctrine, perfect in identity of substance, only expressed with more scientific accuracy of mental and verbal analysis! He would have rejoiced with all the powers of his reason and of his heart, as the Fathers of the ante-Nicene ages would have

---

\* Sti. Bernardi, opp. Ep. clxxi. Ed. Paris, 1667.
† Ibid ut supra.

rejoiced, if they could have heard the definition of Nicea and the more perfect distinctions of the Athanasian Creed.

It remains only to commend to the reader the following pages, which cannot be read without a lively interest, or without deriving both consolation and incentives to the love of God, from the spirit of sanctity which breathes in the life and words of the saint.

The present translation, made by Sisters of St. Mary's Convent, Greenwich, is truly excellent for its pure, easy, and simple English, which reads off, not as a translation, but with the facility of an original.

HENRY E. MANNING.

# First Period

## DOMESTIC LIFE OF ST. BERNARD, FROM HIS BIRTH TILL HIS ENTRANCE INTO THE ORDER OF CITEAUX. (1091-1113)

# CHAPTER I

BIRTH OF ST. BERNARD—FIRST YEARS OF HIS CHILDHOOD—
DETAILS REGARDING HIS FAMILY.

**B**LESSED is the man whose infancy has been watched over, kindled, penetrated by the eye of a tender and holy mother. That glance has a magical power over the soul of the child; it beams forth sweetness and life; and, as the sun's rays mature the fruits of the earth, and sweeten them by the communication of its own substance, so does the mother deposit, in the soul of the child, the sacred character of love.

St. Bernard had this inestimable blessing. His pious mother, Elizabeth, daughter of Count Bernard de Montbar, had been married in her early youth to Tecelin, Lord of Fontaines, near Dijon. This marriage was not concluded without much difficulty. Elizabeth was but just fifteen, and her soul, of which divine grace had already taken possession, was wholly given to God; she longed after the peace of a cloister, and was preparing herself, under the direction of her virtuous father, to embrace the austere rules of a monastic life. But Providence reserved her for another destiny. She was called, against her will, to become a wife and a mother, and to transmit the blessings which had crowned her from infancy to a numerous posterity.

Tecelin, her husband, was capable of appreciating her character, and deeply reverenced her. He was a noble knight, of gentle manners, and full of the fear of God; and, although his important office kept him almost constantly close to the person of the Duke of Burgundy, he preserved the dignity of the Christian life in the court as well as in the camp, and distinguished himself on all occasions by his valor, his uprightness, and his probity.

Divine Providence, which had decreed this union, made it happy and fruitful. Elizabeth gave birth to six sons and one daughter—Guido was the eldest, then Gerard, Bernard, Andre, Bartholomi, Nivard, and Hombeline.

Bernard, the third son of Tecelin, was born in 1071, at the Castle of Fontaines, in Burgundy. His birth had been preceded by a remarkable circumstance. Elizabeth, during her pregnancy, had a dream which terrified her extremely; she dreamed that there was a white dog within her womb, which barked incessantly. "Trembling and disquieted," says a contemporary historian, "Bernard's mother consulted a man of great sanctity, who, at the same moment, found himself filled with that spirit of prophecy which animated David when, speaking of holy preachers, he said to God, 'The tongue of Thy dogs shall bark against Thine enemies,' and he replied immediately: 'Fear nothing; you shall be mother of a child who, like a faithful dog, shall one day guard the house of the Lord, and bark loudly against the enemies of the faith; for he shall be an excellent preacher, and with his healing tongue he shall heal the wounds of many souls.'"

The happy mother, with a thrill of joy, received into her heart the words of the man of God. She had offered her first two sons to the Lord from the moment of their birth, but she consecrated Bernard to him in a more especial manner; and her ardent desire was to transmit to all her children the high vocation which in her youth, she believed, she had herself received.

This Christian mother regarded her maternal duties as a charge intrusted to her by the divine goodness; she considered her children as sacred deposits committed to her care, and for which she was responsible before God. Thus, although of a very delicate constitution, Elizabeth would never leave to a stranger the care of nursing her children. Bound by the cords of her own heart to the source of all love, she transmitted to them, with their mother's milk, the heavenly virtue which was her life.

Tecelin led too chivalrous a life to be able personally to direct the education of his sons. He intrusted this charge with perfect confidence to the enlightened care of his wife, whose views he approved, though he did not fully comprehend their extent and elevation. Having been himself brought up in the profession of arms, and joining, according to the spirit of that age, military habits with devotional exercises, he saw no impediment to forming all his sons for the career which had been one of no little glory to himself; but Elizabeth, more clear-sighted than he, trembled at the danger to which purity of heart is exposed in the camp; and she knew too well the blessedness of the religious life to desire any other happiness for those whom she had brought forth and consecrated to God; she educated her children for heaven, rather than for earth, and taught them early to discern good from evil, to choose the better part, to love, above all things, Him who is love itself—the first Beginning and last End of man. For this purpose she established the perfect order and salutary discipline of the evangelical law in the interior of her house.

"I cannot forget," says one of her contemporaries, "how this illustrious lady sought to serve as an example and model to her children. In her household, in her wedded estate, and in the midst of the world, she, in some sort, imitated the life of a solitary or religious, by her abstinences, by the simplicity of her dress, by her retirement from all the pomps and pleasures of the world. She withdrew as much as possible from the perturbations of the secular state, persevering in fasting, in watching, and in prayer, and making up, by works of charity, for anything that might be supposed wanting in a person bound by the marriage tie and living in the world."

Such an example of life, joined to a conversation ever serious, and, at the same time, full of gentle sweetness, left an indelible impression on the mind of Elizabeth's children. She loved them with an affection altogether free from that natural selfishness which seeks its own enjoyment, she sowed the seed of solid virtues deep in their hearts, without caring to cultivate the brilliant and superficial flowers so fascinating to young minds. History tells us that she exercised them in the constant practice of self-denial and mutual charity, accustoming them gradually, by a discreet moderation, to the mortification of the senses and of the will; so that she established a happy agreement of tastes, habits, and Christian sympathies among her children.

The austerity of this education, tempered as it was by all that is sweet and loving in a mother's heart, developed, at the same time, the extreme tenderness of heart, and the manly and generous character which distinguished the sons of Tecelin. All displayed the noblest qualities as they advanced in age; and, amid these qualities, filial piety ever shone most conspicuously.

Bernard especially, that sweet child so dear to his mother's heart, had fed deliciously upon her words and her inspiring looks. While yet very young he unfolded like a flower under the sunshine of his mother's eye; he set himself, as far as his age permitted, to live like his mother—to pray like his mother; he secretly imitated the things he saw her do—gave bread to the poor, rendered all kinds of little services to his brothers, and to all who approached him; he spoke little; watched himself closely, to keep under his natural vivacity; and he was often seen to steal away to weep over his faults, and sob out some simple, childlike prayer. Bernard showed also, from the earliest age, a wonderful inclination for study. There was something bright and quick in the precocious intelligence which shone forth in his eye, and in the refined and expressive features of his gracious countenance. His open and gentle heart diffused the innocent joy and smiling grace, so lovely in childhood, over his face and person. His hair was golden, his complexion very fair, and his figure slender; his outward appearance exactly resembled that of his noble father; but his soul was the soul of Elizabeth.

In one of his childish illnesses he gave a striking proof both of his patience, and his delicacy of conscience. A woman offered to cure him of a headache which had long baffled all remedies; but the holy child, having caught sight of some superstitions objects in her hand, sprang out of bed, and chased her out of his room with a cry of indignation, because she had sought to cure him by the hateful arts of magic.

Our Lord, it seems, vouchsafed to reward the piety of this true child of Elizabeth immediately and visibly. The pain instantly left him, and the child rose from his bed full of health and intense joy.

Another event contributed greatly to enkindle this simple and vivid faith. "During the blessed night of Christmas, it happened that the young Bernard, seated in deep recollection before the commencement of the divine office, bowed his head upon his breast, and fell asleep; at the same instant, the child Jesus appeared to him in a vision—the Incarnate Word showed Himself to him as if just born again of His Virgin Mother, and as the fairest of the children of men. This wonderful vision so ravished the first affections of the little Bernard, that it lifted him above the state of childhood, and from this moment his mind was convinced, as he still believes and declares, that the hour at which he had this vision was the very hour of our Lord's birth. "In short," adds the friend and contemporary of St. Bernard, "those who have heard him preach cannot fail to recognize the number of graces and benedictions he received on that blessed night; for, from that day forth, he seemed to have had an ever-deepening knowledge of that mystery, and spoke of it with a fuller and more kindling eloquence."

Some years passed by; and the little Bernard grew in age and in grace, before God and man.

# CHAPTER II

### EDUCATION OF ST. BERNARD—DOMESTIC MANNERS OF THE MIDDLE AGE.

At the church of Chatillon-sur-Seine there was a school greatly renowned on account of the new method of teaching which some learned scholastics had introduced. The wisdom of the world was taught there; *secularis sapientia*, the name given to the somewhat equivocal learning of the new masters. The reputation of this school bad attracted a great number of scholars; and Bernard was gifted with so great a capacity for study that his parents determined to send him thither. He made rapid progress; learned to read and write Latin with ease and elegance; cultivated poetry, and became even too passionately attached to literature. But, as he advanced in his studies, he was often pained by hearing religious questions treated with a frivolous subtlety.*

Without being able to account for the feeling of fear which the rashness of some of the masters excited within him, he possessed that quick and unerring tact, that mysterious sense of holiness and truth, which detects, at once, the slightest deviation of the mind. Bernard preserved throughout his life the painful apprehensions which these early studies had excited. It was not that he had no love for dialectics—he devoted himself with great ardor to this art, and acquired therein a remarkable superiority over his fellow-disciples—but he shrank from applying it to the eternal

---

* From the beginning of the eleventh century public schools had been formed in several churches of France – at Rheims, Poictiers, Maus, Auxerre, and other considerable towns. These schools were multiplied in the following century.

principles of theology, and from subjecting mysteries, which must be believed with the heart before the understanding can take cognizance of them, to a cold process of analysis; in short, the faith which had been watered and nourished by his mothers words, he felt to be too sacred a thing to be ventured in the lists of human disputation. Bernard sought a remedy against the chilling effect of profane studies in the reading and meditation of Holy Scripture. He drank in daily, the nourishment of his soul and the light of his understanding, from the living fountain of the divine Word. This exercise, which he never discontinued, wonderfully enriched his memory, while it gave to his style that prophetic tone and that lofty sublimity which characterized his sermons and his writings.

While Bernard was studying at Chatillon, his brothers successively entered upon their military career. This must have been a hard trial to Elizabeth; but at the bottom of her heart there were presages, not to be mistaken by a mother, which softened her grief. She made no opposition to her husband's will; and he did but yield, in some sort, to the force of circumstances, in calling upon his sons to follow his own course; in fact, a warlike enthusiasm, at that time, pervaded Burgundy. This feudal province was governed by mighty dukes, descended from Hugh Capet; one of whom had recently given his daughter in marriage to the famous Alphonso, King of Castille and Leon.* Notwithstanding the distance between the two countries, this alliance constantly attracted a host of Burgundian knights, in search of brilliant adventures, to the Court of Spain. This was the brightest period of Castillian glory. The Cid, who died, as is believed, the same year in which Bernard was born, had filled the world with the fame of his valor; and Alphonso himself, the son-in-law of the Duke of Burgundy, was accounted so accomplished a master in chivalry, that the noblest knights thought themselves happy to be his scholars.

But besides these particular incentives to the chivalrous spirit in Burgundy, there were far graver motives which excited not France only, but all Europe to war. The state of things was so complicated at the opening of the twelfth century, that the

---

* This marriage took place in 1078. Constance, wife of Alphonse IV, was the daughter of Robert, the old Duke of Burgundy, the son of Hugh Capet.

whole west was disturbed. On one side, the growing power of the Normans, now become masters of England and Sicily, piqued the jealousy of the King of France, and most of the great feudatories of his crown. On the other, the serious disputes between the Emperor of Germany and the Pope, on the subject of investitures, had divided Christendom into two parties, each prepared, at any moment, to fly to arms; and these contests had come to such a point of bitter hostility that it was impossible to foresee their issue. Meanwhile, another event came in to supersede these weighty questions, and produced a general convulsion in all ranks of society.

From the year 1095, Peter the Hermit had been traversing the west, with pressing letters from Pope Urban II, urging Christians to hasten to the relief of Palestine. Since that time nothing had been heard of in Europe, but the wonderful exploits of the holy war. The French had reaped a rich harvest of glory—Nice had fallen before them; Antioch, the ancient and stately capital of the East, had been taken after a memorable siege, and the foundations of a new empire had been laid there by a Norman prince. Last of all, Godfrey de Bouillon had won the holy city by the edge of the sword, on the 15th of July, 1099; and the crown of Jerusalem had been unanimously bestowed on him.

Such were the glorious tidings told in the west at the beginning of the twelfth century; we may imagine to what a pitch they must have excited the enthusiasm of its chivalry. The news spread rapidly in all lands, by means of the troubadours, who, in our fathers' times, filled the office now performed by the public newspapers. They went from castle to castle, chanting the deeds of the Christian heroes, to assemblies of noble knights and ladies; and their songs were repeated by the minstrels of the country, and acted by the mimics and jugglers. This was the ordinary amusement of the long winter evenings; for the Castillians took advantage of the necessary cessation of feudal warfare to make their winter quarters in the embattled castles; and there, in his vast hall, amidst his family and faithful vassals, the feudal lord, seated in his chair of state, gave audience to the troubadour, and lent an attentive ear to the exploits of the Christian heroes, and to lamentations over the sufferings of the Church.

It was not the manner of the men of the middle ages to busy themselves with the minute details of daily life, and the host of ephemeral objects whose very multiplicity diminishes their interest. Our fathers could be moved only by great things; and the interest they took in them was manifested after another fashion than by mere words and barren wishes. Every just cause, every serious grievance, found among them zealous defenders, ready to combat to the death in the cause of right and honor. Thus did the sacred cause of the Crusades take possession of noble natures.

There is no doubt that Tecelin, with the character which we know to have been his, would have sent his sons to serve under Godfrey's banner, had their bodily strength been equal to the vigor of their souls; but the two eldest were, at the time of the first Crusade, at that intermediate age which divides manhood from youth, and Bernard was still a child. We know, however, how young hearts burn at the recital of heroic deeds; and they made an indelible impression on the sons of Tecelin. The two eldest had no sooner attained the age of manhood, than they burned with impatience to signalize their valor. A quarrel of the Duke of Burgundy furnished an opportunity. Guido and Gerard were called to the camp of their liege lord. Writers, who were personally acquainted with the family of St. Bernard, agree in their commendations of these two knights, and their young brothers. "The character of the eldest was grave and upright, modest and dear to God; he was endowed with a gift of wisdom, which appeared in his words as well as in his actions. Gerard, his younger brother, was deservedly esteemed; his manners were chaste and simple, and he had a rare prudence, and remarkable presence of mind. As to Bernard, he was the light and mirror of his brethren, and at the same time, the lofty pillar of the Church. The soul of Andrew, the fourth, was simple and honest—fearing God, and flying evil. Bartholomew anticipated in his youth the wisdom of age, and shone in all the beauty of a pure and stainless life. Nivard, lastly, the youngest of all the children, already preferred the blessings of heaven to the goods 'of earth." Hombeline, who was younger than any of her brothers, was a gentle and ingenuous girl; but her pious dispositions sometimes gave way to an inclination for worldly vanities; and we shall see, in the sequel, the effect of this early tendency.

Guido, having now begun his career, took his place in the world, and married a young and devout lady, distinguished both by her beauty and her illustrious birth.

# CHAPTER III

BERNARD FINISHES HIS STUDIES AND RETURNS TO
FONTAINES- DEATH OF HIS MOTHER—TEMPTATIONS
AND CONVERSION.

The mind of St. Bernard had very early come to maturity. By his extreme aptitude, joined to great perseverance, he had mastered the various sciences, both sacred and profane, which were taught at Chatillon; but, what is so rare, his too great ardor for study had not diminished his pious dispositions. Whilst his talents were powerfully developed, faith took deeper root in his soul; or, as he himself says, he tasted and long enjoyed the inward sweetness of a spiritual spring; all the seeds of grace with which his soul was filled, blossomed during this happy season of his life, and gave promise of the great virtues which were afterwards seen in him. There are few men who have no recollection of that mysterious time when the yet virgin soul opens, and produces the first flower of love. Happy when its first sweet perfume rises toward God! This is the time of which the prophet speaks, the time of the soul's adolescence—"And I passed by thee, and saw thee, and behold thy time was the time of lovers."* At this age every young man is a poet; he is a poet because he loves, and because poetry is the natural language of all who love; but poetry does not express herself in words alone; she lives in the pensiveness of silence and of tears; she kindles the eyes; she gives birth to dreams and sighs. We love, and know not what we love—we glimpse it, we invoke

* Ezek. xvi. 8.

it, we seek it everywhere, amid the shadows and reflections of truth and beauty; but our ideal is not upon earth; and hence, that mixture of desire, and love, and sorrow, and hope, blending into an undefinable feeling, which may be compared, in some respects, to that pining of the exile for his native land, which the Germans call *Heimweh*.

The young Bernard passed through the various stages of that poetical age. Alas! it is of short duration; for the flower must fall before the fruit can appear; and between the fall of the flower and the maturity of the fruit there is, in the spiritual as in the natural life, a long uncertain interval—a time of toil, and anxious, heavy labor, which sometimes drags on even to the end of our earthly course! Bernard was in this second period when he left Chatillon to return to his father's house; he was then just nineteen, shining outwardly with all the brightness of youth and genius; he felt no longer within him the transports of his former fervor; his piety, devoid of all consolation, and weaned, so to speak, from all its sweetness, seemed to have no longer either light or heat; the spring-time, with him, was past; the shadows of night were around his soul, and the voice of the turtle was no longer heard therein.

Now began his trials. Hitherto, his chastity, protected by piety and modesty (the two guardians assigned by grace and nature to that precious virtue), had suffered no assault; but the charms of the world, into which he had just entered, excited his senses, and strongly allured a heart full of simplicity, and but too open to outward impressions. He happened one day, says his biographer, to cast his eyes upon a woman whose bewitching beauty had struck him. Bernard experienced a new sensation; his startled conscience awoke in terror; he feared lest the dart should be mortal, and fled at once, he knew not whither; he ran on till he came to a frozen pond, plunged boldly into it, and stayed resolutely in the water until he was drawn out half dead. An act of such resolution was followed by the happiest results; his triumphant virtue acquired fresh strength, and, from that moment, rose more and more above all sensual influences.

Meanwhile, he was struck to the heart by a new affliction—the most poignant that can befall a son—which put an end to all his home happiness. His mother, like a fruit ripe for heaven, was snatched away from him, scarcely six months after his return to Fontaines. Elizabeth was surrounded at that moment by all her family. Neither infirmities, nor length of years, had given any tokens of the approach of death; on the contrary, still fresh and strong in health, both of soul and body, she devoted herself, more and more, to exercises of piety and unwearied charity. "She was often seen," says an ancient author, "alone, and on foot, on the road from Fontaines and Dijon, entering the houses of the poor, visiting the sick, distributing food and medicine, carrying all kinds of succor and consolation to the afflicted; and what was most admirable in her beneficence was that she so practised it as to preserve the utmost possible concealment; she did all her good works in person, without the assistance of her servants; and of her it might be said with truth, that her left hand knew not the bounty of her right." In the midst of these holy exercises, the saintly Elizabeth was called, almost suddenly, out of this world. The circumstances of her death were so touching that we cannot refrain from giving some details of it, from the pen of one of her contemporaries who was present: "Our venerable abbot's holy mother was accustomed to celebrate the feast of St Ambrose (the patron of the Church of Fontaines) with great magnificence; and on this occasion she always gave a solemn banquet, to which the clergy were bidden. God was pleased to reward the particular devotion of this holy woman to the glorious St. Ambrose, by a revelation that she should die on his feast; and, in truth, it was no marvel to see so devout a Christian endowed with the gift of prophecy. She therefore announced to her husband, her children, and her whole assembled household, with the most perfect tranquillity and confidence, that the hour of her death was at hand. They were all confounded, and refused to believe the prediction; but they soon found there was great cause for anxiety. On the vigil of St. Ambrose, Elizabeth was attacked by a violent fever, which obliged her to keep her bed; on the morning of the feast, she humbly desired that the body of our Lord might be brought to her; and, after receiving this holy Viaticum, together with extreme unction, she felt herself strengthened, and insisted that the ecclesiastics who had been invited should sit down to the banquet she had prepared for them. Now, while they were at table, Elizabeth sent for Guido, her eldest son, and commanded him, as soon as the repast should be over, to bring into her room all the clergy who were present. Guido piously obeyed his beloved mother's desire. Behold them all, then, assembled round her bed! Then the servant of God declared, with a serene countenance, that the moment of her dissolution was come. The clerks fell to prayer, they intoned the litanies. Elizabeth herself chanted sweetly with them, as long as her breath lasted; but, at the moment when the choir came to those words of the litanies—*Per passionem et crucem tuam libera eam Domine,* the dying woman, commending her soul to the Lord, raised her hand to make the sign of the cross, and, in that attitude, she rendered up her holy soul, which the angels received, and carried to the abodes of the blessed. There does she await, in peace and rest, the awakening of her body on the great day of the resurrection, when our judge and advocate, Jesus Christ, shall come to judge the living and the dead, and to burn up this world with fire. Thus did her holy soul leave the sacred temple of its body; her right hand remained uplifted in the same position to which she had raised it to make the sign of the cross, a thing which astonished all who were present."

O mother of St. Bernard! O mother seven-fold blessed, and worthy of blessing from all the children of the Church, deign, I beseech you, to guide the pen which ventures to write the history of your son; that the example of his virtue, and the glory of his sanctity, may animate, console, and kindle us who live so poorly in these latter days. Alas! we can scarce believe the wonders of old time, so rare have they become since charity has waxed so cold upon this earth! I pray you, then, O saintly mother, let your Bernard live again in this book, and let his spirit aid the writer. Far from him be vainglory and self-seeking, and the false blaze of human eloquence. Let his words be true and simple, and his narrative faithful and exact! Under your patronage, sweet Elizabeth, he will resume it, and proceed with confidence.

"The happy passage of Elizabeth's soul," continues the monk before cited, "was a subject of joy to the angels of heaven; but on earth it was an occasion of heavy grief and mourning to the poor of Jesus Christ—the widows and orphans to whom she had been a mother." Bernard, above all—but now so happy to be once more with his mother, after so long an absence—Bernard remained like one stunned by so heavy and unforeseen a stroke.

He was attached to his mother by the bonds of grace still more strongly than by those of nature; and his loving heart, full as it was of filial piety and tenderness, seemed deprived for ever of all that gave it joy, and life and happiness.

Overwhelmed by his affliction, he could scarcely find a thought of consolation even in his lively faith, and the eternal promises of God. He was now about twenty, the age at which the son is just beginning to understand the value of a mother: for the child loves her instinctively, childishly; but the young man rationally, conscientiously; joining a peculiar esteem, a boundless respect and confidence, to his affection. Bernard, though surrounded by his brothers, his sister, his aged father, felt alone in the world; his support was gone, his consolation was no longer here below, he saw his mother no more, no longer heard her voice—he seemed in some sort separated from himself.

But his weariness and sorrow were made still heavier by his interior aridity, by the dryness of his devotions, the coldness of his heart, which seemed frozen within him. In this state of darkness, which seems to be the inevitable portion of all souls destined to high sanctity, Bernard was to endure all the trials of the purgative way; for thus, as Holy Scripture teaches, does the Lord try his servants, as silver is tried in the fire, and gold in the crucible. "My son," says the Book of Ecclesiasticus, "when thou comest to the service of God, stand in justice and in fear, and prepare thy soul for temptation."*

Bernard had to struggle against three kinds of temptation, which fasten successively upon the body, the mind, and the soul—by the desire of the flesh, the desire of the eyes, and the pride of life.

The first of these temptations was the more violent, as Bernard had conquered it on a former occasion; but the old and cunning serpent awaited the most critical moment to surprise Bernard's youth, and make a decisive assault. As we have already said, Bernard possessed remarkable personal beauty; his figure was perfectly proportioned, his manners elegant and dignified, his eye full of fire, his countenance sweet and gracious; his gait, his movements, his attitudes, his smile—all were modest, simple,

---

* 1 Eccle. ii, 1.

and noble; his words were naturally elegant, impressive, and persuasive. There was something in his whole person so amiable and so attractive, that, according to the expression of one of his biographers, he was more dangerous to the world than the world to him. We may conceive the numberless perils which must have surrounded such a young man, especially when we consider that his heart was open, expansive, and prone to love. He was fearfully tried.

But divine grace, which assists the humble and strengthens the warrior of Christ, covered Bernard with a shield, which made him invulnerable to all the arrows of the demon of sensuality. Then did the tempter take a more subtle form, and, seeing that Bernard's weak side was an excessive love of learning, he tried to captivate his mind by the desire of the eyes. Imprudent friends (his brothers among the rest), in order to relieve his melancholy, persuaded him to address himself to curious and occult sciences; and they represented to him so forcibly the interest which belongs to this kind of study, that Bernard, naturally inclined to intellectual inquiry, at first saw no objection to what they advised; but the voice of conscience soon warned him of the danger. He saw that the pursuit of science, without any practical end, or any other result but the satisfaction of vain curiosity, is unworthy of a Christian. For, as he afterwards said himself (and here we are citing his own words), 'There are some who wish to learn only for the sake of learning, and this curiosity is ridiculous; others wish to learn only to be considered learned, and this vanity is blamable; others wish to learn only to traffic with their learning, and this traffic is ignoble. When, then, is learning good? It is good, says the prophet, when it is put in practice;* and he is guilty, adds the apostle, who, having a knowledge of the good which he should do, does it not."†

These truly Christian considerations counterbalanced the specious suggestions of those around him.

Still it became necessary to adopt some way of life, some social position, some sphere of activity: it became necessary, in fact, to choose between God and the world. In this alternative Bernard

---

\* Psalm cx.
† James iv. 17.

suffered most painful perplexity, for the secret dictates of conscience contended against all his reflections and all his desires. The tempter took advantage of this condition of his mind to make a last assault, longer and more obstinate than any of the preceding; and this time he directed his insidious temptations to the excitement of thoughts of pride.

In truth, the world appeared in a very seducing shape to Bernard. His family influence and his father's personal services promised him rapid advancement and high distinction in military service; on the other hand, his flexible genius and vast knowledge seemed to call him to the Court, where he had every chance of a brilliant fortune. His grave and studious habits fitted him for the legislature; and his personal merit, as well as the nobility of his birth, opened a way to the highest ecclesiastical dignities. But Bernard still remained undecided; neither the pressing solicitations of his family, nor the urgency of his friends, nor the force of his own passionate desires after great and lofty things, could bend his will and win his consent. Whenever the world smiled on him, the memory of his mother recalled him to the reality of life; and all his schemes seemed to dissolve under the action of an internal power, which brought him either anguish or comfort, according as he obeyed or resisted its mysterious influence. Oh, how cruel is this conflict! How much more torturing this anguish of spirit than all bodily suffering! Amid such tribulations the will is crucified; the soul, crushed on all sides, is freed from all its impurities; it is stripped of its very self, emptied of its very life, till it dies to its tastes, its desires, its will, its appetites, its affections, to all that belongs to it. Not till then can it say with her, who will ever be the model of all perfection, *Ecce ancilla, Domini, fiat mihi secundum verbum tuum*. Then, when the vase is empty and pure, the Holy Spirit fills it, and makes it a vessel of honor before God.

But who shall describe the anguish and deep sadness of a soul under the torture of this crucifixion? Torn asunder by two contrary forces, both at once urging and soliciting his will, Bernard raised his eyes to heaven, and then met his mother's eye, which restored him to calmness, and, at the same time, aroused his conscience. "She seemed to him to be weeping, and reminded him, sorrowfully, that it was not for the vanities of the world that she had brought him up with such tender anxiety; that she had had far other hopes for him while training him with so much care."

One day, while on his way to visit his brothers, who were with the Duke of Burgundy, at the siege of the Castle of Grancey, as he rode along, silently and in deep thought, the world with its perturbations and perpetual vicissitudes seemed to pass before him as a vain show, and suddenly a voice founded in the depths of his heart—"*Come to me all you that labor and are heavy laden, and I will refresh you; take my yoke upon you, and you shall find rest to your souls.*" At these words a heavenly longing took possession of Bernard's heart, and thrilled to the very marrow of his bones. He stopped at a church door, entered it, and, prostrate before the altar, he prayed, with many tears, raising his eyes to heaven, and, in the words of the prophet, pouring out his heart like water before the face of the Lord created At that moment a deep calm fell upon his soul, the breath of God rekindled the lamp of his spiritual life, and Bernard, all on fire with love, consecrated himself for ever to God, and joyfully took upon him the yoke of Him who is meek and humble of heart.\*

Many years after this change from the hand of the Most High, Bernard loved to recall its circumstances, and to relate them to the monks of Clairvaux. "I am not ashamed to confess," said he, "that frequently, and especially at the beginning of my conversion, I have experienced great hardness and coldness of heart. I sought Him whom my soul desired to love; Him upon whom my frozen heart might rest, and gather warmth; and as no one came to help me, and to melt the thick ice which bound all my interior senses in its chain, my soul became more and more languid, weak, and benumbed, giving way to grief, and almost to despair, and murmuring inwardly, 'Who can endure such cold.'† Then all at once, at the first sight, perhaps, of some spiritual person—or, perhaps, at the mere remembrance of the dead or the absent—the Spirit of God began to breathe upon these frozen waters, they flowed again, and my tears served me for food day and night."

---

\* Matthew xi. 28, 29.
† Psalm cxivii.

# CHAPTER IV

### CONVERSION OF ST. BERNARD AND SEVERAL OF HIS FRIENDS.

"I AM come to cast fire on the earth," said Jesus Christ "and what will I but that it be kindled?"*

When that divine fire descends into a soul, it purifies and transfigures it by a process like that of material fire. When it lays hold of wood, first it dries it, and blackens it with dense smoke; then it penetrates by little and little into its substance, consuming all the gross and heterogeneous matter it meets with; lastly, it kindles, transforms, glorifies it, till the wood itself is changed into fire, and partakes of its qualities. Thus Bernard, having passed through all the stages of this purifying process, remained like a lighted torch in the hand of God, prepared to give light to all His Church.

Now, when a man has been thus renewed and animated by heavenly love, he is not slow in becoming an instrument of marvellous efficacy for the salvation of his fellows; and the ever-increasing power which Bernard was called on to exercise over the age in which he lived was manifested from the first moment in which his heart was devoted to God.

The first person whom his example, even more than his words, wrought upon to leave the vanities of the world, was his uncle, the valiant Gauldry, Count de Trouillon. This nobleman had a high military command; he was very rich, and yet more distinguished

---

\* Luke xii. 49.

for his valor than for his liberality. At Bernard's call he quitted the world, attached himself to his nephew as to a father, and continued till his death among the number of his most zealous followers.

After this remarkable conversion, the zeal of Bernard seemed to know no bounds. As the fire which consumes a forest, spreads from tree to tree, lighting up young sapling* and aged trees without distinction, and becoming more intense as it fastens upon each new prey, so Bernard's burning charity kindled brothers, kinsmen, friends, and wrapt young and old, husbands and wives, children and parents, in one holy flame.

Bartholomew was the first to be touched by his brother's exhortations. He was on the point of entering the service of the Duke of Burgundy; but he chose the better part, and hesitated not to enroll himself among the soldiers of Jesus Christ. Andrew, who, as well as Bartholomew, was younger than Bernard, had just received the honor of knighthood, and as he looked forward hopefully to a brilliant career, he heard his brother's words with reluctance, rejected his advice, avoided his presence, was even irritated at his urgency; but, one day, as Bernard was about to renew his endeavors, Andrew exclaimed, in a tone of emotion, "I have seen my mother!" "In fact," adds the historian, "she had appeared to him visibly, and testified by a smile her joy at the holy resolution of her children. Andrew, amazed and moved even to tears, threw himself on his brother's neck, and, instead of a soldier of this world, became a soldier of Jesus Christ."

We have seen that Guido, the eldest of the family, was married; he held a high place in society, and fulfilled the duties of his state of life as a Christian should do; but the urgency with which Bernard strove to withdraw him from the perils of the world, and the obligations of the most legitimate engagements, and the facility with which Guido yielded himself to such painful sacrifices, induces us to believe that some conscientious motive, unknown to historians— it may be, some previous engagement—obliged Guido and the other members of that holy family to consecrate themselves entirely to God. Be this as it may, Guido, constrained by the desire after evangelical perfection, ardently desired to leave the world for Jesus Christ; and he promised to accomplish his purpose, should his wife, as is required by the laws of the Church, consent to it. But the attainment of this consent from a young and tenderly-loving wife and mother seemed almost impossible. Bernard, however, to whom a clearer light was granted, assured him that she would either consent, or that she would be taken from him by death. The proposal was made to her, but no consideration could induce this heart-broken woman to separate from her husband; she used all the inexhaustible resources which her loving woman's heart suggested, to shake Guido's vocation; and his upright and generous character could neither resolve to renounce his calling, nor to overwhelm the mother of his children with such intolerable anguish. The perplexity of so dreadful a trial is more easily conceived than described. The struggle was violent, but it did not last long; a miracle of grace ended it. Guido's wife sent for Bernard; she wished to see him, to open her heart to him. He came, and found her ill, and suffering under a strange anxiety of mind. The voice which had first spoken to her husband's heart is now thrilling through hers. She desires, like him, to consecrate herself to the God of love, who calls her; and now, in the presence of Guido and Bernard, she pronounces her vows, and receives, at the same moment, health of body and peace of mind. The husband and wife made no delay in carrying their holy resolution into effect; and, having made all necessary arrangements, they separated.

Guido became Bernard's disciple,* faithful companion, and inseparable friend. But his wife entered the convent of Juilly, where she persevered in a course of most austere piety, having been placed over a large community of religious women.

Guido's younger brother, Gerard, showed deep displeasure at what had passed in his family. He judged Bernard's zeal by the rules of human prudence, and severely condemned the facility with which his brothers had contracted such serious engagements. This disposition of his brother greatly distressed Bernard, but did not prevent him from going to seek him at the camp at Grancey, where he now was, at the highest pitch of glory and honor. "Gerard," says the chronicler, "was an intrepid soldier, of consummate prudence, and highly valued and esteemed by

---

* Several of those whom Bernard gained to God being married persons, their wives, who entered into their views, retired into a Benedictine convent, near Dijon, the same to which Hombeline, St. Bernard's sister, afterwards went.

all who knew him." He received his brother coldly, repelled him by the specious objections of worldly wisdom, and hardened his heart against the call of grace. Then Bernard, quivering with fraternal charity, with a kind of supernatural energy, placed his hand on his brother's side, and said, in a prophetic tone, "I know, yes, I know well, that nothing but adversity will open thy mind to the truth. Well, the day will come, and that speedily, when this spot which I touch will be pierced by a lance, which will thus open a way for the entrance of those words into thy heart, from which thou now turnest away in disdain."

Gerard declared afterwards, that at the moment his brother spoke these words, he felt as if a dart was already piercing his side; and a few days after this prediction, at the siege of the castle of Grancey, he was, in fact, wounded by a lance, in the very part to which Bernard had pointed. The wound seemed mortal; and Gerard, stretched upon the field of battle, fell into the hands of the enemy, who carried him off to their camp and kept him prisoner. In this sad condition, full of anxiety and grief, Gerard, despairing of life, sent in all haste for his brother. Bernard, however, came not, but sent him this message: "Thy wound is not unto death, but unto life."

The event justified these words. Gerard escaped miraculously from his close imprisonment; and, being freed from his chains, his first care was to break the bonds which held him to the world, to follow his higher calling, and consecrate himself, like his brother, to the work of God.

St. Bernard, having thus become the guide and spiritual father of his brethren, had still no settled plan as to the kind of life he should embrace. The religious life was the great desire of all; but they left the accomplishment of the design, and the determination of the order they were to embrace, to the care of Divine Providence. One day, when they had gone all together into a church, full of desires to know the will of God, they heard this text read from the Epistles of St. Paul: "He who hath begun a good work in you will perfect it unto the day of Jesus Christ."\*
Bernard was struck by these words as by a voice from heaven; and, full of hope, he assembled his friends and kindred, and all

---

\* Philip i, 6.

those who were dear to him, to re-animate their devotion and communicate to them the glorious light and grace which inundated his own soul. Few people could resist his energetic representations, his persuasive words, the force of his example. To some he showed the deplorable delusion of a life wholly of this world; to others, the consolations and inexhaustible sweetness of the religious life; to all, the necessity that every man, and, above all, every Christian should consider seriously the true end of his being, and walk courageously and right onward towards it, and not exchange for a few passing pleasures the eternal joys laid up for the faithful soul. "The zeal which inspires me," said he, "comes not from flesh and blood, but it springs from a desire to labor together at the work of our salvation. Nobility of birth, dignity of presence, grace of person, youth, lands, palaces, high honors, the wisdom even of this world, all this is of the world. But how long will these things last? They will vanish *as* the world, *before* the world—in a moment, you, yourselves, will disappear from the world. Life is short, the world passes away, and you will pass away before it. Why not cease to love what will soon cease to exist?" "O my brother," he wrote to one of his friends, whom he was pressing to join him, "come, without any farther delay, and attach yourself to a man who loves you with a true and enduring love. Death will not part two hearts which the love of God has united. The happiness which I desire for you belongs neither to time nor to this mortal body, and will subsist independently of both. What do I say? It will seem sweeter still when the body shall be destroyed, when time for you shall be no more. What comparison is there between this happiness and the goods of this world? The greatest good is that which can never be taken from us, and what is it? The eye hath not seen it, the ear hath not heard it, the heart of man hath not understood it, flesh and blood are not capable of its enjoyment, the Spirit of God alone revealeth it unto us. Blessed are they who understand this saying: 'Ye are my friends, all things whatsoever I have heard of my Father I have made known to you.'"

On another occasion he replied thus to one who wavered in his resolutions: "Do you wonder that you are ever floating between good and evil, when you have never yet set your foot on the solid rock? Once make a firm resolution to take up the yoke of Jesus

Christ, and nothing will be able to shake you again! Oh, if you did but understand what I mean! Thou alone, O my God, canst reveal to the eye of man what Thou hast prepared for those who love Thee.

*'Let him that thirsteth,' says the Saviour, "come to me and I will give him drink. Come to me all you who labor and are heavy laden, and I will refresh you!'* Can you fear to want strength when the Truth Himself promises to support you? Oh, if I had the happiness to have you as a fellow disciple in the school of Jesus Christ, if I could pour into your purified soul that unction which teaches all truth, with what zeal would I break to you that bread all burning with the fire of love—that spiritual bread which Jesus Christ ever breaks with such profuse liberality to the poor of the Gospel! How joyfully would I shed over you some drops of that celestial dew which the goodness of God reserves for His children, and which I would pray you in turn to pour over me! I can scarcely leave off, so many things have I to say. I pray God to give you the knowledge of His law and of His will."

The influence which Bernard exercised by means of his letters and his burning words was so effectual, so irresistible, that he was soon surrounded by a company of young men, who not only changed their way of life, but bound themselves to him to follow the holy path which God had traced out for him.

Among these noble-hearted men there was one whose conversion was too remarkable not to be specially recorded. A young nobleman, named Hugh, of the illustrious house of the Counts of Mâcon, had been Bernard's school-fellow and early friend; a happy sympathy in thought, taste, and sentiment, had bound them closely to each other, and their souls, ever in harmony together, vibrated in unison like two strings of the same lyre. But when Hugh heard of Bernard's change he was cut to the heart, and he wept as if he had for ever lost him, who was, he heard, dead to the world. Both the friends now sought each other, but with different motives. Hugh hoped to draw Bernard back to the brilliant career of this world; Bernard to gain his friend's soul to God. An opportunity of meeting occurred; both were deeply moved, and they embraced with many tears. It was some time before they could speak; at last they broke silence, but, before they had exchanged many words, Hugh's soul melted into Bernard's, and, pressing him to his heart, he protested that he would live henceforth to God alone, and that they should be ever united in Jesus Christ.

Soon afterwards, however, Hugh's resolutions and his spirit of devotion began to grow faint, owing to the constant opposition of his worldly friends. Bernard heard of it, he flew to Mâcon, found Hugh in a lovely garden, the centre of a group of young cavaliers; a heavy rain had forced them to take shelter under a tree. Bernard approached his friend, and forced him to come with him notwithstanding the storm. "Hugh," said he, "you must brave this storm with me." As soon as they were alone, calmness returned both to the sky and to the soul of Hugh, and from that time no human effort could disturb the happy change thus wrought by God. "This same Hugh," adds a contemporary biographer, "afterwards became Abbot of Pontigny and Bishop of Auxerre—a church which he still rules in such a manner as to prove that he has the merit as well as the dignity of the episcopate."

It was a thing unheard of and unexampled in those warlike times, and, above all, in joyous Burgundy, for a number of young cavaliers to renounce the pleasures of their age, the glory of their name, and all worldly advantages, to embrace the austerity and poverty of Jesus Christ. Bernard himself was astonished at it, and filled with intense joy, which he expresses admirably in one of his letters. "The news of your conversion," he writes to Geoffrey de Peronne, and his companions, "edifies and rejoices the whole church. Heaven and earth thrill with joy, and the faithful bless the Lord for it. That joy is the effect of the mysterious rain which heaven has poured down more abundantly in our days, and of that free blessing which God reserves for his inheritance. The cross of Jesus Christ has not proved barren in you, as in too many others, who are rebellious against God, who put off their conversion, and whom death overtakes in their impenitence. If the angels rejoice over the conversion of a single sinner, how must they thrill with joy at the conversion of so many sinners; and of sinners, too, whose example is most powerful and contagious, inasmuch as they are in the flower of their age, and distinguished in the world by their birth and talents. I had read in the Sacred Scriptures that among those whom God calls to the faith, there are few wise according to the flesh, few mighty, few noble, and now, by a miraculous grace, I behold a thing altogether contrary. I see a great multitude who despise the glory of the world, and trample on the delights of youth and the pride of birth; regarding the wisdom of this world as foolishness, they are insensible to flesh and blood, callous to the tears of their kindred, and count honors and dignities as nothing, so only they may possess Jesus Christ. What reason should I have to praise you if I regarded these glorious deeds as yours! But God alone has changed your hearts, and wrought these marvels in you. It is an extraordinary work of His grace, and since every perfect gift descends from the Father of lights, it is just that all the glory should ascend to Him."

The Church in France, long groaning under extreme misery, received great consolation from these triumphs of the spirit of God; but she dreamed not yet of the riches silently preparing for her, nor of the innumerable fruits of salvation which that new tree should one day bear, whose lovely seed was now germinating in secret. It was thus of old, when all the people of the earth were given over to a frightful idolatry, that twelve Jewish fishermen, despised and persecuted by men, prepared themselves to overthrow the temple of the false gods, and to renew the face of the world. Bernard and his friends retired to an humble dwelling at Chatillon, and applied themselves energetically to the work of their own salvation, that they might thus be more capable of working for the salvation of others.

# CHAPTER V

COMMUNITY LIFE AT CHATILLON—FAREWELL TO THE
PATERNAL HOME—CONVERSION OF NIVARD.

CHATILLON seemed to have been selected by Bernard's holy company because the chosen youth of the province were assembled there. There Bernard himself had spent his brightest years, and there he had many friends, old companions of his studies, and witnesses of his success.

As soon, however, as they were collected in a house belonging to one of their number, Bernard set himself to regulate its internal discipline according to the spirit of the Gospel; and first he turned his zeal against himself, that he might free himself wholly from the old man, and become an example in all things to those whom he had begotten to Christ. He strove to perfect himself in all his ways, to rise, more and more, above all sensuality; fighting incessantly against concupiscence, in order to break all the power of the flesh. His continual exercise was meditation on the sufferings of Jesus Christ. He compared this exercise to the bundle of myrrh which the bride, in the Canticles, gathered, with pious care, to place in her bosom. He speaks thus upon this subject: "For myself, dear brethren, from the first beginning of my conversion, seeing myself to be wanting in all virtues, I took to myself this bundle of myrrh made up of all my Saviour's bitter sufferings, of the privations He endured in His infancy, the toils He underwent in His ministry, the weariness He suffered in His journeyings, His watching in prayer, His fasting and temptation, His tears of compassion, the snares laid to catch Him in His words, His perils among false brethren, the insults, the blows, the mockeries, the nails, the sorrows, in short, of all kinds which He endured for the salvation of men. I have found wisdom to consist in meditation upon these things, and I have discovered that here alone is the perfection of justice, the fulness of wisdom, the riches of salvation, and the abundance of merit; here is that which raises me in depression, moderates me in success, and makes me to walk safely in the royal road between the goods and the evils of this life, removing, on each side, the perils which threaten my way. Therefore, also, it is that I have these things always in my mouth as you know, and that I have them always in my heart, as God knows; they are ever on my pen as all men may see; and the most sublime philosophy, which I have in this world, is to know Jesus, and Jesus crucified."

This divine philosophy, while it enlightened his understanding and blazed forth in his eloquence, was realized in every action of his life, so that he might have said, like St. Paul, to those who followed his guidance—*My brethren, "I beseech you, be ye followers of me, as I also am of Christ"** And so all these souls which were gathered round him walked emulously in the steps of such a master, forgetting worldly delicacy, that they might free themselves from the bondage of the senses; practising rigorous austerities, that they might subdue the flesh to the spirit; and offering themselves daily as living victims for sacrifice. Bernard supported them by his firm and gentle words, enlightened them by his experience, compassionated their weakness, and gave them the counsels needful for their advancement and perseverance. Even his reproofs were mingled with so much love and sweetness, that they excited at once repentance and gratitude, without ever provoking a murmur. He knew also, by his own experience, what kind of temptations are wont to attack those who give themselves up to God; he forewarned them against vainglory, and more especially against the discouragement too common with those who are but entering the way of perfection, and who, though weaned from human consolations, have not yet arrived at the point where purer joys are found. "All of us, as many as have been converted to God," said he, "feel within ourselves, and acknowledge the truth

---

* 1 Cor. iv. 16.

of those words of Holy Scripture—'Son, when thou comest to the service of God, stand in justice and in fear, and prepare thy soul for temptation.'* Now, the first thing which attacks us at the beginning of our conversion, according to common experience, is the apprehension caused by the frightful image of the severe life which we have embraced, and to which we are not yet accustomed. We do not see that *'the sufferings of this time are not worthy to be compared with the glory to come that shall be revealed in us!* † and we shrink from suffering known evils, for a good of which, as yet, we have no evidence. Those who enter religion must, therefore, watch and pray, to overcome this first temptation, lest, borne down by despondency and fear, they come at last (which God forbid) to desist from the good work they have begun. But, after overcoming this first temptation, we must next beware of human praise, which will tempt us to take pride in the holy life to which we have bound ourselves. Endeavor, therefore, my brethren, after our Saviour's example, to rise above all these things."

Such were the wholesome and powerful lessons which Bernard frequently impressed upon the souls under his direction; and thus did he, like a watchful guide, make plain for them the strait way for salvation; removing the obstacles, and arming them against the dangers, which chiefly beset its entrance. This careful and truly evangelical culture failed not to produce its fruit. Then was seen that miracle which the Christian faith alone has ever been able to perform, and which the magic of the world has never been able to imitate —a miracle ever new, and ever wonderful; but which, from its very frequency, escapes the attention of the vulgar, like those miracles of nature which are renewed every day before our careless and inattentive eyes. Then were seen men of different conditions and social position—students, nobles, old warriors, knights, accustomed to the life of a camp; young men, nurtured in luxury; men of the world, who had hitherto known no passion but for glory and pleasure; rich and poor, learned and ignorant, the weak and the powerful— living all one and the same life, walking together by the same rule, in the same path,

---

\* Eccl. ii. 1.
† 1 Rom. viii.18.

crowded closely together, like innocent lambs, under the crook of a shepherd boy!

They were now thirty in number, of one heart and one soul. The interior of their dwelling, says the venerable William of Saint Thierry, realized the picture drawn by St. Paul of the Church of Corinth. Whoever entered that house felt himself surrounded by an atmosphere of heavenly peace; and so deep was the emotion excited, that, falling on his face, he gave glory to God, and confessed that the Lord was truly in the midst of them. "And then, uniting himself to that holy company, he abode within its bosom; or if he went away again, it was to publish everywhere the happiness of these blessed men, and to deplore his own evil fortune in being unable to remain with them."

There was, in truth, something very extraordinary in the union of these men of high distinction, still in the midst of the world, still wearing the dress of the world, and yet giving example of a supernatural life, which rose before God as a sacred holocaust. All applied themselves, under Bernard's guidance, to the serious practice of the evangelical counsels. They gave themselves to fasting, holy vigils, mental prayer, and meditation on eternal truths, supporting each other by the reciprocal practice of a lively and tender charity. Bernard, though one of the youngest, was like a mother or an elder brother among them—he nourished them with love. "The superior," said he, "should be a mother rather than a master, and be rather loved than feared."

This most true idea gave him an immense power over his subjects. His words of love, like a living chain, bound them together, and linked them to his own heart. Around him was habitual silence; but there was no sadness in this silence. On the contrary, it was all living and thrilling with angelic eloquence; the truly wise have a language among themselves, unknown to the rest of mankind; a mysterious and real communication—vivid, rapid, sublime—by means of which souls sympathize, minds speak, affections expand, sentiments are exchanged, thoughts discovered and revealed; the language this of angels, which none but the King of angels, and they who lead an angel's life, can understand. In them a new sense is awakened—the intimate sense of spiritual things—a sense which includes all others, for it is at once a pure eye, a chaste ear, a fine touch, a spiritual taste, and a divine smell. It is not that organ which no man can tame, which at the same time blesses God our Father, and curses man made in His image; it is not the tongue, which serves both to good and evil, to discord and to peace; it is, as we have said, a language which belongs to the children of wisdom, to them of whom it was written, "Blessed are the peacemakers, for they shall be called the children of God."*

Such was the religious life at Chatillon. But, as is its customs, the world could not long leave this chosen little flock in peace. It had begun by excessive praise, now followed loud censure, and, as a contemporary chronicler assures us, grave suspicion. Thus six months had hardly elapsed since their first establishment at Chatillon, when Bernard felt called upon to draw up a regular plan of life in conformity to the spirit which animated his religious family.

At this critical period the saint gave a proof of humility which, perhaps, surpasses all the heroic instances of this virtue in his after-life. It was a custom very generally followed, especially at that time, for men providentially called to the service of God to remain united together in the particular spirit of their vocation, and constitute a new order in the Church. In the very lifetime of St. Bernard several apostolic men founded, with the approbation of the Holy See, different monastic congregations, adapted to the special work to which they had devoted themselves. St. Bruno, having been persecuted at Rheims, retired, in 1086, into a solitude near Grenoble, where, with six companions, he began the celebrated contemplative Order of the Carthusians. Another founder, the pious Norbert, also a contemporary of St. Bernard, instituted, in 1120, the order of the Canons Regular of Premontré. A few years earlier, St. Robert and St. John Gualbert, with a small number of disciples, formed, for a special end, various congregations, which spread widely and rapidly. In 1116, the illustrious Robert of Arbrisselles founded the celebrated Order of Fontevrault. Eight years afterwards, in 1124, St. Stephen and some of his companions laid the foundations of the Order of Grandmont; and lastly, another Robert, the holy Abbot of Molesme, about 1100, had established himself, with his most fervent disciples, in the desert

---

* Matthew v. 9.

of Citeaux, there to revive, in its primitive purity, the ancient rule of St. Benedict.

It is evident that Bernard, surrounded as he was by a numerous company, and already in high estimation for sanctity, might have aspired, like so many other founders, to a separate existence in union with the children whom God had given him. But such was his repugnance to every kind of distinction and pre-eminence, that, with most entire self-abnegation, he prepared to bury himself and his disciples in an order already established. For this purpose they chose the Order of Citeaux, the most severe then existing—the austerity of which was so excessive as to be spoken of even by religious with a shudder of horror and compassion. The congregation of Citeaux had, as we have said, been recently founded by St. Robert, in the dark forests of Beaune, in Burgundy; at the period of which we are writing the first founder was dead, and Stephen Harding, an Englishman of noble birth, was at the head of the community, which he ruled with consummate wisdom. But the ravages of a disease which had decimated the country round, added to the extreme austerities practised there, kept new members from joining them, and the holy abbot mourned over this desolation like a barren mother who despairs of children. It was in this house, thus lacking both subjects and all things necessary for the support of life, that St. Bernard resolved to begin his novitiate with the friends who were with him.

They settled all their affairs like men preparing for death and, having made all their arrangements, Bernard and his brothers went, before their departure, to Fontaines, to bid farewell to their father and ask his blessing.

At that interview occurred one of those agonizing scenes which the strongest human heart can endure but once in the course of a long life. Tecelin had long been anxiously watching his children's path, and although he was expecting an inevitable separation, he had not been able to bring himself to consent to the sacrifice. To lose in one day five sons, whose noble qualities had been his glory and his delight! to be robbed in his old age of the rightful hopes of his whole life! it was too much for an old man bowed down beneath the weight of years. "The thought of this farewell," says an historian, "convulsed his heart, his eyes closed as he gazed on them, his voice failed him, and he almost lost consciousness."

The young Hombeline was shedding floods of tears at her father's side; she had a strong affection for each one of her brothers, but from her childhood, and especially since her mother's death, her deepest and most confiding tenderness had been for Bernard. Now she viewed him as the cause of the ruin of their house and of her own happiness, and, in a tone in which disappointment, love, anger, reverence, and hope were all blended, she conjured Bernard to suspend his plans, she implored him to have some regard to the gray hairs of his father, to the deserted state of his youngest brother, and to have pity on the poor feeble sister whom he had once so dearly loved, and who would soon be left alone and unprotected.

Bernard possessed his soul amid the tortures of this cruel trial. God alone—the God who dwelt within that loving heart—could have given him the supernatural strength to consummate the sacrifice, according to the words of Jesus Christ: "If any man will come after me, let him deny himself and take up his cross and follow me;"* and, "Every one that hath left house, or brethren, or sisters, or father, or mother, or wife, or children, or lands for my name's sake, shall receive an hundred-fold and shall possess life everlasting."

The sons of Tecelin received their father's blessing and departed.

For the consolation of the reader we will anticipate the course of events, and hasten to tell him that, towards the close of his life, the aged Tecelin rejoined his sons, and died of days, in the arms of St. Bernard.

And thus, in requital of a momentary sacrifice, accomplished in the short space of their earthly life, they are inseparably united for all eternity.

Bernard escaped, by his departure from the scenes of all this sorrow, the dangers arising from those strong affections so often fatal to souls like his. But one last stroke remained for his father, which came so visibly from the hand of Divine Providence, as to have sufficed (one might have supposed) to open his eyes to the irrevocable destiny of his family. As they left the castle-yard the sons of Tecelin caught sight of their youngest brother, who was at play with other children of his own age. Guido, the eldest,

---

* Matthew xvi. 24.

embraced him, saying, "My little brother Nivard, do you see this castle and these lands? Well, all this will be yours—yours alone." "What!" replied the child, with more than a child's thoughtfulness, "are you going to take heaven for yourselves and leave earth for me? the division is not equal." From that moment the little Nivard could not be restrained by his father, his relations, or any human influence. He joined St. Bernard, who, with his brothers and companions to the number of thirty, set out for Citeaux.

They journeyed all together, on foot, under the guidance of their beloved pastor, who marched at their head.

This was in 1113.

# Second Period

MONASTIC LIFE OF ST. BERNARD, FROM HIS ENTRANCE INTO THE ORDER OF CITEAUX, TO HIS POLITICAL LIFE, CONNECTED WITH THE SCHISM OF ROME. (1113~1130)

# CHAPTER VI

ORIGIN OF THE ORDER OF CITEAUX—REVELATION CONCERNING ITS FUTURE DESTINY—ARRIVAL OF ST. BERNARD AT THE MONASTERY.

THE religious orders, which succeed each other on the unchanging territory of the Church, are subject to the laws which govern the productions of nature. They grow from feeble and imperceptible seeds; increase, flourish, and bear fruit; then decrease, fade, and fall to the ground. But they have produced a fruit which contains within it the germ of a new seed-time, and which bursts forth vigorously from its decaying sheath, to reproduce its never-failing kind.

Thus the Order of St. Benedict, first devoutly founded, in the sixth century, on Mount Cassino, has been propagated through successive transformations even to our days, casting off at each new phase its former shell, to revive under some other form, adapted to other times and other manners. In the last century, including all the different branches and affiliations, more than thirty-seven thousand monasteries recognized St. Benedict for their patriarch; and from the time of Charlemagne, the western monks generally embraced his rule and discipline. One of the most memorable transformations of the Benedictine order, before St. Bernard's time, was the reform of Cluny, so called from a celebrated monastery of that name, founded about the year 910, in the diocese of Mâcon, by William the Pious, Duke of Aquitaine. This Benedictine congregation was governed for nearly 200 years by St. Berno, St. Odo, St. Mayeul, St. Odilo, St. Hugh, and Peter the Venerable—all illustrious for their learning and deep wisdom; and it extended its fruitful branches over the whole of Europe. It was the central fire of the piety, wisdom, and sublime virtues of the middle age, and the home of its greatest men. The houses of his rule in Italy, France, Spain, Germany, and England, numbered among their simple religious a multitude of princes, cardinals, and sovereigns; and among the humble monks who came forth from Cluny to rule the world, we may count three famous Popes—St. Gregory VII, Urban II, and Gelasius.

This marvellous prosperity continued to increase until the death of the holy abbot, Hugh, in 1109. From that time the Order of Cluny, having come to the highest pitch of its power, daily faded under the burden of its own wealth and grandeur. The abbot, Pons, who succeeded Hugh, opened the door to abuses; and, under his short administration, all the springs of the religious life began to relax. The building bent towards its fall. After the death, indeed, of this unworthy superior, who died of the plague, Peter the Venerable tried to remedy the evils of his rule, and to restore the ancient discipline. His attempt, according to St. Bernard's own testimony, had no lasting success. He was the last illustrious man of this order, which seemed now to have fulfilled its destiny, and which, after his death, is lost in obscurity. But as the sap retired from the branch of Cluny, it was concentrated on another point of St. Benedict's Order; which, at the end of the eleventh century, was already beginning to flourish under a new form. Several Benedictine monks, animated by a strong desire for perfection, retired into the lonely forest of Molesme, on the confines of Champagne and Burgundy; they made themselves little huts with the branches of trees, and formed the congregation of Molesme, under the austere government of St. Robert. But in the designs of Providence, this congregation was to be but the nursery of a more vast and fruitful order. As soon as the establishment of Molesme was developed, the pious Robert, under the inspiration of God, made choice of the most fervent of the monks, and withdrew them like precious plants from Molesme, to transplant them to the desert of Citeaux. There they dwelt together, their number at first being seven—viz., Robert, Alberic, Stephen, Odo, John, Letald, and Peter. Fourteen other religious, from Molesme, afterwards joined them, with the intention of leading a more perfect life; and, in 1099, they finished a small wooden chapel, which they dedicated to the Blessed Virgin, in order to place themselves more especially under the protection of the Mother of the Saviour. This was the grain of mustard-seed, whose fruit, so long deferred, was to fill the earth. Citeaux, situated in the diocese of Chalons, at some leagues distance from Dijon, was at that time an almost inaccessible solitude, the savage wildness of which had never yet been softened by the hand of man. Robert and his companions retired into the depth of the forest, cleared a part of it, and built an oratory, around which they lived in a constant round of labor and contemplation. These religious had at first no peculiar rules or constitutions. They devoted themselves to the literal practice of St. Benedict's rule, without making any change in it. But Robert having been obliged to return to Molesme, his disciple and successor, Alberic, gave a definite constitution to the rising congregation, and the form of life of the ancient fathers of the desert.

The rigid practices of Citeaux all tended to the annihilation of self, to the complete mortification of corrupt nature, to the detachment of the soul from the ties, and its liberation from the bondage of flesh and blood, to its restoration to holy freedom, and its original relation to its first Principle and the invisible world. The chosen souls called to this high spirituality found everything in the discipline of Citeaux to develop the divine sense within them. Calm and sustained labor, rigorous silence, habitual recollection, which intensely concentrated the powers of the soul; removal from all dissipation, from every object calculated to excite the imagination and the senses, punctual obedience, poverty, complete relinquishment of material things—such was the manner of life, sanctioned by the experience of ages, which these holy monks fervently embraced; and they became the more firmly established in it as the bonds of earth fell from them, and they rose each day higher and higher towards the source of eternal joy.

So pure a life could not fail to provoke calumny. The merely rational man does not understand the spiritual man's austerities; he sees no farther than the surface of things, and condemns, as blamable extravagances, the mortifications which tend to purify his earthly life. Confounding, in his ignorance, human nature as it came out of the hands of God, with human nature now contaminated by sin, he asks, if God endowed it with so marvellous a sensibility never to know enjoyment? if God gave it organs, never to be used? if God can take delight in the sufferings of man? This is to ask why Christianity was founded on the cross? why Christ Himself suffered and died? The doctrine of suffering and tears is not an after refinement of Christian morality; it is the expression and promulgation of the very laws and inevitable realities of our earthly existence. This mortal life, which terminates in death, is but a course of sufferings, necessary for the destruction of our perverted nature; blessed are they who give themselves voluntarily to this work, instead of waiting for the last day to do by violence that which should have been the gradual work of a whole life!

The religious of Citeaux took all the evangelical counsels in earnest; and their severe rules were terrifying to nature. Read the description, given by the ancient chronicler of the order, of their way of life. "These holy monks," says he, "wished to live unknown and forgotten in their deep solitude. Their austerities seemed beyond human endurance. They were half naked*—exposed to the most piercing cold of winter and most burning heat of summer. To their continual labor they joined the most painful exercises; vigils, almost throughout the night, the divine office, spiritual lectures, long prayers, and other devout practices, succeeded each other without any intermission." "There was," adds the same author, "neither tumult, nor noise, nor confusion, nor complaint, nor dispute among them, nor intermission in their holy exercises. The Virgin, the Queen of Angels, was the light of St. Alberic, St. Alberic was the light of St. Stephen, St. Stephen was the light of his brothers, and they who received the light yielded instant obedience to those by whom it was given."

St. Stephen, an Englishman by birth, undertook the government of the congregation of Citeaux, on the death of St. Alberic, in 1109. Nothing can be more touching than the account of this father's obsequies; the words pronounced by St. Stephen on

---

\* The Benedictine habit was black or brown. St. Alberic changed it for one grayish white, when he took the Blessed Virgin for their patroness. This was the color of St. Bernard's monastic habit; "the cowl of which is still preserved in the monastery of St. Victor at Paris," says E. Lenain.

this occasion may give us an idea of the intense charity which subsisted among these monks. "Alas!" said he to his brethren, "Alberic is dead to our eyes, but not to the eyes of God. Dead as he seems to us, he lives for us before the Lord; for this is the way of the saints, that, when they go to God by death, they carry their friends with them in their heart, there to preserve them for ever; so that we may say that, death having united him to God, by an eternal and unchangeable love, he has taken us with him to God." The congregation of Citeaux, under the direction of Stephen, began to attract public attention, and to excite the murmurs of the neighboring monasteries. The monks of Cluny, having fallen from their original fervor, loved not to see this new order arise to rebuke their self-indulgence. Hence, accusations, invented by envy, burst forth on all sides against Stephen and his brethren; they were denounced to the whole Church as innovators, who carried ascetism and maceration of the body to excess; they were even accused of introducing schism and division among religious orders.

In these critical circumstances, the patience of the venerable abbot was admirable. Convinced that if this new institute were the work of God it would keep its ground, notwithstanding all the efforts of men, he stood fast in the strict observance of the rule, and only replied to his calumniators by redoubled zeal and vigilance.

Yet his faith was put to a new test, which caused him strange perplexity. We have already noticed, in the preceding chapter, that a mortal malady had made frightful ravages in the country, but nowhere had its effects been so fatal as at Citeaux. Nearly all the religious, already exhausted by excessive austerities, died at the first approach of the malady, and but a very small number of sickly monks remained alive in 1112. "Besides all the various afflictions which overwhelm me," said the venerable Stephen, "my heart is pierced through with anguish when I consider how few religious remain with us, for we are dying daily, one after another, so that the thing which I greatly fear seems on the point to befall us, that this order will perish and die together with us."

This frightful mortality had so stricken the rising congregation that the monks began to fear that there was some truth in the accusations brought against them, and that the austerity of their life was not ordered according to the rules of Christian prudence. St. Stephen's own confidence began to waver, and not knowing what course to take in this painful state of uncertainty, he endeavored to obtain light by a means hitherto unheard of; which denotes, at once, the strength of his faith and the purity of his conscience. The fact which we are about to relate, however strange it may appear, seems to us to possess a character of the greatest authenticity; I will, therefore, transcribe it, with a few omissions, in the simple words of the annalists of Citeaux.

"There was, at that time, a brother who was about to go and receive the recompense of his labors. Then, St. Stephen, being full of the spirit of God, approached him, and said thus, in the presence of all the religious: "You see, my beloved brother, in what affliction, trouble, and depression we are. We believe assuredly that we are walking in the narrow way which our blessed father, St. Benedict, showed unto us, but we are not sure whether that manner of life is pleasing to God, especially seeing that the religious of this country condemn us as persons who have invented new ways of life, and who cause scandal, schism, and division. I am deeply afflicted, also, to see that the number of brethren who daily leave us reduces us to so small a company; and, as God sends us no one to fill the places of those whom He calls to Himself, I fear much that this new institute will end with us. Therefore, in the name of our Lord Jesus Christ, for whose love we have chosen the narrow way set before us in His Gospel, I command you, in virtue of holy obedience, that, when you shall be with God, you return to us, at the time and in the manner which shall please Him, to inform us, according to His will, what we are to believe concerning our state, and the life which we are leading.'

"To these words the dying man simply answered: 'Reverend father, I will do very willingly what you are pleased to command me, on condition that you will aid me with your holy prayers, that I may be able to execute your orders.'

"Some days had elapsed since the death of the religious, and the holy abbot, being at work with his brethren, gave the signal for repose, as was the custom. He retired a little apart, and, having seated himself, and covered his head with his scapular, he began to pray. At that moment the deceased monk appeared to him, all resplendent with glory—he seemed to be raised in the air without touching the ground. The holy abbot asked how it fared with him.

"'I am happy,' replied he, 'and I pray God to render you as happy as I am, for by your wholesome instructions, and your constant care, I now enjoy that happiness and peace incomprehensible, which surpass all the thoughts of men to conceive. And now, in obedience to the command you have been pleased to lay upon me, I return to make known to you, my father, and to all my brethren, the grace and mercy of our Lord Jesus Christ towards this new order. Know, then, and doubt not, that your way of life is pleasing to Jesus Christ. Banish your affliction, or rather let it be changed into joy, for behold God will shortly make known to you the riches of His mercy, and will send you a great number of persons, among whom there will be many noble, wise, and mighty; and they shall so fill this house, that they shall go forth from it like swarms of bees to overspread all parts of the world; and they shall people other monasteries, which shall be the happy fruit of that seed of benediction, which has grown and gathered strength in this place, by the grace of God.'"

"The religious," continues the historian, "having uttered these solemn words, asked and obtained the blessing of him who had been his superior in the school of sanctity, and then disappeared, leaving St. Stephen in an ecstacy of admiration and gratitude. This extraordinary revelation revived the courage of the monks; but another event, which happened at the same time, was looked upon by them as a new presage of the consolations which they expected. A brother had a dream in which he saw a multitude of men, who came to the monastery to wash their clothes, and he heard a voice, which told him that this fountain should be called Enon, the place where the precursor of Jesus Christ baptized. This vision appeared to the holy abbot to have a hidden meaning; and from that time he lived in continual expectation of a great number of persons, who were to come and wash off the stains of their souls in the labors and tears of the penitential life of Citeaux."

This expectation was at last fulfilled. St. Stephen and a feeble remnant of his monks were one day before God in prayer, supplicating, all together, in the fulness of their heart, for the accomplishment of the divine promises.

At that moment, a troop of men, to the number of thirty, with a young man at their head, slowly crossed the forest, and arrived at the gate of the monastery. St. Stephen, his heart full of hope, went to receive them; and they fell at his feet, and earnestly besought admission into the order.

Then did the joy of the Abbot of Citeaux burst forth into a song of thanksgiving: and "such was the effect of this visit," writes William of St. Thierry, "that this house seemed to have heard those words of the prophet—'Give praise, O thou barren, that bearest not: sing forth praise, and make a joyful noise, that thou didst not travail with child: for many are the children of the desolate, more than of her that hath an husband, saith the Lord.'"*

---

* Isaiah iiv. 1.

# CHAPTER VII

NOVITIATE OF ST. BERNARD—HIS PROFESSION—
ENLARGEMENT OF CITEAUX—FOUNDATION OF CLAIRVAUX.

"In the year 1113 of the incarnation of our Lord, fifteen years after the foundation of the house of Citeaux, the servant of God, Bernard, at about three-and-twenty years of age, entered, with thirty companions, into this monastery, which was then governed by the Abbot Stephen, and subjected himself to the sweet yoke of Jesus Christ. From that day, God raining down blessings on this vine of the Lord of Hosts, it produced its fruit and extended its branches to the sea, and even beyond the sea."

Citeaux, which but now was on the point of becoming extinct, like a new-born child condemned to die in the cradle, seemed to have received a new birth on the arrival of Bernard and his numerous company, All entered on their novitiate immediately, with the exception of one, whom St. Stephen put off for two years, on account of his extreme youth. This was the gentle Robert, St. Bernard's cousin, of whom we shall soon have occasion to speak.

From the moment of his entrance on the monastic life, Bernard's chief care was to realize in himself the advice he had given to others. "If thou beginnest, begin well."—"*Si incipis, perfecte incipe.*" In choosing for his retreat the poorest and most obscure of the religions orders, he hoped to remain there, unknown and forgotten of men; and henceforward, desiring nothing but to die with Jesus Christ, he embraced the cross lovingly, attached himself to it resolutely, and carried it generously after the Divine Master to whom he had consecrated himself. Having his eye continually fixed on the high end to which he was tending with all his strength, he frequently said to himself, "Bernard, why hast thou come here?"—"*Bernard, ad quid venisti*?" And as we read of our Lord, that He began to do, and afterwards He taught,* so Bernard worked first at his own sanctification, and practised himself all that he was afterwards to teach to others. His biographers tell, with admiration, of the efforts which he made to overcome himself, and to bring his lively and naturally passionate character into subjugation: he submitted, with perfect regularity, to the most humble and painful exercises of the discipline of St. Benedict; and his virtue daily developed itself so vigorously as to astonish the aged saint who governed this new school of prophets. He had acquired the salutary habit of living interiorly, which rendered recollection easy and continual; and as the life-giving graces which he drew from the invisible source shone forth in his exterior, he seemed always surrounded by a glory of celestial joy; so that, says one of his biographers, one would have taken him for a spirit rather than a man, exemplifying in his person what he afterwards said to his novices: "If you desire to live in this house, you must leave outside the bodies which yon bring from the world; for souls only are admitted here, and the flesh is nothing." The more he tasted the delights of the love which burned within him, and enlightened him interiorly, the more he mortified his senses—his natural life— lest communication with exterior things should become an obstacle to the enjoyment of these ineffable consolations. "And thus the constant practice of mortification gradually became so habitual, that living now only for spiritual things, he saw without seeing, heard without hearing, ate without tasting, and he scarcely retained any feeling for the things of the body." It is said that more than once he drank oil or some other liquid for water without perceiving it; he did not know at the end of his year's novitiate, whether the top of the dormitory was flat or vaulted; neither did he know whether there were windows at the end of the oratory where he prayed daily; one single thought absorbed him entirely and preserved him from puerile distractions. His conscience, becoming more delicate the more he purified it, could no longer suffer any imperfections, and

---

* Acts i. 1.

the highest fault was agony to the young novice. His affection for his mother had suggested a vow to recite the Seven Penitential Psalms every day in her memory. "Once," says the author of "The Exordium of Citeaux," "whilst still in his novitiate, he went to rest without having accomplished the duty which he had prescribed to himself. The next day, Stephen, his spiritual father, being inwardly enlightened, said to him: 'Brother Bernard, to whom did you give the care of reciting your seven psalms yesterday?' At these words, Bernard, astonished that a practice which he had kept secret should be known, burst into tears; and throwing himself at the feet of his venerable guide, confessed his fault and humbly begged pardon for it. Another time, having received a visit from some of his relations who were living in the world, he took pleasure in listening to the news which they told him. This vain curiosity was scarcely satisfied when he began to feel the bad effect of it. Dark clouds obscured the peace of his soul, and, for a long time, he remained without any consolation in prayer, and without joy or strength in his ascetic exercises, until, at last, having seen the greatness of his fault, he threw himself at the foot of the altar, praying and weeping for the return of grace. It was thus that the unction of truth, which inwardly directed and instructed him, purified him from the slightest stains; and in requital of his punctual fidelity to grace, raised him, step by step, to the most sublime perfection.

Meanwhile, even in the year of his novitiate, Bernard, whose constitution was feeble and delicate, fell ill—he could neither eat nor sleep, and often had long fainting fits. "As he eats little," says a contemporary biographer, "he also sleeps little; and, in these two things, he seems to use what is necessary, less to sustain life than to defer death." Besides the natural weakness of his temperament, he hastened the ruin of his health by the excess of his austerities; and he had reason afterwards to regret his want of due discretion in the use of penitential practices. His stomach rejected every kind of nourishment, and his body became so thin, that it seemed scarcely material. But these infirmities did not prevent him from following the common rule; he shunned all singularity, and endeavored to supply his want of physical strength by the fervor of his spirit. His greatest grief was not to be able to share the fatigue and rough work in which his brethren were employed.

He lamented before God the sad incapacity which prevented him from serving the monastery by the labor of his hands; nevertheless, by dint of application and perseverance, he at length succeeded in digging the ground, chopping wood, and carrying it on his shoulders. Whilst he was engaged in these exterior works, his brethren were admiring his profound recollection; he came and went, ready for every service, showing even in the least things an extraordinary zeal; and in the midst of these multiplied and fatiguing occupations, he was ever attentive to the voice which speaks to the heart, ever consumed in the living fire of love, ever in intimate communication with the source of divine light. He always preserved a grateful remembrance of this kind of life once active and passive, which was to him a season of abundant grace and rapid progress. "He declares it still," says the monk already cited; "he avows that it was principally in the fields and woods that he received, by contemplation and prayer, the understanding of the Scriptures; and he is in the habit of saying pleasantly to his friends, that he had never had any other master in this study than the beech trees and oaks of the forest."

It was in these peaceful and fervent exercises that the time of the novitiate passed. The long-desired day of his profession at length arrived; it was in the month of April, 1114, that Bernard and his old companions pronounced their perpetual vows with deep emotion. Contemporary chroniclers simply announce the fact; adding that expressions are wanting to speak of it worthily. One must, indeed, have experienced the joy with which the soul is inundated when it fulfils an irresistible vocation, and have tasted that feeling of happiness and perfect rest, to understand and speak of what passed at this time within these chosen souls. Bernard and his brothers offered themselves to God, without reserve, as victims of expiation and of love, desiring nothing else in this world than to immolate themselves daily to the service and glory of Jesus Christ.

The example of St. Bernard had drawn many postulants to Citeaux, so that the monastery could scarcely contain the great number of persons, of different countries, who begged admission into the order. Historians, astonished at this extraordinary increase, attribute it to the jealousy of certain old religious orders, particularly the monks of Molesme. The unfavorable reports which they spread about the new monastery, as they called it, made it known everywhere, and contributed greatly to draw inquirers thither, who, through the effect of grace, became religious. The number of these last growing daily larger, Stephen was obliged to think about the establishment of a colony. The place, which he considered well adapted for this foundation, had been offered to the Abbot of Citeaux by the lords of the country of Chalons. It was a forest, of which they cleared a part; and, after having raised an humble church, surrounded by cells, Stephen sent thither twelve monks, under the conduct of Bertrand, a man as venerable on account of his piety as of his great age. This was the first filiation from Citeaux; and St. Stephen, in imitation of the ancient patriarchs, wished to give it a symbolical name; he called it *Firmitas* (*Ferté*)—*Firmness*—to mark the. strength and consistency that God had given to the new order. Scarcely was the monastery of La Ferté established, when a second colony of religious was asked of St. Stephen, for the diocese of Auxerre. Although the holy abbot earnestly desired the extension of his order, he was in no hurry to accept the land which had been placed at his disposal; he feared the dangers of too rapid and precocious a development; he consulted his brethren, carefully examined all circumstances, and waited with tranquillity the indications of Providence. But at last, the monastery continuing to fill with novices, he was obliged to decide. Stephen again designated twelve of his religious, and gave them as abbot the celebrated Hugh de Maçon, the most intimate friend of Bernard, and his spiritual son. The merit of Hugh may be estimated by the choice made of him, and the wonderful increase of the monastery of Pontigny under his direction. This house became, as it were, a nursery of holy prelates, who shed the most brilliant lustre on the Order of Citeaux.

Meanwhile, the mother-house, like a hive too narrow to shelter all the bees that multiply within it, was so full of postulants, in the year 1115, that St. Stephen, after having delayed their reception, was again obliged to seek an establishment for these swarms of evangelical laborers. An uninhabited spot, in the province of Langres, had been mentioned to him. This desert was very marshy, and almost inaccessible; there was no doubt that the religious of Citeaux would easily obtain permission to establish themselves there. Consequently, Stephen, although he knew no one in the diocese who could maintain the foundation, proposed his idea to the brothers, and asked their opinion. Some judged this enterprise impossible, on account of the want of every kind of means; others, among whom was St. Stephen, thought that they ought to depend entirely on God for the success of the work. This last advice prevailed. The holy abbot chose, for the new establishment, Bernard's brothers, his uncle Godfrey, two religious, named Gauldry, one of whom was his relation; another named Elbold, of very advanced age; he joined to these, to complete the number of twelve, the monk Walter, and the young Robert, Bernard's cousin. Stephen put at the head of this holy colony him who had been the guiding angel of his brethren, and the consolation of Citeaux. Bernard was then only in his twenty-fifth year; and it was a subject of general surprise that a young man of so delicate a temperament, and who had no experience in worldly affairs, should be chosen as the head of so perilous an enterprise. But his virtue had shone forth in so remarkable a manner, that St. Stephen, better versed than others in the hidden ways of Providence, did not hesitate to uphold this choice, the consequences of which were so happy for the Church.

The day of the departure of the new colony having arrived, the religious designated—whose number was to represent the apostolic college—set out, under the conduct of Bernard, who, having become their abbot, represented Jesus Christ in the midst of his disciples. The ceremony observed under these circumstances was simple and touching. The abbot of the mother-house solemnly placed a cross in the hands of him who was to be invested with the dignity of abbot; then the new abbot, leaving the church, with the cross, and followed by his twelve religious, bade adieu to his brethren, who intoned a solemn chant as they set forth. "As soon as Bernard and his twelve monks," say the chroniclers of Citeaux, "had silently quitted the church, you might have seen tears stream from the eyes of all his brethren, while nothing was to be heard but the voices of those who sang the hymns; and now they could no longer restrain their sobs, in spite of the efforts they made to stifle their tears. It was difficult to distinguished those who were going from those who remained behind, all being in grief and affliction; until, at length, they reached the gate of the monastery, which opened for some, and was closed again upon the others."

Who does not here admire the humble obedience and profound abnegation of these true disciples of Jesus Christ? They separated, without a murmur, from old friends, from faithful companions, with whom they had lived in the world and in the monastery; they quitted a venerable superior, whom they loved as their father; a holy house, which they had chosen for their resting-place; an edifying company, the object of their tenderest affections; and they departed, without knowing whither they were going, what would become of them, nor the sufferings which awaited them! Bernard, always full of vigor in his apostolic path, recovers strength, and strengthens his brethren; he walks before them, like the Good Shepherd; he guides them, consoles them, raises them above all human forethought, and fills them with hope and joy. Long did they wander across an uncultivated country, through dense forests; but they felt neither privations nor fatigues; the tired traveller does not long more earnestly for his home than these men of God sighed after their desert. They, at length, reached this swampy valley; it was an old haunt of robbers, and was called in the country the valley of Absinthea; but Bernard gave it the name of Claire-Vallée—for henceforward it was to become one of the most burning furnaces of divine light.

Bernard and his companions found no difficulty in establishing themselves in a place far from any habitation; and. instead of disputing with them the possession of a retreat which until then had only inspired them with fear, the inhabitants of the neighboring country helped them to clear the ground, and to build little cells—glad to have monks among them whose mortified life touched them with compunction. As soon as they had finished their humble oratory, and the buildings began to take the form of a monastery, Bernard gave it a definite organization. He confided the charge of prior to the monk Walter, whom St. Stephen had particularly designated for that important ministry; he gave to his brother Gerard the office of cellarer, and charged Andrew, his other brother, with the care of the door. Then, having put all the rules of Citeaux in full exercise, he set out, accompanied by a religious, to Chalons to be blessed there as abbot. William of Saint Thierry thus relates this circumstance:—

"When it became necessary that Bernard should receive blessing from a bishop, the see of Langres, in which diocese he was, happened to be vacant; and the brethren, deliberating among themselves where they should take him to be ordained, the high reputation of the famous doctor, William of Champeaux, Bishop of Chalons, induced them to decide on this remarkable prelate. He went, therefore, to Chalons (on Marne) with the monk Elbold. When Bernard, then only twenty-five years of age, entered the episcopal house—his body emaciate, and death painted in his face, whilst the monk who accompanied him was tall, robust, and well-looking—some laughed, others mocked; but some, judging according to truth, were touched with reverence. The bishop, without asking which of the two was abbot, fixed his eyes on Bernard, and received the servant of God as being himself servant of God. From that day and that hour they had but one heart in our Lord; and they visited one another with so much familiarity, that Clairvaux became to the holy bishop as his own house, and Chalons the hospitable retreat of all those from Clairvaux. The diocese of Rheims and all France was excited by the example of William of Champeaux to revere the man of God; for all learned of so pious a bishop to respect him as an angel sent from heaven. It was said, with reason, that a prelate of such high authority must have seen great heavenly gifts and graces in Bernard, since he testified so lively an affection for him, although he was but an unknown monk, who sought only to humble himself." Meanwhile, as it ordinarily happens among men, the inhabitants of the country, who had at first shown great zeal in succoring these poor religious, soon got accustomed to seeing the examples of sanctity which shone before their eyes; and, growing tired of assisting in proportion as they ceased to admire them, Clairvaux fell, by degrees, into extreme distress. The monks, constantly occupied in the building of the monastery, could not possibly earn their bread by their work; and as their establishment had been made after the season for sowing, the land yielded them nothing. It was with incredible trouble that they procured a little barley and millet, with which they made bread—having nothing to eat but the leaves of beech trees, cooked in salt water. The winter came to add new rigors to this frightful condition, and Clairvaux had to sustain evils of all kinds.

"One day," says a pious chronicler, "even their salt failed them." Bernard called one of the brethren, and said to him: "Guibert, my son, take the ass, and go buy salt in the market." The brother replied: "My father, will you give me money to pay for it?" "Have confidence," replied the man of God; "as for money, I do not know when we shall have any; but there is one above who keeps my purse, and who has the care of my treasures." Guibert smiled, and, looking at Bernard, said to him: "My father, if I go empty-handed, I fear I shall return empty-handed." "Go," still replied Bernard, "and go with confidence. I repeat to thee, my treasure will be with thee on the road, and will furnish thee with what is necessary." Upon this, the brother, having received the reverend abbot's blessing, saddled his ass, and went to the market, which was held near a castle called Risnellus. "Guibert," adds the simple chronicler, "had been more incredulous than he should have been; nevertheless, the God of all consolation procured him an unexpected success; for, not far from the neighboring town, he met a priest, who saluted him, and asked him whence he came. Guibert confided to him the object of his mission, and the extreme penury of his convent; which so touched the charitable priest, that he furnished him abundantly with all sorts of provisions." The happy Guibert returned in haste to the monastery, and, throwing himself at the feet of Bernard, related what had happened to him on the road. The father then gently addressed these words to him: "I told thee, my son, there is nothing more necessary to the Christian than confidence in God; never lose it, and it will be well with thee all the days of thy life."

This assistance, however, and several other resources which had been presented them, in a no less marvellous manner, were at length exhausted, and Clairvaux fell anew into all the horrors of complete indigence; the religious, a prey to hunger, cold, and almost insupportable privations, gave way to discouragement, and manifested loudly their desire to return to Citeaux. Bernard himself was overpowered by so deep a sadness at the sight of the moral and physical sufferings of his children, that he lost power to encourage them; so that he ceased even to break the bread of the word to them; and thus, says the annalist of Citeaux, the religious were deprived at once of the bread of the body on account of their extreme poverty, and of the bread of the soul on account of the silence of their holy abbot.

This state of things, which had began before the end of the year 1115, was prolonged during the winter of the following year, and it would be impossible to tell what Bernard had to suffer during these sixteen or seventeen months, in striving to prevent the dissolution of Clairvaux, and to turn to the advantage of the brothers the terrible trial which, in the designs of God, was to confirm for ever their virtue, their confidence, their faith, their patience, and their entire self-abandonment to the care of Providence.

Oh, generous men! who then led you into these barren places to endure the most cruel hardships, but He who came down upon earth to be born in a manger and to die upon the cross? Who put into your hearts the thoughts of quitting your lands, your castles, your friends, your relations, and of despoiling yourselves of yourselves, but the God of love, who, for love of men, gave them his own life?

One day Bernard, bathed in tears, had prostrated himself on the steps of the altar, with his brothers, lamenting before the Lord and imploring aloud the mercy of the Saviour, to whom they had devoted themselves in the simplicity of their hearts.

At this moment they all heard a strange voice which seemed to come from heaven. The astonished brethren listened attentively and heard distinctly these words, which resounded through the church: "Arise, Bernard, thy prayer is heard!"

# CHAPTER VIII

DEVELOPMENT OF CLAIRVAUX—ILLNESS OF ST. BERNARD—
NARRATIVE OF WILLIAM OF ST. THIERRY.

CLAIRVAUX, at the time of its foundation, may be compared to the grain spoken of in the Gospel; nothing, in fact, could have been weaker, humbler, more miserable than this heavenly seed when it was first cast into the field of the Church; it long vegetated without any development; it had to struggle against the most violent storms and tempests; but the principle of life contained within it rendered the work of God indestructible, and, after a profound humiliation and abasement, it made a sudden spring.

The long and cruel sufferings of the religious were, at length, divulged, and excited public compassion; unexpected relief poured in on all sides; and Bernard had soon to apprehend the dangers of too great abundance more than the evils of famine. While the brethren were still in amazement at the superhuman voice which had been heard in the church, two strangers arrived at the monastery, and laid very considerable offerings at St. Bernard's feet. Wagons, laden with provisions, arrived soon afterwards from Chalons; and the desert of Clairvaux, watered by the sweat of these pious cenobites and fertilized by their labor, began to afford regular resources and to supply their urgent necessities.

Bernard, now at ease as to temporal things, and seeing peace and divine virtues flourish among his children, was able to absent himself from the monastery and accede to the frequent entreaties of the Bishop of Chalons, who desired him to preach in the churches of his diocese. These missions exercised an irresistible influence; the whole population flocked to hear the man of God whose powerful words worked wonders; priests, as well as illustrious laymen, not content with reforming their lives, attached themselves closely to the young abbot, and followed him to Clairvaux to embrace the monastic rule. "How many learned men," writes one of the biographers of St. Bernard, "how many orators, how many nobles and great ones of the earth, how many philosophers have passed from the schools or the academies of the world to Clairvaux to give themselves up to the meditation of heavenly things and the practice of a divine morality."

"As he acted rather by the power of faith than by the spirit of the world," says another writer of the same time, "he made easy many things which seemed scarcely more possible than to remove mountains. Grace manifested itself in a remarkable manner by his preaching; by it he softened the most hardened hearts, and he scarcely ever returned without bringing back some fruit of his discourses. Thus making every day new progress, as much by the efficacy of his instructions as by the example of his sanctity; and the nets of the word of God being thrown out on every opportunity by this faithful servant who preached in the name of God, so great a draught was taken at each cast as seemed sufficient to fill the little vessel of Clairvaux. Hence, it happened that in a short time, by the greatest miracle which he ever wrought in his life, this half-dead, languishing man, whose voice alone seemed left to him, rendered this once obscure valley so illustrious, that it truly deserved its name of Claire-Vallée, since it spread, as from the highest summit of Christian virtues, a divine light and brilliancy over the face of the earth." Among the new disciples of the Abbot of Clairvaux, the learned Roger, who afterwards became Abbot of Trois Fontaines, Humbert, the pious Ranald, Peter of Toulouse, the Blessed Odo, afterwards Sub-prior of Clairvaux, and several canons of Chalons and Auxerre, are specially to be noticed. The celebrated Stephen of Vitry came, also, to put himself under the direction of St. Bernard, and entered the novitiate, to the astonishment of every one; but he was the only one of these new monks who did not persevere to the end in the way of God.

The great soul of Bernard seemed to dilate as the number of his children increased; and, making himself all to all, he placed no limits to his solicitude, until, at length, sinking under fatigue, vigils, and excessive labor, he lost his strength, and became subject to violent pains. For a long time his infirmities had been increasing in an alarming manner, and a continual low fever, added to his rigorous abstinence, had enfeebled his body. But, towards the end of the year 1116, the illness proved to be of so complicated a kind as to lead all to fear that his end was near.

Under these sad circumstances, the Bishop of Chalons, William of Champeaux, who was deeply interested in the preservation of the holy abbot's life, hastened to Clairvaux. He was persuaded that a less austere diet, together with repose and care, might restore his health; and, with this conviction, he, on his knees, begged the Chapter of Citeaux to give him permission to have the management of Bernard for one year. The Chapter, touched by the charity of the humble prelate, placed the Abbot of Clairvaux, in an especial manner, under his obedience; and, in virtue of this right, William of Champeaux required that Bernard should be completely released from all care, spiritual or temporal, of the monastery, for the space of a year. He had a separate dwelling prepared for him, without the inclosure of the cloister, and confided the sick man to a doctor, whose directions were to be strictly observed. Unhappily, this doctor, unworthy of the reputation which he enjoyed, had neither skill nor conscience; and the pedantic authority which he exercised over Bernard became the source of more acute pain to him than his physical sufferings. During the ten or twelve months that this sort of exile lasted, Bernard bore, without murmuring or complaining, the brutal treatment of this ignorant quack; and as if God, content with his obedience, wished to show that it is He who withdraws or restores health as He judges fit, without human intervention, and often in spite of it, Bernard began gradually to recover his strength, and was soon convalescent. One of his most faithful friends, he whom we have cited several times—William of St. Thierry—came to pay Bernard a visit during this retreat, and passed several days with him, so as to observe his private and customary manner of life. He has given in his journal an account of all that he saw at Clairvaux; and the picture he draws is so simple, touching, and edifying, that we will give a faithful translation of it here, abridging it but little for fear of lessening its interest.*

"It was at this time that I began to go to Clairvaux and to visit the saint. Having come to see him, with another abbot, I found him in his cell, which was like to the lodges ordinarily assigned to lepers on the high-road. He was then enjoying perfect repose, being released from all care of the house, by command of the bishop and abbots; living in God and full of joy, as if he had already tasted the delights of paradise. When I set foot in this royal chamber, and considered what this lodging was and who lodged in it, I attest, before God, that I was seized with as much reverence as if I had been approaching the holy altar. I felt penetrated with so great a sweetness in entering into communication with this man, and I conceived so ardent a desire to remain with him, to share his poverty and his simplicity, that if a choice had been given me among all kinds of conditions, I should have asked nothing so earnestly as to dwell always with this man of God, to serve him.

"After he had, on his part, received us with gracious charity, we asked him what he did and how he lived in his cell. He replied, with a gentle smile which was habitual to him—'I am happy, perfectly happy, here; for before, reasonable men obeyed me; and now, by a just judgment of God, I obey a man without reason.' This he said of an arrogant doctor, who had boasted he could cure him, and into whose hands he had been put by the bishop, the abbots, and his brethren. We ate with him, and we thought that every kind of care ought to be taken of his health,

---

* The B. William, Abbot of St. Thierry, was one of the most learned men of this great age, as may be seen by his works, collected in the library of the fathers; and by the particular esteem Bernard testifies for him in his epistles. The work which he addressed to the religious of Mont-dieu, where he treats of the advantages of solitude, contains the most sublime principles of the ascetic life. He was so much struck by the sanctity of the Abbot of Clairvaux, that, even during his lifetime, he wrote the most remarkable facts of his history; but this writing, interrupted by the death of William, was, unfortunately, but a single book, and ends before the time when St. Bernard entered public life. Several authors pretend that William laid down his dignity of abbot to embrace the rule of Citeaux. This fact does not appear to us to be proved; for that such was the desire of William is evident, from his correspondence with St. Bernard; but we see, from these same epistles, that the latter always opposed this project of William. -See Bernard, Epist. 79.

the re-establishment of which was so necessary. But seeing that, by the order of the doctor, they offered him food which a person in good health, and dying of hunger, could scarcely eat, we were indignant; and it was with much difficulty we could preserve the rule of silence, and refrain from treating this doctor as a sacrilegious homicide. As to the man of God, he was indifferent to these things; his digestion being so greatly injured, that he was no longer able to discern the taste of what he took.

"Such was the state in which I found the servant of God, and such was his way of life in his solitude; but he was not alone, God was with him; and he enjoyed the company and consolation of holy angels, as has been proved by manifest signs—for one night, as he was praying with extraordinary fervor, and pouring out his soul before God, he heard a harmony of voices, and having fallen into a light sleep, he was awakened by a noise as of a great multitude passing before him. Then, the voices which he had before heard renewed their concerts—he left his cell and followed them. There was not far off, a place full of thorns and briers exceedingly thick—though now it is very different from what it was then—there he saw two choirs, on either side, who alternated their melodious chants, entrancing the holy man. He did not rightly understand the mystery of this vision until several years after, when the monastery was removed to a more spacious place, and the chapel was built on the very spot where he had heard the angelic voices. I remained several days with this great saint, although I was unworthy of such a favor; and, whenever I looked, I was struck with admiration, as if I had been contemplating a new heaven and a new earth; seeing men of our time following in the footsteps, and living the perfect life of our first fathers—the solitaries of Egypt.

"On coming down from the mountain, and entering Clairvaux, the presence of God was visible on all sides; and the silent valley published, by the simplicity and humility of the dwellings, the humility and simplicity of those who inhabited them; and then, penetrating further into this holy place, so full of men, where none were idle, all occupied at some kind of work, there was to be found at midday a silence like to that of midnight, interrupted only by manual labor, and the voices which sang the praises of God. The harmony of this silence and the order maintained was so imposing that even worldly strangers, struck with reverence, not only feared to utter a wicked or idle word, but even to indulge a thought which was not serious and worthy of the holy retreat.

"The desert in which these servants of God lived was surrounded by a thick, dark forest, so closely shut in by two neighboring mountains as to give it the appearance of a deep grotto. . . and although there was so great a number of them, they were, nevertheless, all solitaries; for as a single man, when he lives in trouble and misrule, contains in himself a noisy multitude, here, on the contrary, by unity and calmness of spirit, all preserved solitude of heart."

Such was this illustrious school of Christian wisdom, under the conduct of the Abbot Bernard! Such was the fervor and the holy discipline of this very bright and very dear valley (*in ejus clarissima et carissima valle*); the servant of God having well regulated all things, and offered a tabernacle to the Lord, according to the model which had been shown him on the mountain, when he was with God in the desert of Citeaux, like Moses in the cloud.

"Would to God that, consenting to be a man with men, he had been as gentle, discreet, and careful towards himself as he was towards others! But no sooner was he released from the year's obedience he promised to the Bishop of Chalons, than, as an unbent bow returns to its first state, or as a torrent, breaking through its bank, returns to its own course with increased impetuosity, so did he return to his austerities with new ardor, in order to revenge himself, in some sort, for his forced repose, and to make up for the interruption of his penance."

It was in the beginning of the year 1118 that Bernard returned to his duties as abbot, to the great joy of his brethren. His health was not re-established, and his body, far from having recovered strength during his long seclusion, seemed thinner and more extenuated than ever. But his mind, freed in so great a degree from material ties, exerted itself with more power and vigor. It was inconceivable, that with a form so frail, he should possess so powerful a voice and such wonderful activity. He had no sooner returned to his charge, than Clairvaux was re-animated with a new life; the words and the example of the holy abbot communicated to the religious an ardent zeal for sanctification and spiritual perfection. New disciples, chiefly of noble extraction, came almost daily to join the old; men of great consideration in the world, either for learning or valor, exchanged at Clairvaux their perishable advantages for the treasure of evangelical sufferings; and whilst the number of the religious increased in so wonderful a manner, their virtues, their holiness, their angelic life was a spectacle still more admirable.

We will here give our readers some passages of a letter, which will complete the description of Clairvaux, and make the holy work of Bernard, founded in this desert, better appreciated. This remarkably beautiful letter, preserved in the annals of Citeaux, was written by the monk Peter de Roya, who, after having renounced worldly grandeurs, tasted, under the direction of Bernard, the purest delights of piety.

"Although the house of Clairvaux is situated in a valley, its foundations are upon the holy mountains. It is there God shows Himself wonderful, and works extraordinary things for the glory of His name; it is there the unwise recover wisdom; it is there the inward man is renewed, whilst the outward man is destroyed; there the proud become humble, the rich poor, the ignorant acquire knowledge, and the darkness of sin is dissipated by the action of light; there there is but one heart and one soul among the multitude of men who are gathered from so many different countries. They are filled with a spiritual joy, in the hope of the eternal beatitude of which they have a foretaste even in this life. By their vigilance in prayer, their recollection, and humble attitude, may be seen how great is their fervor and the purity of soul with which they commune with God, and the intimate union they contract with Him. The long pauses they make in the office in the middle of the night; the manner in which they recite the psalms and apply themselves to the reading of the sacred Scriptures; the profound silence they maintain when they listen to God, teaching in the depths of their heart—all this sufficiently shows the consolation they enjoy. But who would not admire them at their labor? For when the whole community goes to or comes from work, they walk with simplicity and in order, like to an army in battle array, covered with the arms of humility; they are bound together by the bond of peace and fraternal charity, which is joy to the angels as it is the terror of devils.

"And so mightily does the Holy Spirit sustain them in their labor by the unction of His grace, that although they have so much trouble and fatigue they bear it with as much patience as if there were none.

"There are some among them who held in the world a distinguished rank, who were surrounded with splendor, and renowned for their learning; these now humble themselves only the more profoundly as they were before more exalted. When I see them in the fields handling the spade, the fork, and the rake, or in the forest with the axe; when I think what they have been, what they now are; they would have appeared to me, had I judged them with the carnal eyes, as fools and madmen, deprived of speech and language—the opprobrium of men, and scorn of the people. But when I look upon them with the eyes of faith, I regard them as men whose life is hid with Christ in God. I see among them a Godfrey of Perrone; a William of St. Omer; and so many other great men, whom I once knew in the world, and who now allow no trace to be seen of what they were; whilst before time they bore themselves proudly, being then but whited sepulchres, full of dead men's bones, now they are sacred vessels containing the treasure of all Christian virtues."*

Such was the glory of the monastery of Clairvaux, in the year 1118.

---

* This edifying narrative recalls impressions we ourselves have felt in a house of St. Bernard, at the Trappist monastery of Mount Olivet, in Alsace, where we had the happiness of making a delightful retreat. The angelical life of the disciples of St. Bernard would appear almost fabulous in times like our own, if we had not still the means of ascertaining its exact truth; and this leads us to render our testimony of what we have seen, known, and admired. We join to it the expression of our gratitude to the reverend abbot, and the profound respect we entertain for him and the holy religious of the monastery, who received us with so much kindness, and gave us so much edification, of which we shall never lose either the fruit or remembrance.
Among the various reforms of Citeaux, which have been made in the course of centuries, that of La Trappe is, undoubtedly, the most conformed to the primitive spirit of the order of St. Benedict. Its founder was the celebrated Abbot de Rancé, who died, in the odor of sanctity, in the year 1700. It is a touching spectacle, and one which cannot fail to excite emotion in any visitor, this assemblage of venerable monks, either silently working in the fields, or immovable as statues in the stalls of their humble church, intoning a grave psalmody. These are schools in which it would be well to learn to become a Christian.

Towards the end of this same year, Bernard had the happiness of seeing his old father, who, by a movement of grace, came to join his sons, and share their destiny. Tecelin took the religions habit, and not wishing that any difference should be made between him and the other monks, he humbly practised all the exercises of the order, and shortly after closed his noble career by the happy death of the just.

But this joy which the Lord granted to Bernard, was followed by an event which deeply wounded his soul, and caused him to pour forth, in a memorable epistle, accents of the most lovely and tender charity.

# CHAPTER IX

HISTORY OF ROBERT—LETTER OF ST. BERNARD—FIRST MONASTERY OF THE FILIATION OF CLAIRVAUX—GENERAL CHAPTER OF THE ORDER OF CITEAUX.

ROBERT, Bernard's cousin, had been consecrated to God from his birth, and his parents had destined him for, and promised him to the Abbey of Cluny. But having attached himself to St. Bernard, and, in a manner, identified his soul with his, he followed him to Citeaux, although he had not then attained his fourteenth year. Not being able to live separated from him, he obtained the favor of remaining in the monastery without taking the habit, or even being admitted among the number of the novices, on account of his youth. It was two years later, at the time of the foundation of Clairvaux, that, by means of prayers and entreaties, Robert, then scarcely sixteen years of age, obtained permission to make the solemn vows in the hands of the holy abbot. This young monk, a model of purity and candor, flourished like a lily in the valley of benediction; and the oldest religious compared him to that child in the Gospel whom our Lord presented to the Apostles as the model of Christian perfection—so that he was to Bernard an object of peculiar predilection and tenderness.

The choice that Robert had made of the Order of Citeaux had much offended the religious of Cluny, who believed that they had a right over this child. Besides this, Robert was rich, and his inheritance excited the avarice of these degenerate monks. They sought, therefore, an opportunity of gaining him; and, in order to succeed better, they abused the confidence of the Holy

See and obtained a decree which permitted Robert to pass from Clairvaux. Furnished with this title, and profiting by the absence of Bernard, the emissaries of the Abbot Pons, of Cluny, came to the young monk and persuaded him that his spiritual father tyrannized over him by an excess of austerities, and, at length, they succeeded in carrying him off with them without the knowledge of the Abbot of Clairvaux.

It is easy to judge how great was the grief of Bernard, to imagine the agony of his maternal heart, when on his return to the monastery, he sought the child of his heart, the child that had been taken from him! A mother alone is capable of comprehending a grief like this. Bernard remained long without uttering a word, reproaching himself with having, perhaps, discouraged this soul which might have required more tenderness; and addressing himself to God alone during nearly a year, he entreated Him unceasingly, with lamentations and tears, to restore to him his much-loved child, the son whom he had begotten in Jesus Christ! At length, going out one day into the fields with the monk Godfrey, he could no longer contain the fulness of charity, which poured forth, like deep waters overflowing their banks. He bade the monk write, then dictated to him that wonderful letter— the burning effusion of a soul kindled with love—which is justly regarded as a masterpiece of tenderness and eloquence.* We will here translate the principal passages of it:—

"I have waited long enough, my dear son Robert, and perhaps I have waited too long, in the hope that God would deign to touch thy heart and mine, inspiring thee with sorrow for thy fault, and giving me the consolation of thy repentance; but since my hope is vain, I can no longer hide my sadness nor restrain my grief. Wherefore, despised though I be, I come to recall him who despises me, and to ask pardon of him who ought rather to ask pardon of me. But deep affliction deliberates not, blushes not, reasons not, fears not to debase itself; it follows neither counsel, nor rule, nor order, nor measure; every faculty of the mind

---

* There is a tradition that while St. Bernard dictated this letter in the open air, a heavy rain fell, without Bernard discontinuing or the paper being wetted. This circumstance, joined to the sublime character of the letter itself, was looked upon as miraculous; and an oratory was afterwards built on the very spot where the saint had seated himself while he dictated this epistle.

is occupied solely with the means of softening the evil endured, and of recovering the good which may restore happiness. Thou wilt say that thou hast not despised me, that thou hast offended no one! Be it so, I allow it; my design is not to dispute, but to finish all disputes. Yes, the blame should be given to him who persecutes, not to him who flies persecution. I forget the past, I will not recall the motive or the circumstances of what is done, I will not examine which of us two has reason to complain; I would blot out even the remembrance of it; I speak but of that which alone afflicts me, unhappy that I am, no longer to see thee, to be deprived of thee, to live without thee! Thou for whom death would be life, and to live without whom is death!\* I ask thee not why thou didst go, I only ask thee why thou art not returned. Return, I pray thee, and all will be peace; return, and I shall be happy, and shall sing with joy, 'He was dead and is come to life again, he was lost and is found!' I will grant that thy departure was my fault; yes, I was too rigid, too severe: I was not sufficiently careful of a tender and delicate youth. I might, perhaps, allege in my justification that it was my duty to use firmness in order to repress the sallies of impetuous youth, to form a young novice to virtue, and to habituate him to discipline, according to those words of Scripture: 'Chastise thy son, and thou shalt save his soul.' (Prov. xxiii. 13.) 'For whom the Lord loveth He chasteneth; and He scourgeth every son whom He receiveth.' (Heb. xii. 6.) 'Better are the wounds of a friend than the deceitful kisses of an enemy.' (Prov. xxvii. 6.) But, once more, I consent to be considered the guilty one! . . . O my son, consider the manner in which I endeavor to recall thee! It is not by inspiring thee with the fear of a slave, but the love of a son, who throws himself with confidence into the arms of his father; and, instead of employing terror and threats, I use only tenderness and prayers to gain thy soul and cure my grief. Others might, perhaps, try another way; they would think that they ought to affright thee by the image of thy sin, by the fear of the judgments of an avenging God. They would reproach thee, doubtless with the horrible apostasy which has made thee prefer a fine habit, a delicate table, a rich house, to

---

\* Mi miserum quod te carco, quod te non video, quod sine te vive per quo mori, mihi vivere est; sine quo vivere, mori.

the coarse dress which thou didst wear, to the simple vegetables which thou didst eat, to the poverty which thou hadst embraced. But knowing thee to be more easily moved by love than by fear, I have not thought well to press him who comes forward of himself; to frighten him who trembles already; to confound him who is already confounded. Moreover, if it be strange that a young religious, full of reserve and modesty, should have dared to violate his vows, and quit the place of his profession, against the will of his brethren, and without the consent of his superiors, how much more strange is it that David should have fallen in spite of his holiness; Solomon in spite of his wisdom; Samson in spite of his strength! Is it surprising that he who found the way to corrupt our first parents in the midst of Paradise should have seduced a young man in the midst of a frightful desert? Again, he has not been seduced by beauty, like the ancients of Babylon; overcome by avarice, as Giezi; blinded by ambition, like Julian the Apostate.

"He only fell because he allowed himself to be dazzled by the glare of a false virtue, and by the counsel of some men of authority. Alas, a wolf in disguise approached a poor sheep who fled not, because he knew him not. What, said he to him, is God pleased with our sufferings? does Scripture command us to shorten our days? Ridiculous observances! digging the earth, cutting wood, and carrying the mire. Besides, why does God create meats if he has forbidden us the use of them? Why does He give us a body if we are not allowed to nourish it? What reasonable man would hate his own flesh? Such were the specious discourses which struck a too credulous young monk. Led astray by the seducer, he allows himself to be led to Cluny. There they cut his hair, they shave and wash him: they take away his coarse and worn habit; they give him others very costly; they receive him afterwards into the number of the religious; they place him above others; they give him precedence of several elder men; the whole community applauds and congratulates him, and triumphs as for a victory, of which he is the prize. O sweet Jesus! what have they not done to ruin a poor soul? And how could he fail to be softened by so many flatteries, puffed up by so many distinctions? Could he then enter into himself, listen to the voice of conscience, know the truth, and remain humble? Poor foolish one! Who then has bewitched thee so as to render thee deaf to my prayers? Why disquiet thyself concerning the promises made by thy father,* for which thou art not responsible, and forget vows which thou thyself hast pronounced, and of which thou wilt render an account to God? In vain they will flatter thee with being absolved by the dispensation from Rome; thou art bound by the Word of God Himself. 'Whosoever,' says He, 'having put his hand to the plough shall look back, is not fit for the kingdom of God.'. . . If thou hast only left this to lead a more perfect, a more austere life, remain in peace, and say with the apostle that thou forgettest what is behind to press forward towards the end, to the happiness for which God destines us. But if it be not so, blush and tremble; for is it not looking back, is it not being a prevaricator and an apostate (pardon me the word), to degenerate from thine ancient way, either in food, or clothing, or by adopting an idle, dissipated, vagabond, and licentious way of life? I do not intend to intimidate thee, but to instruct thee as a son whom I love with tenderness; for though thou mayest have many masters, thou hast, nevertheless, no other father than me. Yes, if I may be allowed to say it, it is I who have begotten thee in religion by my lessons and example; it is I who have nourished thee with milk, ready to give thee stronger meat if thou hadst had more strength. But alas! thou hast weaned thyself before the time; and now I fear that all that I have gained by my patience, rendered fruitful by my words, strengthened by my prayers, may be lost and dissipated; and to what am I reduced? I deplore less the loss of my trouble than the misfortune of a son who is losing himself; I complain that a stranger, without pain or labor, should despoil me of the glory of having formed thee. I grieve as that woman whose child was taken from her whilst she slept, and put by her companion in the place of her own that she had stifled. This is what they have done to me in tearing thee from my bosom; such is the loss for which I weep; this is what I ask to be given back to me. Could I forget my own offspring? Could I feel other than the most cruel anguish when they separate from me the half of myself?. . . Come, soldier of Jesus Christ, arise; shake the dust from off thee; return to the combat, and cause the shame

---

* The simple promise of parents did not bind the child; it was necessary, according to the rule of St. Benedict, that they should make the solemn oblation of him, in the prescribed form, and then he was clothed in the monastic habit.

of thy defeat to be forgotten, by redoubling thy courage. There are many combatants who persevere unto victory; but there are few who, after having given way, return to the encounter. Since, then, rarity enhances the price of all things, what joy would it be for me to see thee capable of a valor which few can reach? Moreover, if courage fails thee, whence comes it that thou fearest where there is nothing to be feared, and that thou fearest not where everything is to be feared? Dost thou hope to escape the enemy by flight? Thy house is already surrounded; the enemy has already seized the outposts; he mounts to the assault; he is almost upon thee, and thou sleepest; and thou thinkest thyself in greater safety alone than in the midst of thy company; without arms, than clothed in thine armor. Awake, rejoin quickly those whom thou hast left, and thou wilt be invincible. . . It is Jesus Christ who is fighting at our head; it is He who cries to us, 'Have confidence, I have overcome the world' And if God is for us, who shall be against us? Oh, blessed war made for Jesus, with Jesus! where neither wounds, nor defeats, nor death, nor anything, save a shameful flight, can deprive us of victory. It is lost by flight, but not by death. Happy he who falls with his arms in his hands; he dies but to be crowned! Unhappy he who, by flying, abandons both the victory and the crown! God grant, my much-loved son, that thou mayest be preserved from this misfortune, and that thy heart may be softened by my words. Should it be otherwise, alas! this letter will only add to thy fatal condemnation."

These earnest and piercing words did not produce an immediate effect. Perhaps they did not reach Robert immediately. Certain it is that St. Bernard wrote them towards the close of the year 1118, and that it was not till 1122 that he had the comfort of receiving once more his young disciple, who was sent back by the successor of Pens, Peter the Venerable, in the first year of his administration. We learn from one of his letters, that he not only had it at heart to perform this act of justice, but that the particular esteem which he felt for St. Bernard led him to send him several other religious of Cluny, who wished to remove to the monastery of Clairvaux. Robert lived sixty-five years after his return, in the most perfect observance of rule, according to the testimony of John the Hermit, a contemporary author, and he was finally chosen to rule the abbey of Maison Dieu, in the diocese of Besançon.

The valley of Clairvaux had long been too narrow to contain the fervent religious, who crowded every day in increasing numbers around the holy and paternal heart of Bernard. It became necessary to form fresh channels from this overflowing spring to water the Church, and spread abroad his virtues.

In the year 1118, Clairvaux gave birth to two houses, which reflected, in a wonderful manner, the image of their mother. The first was established at the request of William of Champeaux, in the diocese of Chalons, and received the name of the Three Fountains (*Trois Fontaines*). St. Bernard, according to the custom of the order, sent twelve brethren thither, and gave them the illustrious Roger for their abbot; the same whom he had converted at Chalons shortly before, and who was generally esteemed for his wisdom and humble piety. The second foundation followed all the phases of that of Clairvaux. St. Bernard sent the usual number of monks to seek some place suited for their establishment in the diocese of Autun. They stopped at Fontenay, where, with the assistance of the inhabitants, they built a sanctuary to the glory of Jesus crucified. The monk whom the Abbot of Clairvaux placed at the head of this colony was Godfrey, one of his earliest companions. This perfect disciple of so perfect a master, says the Chronicle, established a way of life at Fontenay, so exactly conformed to that of Clairvaux, that no difference between them could be discerned; Fontenay, like Clairvaux, deserved to be called by a great pope—the wonder of the world.

William of Champeaux had powerfully seconded Bernard in all his undertakings; he had himself erected the celebrated Abbey of Canons Regular of St. Victor, near Paris, where, for a long time, he taught the sacred sciences, with great success. But at the close of this same year, 1118, this prelate, full of merits and of days, happily finished his course, and entered into the joy of his Lord.

At the beginning of the following year, Stephen, the holy Abbot of Citeaux, assembled, in his monastery, all the abbots of the order, which then numbered twelve. This assembly, designated in ecclesiastical history by the name of the first general chapter of Citeaux, gave a definitive form to the constitutions of the order, and regulated, in the great *Charter of Charity*, the usages of all the monasteries which were affiliations from Citeaux, in order to transmit them, pure and entire, to posterity.

The institution of these chapters, designed to maintain union and the bond of brotherhood among the different houses of the same congregation, appeared so beautiful that the older religious orders subsequently imitated it, and thereby acquired immense influence. Bishops, popes, kings, and emperors came to solicit their aid, and to place themselves under the protection of these venerable men, who were justly entitled the lofty pillars of the Church.

Bernard was at this time but eight or nine and twenty; but his wisdom and experience stood him in the stead of gray hairs; and such was the mastery of his mighty eloquence over the assembly of aged men, that henceforth he was listened to and consulted as the oracle of Citeaux. After his return to his monastery, he applied himself with fresh zeal to the advancement of his brethren in perfection; and not content with securing the welfare of his order, he conceived the design of laboring for the revival of the ancient monastic spirit throughout the Church, and of reestablishing everywhere the purity of the primitive times. To renovate the world by the fervor of Christian piety, and to this end to form men to serve as fit instruments of the Holy Spirit; such was his idea—such the object of his ardent desires.

But such manifold labors, without any interval of repose, shattered his frail constitution. He was obliged a second time to leave his beloved community, and to suspend his laborious ministry for a season. This separation was to him a most painful sacrifice; he beheld his plans, his labors, his undertakings, suddenly checked by a lingering sickness; and had the heavy trial of being compelled to remain inactive, and to relinquish a number of works at their very commencement. But this sickness formed part of the design of Providence, and concurred in the preparation of a new order of things; the cell, in which the holy monk lay upon his miserable pallet, was to be the centre of a sphere of action which, daily widening farther and farther, was to extend, at last, to the utmost limits of the Church.

# CHAPTER X

ANOTHER ILLNESS OF ST. BERNARD—VISION—FRUITS OF HIS RETIREMENT.

SICKNESS is, to common souls, an occasion of weakness and slackness, which relax the springs of the spiritual life. To strong souls it is, on the contrary, an exercise of courage and patience, by means of which the Christian overcomes himself, tames his inferior nature, and learns to imitate the patience of Him who suffered for ns—*to leave us an example.*\*

St. Bernard, constrained by his cruel sufferings once more to isolate himself from his brethren, and abstain from all active exertion, entered, so to speak, into the spirit of this involuntary position, and fulfilled its duties with a masculine and magnanimous courage. Believing himself to be useless to all, and struck as it were with barrenness, he renounced himself more entirely than ever, took up his cross, and prepared tranquilly for death; the thought of which animated him with hope, and filled him with joy. But the more closely death grasped this extraordinary man, and threatened to strip him of his natural life, the more did the spirit of God redouble and multiply the supernatural strength of his soul.

One day, however, his sufferings became so excessive that, no longer able to bear up against them, he called two of his brethren, and begged them to go to the church and ask some relief of God. The brethren, touched with compassion, prostrated themselves

---

\* 1 Pet. ii. 21.

before the altar, and prayed with great abundance of tears. During this time, Bernard had a vision, which ravished him with delight. The Virgin Mary, accompanied by St. Lawrence and St. Benedict, under whose invocation he had consecrated the two side altars of his church, appeared to the sick man. "The serenity of their faces," says William of St. Thierry, "seemed the expression of the perfect peace which surrounds them in heaven." They manifested themselves so distinctly to the servant of God, that he recognized them as soon as they entered his cell. The Virgin Mary, as well as the two saints, touched with their sacred hands the parts of Bernard's body where the pain was most acute; and, by this holy touch, he was immediately delivered from his malady; and the saliva, which till then had been flowing from his mouth in a continuous stream, ceased at the same time.

St. Bernard had previously had a dream, which had already taken from him the expectation of approaching death. He saw himself standing on the sea-shore, waiting for a ship in which to embark; but the ship, which seemed still to approach the land, vainly attempted to reach it, and at last disappeared, without Bernard being able to embark. This dream, confirmed by a marvellous vision, seemed to announce to the saint that the time of his departure from this world was not yet come. But the weakness of his constitution, and his state of extreme exhaustion, did not long permit him to administer the affairs of his community. He was obliged to remain shut up in his cell, where meditation on Holy Scripture and continual prayer filled his soul with ever-increasing light and glory.

It was at this period that he composed his treatise on the different degrees of humility and of pride; and this work, the first which he published, became a source of trouble and opposition to him.

In this admirable work, St. Bernard recalled science into a long-lost path by replacing it on the basis of the interior life, and founding it on ascetical experience, justified and confirmed by the Word of God.

Humility is the point whence he set forth; it is, according to him, the condition of acquiring the science of truth. But it pre-supposes the knowledge of truth, for it is formed in three ways—by the knowledge of ourselves, by the knowledge of our neighbors, and by the knowledge of the absolute Truth. This being laid down, he shows the reciprocal relations of the different degrees of science with the corresponding degrees of humility; whence he deduces, with great logical force, the twelve degrees of humility of St. Benedict's rule, which he contrasts with as many degrees of pride. This work, begun for the instruction of monks, was immediately followed by another, which is simply a collection of four homilies, commonly known under the name of *Super Missus Est*. Bernard called them, *Praises of Mary*. This last tract, the production of a loving and tender heart, was only to be appreciated by loving souls. We read in the history of Citeaux the account of the violent attacks to which St. Bernard was exposed. "As there will be always people in the world," says the historian, "who have no greater pleasure than to carp at the works of others, and pass rigid censures upon them, there were persons who condemned this treatise (*de Gradibus humilitatis*). But it was not only obnoxious to the censure of the curious, even illustrious and celebrated doctors had some fault to find with it."

Among these doctors, indeed, was the learned Hugh de St. Victor, justly celebrated for his erudition and deep piety. But he, unlike obscure slanderers, addressed himself directly to St. Bernard, and asked an explanation of certain difficult passages. He was the only person also, to whom St. Bernard made any reply; for hitherto he had preserved an humble and constant silence. But, in his letter to Hugh, he sets the seal of humility on the very work which treats of that virtue, by retracting a passage in which he had cited the sense of a passage of Scripture instead of the sacred text. He declares further, that in speaking of the angels he had ventured an opinion which he had not found in the ancient Fathers. "Nevertheless," adds he, "though the explanations we give of the words of Scripture be not drawn from the holy Fathers, they are not therefore unlawful, provided they be not contrary to the sentiments of the Fathers and the rules of the faith." Notwithstanding these discussions—and, perhaps, even because of these discussions, by which the enemies of St. Bernard sought to bring discredit upon him in the eyes of the Church—his name acquired a greater celebrity, his works were spread abroad, and soon obtained universal assent. Many wished to see the man whose writings, so full of light and unction, had excited so unjust a clamor; and hence the great number of visitors who from this time followed each other to Clairvaux. They were never wearied of admiring the humble monk who, still in early youth, had peopled the desert with a numerous troop of angels rather than men; and who, from the depth of his retreat, cast forth so sweet a light over the whole Church. He was regarded, from that time forward, as a saint; he was cited as the model of religion, the glory of the priesthood, the scourge of heretics. Still sick and unable to mount the pulpit, he lived apart in the same cell which the Bishop of Chalons had caused to be built for him; and then, although deeply engaged in meditation on eternal truths, he was accessible to every one, and received without distinction, and with a serene and affectionate cordiality, all those who came to see and consult him upon all kinds of affairs. Hardly a day passed in which he did not receive either new guests, or letters which required long answers. He often sighed in secret over this multiplicity of cares which left him no repose. But he remembered also that divine charity cannot, and must not remain inactive; and that to sacrifice our own repose to our neighbor's peace, is to serve God and imitate Jesus Christ.

This sincere charity, joined to a complete self-abnegation and a rare capacity for business, drew to him a great number of persons of consideration, who made him the umpire of their differences. Priests and laymen alike came to consult him; and princes, prelates, and even kings, had recourse to the man of God as to an oracle. His light began to shine as the morning dawn. Every just, useful, lawful undertaking was acceptable to him—inflamed his zeal, excited in him an earnest and devoted sympathy; and whenever he undertook any cause, however unimportant, he took it deeply to heart and prosecuted it with indefatigable activity. It was wards sinners especially that he exercised his ardent charity. He urged them, like St. Paul, in season and out of season, by the most ingenious solicitations of tenderness, by the most vivid representations of truth. But yet, when he had to deal with an oppressor, or to maintain the rights of innocence and justice, he became inflexible as a rock, and his will was as firm as an immovable pillar. He acknowledges this himself in one of his letters. "The way of tenderness," says he, "is that which is most habitual to me; but when men abuse gentleness, and the oil of charitable remonstrance falls uselessly upon them, we must use stronger remedies, and employ the strength of wine; for if the enemies of holiness and justice have hardened brows, ours must be harder still; because there is nothing so hard but it will yield to that which is harder; and God himself, speaking to the prophet Ezekiel, promises this—He will give him a brow harder than that of his enemies.'"

This Christian severity, which is indeed inseparable from true charity, had many important results. We will cite here two examples only, taken from the letters of St. Bernard himself.

Thibald, Count of Champagne, a just and virtuous prince, had, in consequence of false reports, confiscated the property of one of his vassals; and, refusing to listen to his justification, he banished him, and reduced him to such a state of misery that his wife and children were obliged to beg their bread. This unfortunate vassal, whose name was Humbert, had exhausted all his endeavors in vain to appease his prince; 'he came at last to Clairvaux, and besought the holy abbot to intercede for him. Bernard, touched with compassion, first begged two prelates to write, in his name, to the Count of Champagne, on behalf of Humbert; but as their letter had no effect, he wrote himself, in these words: "I am grateful for the interest you have taken in my illness because it is inspired by the love you bear to God; yet I have reason to be surprised that, loving God, and loving me for God's sake, you should refuse a favor which God alone had inspired me to ask of you.

"Assuredly, if I had asked you for gold, or silver, or some other favor of that kind, you would not have refused me. Why, then, do you judge me unworthy of a favor which I solicit less for my sake than your own? Know you not that threatening of God—'*The time cometh when I will judge justices?*' How much more injustices? Do you not fear that which is written—'*With the same measure that you mete to others you shall be measured?*' Do you doubt whether it be easier to God to despoil a prince, than for a prince to despoil his subject?'"

This letter, of which we cite only a single passage, had an immediate effect. The Count of Champagne examined into his vassal's case, and gave a judgment which re-established him in his rights and possessions. But the prince's advisers, interested in the maintenance of the former sentence, raised obstacles in the way of Humbert's restoration. St. Bernard then wrote to him again: "What faithless counsellor hath attempted to shake the invincible firmness of your soul by his base advice? Whoever he be, he is a false friend, a traitor, a dangerous courtier, who sacrifices your honor to his passions. I conjure you, by the mercy of God, to prevent the impious from triumphing over the affliction of the poor, and deign to command that restitution be made without delay, of their rightful inheritance, to the wife and children of Humbert."

This affair was hardly accomplished, when St. Bernard had to make the truth known, on another occasion, to the Count of Champagne. This prince had made very severe regulations to repress the intolerable abuse of judicial combats; and laws, still imbued with the prejudices of the middle ages, fell severely on the victims of these duels. St. Bernard complains of this to Count Thibald: "It is but a short time since, in a duel which took place in presence of the Provost of Bar, the vanquished combatant was condemned by your sentence to lose his eyes. But as if he were not already unfortunate enough in his defeat and loss of sight, your officers have also taken possession of his property. Yet you are bound in charity to leave him wherewithal to support his sad and languishing existence. Besides, the fault of the father ought not to be visited upon the children, nor should it deprive them of their inheritance."

The frankness of St. Bernard, and the holy boldness with which he raised his voice in behalf of justice, were at the same time accompanied by such profound meekness and perfect disinterestedness, that his words had the authority of an oracle. The young abbot had retained from his early education a noble refinement of tone and manner, and a delicacy of language which, added to his mental endowments, spontaneously won all hearts. Every look, every movement, shed the glory of grace, benevolence, heavenly life, around his person; and every word of his bore its fruit. "He had always," says an ancient author, "consolation for the afflicted, help for the oppressed, counsel for the troubled in mind—a resource for every necessity, a balm for every sickness."

So many virtues and eminent qualities, all consecrated to the service of the Church, could not remain hidden; they shone more and more brightly every day; and, at the period of which we are now writing, the name of St. Bernard is seen to beam as a beneficent star on the horizon of his country. His correspondence attests the relations subsisting between him and the principal personages of his time, not only in France, but in Italy, Germany, Portugal, and even Asia. The monastery of Clairvaux had become a sacred spot to which curiosity, no less than piety, attracted a crowd of illustrious strangers. They came to contemplate the ancient marvels of the desert in the heart of France. Besides this edifying spectacle, many miracles were spoken of as having been wrought by the saint. It was well known that a child from the neighborhood of Clairvaux had been presented to Bernard in a state of extreme suffering; his arm was paralyzed, his hand withered. Bernard prayed, made the sign of the cross upon the child, and restored him to his mother perfectly cured. A no less extraordinary cure was wrought on a rich man named Humbert, who afterwards became a religious, and was the first abbot of the monastery of Igny. This man, to whom Bernard bore a particular affection, was so terribly afflicted with epilepsy as to fall into fits seven times a day. Bernard prayed for him whom he loved so much. From that moment, Humbert was cured, and never again to the end of his life experienced a single attack of the sickness. It is also related that, being at Foigny, in the diocese of Laon, on the day of the dedication of the new church of the monastery, which he had founded there, this church was filled with so incredible a multitude of flies, that their buzzing disturbed the devotions of the faithful; and as there was no other way of getting rid of them, the saint cried, *"Excommimicabe eas!"* The next day they were all found dead; and their number was so great that they blackened the pavement, and were carried out of the church in shovels. To which a chronicler adds, that "this miracle was so well known, and so celebrated, that the curse of the flies of Foigny passed into a proverb among the people around, who had come from all parts to assist at the dedication of this church." One day, several knights, on their way to a tournament, passed by Clairvaux, and asked a night's lodging in the monastery. It was towards the end of Lent; and Bernard, while he lavished the duties of hospitality upon his guests, did not conceal from them the extreme pain he felt to see young Christians full of such frivolities at the solemn season of the year when the Church is mourning in retirement and penance. "I ask a truce of you," said he, "till after holy Lent." But the knights, impatient to distinguish themselves at the tournament, could not resolve to accede to his desire. "In that case," said St. Bernard, "I shall ask this grace of God, and I have a firm confidence that I shall obtain it." He then ordered wine to be served to them, blessed the cup, and said: "Drink to the health of your souls!" They drank, and soon afterwards took leave of the holy abbot. But they had scarcely set forth when their consciences began to trouble them, and they communicated to each other the emotions they experienced, and the strange anxiety of their minds. What they had seen and heard at Clairvaux absorbed them entirely; and tears of regret and tenderness moistened their eyes when they compared the vanity of their lives with the grave and holy lives of these servants of God. All, with one accord, turned back again; and, influenced by a holy desire after perfection, they stripped off their armor, laid aside their rich garments, and prostrated themselves at Bernard's feet, to consecrate themselves to God. They vowed the rest of their lives to the tranquil exercise of the spiritual warfare of the children of Jesus Christ. "Some among them," adds the biographer, "are still fighting in the service of God; many more already reign with Christ in heaven, having been delivered in this world from the bonds of their mortal bodies."

# CHAPTER XI

LABORS OF ST. BERNARD—HIS RELATIONS WITH THE
CARTHUSIANS—JOURNEY TO GRENOBLE AND PARIS.

MEEK and humble amidst the reverence which surrounded him; simple, calm, and patient amidst the multiplied cares and business which absorbed his time, Bernard, in proportion as he saw his sphere of activity enlarge, concentrated himself the more intensely within, and kept up, with increasing watchfulness, the living and ceaseless communication of his soul with God. Love, like a bright and consuming fire, neutralized in him the dangerous influence of an immense popularity, while, at the same time, it endued his words with unction, clearness, and strength. His disciples, daily increasing in number, peopled the valley of Clairvaux; and, notwithstanding the successive enlargements of the building, the monastery could no longer contain the multitude of new monks, whose number now amounted to seven hundred. The elder monks were obliged to give up their places in the Church, the novices alone being admitted to say office there. The seeds of so abundant a harvest could not fail to be carried far and wide. On all sides religious formed in the school of St. Bernard were sought after; and that province counted itself fortunate which could obtain some of these men, so rich in virtue, and so largely endowed with that attractive grace which brings down blessings from heaven and diffuses them over the earth. Paris, Chalons, Mayence, Liege, several cities in Flanders, Germany, Italy, and Guienne, already boasted offshoots from Clairvaux; and from the year 1122 Bernard had been travelling into different countries to found establishments, and connect them together by the sacred bonds of Christian brotherhood. His cares, far from overwhelming his frail existence, seemed, on the contrary, to fill him with ever-increasing strength. He had become the soul and centre of the whole order of Citeaux, and—to use the words of one of his ancient biographers—as rivers return to the sea whence they came forth, so all, whether of good or evil, that befell his children, returned without fail to him, by the tidings he received from them, and the advice he gave them in return. But besides these labors—besides his journeys, and the vast correspondence which he kept up with the houses of his order, with the prelates who sought his advice, with learned men who consulted him on doubtful questions, with the multitudes who opened their consciences to him—he found time to write long letters to his friends, and to send them treatises which he composed for their benefit.

It is in these writings, the spontaneous effusions of his heart, that the spirit of St. Bernard should especially be studied. We will quote here the celebrated letter which he addressed, in 1122, to the religious of the great Chartreuse, near Grenoble; we shall admire therein his sweet serenity amidst the most overwhelming occupations, as well as the sublime height of contemplation to which he rises. The length of this letter compels us to abridge it:—

"Brother Bernard, of Clairvaux, wishes eternal salvation to his most venerable fathers and most dear friends, Guignes, Prior of the Chartreuse, and all the holy religious of his community.

"Your letter has given me the more joy, that I have been long desiring it. As I read it, I felt a fire kindling within my soul—a ray, methought, of that which our Lord brought upon earth. Oh, what must be the fire of that divine charity with which God consumes your hearts, since the sparks which issue from it are so intense! Blessed be you, of the Lord, for your goodness in writing to me first, and thus giving me courage to write in my turn! I should never have dared to begin, however much I might have desired it. I feared to disturb your holy repose, to suspend your secret communings with God, to interrupt that sacred and perpetual silence which surrounds you, to distract, by useless words, ears ever attentive to the voice of heaven.

"But charity is bolder than I; she is the mother of the tenderest friendships; and when she knocks at the door, no repulse is to be feared. Oh, how happy I am, to have paid a passing visit to your dear mountains, whence I have derived so mighty an aid! Yes, I shall ever number among my most solemn seasons, and everlastingly commemorate, that day on which I first found a home in your hearts."

After this loving preface, St. Bernard treats of divine love, and the different degrees by which we ascend to it.

"'God is love,' says St. John.[*] Love is that eternal law which created the universe; and which, by its wisdom, rules and governs it. And nothing is without this law, not even that supreme law of which I speak; which, all uncreated as it is, receives a law from itself. But the slave and the hireling make to themselves a law different from that of the Lord, inasmuch as the one loves not God, and the other loves something else more than God. Both make themselves a particular law; but they cannot make it independent of the unchangeable order which the eternal law has established. They imitate, or, as it were, parody the Creator, by serving as a law to themselves, and taking their own will for their rule of conduct. But this yoke is heavy and insupportable; for it is an effect of the divine law, that every man who refuses to subject himself to it, becomes his own tyrant; and, by shaking off the yoke of divine charity, he falls, necessarily, under the overpowering weight of his own will. As, therefore, we are carnal, and born of concupiscence, our love must inevitably begin by the flesh; but if it be guided by order and by grace, it will rise, by progressive degrees, to the perfection of the spirit. Thus, man begins by loving for himself, because he is carnal, and has no taste for anything out of himself; then, seeing that he cannot stand alone, he is forced to have recourse to God, to seek Him by faith; and he loves Him as a good necessary to himself. In this second degree, he loves God, it is true; but he loves him for himself, and not yet for God. Lastly, urged by his own necessities, he continues seeking God; he is occupied with Him in his thoughts, his meditations, his reading, in the practice of obedience—so that by this commerce and familiarity, if I may so express myself, he learns to know God

---

[*] 1 John iv. 16.

better, and thereby finds Him to be more and more worthy of love. He tastes how sweet the Lord is, and thus he passes on to the third degree, in which he loves God for His own sake, and no longer in relation to himself. The fourth degree will be certainly attained when the faithful servant shall enter into the joy of his God, and be inebriated with his chaste delights. Then shall this holy ecstacy plunge him into an entire forgetfulness of himself, and he will be henceforth one spirit with God."

St. Bernard did not confine himself to keeping up, by letter, the sentiments of love and esteem which he bore to the religious of the Chartreuse. That order had arisen a few years before that of Citeaux, and, both following a similar way of life, had developed in solitude, amid persecution and suffering. For this reason St. Bernard bore a particular affection to the disciples of St. Bruno; and, towards the end of the year 1123, being unable longer to resist their solicitations, he took advantage of a journey which he was compelled by the interests of his order to undertake, to go to Grenoble, where St. Hugh, who was then bishop of the diocese, received him as a messenger from heaven.

This prelate, venerable for his sanctity as well as for his extreme old age, prostrated himself before the Abbot of Clairvaux, who was then only in his thirty-second year; "and these two children of light," says a contemporary writer, "united together so as to form but one head and one soul, being linked and bound together by the indissoluble bonds of the charity of Jesus. They both experienced the sentiments of the Queen of Sheba when she visited King Solomon—each being delighted to find in the other far more than fame had reported of him."

The servant of God, accompanied by several monks, hastened to climb the rocks and wild mountains, on the summit of which the Carthusians had placed their cross and their cells. This visit caused so deep and joyful an impression, that the memory of it remains fresh and vivid to this day— centuries have not been able to obliterate its traces.

An anecdote is, however, recorded of this memorable visit, which must not be omitted. One of the Carthusians—the prior, as it is said, of the monastery—was scandalized at the brilliant equipage of St. Bernard. He arrived, in fact, mounted on a horse magnificently caparisoned; and this appearance of luxury had painfully affected the good religious, who could not understand such ostentation in a monk professing poverty, and having the reputation of a saint. The Carthusian, who could not conceal his feelings, opened his mind to a monk of St. Bernard's company, and frankly told him his thoughts. But the holy Abbot of Clairvaux, having been told of his distress, immediately asked to see the horse upon which he had been riding, ingenuously confessing that he had never noticed it, but had accepted it, just as it was, from the monk of Cluny who had lent it to him for the journey. This simple explanation, which shows to what an extent St. Bernard had mortified his senses, greatly rejoiced and edified the pious community.

At the same time, the beginning of the year 1123, Bernard made his first journey to Paris, whither he was summoned by the affairs of his order. He had scarcely arrived in the capital, where his name was already justly celebrated, when he was pressed to deliver a discourse in the schools of philosophy and theology. He yielded to this invitation, and having to speak before a numerous assembly, he prepared himself with care, and pronounced a learned dissertation on the most sublime questions of philosophy. But when he had finished his discourse, the audience remained cold and unmoved; St. Bernard withdrew in sadness and confusion; he shut himself up in an oratory, where he sighed and wept abundantly before God. On the morrow, St. Bernard presented himself again in the same school; "but this time," says the author of the Exordium of Citeaux, "the Holy Spirit spoke by his mouth, and guided his lips; and the admirable discourse which he pronounced made such an impression that many ecclesiastics, being deeply moved by it, placed themselves under his direction, and followed him to Clairvaux, there to serve God under his guidance."

# CHAPTER XII

SERVICES RENDERED BY CONVENTS—CONVERSION OF
HOMBELINE—DEATH OF GAULDRY.

BERNARD returned to Clairvaux laden with these precious spoils, and immediately resumed the government of the monastery—applying himself, by his example and his daily preaching, to the instruction of his brethren, and their perfection in the way of the saints. But the spiritual cares to which he devoted himself with boundless zeal, did not prevent his providing also for the material wants of the country in seasons of distress. A long drought, followed by a terrible famine, had long desolated Burgundy; and this scourge now falling heavily upon the rest of France, the populace, always cruel when pressed by hunger, broke out into unrestrained murmurs and threats. In this sad condition God seemed to renew at Clairvaux the miracle which he wrought formerly in Egypt. This desert, thanks to the provident care of St. Bernard, became a very granary of plenty to all Burgundy; and we read that St. Bernard adopted as many as three thousand poor men, whom he marked with a particular sign (*accepis sub signaculo*), pledging himself to support them as long as the famine should last.\* This example was followed by the neighboring monasteries, and brought extraordinary supplies to the province.

---

\* Not long ago a similar fact occurred in Switzerland, which was related to us by the inhabitants of the place. It is well known that the Capuchin Fathers live wholly upon alms, and that, in times of distress, when in want of necessaries, they ring their alms-bell, which never appeals in vain to public charity. During the famine of 1816, the village of Domach, near Basle, being in absolute destitution, the bell of the convent

Such was the noble use made of those riches which the frugality of the religious and the piety of the faithful caused to abound in monasteries. Religion, which makes itself all things to all men, administered the public funds during the minority of nations; she gave back as interest what she secured as capital; she received the superfluity of the rich to satisfy the wants of the poor; and, thanks to monastic institutions, the evil of mendicity was never, in the middle age, what it has become in our times.

This was, however, but an accessory to the greater benefits which society derived from the monastic system. Not to mention here the moral and material resources which these institutions afforded to the country, by the cultivation of waste lands, by a wise distribution of alms, by the impulse given to agriculture, to the useful arts, to science, to all kinds of labor, and, above all, by the spirit of civilization diffused over the population, which gathered successively around the convent as around a focus of life and benediction; we would only here recall one single benefit to mind, because it touches upon a question now in debate, and will give occasion to relate a beautiful trait of St. Bernard's life.

These monasteries, so worthy of all admiration, exercised their blessed influence especially on the penitential system. They were, in the true sense of the word, houses of correction, in which criminals were not only confined to prevent them from injuring others, but were subjected to the vivifying action of religion, which alone can change the morals, by transforming the heart. Hence, the facility with which monks obtained the pardon of a criminal on condition that they should detain him in their convent, and answer for him to society. St. Bernard loved these works of mercy, and often obtained most remarkable results from them. One day, as he was going to visit the Count of Champagne, he met the sad procession which was leading a malefactor to his death. Bernard, touched with compassion, threw himself into the midst of the crowd, and took hold of the cord by which the criminal was bound. "Trust this man to me," said he, "I wish to hang him with my own hands." And he led him by the cord to the palace

---

was rung, and brought in Bnch abundant supplies that the Capuchins were enabled to feed the whole village, and a number of the poor of the neighborhood. This is the testimony of the grateful people at the present day.

of the Count of Champagne. At this sight, the terrified prince exclaimed: "Alas, reverend Father, what are you doing? You do not know that this is an infamous wretch who has deserved hell a thousand times already. Would you save a devil?" But Bernard gently replied: "No, prince; I do not come to ask you to leave this unhappy man unpunished. On the contrary, you were about to make him expiate his crimes by a speedy death. I desire that his punishment should last as long as his life, and that he should endure the torments of the cross to the end of his days." The prince was silent; St. Bernard then took off his tunic, clothed the criminal with it, and brought him to Clairvaux, where "this wolf," says the chronicle, "was changed into a lamb;" he was called *Constantine*, and he well deserved that name; for he persevered for more than thirty years, and died at last at Clairvaux, in a most edifying manner.

Such conversions were not unfrequent, and the elements of the monastic orders, which purified the modern world, presented the most marvellous mixture of all that was brightest and most hideous, purest and most vile, in society. Convents were sacred asylums—cities of refuge—whither those retired whom the world renounced, as well as those who renounced the world; they buried themselves together in one common grave, to rise again together to a new life; thus realizing the words of the prophet—" The wolf shall dwell with the lamb; the leopard shall lie down with the kid; the calf, the lion, and the sheep shall dwell together, and a little child shall lead them.*

These things happened about the year 1124. But before we pursue the course of time, we will narrate two facts which relate to the private life of St. Bernard. We have not forgotten Hombeline, his sister, who was living amid the pomps of the world, its varieties, and its pleasures. This noble lady, on hearing of the great reputation of her brother, came one day to pay him a visit, with a grand equipage. She stopped at the gate of the monastery, and asked to speak to the reverend Abbot of Clairvaux. But he, disliking the luxury which she displayed in her equipage, could not make up his mind to see her; and her brothers, following his example, refused also. On this, Hombeline, touched to the heart,

* Isa. xi. 6.

loudly expressed her sorrow. "I know I am a sinner," cried she, melting into tears; "I know I am a sinner; but did not Jesus Christ die for such persons as I am? If my brother despises my body, let not the servant of God despise my soul. Let him come, let him command, let him order—I will obey him; I will do whatever he desires me."

At these affecting words, the gate of the monastery opens, and St. Bernard presents himself, accompanied by his brothers. He had a serious conversation with Hombeline; he recon- tiled her with God, and gave her for the rule of her life that which her mother had kept during her married life. Hombeline, struck with veneration and full of joy, returned home entirely changed by the power of grace; and afterwards, being free from the marriage bond, she took the religious veil, and died in the odor of sanctity.*

This conversion, according to the testimony of historians, caused a lively sensation among the ladies of the world, and became an example to many others. But the joy which it occasioned to St. Bernard was diminished by the loss of Gauldry, his uncle, the first of his companions, who died this year at Clairvaux. Of the circumstances of his death interesting particulars are recorded.

We quote the words of a contemporary author:—

"After Gauldry had lived some years at Clairvaux, in great fervor of spirit and ardent zeal for the practice of every virtue, he passed from this life to a happier world. But about an hour before his death, he was suddenly agitated; he shuddered, and his whole body trembled in a frightful manner, after which he became calm, and expired with a serene and tranquil countenance. The Lord would not permit the holy abbot, who had been grieved at this occurrence, to remain ignorant of its cause. Gauldry appeared to him one night in a dream, and when he questioned him as to his present state, he replied that he was perfectly happy. Then the saint asked him what was the cause of the horrible agitation which he had suffered before his death, and Gauldry told him that at that very moment two devils had endeavored to throw him into a pit of immeasurable depth; but that St. Peter having

---

* Some writers say she was married to a brother of the Duchess of Lorraine. The day of her death is mentioned in the Annals of Citeaux, at the date, 21st Aug., 1141.

come to his aid, the demons had relaxed their hold on him, and that he had experienced no further trouble."

The apparition of the religious, after their death, was by no means rare; and the history of Citeaux relates numerous examples, to which we may probably have occasion to recur.

# CHAPTER XIII

REMARKABLE CONVERSIONS—SUGER, ABBOT OF ST. DENIS—
HENRY ARCHBISHOP OF SENS—STEPHEN, BISHOP OF PARIS—
DISPUTES OF THE LAST WITH KING LOUIS LE GROS.

TRUTH, like light, wounds the feeble sight, and at first excites a movement of repulsion; but though it may be impeded in its solemn promulgation at first, nothing can extinguish its brilliancy, nor hinder its final triumph through the world.

Thus St. Bernard's *"Apology,"* which he published about this time, had excited a violent reaction in all directions; yet at the same time it aroused more than one conscience, and laid up in men's souls a seed of grave and fruitful words, which, after the final effervescence had passed away, produced salutary effects.

One of the conversions due to this work, which caused the greatest edification in the Church, was that of the celebrated Suger, Abbot of St. Denis, and minister of Louis le Gros. "I have not seen it with my own eyes," said St. Bernard, "but I have heard it related that this cloister was surrounded by soldiers and filled with petitioners and intriguing courtiers; that it re-echoed with the tumult of worldly affairs, and even that women had free admittance there. I ask, how can the mind be absorbed in God amidst such disorders?" These abuses had by degrees become rooted in the monastery through concessions made to the spirit of the world; and in the time of Suger this celebrated abbey was considered as a kind of pleasure house to which the king and queen made long and brilliant visits.

The monks of St. Denis had been for a long time habituated to this sort of life, and had preserved nothing of their vocation but its outward decorum and observances. But Suger, amidst all his prosperity, was neither happy nor at ease. His noble and upright soul, however he might be stunned by the engrossing effect of business and pleasure, remained open to the voice of truth, and possessed a deep sense of the dignity of the Christian character. He had heard divers opinions of the famous "*Apology*," and, at length, he examined it for himself. As he read, a ray of grace touched his heart, and made it tremble. He blushed for shame; he made a resolution to reform his monastery, and also to reform himself. The monks, who had fallen into relaxation in consequence of his example, aroused themselves at his voice. The house soon assumed a new aspect, and the world was astonished at so sudden a conversion.

But St. Bernard, at the sight of this change, and at the prospect of the influence which such an example would exercise upon a number of other congregations in France, could not contain the expression of his joy. He wrote to Suger, congratulating him, and compared his success to that of the general of an army: "When the valiant captain," said he, "perceives that his men recoil, and that the swords of the enemy are cutting them in pieces, he prefers to die with them rather than survive with dishonor, though he might avoid the danger. For this reason he stands firm in the strife, fighting vigorously, mingling in the ranks, facing danger and death, to affright the enemy; whilst with his voice and his sword he inflames the courage of his followers. He confronts him who strikes, he defends him who is about to perish. In short, despairing of saving all, he would at least die for each; and whilst he attempts to arrest the progress of the conqueror, whilst he raises those who fall, and rallies those who fly, it sometimes happens that his valor, contrary to all expectation, turns the tide. In turn, he disperses the forces of the enemy; he triumphs whilst they seemed to be on the point of obtaining the victory; and his warriors, whose defeat appeared to be certain, repose joyfully at last in the arms of victory. . . Yes, this wonderful change is the work of the Most High! Heaven rejoices at the conversion of one sinner!

How much more over that of a whole house? and such a house as yours! The Saviour is angry with those who convert a house of prayer into a den of thieves; He will bless him who restores to God His own abode, who changes an arsenal into a heaven, and out of a school of Satan makes a school of Jesus Christ."

The thrilling words of St. Bernard did not resound only in the bosom of the monastic orders; they stirred also the hearts of the high secular clergy, and recalled worldly bishops into the apostolic path.

Henry, Archbishop of Sens, was the first who opened his heart to the holy monk of Clairvaux. Resolved to put an end to a kind of life unworthy of a prelate—but too much engrossed with exterior things to comprehend the extent of the pastoral obligations—he wrote to St. Bernard to ask for some instructions upon the duties of the episcopate. This request alarmed the humility of St. Bernard. "Who am I,*"exclaimed he, "that I should dare to teach a bishop? and, yet, how can I dare to refuse him? The same reason inclines me to grant and to refuse. There is danger on both sides; but, no doubt, there is most in disobedience."* St. Bernard then dispatched to the archbishop, under the form of a letter, a treatise on the duties of bishops. It contains truths and details of matters which are very interesting. We shall here give a rapid analysis of it, together with some extracts.

The letter begins with a parallel between good and bad pastors. Ambition and cupidity, whence arise simony, are the two wounds which gnaw the body of the Church. After having developed this idea, he thus addresses the archbishop himself: "As to you, bishop of the Most High, whom do you desire to please—the world, or God? If the world, wherefore are you a priest? If God, why are you a worldly priest? We cannot serve two masters at once. To desire to be the friend of the world, is to declare oneself an enemy of God. If I please men, said the Apostle, I shall not be the servant of Jesus Christ. For, in short, if the priest be the shepherd, if the people are his flock, is it reasonable that there should be no distinction seen between them? If my pastor imitates me, who am one of his sheep, if he walk with his back bent, his face

---

* This work is placed amongst those of St. Bernard, and is entitled "*De Officio Episcoporum.*"

looking downwards, his eyes turned towards the earth, seeking to fill his belly whilst his soul is famished, where is the difference between us? Is it fitting for a pastor to gratify his appetites like a brute beast, to grovel in the dust, to tie himself down to the earth, instead of living according to the spirit, and seeking and tasting the things of heaven? The poor murmur. . . your horses, say they, amble under housings studded with gold and precious stones, whilst we walk barefooted; your mules are richly caparisoned, adorned with buckles, chains, bells, and long trappings, shining with golden nails and jewels, whilst you refuse to your neighbor wherewithal to cover his nakedness! Tell us, O bishop, of what use is gold, we say not in the temples, but upon the harness of your horses. Though I did not name these disorders, the misery of the poor would proclaim them aloud."

The conversion of the Archbishop of Sens, and that of the Abbot Suger, greatly augmented the reputation of St. Bernard; and, from this time, he had to defend himself against the honors which were offered to him on all sides. The city of Chalons, and afterwards that of Langres, the sees of which were vacant at this time, sought him for their bishop, and made many attempts to conquer his resolution never to accept any ecclesiastical dignity. At a later period he was declared Archbishop of Rheims, by the election of the clergy, and the acclamations of the faithful; but he decidedly refused this dangerous post, and was even obliged to have recourse to the authority of Rome, that he might not be forced to yield to the persevering desires of this noble Church.

A mission of another kind, more suited to his extraordinary vocation, now presented fresh food to the zeal of the man of God. The Bishop of Paris, Stephen de Senlis, a courtier and especial friend of the king, has been touched by the preaching and the writings of St. Bernard; but the example of Suger and the Archbishop of Sens had produced so vivid an impression on his mind, that, putting an end to his long hesitation, he left the court, that he might henceforward employ himself altogether in the care of his flock. This unexpected retreat displeased King Louis VI, who loved Stephen, and had heaped favors upon him, in order to retain him near his person. This prince, whose character was imperious and irascible, could not endure contradiction; the affection which he had entertained for the prelate was now changed to hatred; and, before long, he excited perpetual annoyances around him, and persecuted him with ever-increasing violence. Some clerics whom the bishop had displeased, by the re-establishment of a more severe discipline, aggravated the king's displeasure against him, and succeeded, at last, by means of intrigues and false reports, to cause their bishop to be brought before the secular authority, which deprived him of his property.* Until this time the prelate had borne this ill treatment with unalterable patience; but he thought that he ought not to abandon the wealth of his church to the will of the temporal power; and after having, in vain, tried remonstrances and threats, he laid the king under an interdict, and, retiring to Sens, placed himself under the protection of his metropolitan. The two prelates went together to Citeaux, where the great Chapter of the abbots of the order was then assembled. They declared their grievances to this venerable meeting, and demanded its protection and assistance against the usurpations of the King of France. The Chapter deliberately examined the cause of the Archbishop of Paris, and acknowledged its justice; and they decided, in consequence, that a letter should be written to the king, in the name of all the abbots of the order, and that it should be presented to him by St. Bernard and Hugh de Pontigny.

St. Bernard drew up this address, which was as follows:—

"Stephen, Abbot of Citeaux, and the General Chapter of abbots and religious of the same congregation, wish to the most illustrious Louis, King of France, health and the peace of Jesus Christ.

"The King of angels and of men has given you a kingdom upon earth, and has promised you another in heaven, if you reign with justice here below. We wish that you may receive it, and we ask it for you. But, why do you, at this time, so strongly resist the effect of our prayers, you who formerly sought them with such humble earnestness? How shall we raise our hands towards the Spouse of the Church, when you are grieving her so boldly, and without any cause? The Church is now attacked by the prince who was formerly her defender. Do you well consider whom you

---

* Mabillon asserts that the malcontents were reported to have carried their animosity so for as to attempt the life of their bishop.

are insulting? It is not the Bishop of Paris, but it is the Supreme Lord of heaven and earth—the terrible God who gives life and takes it away; who, in short, has declared that he who despises His ministers despises Him. . .

"We counsel you, we conjure you, by the fraternal relation which you desire should subsist between us (a relation which you have violated on this occasion), to put an end to this great scandal as soon as possible. But if we have the misfortune not to be heard, if you reject the advice of your brethren, who, each day, offer up their prayers for you, for your children, for your kingdom, know that our lowliness, all powerless as it is, will not forget the interests of the Church, and of its minister, the venerable Bishop of Paris, our father and our friend. He complains to poor monks of a powerful king, and prays of us, by the tie of brotherhood that exists between us, to write to the Pope on his behalf. But before we do this, we have thought it most fitting to address ourselves directly to your Excellency.

"If God inspire you to follow our advice, and accept our mediation, to reconcile yourself to your bishop, or, more properly, to God Himself, we shall be ready to undergo any sort of fatigue, and to go to any place you please, provided only we may obtain this result. But if our advances are not accepted, we shall know how to assist our friend, and serve a bishop of the Lord."

The holiness of these monks, says a modem historian, must have made a deep impression on the mind of the king; for a letter, written with so much freedom, not to irritate him. But he was, on the contrary, touched by their prayers and their firmness; and still more, he was alarmed at the anathema with which he was threatened. The fear that the Pope would confirm this anathema, immediately produced a happy issue to the objects of the deputation; and the king promised to restore to Stephen the patrimony of which he had deprived him. But these good dispositions lasted but a short time, and had no beneficial result; for the Pope having taken off the interdict, Stephen became once more the object of the monarch's unjust resentment. Believing that he was blameless in a matter which the Pope did not punish, he left the wealth of the city of Paris under sequestration, and paid no further attention to the earnest entreaties of the abbots of Citeaux. St. Bernard and Hugh de Pontigny informed the Pope of the state of things. They did not hesitate to write to him that the honor of the Church had been sacrificed under the Pontificate of Honorius. "Already," they added, "had the humility, or, rather, the firmness of the bishops appeased the anger of the king, when the authority of the sovereign Pontiff came in to crush the courage of the bishops.". . . "Your brief," they add in another letter, "is the cause not only of their retaining what they have taken, but it also renders them bolder in robbing what remains.",  ,

The obstinacy of the king proved fatal to him. St. Bernard had vainly, on several different occasions, exhorted him to peace.

"You have despised the terrible God, by despising the supplications of His bishops," said he to him one day, with all the boldness of a prophet. "Well, then, expect the chastisement which your crime deserves. Your eldest son will be taken away—he will die an early death."

This prediction was followed by the event. Philip, the presumptive heir to Louis VI, who had already received the royal unction, and who was the object of the love and well-founded hopes of his father and all France, was killed, soon afterwards, by a fall from his horse, in 1131.

The unhappy king was struck with consternation, but peace was restored to the Church of Paris.

Suger himself thus relates this fatal accident, in his "Life of Louis le Gros:"—"Two years afterwards," says the Abbot of St. Denis, "the young prince, who was about sixteen, was riding one day in a faubourg of the city of Paris (Rue du Martroy St. Jean, near the Grève); suddenly a detestable little pig threw himself into the way of the horse; he suddenly fell, threw his noble rider against the curb-stone, and stifled him by the weight of his body. All hurried to raise the half dead and tender youth, and to carry him into a neighboring house. Towards night he expired. On this very day the army had been assembled for an expedition; so that all these warriors, as well as the inhabitants of the city, were struck with grief, and poured forth sighs and groans. As to the despair of the father and mother, and their friends, no words can describe it."

# CHAPTER XIV

CONTINUATION OF THE FORMER—CONVERSION OF THE DUCHESS OF LORRAINE, OF BEATRICE, OF ERMENGARDE, COUNTESS OF BRETAGNE—THE VIRGIN SOPHIA—PRINCE HENRY OF FRANCE—AMADEUS, PRINCE OF GERMANY.

CHRISTIANITY has, like the ancient people of God, its deplorable epochs, in which kings and people, and even the ministers themselves, appear to be clothed *in vice*, as the prophet says, *like a garment*. Their unfaithfulness had long ago opened the sanctuary to the passions of men; avarice had become the idol of the world; princes sacrificed to it both honor and justice; and the people, too susceptible to the fatal impulse, followed their example, whilst they murmured against them. Such evils could not fail, in their development, to produce those inevitable scandals of which the Apostle spoke. We shall soon behold them ravaging the field of the Church. But, at the same time that iniquity abounds in the fullest measure, heavenly virtues also descend upon elect souls, and never-failing grace prepares, beforehand, powerful weapons to combat with evil, and oppose an insurmountable barrier against it. Already had the monastic spirit, regenerated in the Order of Citeaux, re-awakened the sacerdotal spirit. The most eminent members of the secular clergy were now laboring to transmit to the lowest degrees of the hierarchy, the sacred spark which they had received from on high. From the mouth of the priests the life-giving word spread through the multitude, and communicated to them a new spirit. But here the action is two-fold: it must, at one and the same time, descend from the summit of the social body and from the pulpit of the Church. The people never yield to truth, but when, to the word which announces it, there is united the authority of example. Now, the effect which the monastic spirit has produced in the priesthood, the sacerdotal spirit must produce in the principal organs of social life. It is, above all, by means of woman that piety is first awakened and spreads its mysterious influence over society.* We have said elsewhere that woman is one of the grand instruments of which Providence makes use to prepare the way for civilization; she bears within herself the seed of the future moral being of nations; and should she prove false to her high mission, society would perish. Let us trace the course of Providence:—A simple monk, transformed by the Spirit of God, renews the spirit of the monastic order. This reform, imperceptible at its birth, spreads itself over the world, and rouses against itself all the passions which it would destroy. Mighty souls rally, and form a close camp, in opposition to that of the world; the sentinels in advance arouse each other; the chiefs are ready for the combat; but the masses are not yet excited. The divine action must pass from pontiffs to kings, and from kings to people; women of rank are the intermediate agents in affording organs of grace to the Church, and models of virtue to the world.

Adelaide, Duchess of Lorraine, was one of the first trophies of St. Bernard. This illustrious lady, according to the account of William of St. Thierry, saw the servant of God in a dream, and placed herself under his direction, after having changed her way of life; for she had been formerly filled with the love of the world; and she *now confesses that the man of God had delivered her from seven horrible demons.* There are not many remains of her communications with her director; but what do exist show the extent of the influence which he exercised over her in the cause of peace and justice. "I give thanks," writes he, "for the pious affection which you exercise towards the servants of God; for when we perceive the least spark of celestial charity lighted up in a heart of flesh, which has hitherto been the dwelling-place of passion and

---

* "In the whole evangelical history," says M. de Maistre, "women play a very remarkable part; and in all the celebrated conquests made by Christianity, either over individuals or over nations, there has always been some woman's influence."

pride, we must certainly believe that it is a divine gift, and not a human virtue. I pray you," he adds, in conclusion, "to salute the duke, your husband, from me; and I exhort you both, for the love of God, to give up the castle, on account of which you are making preparations for war, if you discover that your claims are ill-founded. Remember that it is written—'What profit is it to a man, if he should gain the whole world, and lose his own soul?'"

Another lady, concerning whom history furnishes but few particulars, seems to have aided the views and labors of the servant of God, as well as the Duchess of Lorraine. One single letter mentions the part taken by her. "You desire to know," writes St. Bernard to the pious Beatrice, "what is the state of my health, after my journey, and the new establishment which I have just completed. To reply in few words, I will tell you that my monks have passed from a savage desert to an agreeable house, provided with all things necessary. . . I left them very happy; and as to myself, I returned here in good health; but since my return, I have had an intermittent fever, which reduced me to extremity. God, however, soon restored my health; and at this time I am better than before."

The encouragement and the tender care which he lavished on the souls which he brought into the ways of God, are shown most admirably in his letters. "Of a truth," he writes to a person of quality whose name is unknown, "of a truth there is no true and deep joy of which God is not the inexhaustible source; and all other joy, compared with this, is only sorrow. . . . I call on you to be my witness, did not the Holy Spirit tell you this, in the bottom of your heart, before I spoke to you? Was it humanly possible for a young woman like you, handsome, graceful, of a noble birth, to raise yourself above your age and sex, to despise all that flattered your senses and your vanity, unless an invisible power had sustained you, unless sweeter pleasures had given you a disgust to the things of the world?"

But among those interior souls with which Bernard held frequent and private communications, the one to whom he seems to have been especially attached is Ermengarde, Countess of Brittany. The letters which he addressed to her exhibit the union of spirit which existed between them; and we may admire here most affecting proofs of the pastoral tenderness which, under an austere disguise, animated the heart of the holy monk.

Ermengarde, a woman of superior merit, had for a long time vegetated in the tepid and common path in which the spirit of the world and the spirit of piety agree together to tolerate each other, and mutually to give up their rights to satisfy, if it were possible, both grace and nature. But a strong mind cannot breathe long amidst so insipid and disgusting an atmosphere. Ermengarde felt the desires and the wants of a heart which the world could not satisfy. She had previously applied to the Cardinal de Vendome, and followed his counsels; but she needed a saint to guide her to the sublimest heights of sanctity. God sent her Bernard; he was a man chosen amidst thousands, as Scripture says, who was to raise her above this world, and point out to her the road to the heavenly country.

I give some extracts from two letters, the only ones which have been preserved; they will suffice to make us comprehend that chaste and living union which the Spirit of God alone can create between holy souls:—

"Bernard, Abbot of Clairvaux, salutes his beloved daughter in Jesus Christ, Ermengarde, formerly Countess of Brittany, now an humble servant of God; and assures her that he entertains towards her every feeling of pure and Christian affection.

"Why cannot I make my mind as visible to you as this paper, that you may read in my heart the sentiments of love with which the Lord inspires me, and the zeal which He gives me for your soul. You would discover there what no tongue or pen could express. I am with you in spirit, though absent in body. It is true that I cannot show you my heart; but if I cannot manifest it to you entirely, you may still, if you will, understand it; you have only to dive into your own to find mine, and attribute to me as much love for you as you find there for me. Humility and modesty will not allow you to believe that you love me better than I do you; and you must think, on the contrary, that the same God who inclines you to love me, and to be guided by my advice, gives me an equal ardor to respond to this affection and a tender interest in your service. Understand, then, how you have kept me near you ever since my departure; for myself I may say, with truth, that I did not leave you when I left you, and that I find you wherever

I am. This is what I thought I could write to you in a few words, being still on my journey. But I hope to write at greater length when I shall have more leisure, and God shall give me the means."

The second letter breathes, still more than the first, the sweet, harmonious tone of spiritual love:—

"My heart," writes St. Bernard, "is full of joy to learn the peace of yours. I am happy, because I know that you are happy, and your tranquillity occasions mine. This peace which you enjoy, proceeds in no degree from flesh and blood. You have renounced your greatness, to live in humility; you have given up the advantages of your birth, to lead an obscure and hidden life; you have resigned riches to embrace poverty; in short, you have weaned yourself from the delights of your country, and the consolations of a brother and a son. After all this, is it not clear that the joy of your soul is a gift of the Holy Spirit? By the fear of God, you have long ago conceived the spirit of salvation; but you have brought it forth in these latter days, and love has cast out fear. Oh, how much I should love to speak, face to face, with you on this subject, instead of writing! Truly, I am angry with my occupations for preventing me from going to see you; and I rejoice when I see any opportunity which may procure me this happiness. These are rare, I confess; but this rarity itself makes them more dear and valuable to me. I am hoping, however, that such an occasion may soon present itself; and I enjoy, beforehand, the sweetness of our meeting."

We read that the Countess Ermengarde, this daughter so intimately united to the heart of Bernard, became celebrated for her labors of piety, and for the abundant alms which she poured into the bosom of the poor. She contributed largely to the extension of the Order of Citeaux; and built, on her own domain, a vast monastery for one of the colonies from Clairvaux. It was there that her holy director loved to take some repose, during his apostolic journeys.

Many other elect souls, from different ranks of society, embraced, at the voice of St. Bernard, the counsels of evangelical perfection. Some, still detained in the world by lawful ties, edified it by their gentle virtues, and shed a reflection, as from heaven, over the face of society; others, more happy in their freedom from all engagement, broke with the world, to devote themselves to God alone, bringing many souls captive in their train.

Amongst these we shall only mention the virgin Sophia, on account of the especial interest which St. Bernard took in her. We have no particulars of her life, and know not the origin of her connection with the Abbot of Clairvaux. Most of the miracles of grace are performed in secret, love obscurity, and remain unknown among men. History only details brilliant actions; and those humble virtues which spread perfume over the Church, escape from its inquiries. The letter to Sophia contains too much useful information to be passed over in silence. We give some fragments of it:—"You are most happy to have distinguished yourself from those of your rank, and to have raised yourself above them by the desire of solid glory, and by a generous contempt of false glory, and are more illustrious by this distinction than by the splendor of your birth. . . When the women of the world, adorned like palaces, pour forth their raillery against you, answer them thus—'My kingdom is not yet come, but yours is always ready.' Or answer them—'My glory is hidden with Jesus Christ in God; and when Jesus Christ, who is my glory, shall appear in His glory, I shall also appear in my glory with Him.'. . . And, besides paint, and purple, and ornament, many possess beauty, but they do not give it; for the beauty we derive from our dress, and which we put off with it, is the beauty of the dress, not that of the person who wears it. Let other women borrow foreign beauty when they find themselves deprived of that which is their own. They clearly show that they are deficient in the true and interior beauty, even because they adorn themselves with so much care to please madmen. As to you, my daughter, consider as unworthy of you a beauty which is derived from the skins of beasts, or the labors of worms. The true beauty of anything resides in itself, and depends not upon anything apart from itself. Chastity, modesty, silence, humility—these are the ornaments of a Christian virgin. Oh, how many graces does chaste modesty shed over the countenance! How much more lovely are these charms than pearls and jewels! As to you, your treasures depend not on the body which withers and corrupts; for they belong to the soul, and they will share its immortality."

The example of these great souls, and their wide influence, propagated the spirit of piety, like an electric spark, through all ranks of society; thrones, as well as cottages, brought forth fruits of grace. Prince Henry,* a son of King Louis le Gros, came to Clairvaux, to see St. Bernard; and as he conversed with the servant of God, he felt himself touched with so ardent a desire to live with him, and embrace his way of life, that he dismissed his numerous suite, and declared, to the great astonishment of the world, that he would never quit the monastery. Bernard, before receiving him into the novitiate, subjected him to long and humiliating trials; he employed him in the hardest labors, even in the office of cook; but the prince persevered in these exercises, and became one of the humblest of the monks of Clairvaux. It was not till long afterwards, and not without strong resistance, that he at length accepted the bishopric of Beauvais; and, still later, he was raised to the see of Rheims, where he rendered immense service to the Church.

To these glorious conquests we may add another—that of Amadeus, a young German prince, a near relative of the Emperor. On the death of the latter, Amadeus became disgusted with transitory greatness, threw off all the insignia of his dignities, and retired to Clairvaux. He remained there for the rest of his life, edifying these simple monks by his meek virtues.

It would be impossible to enumerate here all the great examples of abnegation, humility, and generous virtue which occurred every day; each vieing with the other in virtue under the irresistible influence of the Abbot of Clairvaux. Compelled by the business of his order to make frequent journeys, he sowed the seed of heaven as he passed along, and gathered into the garners of Clairvaux a rich and precious harvest. "If one should attempt to relate all these things with the tongue or the pen," says the chronicler, "one would run the risk of exciting the incredulity of those who have no relish for holy things."

---

* Louis le Gros had, besides Philip, who was just dead, six sons—Louis le Jeune, who succeeded him; Henry, who became a monk at Clairvaux; Robert, Count of Dreux; Rolin, Lord of Courtenay; Philip who received Holy Orders; and a daughter, named Constance.

And if piety was thus renewed in the world, and sprang up, as it were, under the footsteps of this apostolic man, we may judge what would be the divine fruit it produced at Clairvaux, and the wonders which the monastery must have presented. Bernard, like a shining light, enlightened this vast solitude, and fertilized it by his word, by his glance, by his example, by his presence alone. It would need a book to be written on purpose to trace the history of this admirable assembly of men, who were climbing together the sublime heights of Christian perfection. We will limit ourselves to some simple traits which are related of the lay brothers of Clairvaux; they are the most obscure and the least known, but not the less edifying, and we have pleasure in bringing them forward.

There was at Clairvaux, say the annalists of the order, a lay brother, of great virtue, and wonderful in his obedience, who had learnt in the school of the Holy Spirit to be meek and humble of heart. Every one gave this testimony of him, that he had never been seen to be impatient, or out of humor, whatever ill usage he might receive. He prayed, on the contrary, for those who accused him, and he had acquired the habit of saying a Pater for every one who accused him, whether justly or unjustly, at the Chapter. One day, having been sent out on some business, he was obliged to go all alone into a thick forest; and, when he was least thinking of it, he was assailed by a troop of robbers, who took away his horse, and unfeelingly stripped him. The robbers having left him, he prostrated himself before God, to entreat of Him to pardon this sin. But one of them, anxious to see what this poor brother was doing, after they had left him in so deplorable a condition, cautiously approached and watched him from a distance. And when he saw that he was in prayer, he returned directly to his companions, and said, striking his breast: "Woe to us, miserable and condemned wretches as we are, we deserve death, for we have ill-treated a saintly man: he is a monk of Clairvaux." The robbers no sooner heard these words than they were touched with compunction, and, returning to the place where they had left him, they found the monk still prostrate, praying for them. They restored him all they had taken away, and humbly begged pardon for their faults.

Another lay brother, a man of great simplicity, and *prompt to obey,* had the care of the bullocks upon one of the farms belonging to Clairvaux. Now, says the chronicler, this man one day saw Jesus Christ, who assisted him in his work. From this moment, burning with a desire to die, and to join *Him who walks with simple souls*, he fell ill, and the seventh day, being in his agony, St. Bernard paid him a visit to bid him adieu, like a beloved and cherished child who was setting out for his heavenly home; and, after having received his paternal blessing, the brother calmly breathed his last sigh; and St. Bernard bore witness of him that God had truly walked with him.

Amongst those humble brothers there was another whose life and death were often cited by St. Bernard himself. It was a monk who, for many years, had suffered the most dreadful pains with an invincible patience—an ulcer devoured his flesh, and had already reached his bones. But no complaint ever proceeded from his mouth; and when, at length, he seemed on the point of expiring, his strength suddenly returned, and the sick man, as if inebriated with a heavenly wine, began to intone hymns and songs of triumph, and, with a strong and sonorous voice, gave thanks to God. And thus this purified soul departed, ceasing to sing only when he ceased to live, and finishing in the heavenly Jerusalem those joyful canticles which he had begun on earth.

But St. Bernard, exhausted both by cares and troubles again fell sick. Obliged to isolate himself in his old abode, he sent to beg William de St. Thierry to come and see him. He was his intimate friend, the confidant of his thoughts; he was also ill, but he came to Clairvaux; they both wanted to see and support each other, and to suffer together. William has left in writing the impressions left on him by this visit; and thanks to the naïveté of his chronicle, we are able, in some degree, to be present at the familiar conversation of these two great men.

# Third Period

## POLITICAL LIFE OF ST. BERNARD

# CHAPTER XV

WILLIAM DE ST. THIERRY RELATES WHAT PASSED DURING HIS STAY AT CLAIRVAUX—ST. BERNARD'S TREATISE UPON "GRACE AND FREE WILL"—THE SAINT IS CALLED TO THE COUNCIL OF TROYES.

"I was sick at our house at Rheims," relates the blessed William de St. Thierry, "and the illness began to exhaust me altogether, when Bernard sent his brother Gerard, of happy memory, to me, and invited me to come to him at Clairvaux, where, he assured me, I should either recover or die very soon. I received as from God the favor which he granted me—to die with him, or to live some time in his society; and I knew not which of the two I should have preferred. I went directly, but with great suffering and difficulty. As soon as I arrived, I felt the effects of the holy abbot's promise, and, I confess, it was in the way which I desired; for I was healed of my great and agonizing malady; but my strength returned but slowly. My God, what blessings did I reap from this weakness! for Bernard being ill all the time I was at Clairvaux, his infirmities afforded him leisure to assist me in my needs; so that, being both in suffering, we remained together all the day long, entertaining ourselves with spiritual medicine and remedies against the conqueror of the soul.

"He explained to me at this time many things in the Canticle of Canticles; but he expounded only its moral and practical sense, without speaking of the more profound mysteries which are contained in this sacred book, because I desired him and entreated him to do so; and, fearing that what he said should escape my memory, I wrote every day whatever God had engraven on my mind, so that I could remember it. He communicated to me, with unequalled kindness and with perfect freedom, all the lights which he had received from grace and acquired by experience; and he took pains to make me understand many things of which I was ignorant, and which can only be known by the practice of divine love.*

"When Septuagesima Sunday was approaching, I felt well enough on the preceding Saturday to be able to rise from my bed without help and walk about the house, and I began to prepare to return to our abbey. But the saint, when he heard of my resolve, prevented me from executing it, and expressly forbade my thinking of it till Quinquagesima. I submitted with less pain to this order, as it was agreeable to my will, and seemed necessary on account of my weakness; and when I wished, after Septuagesima, to abstain from meat (having eaten it till then, by Bernard's order), he still forbade me to do so, and would never permit it. In this point I did not think I ought to acquiesce in his opinion, and I did not attend to his orders nor his entreaties. We separated then on the Saturday evening, he going to the choir, and, without saying another word, I to my bed. Immediately after lying down, my malady returned upon me with extraordinary violence, and I suffered so cruelly at night, that the pain got the better of all my powers of patience and resignation; and, in short, despairing of life, I thought I should never live till morning to see once more the great servant of God. After having passed the night in this anguish, I sent very early to entreat him to come to see me. He came directly; but with the severe countenance of one who

---

* The sublime book of the Canticles can only be understood by those who have some experience in the mystery of love. St. Bernard gives the key of this mystery in these words:—"We must consider the expressions of the Canticle of Canticles less than the affections. Love speaks in all; and if any one would understand what we are saying, he must love. It is in vain that he who loves not, approaches to listen to the words we read; for these burning words will never be comprehended by a heart of ice... This sweet colloquy," says he, "demands chaste ears, and when you think of the two lovers, do not picture to yourself a man and a woman, but the Word and the soul, or rather Jesus Christ and His Church, which comes to the same tning; for the Church does not signify one soul alone, but the union, or rather the unity of many souls." We shall return hereafter to the magnificent commentaries which St. Bernard composed on this sacred book.

reproves, rather than with that sweet and charitable compassion which he was accustomed to show towards me. He said, however, with a smile, 'Well, what will you eat today?' and I, who knew before he spoke that my disobedience of the preceding day was the real cause of my increased illness, replied, 'I will eat whatever you are pleased to order for me.' 'Well, be at ease,' said he, 'you will not die yet;' and he went away. What shall I say further? At the same moment my illness left me, and all that remained was a lassitude which prevented me from rising that day; for the sufferings I had endured were very great, and I never remember to have felt the like. But on the following day I was perfectly well; and having also regained my strength, I returned a few days afterwards to my monastery, with the blessing and kind favor of my host."

St. Bernard took advantage of the short moments of repose, which his sufferings compelled him to take, to write a treatise upon *"Grace and Free Will."* It was called forth by the following circumstance: He was conversing one day with his brethren, upon the marvellous effects of grace, and he added, in a tone of deep thankfulness, that grace had always prevented him in good—and that all good owes to grace its beginning, its progress, and its perfection. At these words, one of his auditors observed, "If grace does everything, what will be our reward—where our merits, where our hope?"

St. Bernard replied, with St. Paul, "God has saved us by His grace, and not by works of justice, which we have done." —Tit. iii. 5. "What," continued he, "do you think to be the author of your merits, and to save yourself by your own justice; you who cannot even pronounce the name of Jesus, without the grace of the Holy Spirit? Have you forgotten the words of Him who said, 'You can do nothing without me'? (John xv. 5;) and again, 'This depends not upon him who willeth, nor upon him who runneth, but upon God, who showeth mercy?' But, you will ask me, what then becomes of free will? My reply shall be brief, *'It works out its salvation.'"* But the holy doctor thought it advisable to treat this delicate question more maturely; and he wrote, on this occasion, the remarkable work of which we are about to give a succinct account.

He first lays down, with St. Augustine, that every good action supposes the co-operation of the human will with divine grace; and that the work of salvation cannot, therefore, be accomplished without the concurrence of these two things—grace and freedom—grace which gives, and freedom which receives, which admits, which acquiesces, which consents; so that to work out our salvation is to consent to grace—*consentire enim salvari est.* Nothing then but the will—that is, the *free* and *unconstrained* consent of the will, can make a man either happy or miserable, according as he turns to good or to evil. This consent, therefore, is, with great reason, called free will, as well on account of the inalienable freedom of man as because of the inseparable judgment of the reason which always accompanies its exercise. This consent is free in itself from the nature of the will; and is a judge of itself because of the nature of the reason. "How, indeed," continues St. Bernard, "could good or evil be justly imputed to him who is not free, since necessity serves as a lawful excuse in all cases? Now, it is certain that where there is necessity there is no longer freedom; that if there be no freedom there is no merit, and, consequently, neither reward nor condemnation. Every action which is not performed with the freedom of a voluntary consent, is destitute of merit. Hence, the actions of madmen, infants, and sleeping persons, are accounted neither good nor evil; because not having the use of reason, they have not sufficient light for the exercise of their will, nor, consequently, of their freedom."

After having clearly defined the freedom of the will, and the different conditions in which it may be found, St Bernard considers it in its relations with grace. "For I say not," adds he, "that by freedom we have the volition of good or the volition of evil; I say only that we have simple volition; for the volition of good is a gift, and the volition of evil is a fault; but the simple act of volition is precisely that by which we are capable of good or evil. Thus, of ourselves we will; but it is of grace that we will what is good."

"It is grace alone," he continues, "which excites free will by inspiring good thoughts; which perfects it, by changing its affections; which strengthens it, to accomplish the good begun; which supports it, lest it fall. Now, in all these operations grace so acts that, in the beginning, it prevents the will, and afterwards continues to accompany it. Both concur to the perfection of the work which was begun by grace, so that they work simultaneously, not one after the other; grace does not one part, and freedom another but each by one and the same act does the whole work."

St. Bernard continues, in a manner befitting these high questions, to determine the relations and points of contact between freedom and grace; then setting out from these premises, he thence deduces the whole doctrine of justification. "O man," says he, "when non-existing thou couldst not create thyself; a sinner, thou couldst not justify thyself; dead, thou couldst not raise thyself to life. No one can doubt these truths except he be ignorant of the justice of God, and seek to establish his own. And who is ignorant of the justice of God? He who attributes to himself any merits but those which proceed from grace.

"We are asked, in what do our merits consist? I reply that the concurrence of our will with the grace which justifies, is imputed to us as merit. As the regeneration, the reparation (*reformatio*) of our inward being cannot be accomplished without the acquiescence of our free will, that acquiescence, that consent, constitutes our only merit. Thus, our merits are fastings, vigils, continence, works of mercy, and all the other practices of virtue by which our inward man is renewed, day by day, in proportion as our languishing affections are purified in the love of spiritual things, and our memory, sullied by the memory of past sins, is cleansed by the holy joy which follows holy deeds. These three things chiefly contribute to the renewing of the inward man—a right intention, pure affections, the memory of good deeds. But in as far as it is the Holy Spirit who works these good dispositions within us, they are the gifts of God; in as far, on the other hand, as they require the consent and concurrence of our will, they are imputed to us as merit. To sum up all in one word, with St. Paul, 'it is those whom He has justified, not those whom He found just, whom God glorifies in heaven.'—Rom. viii. 30."

Such is the substance of that work of St. Bernard, which the Bollandists call the golden book. The most subtle and complicated questions of theology are there explained with clearness and unction—grace, and its divers operations, its force, its effects, its influence on man; the human will, its freedom, its impotence, and weakness, in consequence of original sin; the agreement of freedom with grace; the gifts of God and the merits of men; justification by Jesus Christ—all these various points, developed according to the unchangeable principles of the Church, present, under St. Bernard's pen, the ever-ancient truth under a new form— *nove, non nova.* \*

Meanwhile, Bernard, not yet restored to health, had scarcely resumed those functions, to which his love for his brethren continually urged him, when he was summoned to a council to be held at Troyes, in the beginning of the year 1128. Some legal business of the Bishop of Paris, and various other necessities of the French Church, had determined Pope Honorius to assemble the Prelates of France, under the presidency of his legate, the Cardinal Bishop of Albano.

The cardinal wished St. Bernard to be present at this council, and wrote to urge him to come. But Bernard had resolved never again to leave his solitude, nor to undertake, without urgent necessity, affairs which seemed to him unsuited to his vocation. His continual infirmities gave him a right to refuse; and, in this determination, he wrote to inform the apostolic legate of his condition and his sentiments. We cannot refrain from citing some passages of this letter: "I was ready," says he, "to obey you; but my body could not follow my spirit; and my flesh, burnt up with fever, exhausted by sweatings, could not answer the demands of the willing spirit. Let my friends judge if this excuse be sufficient, who make use of the obedience I have vowed to my superiors to drag me so often from my cloister and plunge me again in the world. It is, say they, an important matter which obliged us to summon you. But why then look to me? These matters are either easy or difficult. If easy, they can be done very well without me; if difficult, I shall not be able to manage them; unless, indeed, they

---

\* It would seem that the holy Council of Trent had the work of St. Bernard in view in its exposition of the doctrine of justification; for it reproduces it almost word for word. How admirable is it to see in the Catholic Church this continuity of the same spirit in the perpetuity of the teaching body. "We expound," says the Council of Trent, " the true and wholesome doctrine of justification, as it emanated from the sun of justice, Jesus Christ, the Author and Finisher of our faith, as the apostles left it to us, as the Catholic Church, by the inspiration of the Holy Ghost, has ever held and taught."

imagine me to be more capable of them than another. In that case, how has it happened, O my God, that I am the only one in whom Thou hast ever been so mistaken as to have hidden him under a bushel, who should have been placed upon a candlestick; or, to speak more plainly, why didst Thou make me a monk? Why hast Thou hidden in the secret of Thy house a man so necessary to the world? But I perceive that in thus complaining I am getting a little out of humor. I declare to you, then, reverend father, that, notwithstanding my repugnance, I will submit quietly to the orders you give me, leaving it to your discretion to spare my weakness."

But neither his sufferings, nor his need of retirement, nor his earnest remonstrances could procure a dispensation from attendance at the council. He received a formal summons; and, thenceforth, obedience triumphed over all other considerations. He set out for Troyes, in the middle of winter, and took his place in the venerable assembly. It was under his inspection that the council regulated the differences of the Church of France, and promulgated several canons on the reform of clerical morals. These regulations, which have not reached our time, are praised by contemporary historians for their energy and wisdom. The council was on the point of terminating its labors when a memorable incident prolonged its session, and gave new importance to its labors.

# CHAPTER XVI

INSTITUTION OF THE TEMPLARS—RETURN OF ST. BERNARD TO CLAIRVAUX—HUMILIATIONS WHICH HE EXPERIENCES—HIS LABORS AND DAILY PREACHING.

In every age of Christianity new wants arise, a new spirit manifests itself. The Church, like a provident mother, foresees and sanctifies these wants. Her infinite power of love never sleeps; she brings forth, she creates without ceasing, she offers new resources for each new exigency; and it would be impossible to point out, among the various necessities which have agitated men and ages, any tendency, any misfortune, any fault, any need which has not found its medium, its remedy, its balm, its proper form, the object corresponding to the desire of the period, in the bosom of the Church.

At the beginning of the twelfth century, the recent conquest of Jerusalem had kindled in the world an enthusiasm which was, at once, military and religious. The Crusades themselves had been but the development and the working out, as it were, of a sublime idea, which was to produce what the sceptre of Charlemagne, and the policy of his successors, had been slowly preparing—the fusing together of the different races of Christendom. This idea was not yet unveiled in all its clearness; but it gleamed over the holy sepulchre when it served as the rallying point of Christian nations; it presented the same goal to all; and to attain it, all ranks were confounded together—the prince and the priest, the knight and the single burgess, made common cause under the banner of the cross.

Hence the general character and spirit of that period, a spirit which is always analogous to the object to which it attaches itself, and the end which it pursues. This end was twofold; it was at once earthly and divine. The earthly Jerusalem appealed to those who aspired to the Jerusalem in heaven; and these two mingled ideas excited to tears of devotion and deeds of chivalrous valor. Religious were inspired with knightly zeal; knights with religious ardor; the soldier became a monk in the prospect of the heavenly Zion; the monk became a soldier for the deliverance of the earthly Zion: the two swords were drawn together to fight in the same cause; and this alliance, first contracted in the minds of men, passed inevitably into the manners of the age, and entered into the constitution of society. Hence the origin of those orders, at once monastic and military, upon which the Church laid her hand at their birth, to legitimatize them, and communicate to them, by her sanction, a supernatural direction and a vital energy.

The Hospitalers, better known under the name of the Knights of Malta, had already reproduced, immediately after the first crusade, the ancient Order of St. Lazarus—a remnant of which had never ceased to exist at Jerusalem, for the care of the sick and the protection of pilgrims. But the Holy Land needed a special and better organized force to oppose a permanent rampart against the infidels, to watch over the security of the roads, to facilitate communication, and to guide the pilgrims, who converged from all parts of the world, towards the glorious sepulchre of Christ.

Several French knights, of the company of Godfrey de Bouillon, had associated themselves together for this noble end, about the year 1118; and, as they had obtained from the King of Jerusalem a dwelling on the site of the ancient temple, they were thence named Knights of the Temple (*Milites Templi*). They lived in community, subject to military discipline, under the command of Hugh de Paganis, their first Grand Master. Their device was that verse of the Psalmist, "*Non nobis, Domine, non nobis, sed nomini tue da gloriam.*"

Ten years, however, after the formation of this association, it still numbered but nine members, and this little knot of devoted men had not yet been able to increase or develop itself. At length, about the year 1128, they came to Rome, with letters from the Patriarch of Jerusalem, to ask of the Pope a rule of life, and that high Roman sanction, without which nothing takes root or prospers in the Church. Honorius understood the importance of an institution so suited to the wants of the time, and charged the French bishops, then assembled at Troyes, to examine it, and give it a definite form. Hugh de Paganis, at the head of the Templars, therefore, presented himself before the council; and, in words of burning zeal, unfolded the design of their order. "The Church," he said, "had bulwarks enough against the malice of spiritual foes; but she needed a particular aid against her visible enemies, especially in the east, where the infidels made the holy places almost inaccessible." He added, "that after long trial his companions believed themselves able to devote themselves to this glorious mission, and that the time would come when the whole world would reap the fruit of their institution." These words and these promises excited the sympathy of the Fathers of the Council; all applauded the generous project of Hugh, and they charged the Abbot of Clairvaux to draw up the statutes of the order. St. Bernard, although sick, and impatient to return to his cell, felt his strength return for the accomplishment of the work which had devolved upon him; he entered into the spirit which animated the Templars, and gave them a rule breathing military ardor and monastic fervor. This rule resolved itself into the formula of the oath taken by the knights at their profession.

We transcribe it here, as an historical monument which belongs to the memory of St. Bernard:

"I swear that I will defend by my word, by my sword, by all means in my power, and even with my life, the mysteries of the faith, the seven sacraments, the fourteen articles of faith, the Apostles' creed, and the creed of St. Athanasius, the Old and New Testaments, with the explanations of the holy Fathers received by the Church, the unity of the Divine nature, and the trinity of persons in God, the virginity of the Virgin Mary before and after the birth of her Son.

"Furthermore, I promise obedience and submission to the Grand Master of the Order, according to the statutes of our blessed Father Bernard. I will go to fight beyond seas, as often as there shall be necessity. I will never fly before three infidels, even though I be alone. I will observe perpetual chastity. I will aid by my words, my arms, and my deeds, all religious persons, and especially the abbots and religious of the Cistercian Order, as our brethren and particular friends, with whom we are especially united. In witness whereof, I willingly swear that I will keep all these engagements. So help me God, and his Holy Gospels."

We see by this act, as well as by many other documents, the veneration and gratitude of the Templars towards him whom they regarded as their father and protector. "Go," said St. Bernard to them, "go forth, brave knights, pursue with an intrepid heart the enemies of the cross of Jesus Christ, well assured that neither death nor life will be able to separate you from the love of God which is in Jesus Christ. In all perils and on all occasions repeat these words of the apostle, 'Living or dead we are God's.' Conquerors or martyrs, rejoice, you are the Lord's."

In a tract, which he published some time afterwards, St Bernard passed an eulogium on the soldiers of the new order, and describes, with great satisfaction, their morals and way of life. He extols their obedience, which is such, says he, that none among them moves but at the order of his superior; they receive food and clothing from him; they live in common without wife or children; and that nothing may impede them in the way of angelic perfection, none among them possesses anything as his own; and their principal endeavor is to preserve the unity of the spirit in the bond of peace. They are never idle; for when not at war, which, says St. Bernard, *is seldom the case*, they are busied in mending their arms or their clothes, for fear of eating the bread of idleness. Every fault is punished, even a light word, a useless action, an immoderate fit of laughter. The chase is forbidden them, vain songs, chess, dice, and other worldly amusements, are banished from their society. But at the approach of battle, clothed externally with ungilt iron armor, and internally with the armor of faith, they are bold as lions, and fall upon their enemies without fear either of their numbers or their cruelty.

After reading this magnificent testimony, it will be asked how an institution so pure in its origin could so speedily have reached such a deplorable end? The fact is, that it had not existed a century before the Templars, enriched by the rights and wrongs of war, had become odious to the whole world. An English writer of the twelfth century, of sense and sagacity (John of Salisbury), complains loudly of the malversations and sacrilegious covetousness of which the Knights of the Temple were, even in his day, accused. They embraced the priesthood and canonical functions solely to appropriate to themselves the benefices attached to them; "so that," says this writer, "they whose profession is to shed human blood, are daring enough to administer to the faithful the blood of Jesus Christ." Did the Templars add to this crying abuse of things sacred, the mixing of the gross alloy of oriental heresies with the Christian doctrine? This would seem to result from the facts which came to light two centuries later. But the energetic protestations of the last Grand Master, at, his dying hour, will always leave a veil of obscurity upon this page of history.*

Meanwhile, the prelates of the Council of Troyes, after having approved the statutes of the new order, separated, satisfied with their work, and happy to return to their homes. St. Bernard had sighed more than any after his beloved solitude. "Have pity on me," he wrote to some fervent religious, "have pity on me, you who have the blessing of serving God in an inviolable sanctuary, far from the tumult of business. As to me, wretch that I am, condemned to continual labors, I am like a little unfledged bird, almost always out of its nest, exposed to storms and tempests."

In fact, a storm of sufficient violence menaced him, and had already begun to growl around his head; on account of certain measures taken by the council, unjust reproaches pursued him to his cell. Several ecclesiastics, whose interests had suffered, accused the Abbot of Clairvaux of having provoked untimely severities; they revived old grievances, and added new reproaches to them, so that complaints, repeated without examination, and carried from mouth to mouth, became general; and some bishops, alarmed at the power of a simple monk, denounced him at Rome, where the whole College of Cardinals found fault with him. The Pope himself, alarmed at these complaints, ordered the celebrated Cardinal Haimeric, the Chancellor of the Roman Church, to remonstrate with St. Bernard.

The cardinal wrote him a severe letter in consequence. He reproached him with meddling too much with things which belong not to a monk, and advised him for the future to remain

---

* The Order of Templars, founded in 1128, was abolished in 1311, by Pope Clement V. Their legal existence, therefore, embraced a period of only 188 years.

in his monastery. "There are various professions in the Church," said he, "and as all things are at peace when every one remains at his post and in his place, so all is confusion and disorder when any one overpasses the limits of his position. It is not fitting," adds he ironically, "that noisy and troublesome frogs should issue from their marshes to trouble the Holy See and the cardinals."

St. Bernard received this letter with humility, but replied to it with holy boldness:—

"How long will truth be hated, even in the mouth of the poor? Must misery itself be the object of jealousy? I know not whether I ought to congratulate or compassionate myself for being looked upon as a dangerous man, because I have spoken according to truth, and acted according to justice. What has there been in my conduct to offend your colleagues?" Here St. Bernard enters into long details concerning the different acts of the course in which he had borne a part. He continues as follows: "If I have done anything wrong, it was in being present at these assemblies—I, who was born for the obscurity of a cloister, and who, being a monk, ought to express by my demeanor what I am by profession. I was present, I confess; but I was called, and even dragged thither. If many have been shocked at this step, I have been no less shocked than they. In conclusion, I can see no one who can better spare me this sort of affairs for the future than yourself—you have the power and the will to do it. Henceforward I conjure you so to act that both you and I may be content—you by maintaining order, I by caring for the salvation of my soul. Let these troublesome frogs be forbidden then to come out of their holes, to leave their marshes! Let them be heard no more in assemblies! Let neither necessity nor authority constrain them again to intrude themselves into worldly affairs! This, perhaps, will be the way to put an end to the accusations of pride and ambition, of which I am the object. If, then, by your authority, I can obtain the grace to remain in my cloister, I shall live in peace, and leave others also in peace."

Cardinal Haimeric was touched by a tone at once so firm and so modest; he opened his eyes to the truth, and rendered due justice to St. Bernard. The other cardinals, now better informed, and a number of prelates, after their example, repaired their fault by a contrary line of conduct, and great demonstrations of respect.

Elsewhere, the accusations which had been so lightly received, fell to the ground of themselves when the truth came to light. The deeper had been St. Bernard's humiliation, the more were his disinterestedness and his wisdom now extolled. Such is the fate of men of God; they float like the fisherman's bark on the deep ocean, which now threatens to ingulf them in its depths, now raises them on its billows to the height of heaven! The reputation of St. Bernard never shone with a purer lustre than after it had passed through this trial of humiliation. Every one hastened, as it were, to make amends to him for his sufferings, and loudly lamented the unjust prejudice which had been raised against a man now venerated as a saint.

While the world thus busied itself in such different ways about him, the servant of God, in the retirement of his cloister, knew nothing of what was passing in the world. He was wholly given up to the contemplative life, and the instruction of his brethren. "The cloister," said he, "is a true paradise. Oh, how sweet and precious a thing it is to see brethren dwelling together in perfect concord, and living in community, in the strictest union of heart and spirit!" "For us," said he again, "who have renounced greatness, to live abject and unknown in the house of the Lord, let us remain at our post; and this post is abasement, humility, obedience, voluntary poverty, peace, and joy in the Holy Ghost. Our portion is to remain in submission to our observances and discipline, to love retirement and silence, to exercise ourselves in vigils, fastings, prayer, manual labor; it is, beyond all this, to love one another, because charity is the most excellent of all virtues."

The latter half of the year 1128, and almost the whole of the year following, passed amid these holy exercises. Bernard, wearied and disgusted with the public affairs in which he had been forced, against his will, to take an active part, had firmly resolved never again to leave his monastery without absolute necessity.

"My resolution is taken," he wrote to the Chancellor of the Roman Church; "I will never more quit the cloister, unless the affairs of our order oblige me to do so, or I receive a formal order from superior authority." But his profound retirement could not free him from the crowd of occupations brought upon him by his friends. His cell was a sanctuary, whither they came to consult him as an oracle. Theologians, learned men, eminent personages of all kinds, submitted to him questions discussed in the schools, or sent him their works before they exposed them to the dangers of publicity. Bernard thus kept up an immense correspondence; and an admirable feature of that period, as Baronius remarks, was the strict friendship and sweet literary fellowship which then united all men of talent together. Among the learned men who were closely connected with St. Bernard, we may instance Peter the Venerable, the author of a number of theological treatises and sacred poems; St. Norbert, the founder of the order of the secular canons, afterwards celebrated under the name of Premostratensians. Richard of St. Victor sends a book upon the Holy Trinity to the holy Abbot of Clairvaux, to ask his opinion of it; Hugh, surnamed the Augustine of his age, another religious of the convent of St. Victor, at Paris, consults St. Bernard on several cases of conscience; Peter, Cardinal Deacon of the Roman Church, asks him for some edifying book. St. Bernard replies: "I have never, methinks, written any work of piety worthy of the attention of your eminence. Some religious, it is true, have collected fragments of sermons as I preach them; you may get these, to cure yourself of the wish to read them." As to the questions proposed by Hugh of St. Victor, they are of little interest in themselves, but they indicate the tendency and progress of dialectics in the schools. St. Bernard replied by a long treatise, in which he grounds his opinion upon that of St. Ambrose and St Augustine, whom he calls the two pillars of the Church.

In all St. Bernard's writings, as well as his words, we discover at once the simplicity and the sublimity of truth. It could not be otherwise with a man whose life was the very expression of truth. But the sacred fire which beamed in his kindling eye, which animated his letters, which shone in his style, never cast a brighter light than upon the pages of Holy Scripture. His words were the very substance of Holy Writ. He had drawn from the sacred text, as he says himself, a substantial and strengthening nourishment, *as the grain is separated from the straws, the kernel from the husk, the honey from the wax, the marrow from the bone.* He began, at the period of which we are writing, to explain the *Canticle of Canticles* in his daily instructions; but we can form no idea of the effect produced by his sermons on the vast assembly of the monks of Clairvaux. His eloquence, according to the testimony of his contemporaries, was distinguished as much by its depth of wisdom as by its brilliancy of style; so that those who listened to his burning words, thought they heard, not a man, but an angel from heaven. His voice, although soft, was so flexible, that it seemed to give forth melodious sound, now sweet and gentle, now severe and terrible, according to the spirit, at whose touch the fibres of his soul vibrated. We have said that notwithstanding the weakness of his constitution he preached every day; he always preached at great length; and what remains to us of his discourses we owe to the diligence of the monks who wrote them down from his mouth. These imperfect abstracts can give no adequate idea of his preaching; yet the sermons upon the Canticle of Canticles are justly esteemed St. Bernard's masterpiece. The mystical life and the sublime mysteries of love are there set forth with a grace and delicacy so perfect that, as we read these ardent pages, the Holy Spirit seems to take possession of our whole soul. St. Bernard, however, would not have all persons, without distinction, read the Book of Solomon. The mystery of the Divine union, under the veil of a nuptial alliance, cannot be understood, he said, but by chaste souls and loving hearts; "for as it is in vain that the light strikes upon closed eyes, so, according to the apostle's words, the natural man cannot understand what belongs to the Spirit of God; the Holy Ghost, who is the source of wisdom, withdraws Him from those whose life is impure."

The eighteen months which St. Bernard had spent amongst his religious had carried the monastery to the highest point of perfection. Sanctity flourished in this numerous assembly of the children of God, as in the brightest days of the primitive Church; and the holy abbot himself had found renewed gladness of spirit and strength of body, in the peaceable and regular exercises of the ascetic life.

But a course so sweet and tranquil is not the portion of the saints. He was soon obliged to interrupt his instructions, suspend the interpretation of the sacred Canticles, and leave the paradise of his solitude to embark, once more, on the wide ocean of the world. The ship of St. Peter, the sport of tempests, had long been struggling with the elements unchained against her.

In this serious emergency, all those interior men whom Providence had been training in secret, were called to take a more direct part in public affairs.

St. Bernard's life belongs henceforth to the history of his age. He communicated to it its movements and direction; and here a new period commences.

# CHAPTER XVII

### STATE OF PUBLIC AFFAIRS IN THE TWELFTH
### CENTURY, (1130-1140)

THE great social question to which Christianity gave birth, and which has re-appeared under different forms in every age of the history of the Church, is that of determining the complicated relations of the spiritual and temporal power. This question was particularly prominent in the middle ages. Charlemagne and Otho the Great had, if not resolved, at least skilfully adjusted it. Both of these princes received the imperial crown from the hands of the Pontiff; and in return, the Popes themselves accepted the tiara with the consent of the Emperor.

In this manner the reciprocal dependence, and the points of contact of the two powers, have been established—one of which, placed at the head of political society, is commissioned to govern all temporal things; and the other, at the summit of Christian society, is charged with the government of minds. A double knot was intended to seal their mutual alliance; the kingdom of God was to be the foundation and sanctifying principle of earthly dominion, the latter concurring, according to the expression of St. Gregory, to the edification of the heavenly empire. But such a harmony, however ingenious in its idea, and in its application to the social theory, is not easy to realize, or to maintain in practice. It will be possible so far only as the two centres of authority, at once united, yet distinct, like the soul and the body, shall obey the same law, and accomplish it within the limits of their own sphere. Now, the limits between these two orders of things, between the physical and the spiritual sphere, cannot be more exactly determined in society than in the individual. The body and the soul, although each of these terms is developed according to particular laws, partake of one and the same life; they constitute together the personality of the man, as of society; and it is no more possible to identify than to separate them—their identification would lead to pantheism; their separation would entail death. There exists, then, between them relations, multiform, necessary, and perpetual; and if these relations are discordant, if the body and the mind, if the heavenly and the earthly principle, in the individual as in society, are in opposition and revolt, this belongs to the present condition of man, and the original overthrow of human nature. Hence the inexplicable difficulty of a thesis which we find at the bottom of all political and religions revolutions.

The Emperors of Germany, representatives of the temporal power in the west, did not remain faithful to the mission which Charlemagne had received from Providence. Turning to their own aggrandizement the high position which the Sovereign Pontiffs had accorded to them for the general interests of Christendom, they arrogated to themselves untenable rights over the Papacy, and sought to make it the instrument of their personal ambition.

This rupture of the equilibrium between the two powers, rendered a reaction inevitable.

Gregory VII, strong in his conscientiousness, and endowed with prodigious energy, gave the signal for enfranchisement, and undertook, with a perseverance which was perpetuated in his successors, the difficult work of disengaging the Church from the yoke of the empire. Hence arose the memorable debates known in history under the title of the disputes about investitures.

The abuses which the course of years, and the manners of barbarous nations, had introduced into the discipline of the Church, were to be cut up by the roots—abuses which had been, in a manner, legitimatized under the patronage of the temporal power. Princes, supported by the unjust pretensions of the emperors, had gradually usurped the privilege of nominating bishops; then of investing them with their functions by the ring and crozier, signs of episcopal jurisdiction. Hence it happened that the bishoprics too often fell into unworthy hands; sovereigns were seen selling them to those who bid highest for them, or bestowing them as rewards on greedy courtiers. Hence the clamors which were heard at that time against the morals of the priesthood, and of the princes of the Church; the episcopate had fallen into an alarming disrepute; and, a greater number of mercenaries having intruded themselves into the august functions of the altar, paralyzed the action of religion. From time to time the Church had protested against the causes of these deplorable abuses. Already in the eighth and ninth centuries, the Councils of Nice and of Constantinople had formally forbidden the investiture of bishops by lay authorities. But these prohibitions, being destitute of a sufficient sanction, were ineffectual. The emperors of Germany, jealous of a prerogative which was to them a source of influence and wealth, attempted, until the time of Gregory VII, to subjugate the Popes, as well as the bishops and the abbots of monasteries. St. Gregory VII thought he could not shake off this yoke without energetically directing the united forces of the spiritual power against the pretensions of the emperors. It was then that this admirable Pontiff was seen re-asserting his lawful supremacy, and restoring its inalienable rights to the Holy See. The Pope, by condemning investitures, did not merely intend to prohibit the feudal ceremony of bestowing the ring and the crozier; but he loudly asserted the liberty of elections, and the independence of the priesthood. To purify the Church, by delivering it, by the weapon of excommunications, from mercenary and unworthy pastors; to sanctify it, by re-establishing the ancient discipline, and reforming the morals of the priesthood—such was Gregory's noble idea; and he pursued its realization with a truly apostolical vigor, notwithstanding the formidable opposition of ambitious princes and covetous ecclesiastics. These long quarrels had been embittered by the equivocal position of the bishops, who, on the one hand, administered spiritual things, and, on the other, held feudal grants of land from the empire. Princes maintained, with some show of justice, that prelates, when they took possession of cities, castles, and crown lands, were bound, in quality of vassals, to take the oath of fealty at the hands of the sovereign, and to receive from him, not the episcopal jurisdiction, but the investiture of the fief, by ring and crozier. The Pope, in opposing that form of investiture, attacked, especially, the abuse connected with it, which consisted in the practice of princes giving this investiture to persons not yet consecrated; and thus, in a manner, compelling the consecration of those elected, who had received beforehand the insignia of the episcopate. The pretensions on both sides were justified by titles and precedents; and the historians, who have sought to throw the odium of the strife on the inflexible pertinacity of the Popes, have not gone to the bottom of the question, or examined its results. No doubt, in our day, the question seems easy of solution, by the sacrifice, on the part of the bishops, of their temporal possessions. But the state of things in the middle ages cannot be viewed by the light of modern politics. The Church has necessities which change with time, and with the phases of humanity. The high mission for the civilization of the world requires an independence, which is sometimes possible only under certain material conditions. And if, even in our day, good men acknowledge the importance of preserving to the See of Rome the territories which secure her independence, and give her an elevated position, which raises her above the contradictory influences of political events, we may well conceive that, in the middle age, amidst the social vicissitudes, the fluctuation of nations, and of never-ceasing warfare, it was fit and necessary that bishops should have a dignified, stable, and permanent position, in order to consolidate Christianity upon the shifting soil of Europe.

It may be, too, that the temporary union of the two powers in the same hands, at the period of the formation of the modern European states, has brought benefits to society of which posterity is not sufficiently aware. In those dark times an immediate contact of the two centres was needed, not, as it is commonly said, to subjugate the State to the Church, as the body is subject to the soul; but to place them in communication, in living union; to fertilize one, as it were, by the other; to engraft the new men upon the old trunk of Christendom, that the Christian sap might penetrate the pagan and barbarian elements, and a homogeneous life circulate through the different members of the modern societies, which, in fact, compose at once the State and the Church.

However this may be, it is an undeniable fact that the European states received their constitution, their organization, their fundamental laws, from the Church. It was the popes, the bishops, the monastic orders, who by the immense resources at their disposal, opened the schools, and founded the institutions whence civilization flowed; and, assuredly, if to their temporal possessions the bishops had not attached ideas of mission from above, of charity, of rigorous justice, and sacred political right, they would never have resisted unto blood in the maintenance of their temporal rights. We do not pretend to justify avarice and cupidity; we would simply account for historical facts; and when we see a St. Gregory, a St Anselm, a St. Thomas of Canterbury, and so many other great men of the same period, struggling for their worldly possessions, which, at the same time, they trampled under foot; choosing to die rather than abandon the perishable goods of the Church, and yet living in extremest poverty; we say with confidence that in this fact a divine idea is contained. This also explains the pertinacity of the popes in wresting from princes the right of investiture, without yielding to them the temporal rights of bishops in return. The strife was long and bloody; but amid all the confused questions which it raised, it had one clear and decisive result which bore upon European civilization. The religious liberty claimed by the Church gave birth to political liberty; and the era of the enfranchisement of the commons follows immediately after the conflict of the papacy with the empire for the enfranchisement of the Church. In the twelfth century all these ideas were maturing, and a deep and general renovation was working in society, amid the downfall of all existing power.

We do not purpose to retrace here the wars of the two Henrys—the schisms, the humiliations, the frightful vicissitudes which Rome and the empire alternately underwent. At the point where we take up the narrative, the great contest regarding investitures was for the moment at rest. The Pope and the Emperor concluded at Worms in 1122 the famous concordat, by which the independence of the Church was recognized. Henry V, exhausted by his own triumphs, and acknowledging at last the impotence of material force against the power of the Church, consented to relinquish the right of investing prelates by the ring and crozier; he bound himself to restore the temporalities to the bishops, to respect the freedom of elections, and especially to assist the Roman Pontiff. Pope Calixtus II, on his side, granted to the prince a legitimate influence in election, excluding all simony and compulsion; he agreed that the bishop elect should receive investiture of his temporalities by the sceptre only, not as formerly before episcopal consecration, but six months afterwards. Thus was terminated, by this memorable treaty, a murderous conflict, which had lasted fifty-six years, and which five Popes, successors of Gregory VII, had maintained with unwearied perseverance.

But though the belligerent powers laid down their arms, the strife of minds ceased not; the impulse was given; the idea of enfranchisement, first raised in the strife between the Church and empire, was reproduced under a thousand forms, in every Church, in every state, and on all sides mind revolted against material force. In Germany, in France, in Italy, in England, in Spain, the watchword of enfranchisement, as in our days of liberty, was repeated, without any precise assignable limit to the progress claimed by the spirit of the age, which was forcing the whole order of society into new forms. We shall see hereafter the coincidence of this social movement with the strides taken by the development of human reason in the twelfth century. The idea of liberty had been conceived, and the period of pregnancy—if we may so speak—was neither less critical nor less perilous than the pangs of birth.

At the present epoch of our history, the state of affairs was singularly complicated by two schisms which broke out at the same time in Rome and Germany. The Emperor of Germany, Henry V, was lately dead. The princes assembled at Mentz to choose his successor, found two claimants to the crown—the first, Frederick of Suabia, better known by the name of Hohenstauffen, the grandson of Henry IV, and nephew of the late emperor, seemed to have legitimate claims on the crown; but his competitor, Lotharius of Saxony, had in his favor the advantage of having abstained from fighting in the ranks of the Pope's adversaries; he was a prince already advanced in age, less valiant than the Duke of Suabia, and less fitted than he to rally around him the different states of the empire; but through the favor of the ecclesiastical electors, he obtained the crown, to the exclusion of the race of Hohenstauffen. Frederic only submitted to this election by standing his ground with arms in his hands; but his brother Conrad assumed the title of king, and prepared to dispute the crown with Lotharius. He crossed the Alps and entered Italy, where the two

Henrys had numerous adherents. This country was at that time a prey to complete anarchy. The wars, of which Italy had been the principal field of battle, had dismembered her territories and increased the number of contending parties; every small state and town aspired, as it were, to become independent, and all together endeavored to separate themselves from Germany in order to lay the foundations of their independence. Milan, above all, puffed up with the success of its arms, sought-to bring all northern Italy under its authority—to form one homogeneous kingdom, of which it was to be the capital. One man alone was wanting to realize these vast designs, and the Milanese believed they had found him in the person of Conrad of Hohenstauffen. This prince was, accordingly, enthusiastically welcomed at Milan. The Archbishop Anselm placed the iron crown on his head, and he was proclaimed King of Italy throughout the whole of Lombardy. The most considerable cities opened their gates at his approach, and Conrad already nourished the hope of being crowned emperor at Rome, when he learnt that Pope Honorius had declared in favor of his rival. The excommunication of Conrad, and of the Archbishop Anselm, who had crowned him by his own authority, followed upon the proclamation of Lotharius; and this intelligence, the terrible consequences of which had been felt in the preceding reigns, stopped the new king in his triumphal course, and paralyzed all his efforts. He retired to an obscure town, where he lived for some time without giving umbrage to Lotharius, when another schism rekindled his ambition, and threatened all Christendom with the calamities of a religious war.

Pope Honorius died on the 14th of February, 1130. Long before his death, the rich and powerful Cardinal Peter di Leone had gained the votes of several cardinals to insure his election to the Apostolical See. He was the grandson of a converted Jew, who had taken the name of Pope Leo IX, to whom his family had rendered some services. The influence which this family had possessed at Rome for many generations, and the apparent virtues of Cardinal Peter, had gained him a number of adherents. Peter had made his course of studies at Paris, where he was distinguished for his lively genius and brilliant qualities. His virtue at that time appears to have been solid; for, renouncing the pomps of the world, he listened to the counsels of St. Bernard, and soon after became a monk at Cluny; but being recalled to Rome by Pope Calixtus II, and promoted to the cardinalate, he was charged with several important legations, which inflated his vanity and afforded him the means of augmenting his fortune, which was already enormous.

The more prudent members of the College of Cardinals were in great apprehension of an election, which they were aware would at once give a fatal preponderance to the temporal power; and, foreseeing the success of the intrigues which they knew were at work, they met together before the Pope's death was made public, and although they were in the minority, they elected, with an unanimous voice, Cardinal Gregory—a prelate of firm character and irreproachable life—under the title of Innocent II.* This election was made in private: many of the cardinals were absent, and the usual forms could not be observed. Therefore, as soon as it was made known, those cardinals who were of Peter di Leone's party declared the election null; and, assembling together, thirty in number, in the Church of St. Mark, they proclaimed him Pope who had long held the suffrages of the Roman princes and people. Peter took the name of Anacletus II., amidst the acclamations of the multitude, and received the tiara in the Church of St. Peter. In the meanwhile, the Bishop of Ostia consecrated Innocent II, and gave him the pontifical insignia; but as the adherents of the two Popes came to open hostilities, the Roman troops (paid by Anacletus) marched against Innocent, who, to escape the popular fury, took refuge in the fortress of the powerful family of the Frangipani, who had declared in his favor.

This schism plunged the turbulent city of Rome into a state of great anxiety, and its terrible effects were dreaded throughout Christendom. Anacletus was now master of Rome. The principal cities of Italy—and, above all, those which had espoused the cause of the race of Hohenstauffen —Milan, Capua, and Benevento successively declared in his favor. The Normans of Sicily recognized his authority, and even pledged themselves to defend his

---

* Notwithstanding the clamors which the election of Innocent excited among the adherents of Anacletus, we cannot find in their writings any reproach or recrimination against the person of Innocent. His election was attacked, but his character was universally respected.

cause; whilst Innocent, who could only count among his partisans a small number of the faithful in Rome, remained shut up in the fortress with the cardinals who had elected him, awaiting from God alone that succor which was needful to the Church at this critical moment.

Anacletus had already written to Lotharius, to the King of France, and to the other Christian princes, announcing his exaltation to the pontifical throne, and informing them of the schism which afflicted the Holy See. To these letters he added another, addressed to the French bishops, wherein he passes a remarkable encomium on the Gallican Church. "This Church," he says, "has never been surprised by error; never has she been stained or dishonored by the contagion of schism; ever faithful and sincerely devoted to God, she has carefully maintained harmony and union with the Roman Church, whose glory she has ever made it her duty to augment by continual proofs of submission." Anacletus, full of confidence, having thus satisfied all necessary forms, awaited with impatience the reply of the Christian powers.

Pope Innocent, in the meanwhile, who had been shut up since the month of February, no longer feeling himself secure in Rome, found means of escaping after Easter— which, in the year 1130, fell in the month of March. He embarked secretly on the Tiber, with all his cardinals; and, after a successful voyage, arrived at Pisa, whence he passed over to Genoa, and from thence went to France. He sent deputies to announce his arrival to the king, and inform him of the state of affairs in Rome. But neither the king nor his minister, Suger, knew which side to take in so difficult a matter. Any act in favor of either Pope might tend to serious consequences; and it was impossible to discern which was the side of right and justice amid the clamors and pie- tensions by which Christendom was divided. Louis VI was unwilling to trust his own decision, and before he pronounced his opinion, he was desirous of submitting the affair to the investigation of a national council. To this end, he convoked the bishops, prelates, and abbots of the kingdom, in the town of Etampes. But that man on whom the eyes of the Church had long been fixed, on whose brow shone the light of sanctity, and who, in Rome, as in France, was revered as the oracle of truth, could not be dispensed from appearing at the council. The king himself wrote a most pressing letter to him, urging him to come to Etampes; and several of the most influential bishops joined their entreaties to those of the monarch to prevail on the humble monk to leave his retirement.

St. Bernard did not hesitate, when he saw the perils of the Church. He came to Etampes, where the king, the bishops, and the princes, who were assembled in great numbers, received him as an angel from God. After all had celebrated a solemn fast, they began their sitting, and it was unanimously agreed that the solution of this important question should be left to the man whose word would be to all a testimony of the Divine will. St. Bernard, as the historians of the council relate, accepted, with fear and trembling, the awful commission which the august assembly had imposed upon him. He dared not refuse. He impartially examined the titles of the two elections, the quality of the electors, and the merit of the elected. He spoke in the name of all; and all present heard him as the organ of the Holy Ghost. But when he had proclaimed that Innocent II. was the real Pope and the sovereign head of the Church, the whole assembly rose, and confirmed by universal acclamation the choice of St. Bernard, and the rights of the legitimate Pontiff.

# CHAPTER XVIII

CONTINUATION OF THE SCHISM AT ROME—ST. BERNARD CAUSES INNOCENT II TO BE RECOGNIZED BY THE PRINCIPAL CHRISTIAN POWERS—THE ANTIPOPE, ANACLETUS, FOUNDS THE KINGDOM OF SICILY.

The holy monk of Clairvaux, with no other strength than that which was given him from on high, had thus dispersed, with one word, the cloud which had overshadowed Christendom. After the example of his Divine Master, he commanded the winds and the waves, and no power could resist the voice of the messenger of God. Thus, in the darkest times of the Church, rays of light always proceed from some part of the horizon, which shine in darkness, and rule the destinies of the human race. Henceforth, St. Bernard, in the strength of his mission, was to instruct kings and pastors; and disperse, with the breath of his word, the vain designs of the enemies of God.

The King of France had already acknowledged the head of the Church. His faithful minister, Suger, and many illustrious prelates, presented themselves before Innocent II, to offer him the homage of their sovereign. The latter shortly after visited the Pontiff in person. Accompanied by the queen, his sons, and a numerous suite of princes and prelates, amongst whom was the humble Bernard, Louis VI proceded to the small town of St. Benoît-sur-Loire, where he awaited Innocent II; and there, *"like a truly faithful prince"* says the historian, *"he lent his crowned head before the successor of St. Peter, and prostrated himself at his feet."* Many affairs relating to the Church of France were settled in this interview; and the king promised the Pontiff that he would give him effectual proofs of his attachment on all occasions.

Since the decision of the Council of Etampes, the French Government awaited, from day to day, the resolutions of the kings of Germany and England. The latter remained in a state of indecision, which was increased by the conflicting opinions of the English bishops. The most influential of their number were inclined to favor the pretensions of Anacletus; whether it was that they had been captivated by his insinuations, or that they feared the firm and inflexible character of which Innocent had given proof during the pontificate of his predecessor; however it may have been, it was thought expedient, at this critical moment, to send St Bernard to Henry I to enlighten his conscience, and gain him over to the cause which had triumphed in France. This mission was completely successful. The King of England attributing his irresolution to motives of conscience, St. Bernard said to him, with the boldness of an apostle: "You hesitate to acknowledge Pope Innocent, from the fear of committing sin! Well, you may be uneasy about the other sins for which you will have to answer; but as to this one, I take it upon myself, and I will answer for you before God."

These words astonished the king, and put an end to his perplexity. He hastened to acknowledge Innocent II; and, docile to the advice of the holy Abbot of Clairvaux, he went to visit the Pontiff at Chartres, loaded him with presents, and promised him obedience, in his own name and that of the subjects of his kingdom. Lotharius, King of Germany, was not slow to follow the example of France and England; and in an assembly of German prelates, convoked at Wurtzburg, Innocent II was proclaimed the lawful Pope. Spain likewise submitted to Innocent; and, thanks to the active interference of St. Bernard, all the other Christian princes successively recognized the same Pontiff and neutralized the effects of the schism. "I have engaged the kings," St. Bernard wrote on this occasion, "to destroy the counsels of the wicked. I have engaged them to exterminate every power which seeks to raise itself above the wisdom of God. Our labor has succeeded. The kings of Germany, France, England, Scotland, Spain, and Jerusalem, have espoused the cause of Pope Innocent. The people and the clergy of all these kingdoms acknowledge him as their father and their head; they all concur together to preserve the unity of one spirit in the bond of peace."

However, Anacletus' party was not to be intimidated by these serious reverses. He had zealous auxiliaries in several countries, especially among the higher clergy, who used every effort to insure the triumph of their cause, notwithstanding the evils which afflicted the Church. The representative of the schismatics in France was the former legate of Pope Honorius, Gerard, Bishop of Angoulême, who, having been deposed from his office of nuncio by Pope Innocent, on account of his reprehensible conduct, attached himself, from a spirit of opposition, to the antipope, who restored to him the title of legate. The whole province of Aquitaine was oppressed by this bishop, and Duke William, who acted by his directions. Whoever refused to acknowledge Peter di Leone as Pope, was exposed to cruel persecutions; bishops were exiled from their sees; others were condemned to banishment or heavy fines.

"This perfidious old man," says an historian of the time, "had sowed the seeds of discord in the province of Bordeaux. Like the ancient serpent, he tormented the prince by his treacherous suggestions, and breathed into him the spirit of disorder and revolt."

The schism, supported by violence and seduction, spread through the south in proportion as it was checked in the north, and threatened to break Catholic unity in the provinces over which the Duke of Aquitaine exercised his despotic rule. Bordeaux, Tours, Auch, and the beautiful provinces inclosed between the Pyrenees and the Loire, and bordered by the ocean, were then under the jurisdiction arrogated by the legate of the antipope. St. Bernard, who, like the Apostle of the Gentiles, was burdened with the care of all the churches, was alarmed at this imminent danger. He would have desired to go in person to the scene of discord, to stifle it in its birth and confound its authors; but as he was detained by the Pontiff for affairs of no less importance, he addressed an admirable epistle to the Bishops of Aquitaine, in which he exposes the real state of things, and discusses the motives which rendered valid the election of Innocent II This epistle is too long to insert at full length; we shall cite the passages which throw most light on this part of our history.

Virtue, which is acquired in peace and tried in adversity, triumphs in time of victory. This is the time, my most reverend Fathers, to signalize your virtue. The sword, which threatens the whole body of the Church, is hanging over your heads; the nearer it is, the more it is to be feared, and the more dangerous and mortal will be its blows. How foolish and vain is the passion of this old man, who dishonors his age and his priesthood for an ephemeral title, and a power which will pass away from him! What an abominable crime to re-open by a schism the wound in our Saviour's side, whence flowed that blood and water which united all nations in one faith! Can any man divide them without becoming the enemy of His cross, and the accomplice of His death? O fierce passion! I have already said it, and he does not deny that he had the impudence to endeavor to obtain the object of his ambition from the lawful Pope; and it was only when he was piqued by his refusal, that he espoused the cause of the schismatic. And with that sacrilegious hand he holds a power which he now uses to pierce the Saviour's side, and ravage the Church! But one day he shall look on Him whom he pierced... However it may be, the oracle of the Holy Ghost shall be accomplished; it must be that scandals come, but nevertheless, woe to that man by whom the scandal cometh! And who is the miserable author of the scandal, if not he who, in spite of the canonical election of the head of the Church, has taken possession of the holy place, not because it is holy, but because it is exalted? The pretended election by which he justifies himself, or, rather, the faction which has elected him, only serves as a pretext for his malice... In fact, the fundamental rule of the common law in this matter is, that after a first election there cannot be a second. The first had been made; therefore, the second was null. Even supposing that some of the prescribed formalities had been wanting in the first election, as the defenders of the schism assert, was it lawful to proceed to a second election without having examined the defects of the first and annulled it by a valid judgment? Besides this, there are two cases in dispute: one regards the personal merit of the two competitors; the other relates to the form of their election. As to the person, that I may not be treated as a detractor or a flatterer, I shall not repeat what is said everywhere, and cannot be denied, that the life and reputation of the Pope are above slander, whilst his rival is not secure from the tongues of his own friends. And as to the formalities of the two elections, that of Innocent is the first in the order of time, the purest with regard to those who have elected him, and the most canonical according to the rules of justice. As far as regards the priority, nobody can dispute it; and the election was made by the most sound portion of the cardinals, bishops, priests, and deacons, to whom appertains the right of naming the Pope. Thus, according to the ancient constitutions, the number of votes was sufficient to render this election valid. Moreover, was not Innocent consecrated by the Bishop of Ostia, to whom this privilege is reserved? If, then, there is more virtue in the person elected, more integrity in the electors, more order and legality in the forms of the election, by what fatal obstinacy do they endeavor to substitute another election made against all the rules of justice, against the will of good men, and contrary to the desires of the universal Church?"

This energetic declaration dissipated the doubts and revived the courage of the bishops to whom it was addressed. But the Duke of Aquitaine, and his perfidious counsellor, paralyzed all their efforts to restore peace and unity. The disordered state of these unfortunate provinces continued on the increase, and St. Bernard, inflamed with zeal for the house of God, was obliged, to his great sorrow, to defer his journey to Aquitaine, whither he was called by the oppressed faithful. Pope Innocent had charged him with another mission; he was summoned to accompany the Pontiff to Germany. Innocent II, from the time of his acknowledgment by all the Catholic powers, had unceasingly turned his thoughts towards Rome; and, henceforth, only aspired to sit on the chair of St. Peter. Now, amongst all the princes of Christendom, the King of Germany was the most personally interested in opening to the Pontiff the gates of the capital of the world; for in that ancient metropolis of Christendom, he was destined, like Charlemagne, to receive the imperial crown. Innocent, therefore, addressed himself to Lotharius, to obtain an interview, in order to concert with him a plan for traversing Italy, and making himself master of Rome. The conference was fixed for the month of October, in the same year, in the town of Liege. Lotharius went thither with the principal lords of his empire, and a numerous suite of men-at-arms, to await the Pope. The latter arrived a few days later, accompanied by St. Bernard and a pompous retinue of cardinals and Roman prelates.

He made his entry into the town amidst an immense concourse of people, and a tumultuous manifestation of popular piety. The King of Germany seemed, on this occasion, desirous of proving to the people the perfect reconciliation of the papacy and the empire. He walked humbly on foot alongside of the Pope, *holding, with one, hand, the bridle of the white horse on which Innocent was mounted, and with a, wand in his other hand he opened a way through the crowd which thronged around him.*—Suger. Viter. Lud vi. On the following Sunday, the Pontiff celebrated a solemn mass, in the presence of the king and his family, and mutual protestations of concord and attachment were made on both sides.

But these outward demonstrations had been made, perhaps, rather too ostentatiously and affectedly not to leave some cause for vague presentiments. Disinterestedness was not one of the virtues of Lotharius; and if he granted the Pope an army to lead him to Rome, it was sure to have been on exorbitant conditions. In fact, the forebodings of the Roman Court were shortly after justified; but they were realized to an extent beyond what had been apprehended. Lotharius, when he had promised the Pope the assistance of his arms, haughtily claimed for himself the privilege of investiture, which his predecessors had exercised before the concordat of Worms. He thought that the precarious position of the Pope would secure a successful answer to his untimely demand. But he was deceived. Innocent remained inflexible, in spite of the threats and anger of the king; but his situation was most perilous; and the Roman prelates, struck with dismay, trembled on beholding the Sovereign Pontiff defenceless in a German city, surrounded by a strong army. Their remembrance of the outrages which Henry V had offered to popes and cardinals was too recent not to excite terrible apprehensions; and they believed this to be a far more fearful snare than the dangers from which they had escaped in Rome.

However, the storm did not break forth; St. Bernard was there to allay it. Full of holy boldness, he opposed himself, like a wall of brass, to the unjust pretensions of the crown, and combated them with the arms of his irresistible eloquence. He recalled to the mind of Lotharius his former engagements, and the promises to which he owed his elevation to the throne; he reminded him that if the Church, at that moment, stood in need of the arm of the empire, the empire, on the other hand, no less needed the support of the Church. Lotharius was silent; he consented not to press his claims any further; but he evinced his dissatisfaction, by breaking off the negotiations relative to the campaign in Italy. It is true that in the present critical situation of the empire, the capture of Rome would not be so easy. The antipope had displayed great activity during the absence of Innocent, and had provided himself with numerous resources. Being now master of Rome, he had augmented its troops and defences; he relied on the north of Italy, whose people were devoted to his cause; and in the south, a remarkable event seemed destined to consolidate his power.

We have already said that the Normans of Upper Italy were the first to acknowledge the election of Anacletus. This bold people, finding themselves too much circumscribed in the beautiful province which they had conquered from France, had settled in Calabria and Apulia, under the guidance of William Bras-de-Fer, and Humphrey, son of Tancred de Hauteville; but in 1061, Robert Guiscard, the Norman, and Duke Roger, having no more enemies to oppose them, aspired to erect their vast conquests, in Italy and Sicily, into a kingdom. Roger II, son of the latter, was destined to accomplish this design. Until that time, Sicily had never had a national existence; it had never obeyed one master; and, during a lapse of many centuries, it had been, in turn, invaded and possessed by foreign nations.* Duke Roger II, after

---

* Since the fabulous times, the coasts of Sicily have been invaded by almost all the celebrated nations of antiquity, who have left lasting traces of their inroads. Hence, we may account for the historical interest and the original traits which are to be met with in that country at the present day; and which, by their infinite variety, form a kind of mosaic, worthy of being studied, on account of its contrasts. "The traveller," says a judinous writer, who has visited this country, "will meet with ruins and monuments; but the living reality would not suffice to satisfy him. He will see vestiges of every age; he will recognize the footprints of the several nations who have ruled over it; he will read its history in its monuments—an immense volume, in which the different epochs are represented by a temple, a basilica, or a fortress; he will pass from shapeless Cyclopean and Phoenician fabrics to Doric temples, raised by the Greek colonists; Roman arenas, Moorish castles, Norman chapels, and sombre dungeons of feudal times; and, alongside of the pompous ruins of departed glory, he will behold scenes of frightful misery."—Travels in Sicily, by Baron de Bussière.

the entire defeat of the Saracens, resolved to unite, under his sceptre, his Italian possessions and the rich provinces of the ancient Trinacria; and, according to the spirit of the age, he addressed himself to the Pope to obtain the royal crown, together with the title of king. The schism seemed to offer him a favorable opportunity for concluding, without onerous conditions, this great affair, which he had unsuccessfully negotiated under the pontificate of Pope Honorius. The prudent delays which the Pontiff had opposed to Roger's impetuosity, and which the politics of the empire rendered necessary, doubtless influenced the determination of the Normans in favor of Anacletus. However it may have been, the latter promised the pontifical sanction to the election of the kingdom of Sicily and Italy, in return for Roger's formal engagement to lend a helping hand against the pretensions of Innocent. The authentic act was drawn up; and it is asserted, from some documents found in Roger's papers, that, in order to attach the kingdom of Sicily more closely to the cause of the Holy See, the schismatical Pope promised him the dignity of patrician of Rome, and, perhaps, even the crown of the German empire. After this treaty, during the Christmas festival of the year 1130, Duke Roger went to Palermo, where he received the crown from the hands of a cardinal legate of the antipope, and took the title of *King of Sicily, by the grace of God,* which was afterwards confirmed to him by the lawful Pope.

It may easily be conceived how much the affairs of the Church and the empire were complicated by this event. Anacletus had established in some sort a mutual relation between his cause and that of the new kingdom. He found in Roger a powerful defender, who was doubly interested in the triumph of the antipope, as he had to fear the vengeance of Lotharius and the success of Innocent. Moreover, the pretensions of Conrad of Hohenstauffen were aroused by the death of Pope Honorius. His numerous partisans in Italy declared in favor of Anacletus, solely because Innocent II had been acknowledged by Lotharius. Anselm, the Archbishop of Milan, who had crowned Conrad, drew the province of Lombardy into the schism, and persuaded the Milanese to take up arms in order to oppose any attempt that Lotharius might make in favor of Innocent. They were resolved to defend the passage to Rome, with the assistance of the Normans and Sicilians.

By these various incidents, the interests of the King of Germany were necessarily united to those of the lawful Pope; and, notwithstanding their differences, they were obliged to come to an understanding, in order to act in concert. They had the same enemies to contend with; the interests of both were compromised by the league of the schismatics and of the malcontent subjects of the empire; and they both had to oppose a schism whose head-quarters were in Italy, and which served as a rallying-point for all parties. A war became inevitable. But the weak Lotharius could not make up his mind to take the field; and, irritated by the Pope's conduct in the affair of investitures, he let him depart without touching on the principal object of the conference of Liege Innocent left Germany, dissatisfied with Lotharius, but thankful that he had escaped the snare, and resisted pretensions which would have again troubled the security of the Churches. He returned to France, and suffered events to take their course, in the firm persuasion that a campaign in Italy would be the inevitable result of the state of affairs. In the mean time, St. Bernard, after urgent entreaties, obtained permission to return to Clairvaux, to recover from his fatigues, and satisfy the ardent longings of his brethren. He had hardly arrived there, when he received a visit from the Bishop of Paris. That prelate came, in a state of deep affliction, to inform him of a horrible crime, which had filled all Paris with consternation, and called for severe measures.

# CHAPTER XIX

ASSASSINATION OF A MONK—ST. BERNARD PURSUES THE AUTHORS OF THE MURDER—HE RECEIVES A VISIT FROM POPE INNOCENT II AT CLAIRVAUX—HISTORY OF DUKE WILLIAM—COUNCIL OF RHEIMS.

The successive reforms which the Bishop of Paris had introduced into his diocese, had long provoked the murmurs of worldly ecclesiastics. Jealousy fomented discord between the pastors of the flock; and the pious intentions of the bishop were universally frustrated by the intrigues of some members of his own clergy. But these difficulties did not abate his zeal, or bend his firmness. He had near his person a venerable monk, named Thomas, Prior of the Monastery of St. Victor, in Paris, who acted as his spiritual director, and lent him the aid of his experience in the execution of his wise decrees. This religious, who was a meek and learned man, was deservedly trusted and esteemed; and, on this account, he was a fitting subject for the resentment which had been aroused by the bishop's reforms.

Among the number of those who were distinguished by their implacable animosity was the Canon Thibaut Nautier, Archdeacon of the Church of Paris. His intrigues and malversations had more than once awakened the vigilance of the Prior of St. Victor, and he was only sheltered from the pursuit of justice by his high position, which he had so much abused. Thibaut meditated revenge; and, in order to gratify his passion, he scrupled not to arm his own nephews. One day, when the bishop, accompanied by Thomas, was returning from a diocesan visitation, they were attacked at the gates of Paris by the nephews of the archdeacon, and Thomas fell, mortally wounded, into the arms of his bishop, who held him in his embrace to defend him. He died, pardoning his murderers. They took to flight, and their uncle had the audacity to solicit absolution for them from the Pope. At this time, Stephen, overwhelmed with sorrow, came to Clairvaux, to obtain St. Bernard's intervention with Innocent. But we must hear the account of the crime from his own lips. In the following simple and moving terms he informs the Pope, in a letter dated from Clairvaux:—

"The learned Thomas, Prior of St. Victor, a monk of great piety, went on a journey one Sunday, by my orders, together with several other monks. He was doing the work of God in a spirit of charity, when he was cruelly murdered in my arms, thus becoming the victim of justice and obedience. . . . The sobs, which are mingled with my words, say more than anything I could write to you. It is enough to recount simply what has happened in order that your paternal heart may feel the weight of my affliction. Alas! I have now neither strength nor light. I have lost all in losing him for whom I weep. I have the title of bishop, but he fulfilled the duties thereof; he refused the honor, but he bore the burthen. If Thibaut Nautier has recourse to your Holiness, I beseech you to let him know that God has heard the voice of my tears. His nephews were the instruments of the crime; but he was the author, and, doubtless, the instigator. I pray your Holiness to give no credit to his recital until you are thoroughly informed of the truth."

St. Bernard, inflamed with zeal, wrote to Innocent on the same subject, and his words are burning with all the eloquence of holy indignation. "It is said that the cruel beast which devoured Joseph has taken refuge with you, most holy Father, to escape from the pursuit of our faithful dogs! What an excess of folly! A wandering, terrified assassin, runs to the place where he has most to fear! What, does he mistake the seat of justice for a cave of robbers? Dost thou dare, thy mouth reeking with the blood thou hast shed, to appear before the father's eyes after having killed the child on his mother's breast? If he comes to ask penance, he must not certainly be rejected; but if he only demands an audience, grant it, holy Father, yes, grant it to him. But grant it as

Moses granted it to the idolaters, as Phineas to the fornicators, as Matathias to the unfaithful Jews; or rather, to remind you of your predecessor's example, receive him as Peter received Ananias and Sapphira."

St. Bernard's zeal, in calling for the chastisement of the culprit, had not only for its object the repression of a single crime, but, seizing every occasion of rooting out abuses from the field of the Church, he stirred up vigorous measures to insure the triumph of justice. There are few documents extant, relative to the result of this matter; but we may judge of its importance by the fact, that several prelates assembled with the Abbot of Clairvaux, in order to consult as to the best means of repressing the licentiousness of a portion of the clergy, and stemming the torrent of passions by which the Church was overwhelmed. The Pope sanctioned the decrees of this assembly, to which he added some resolutions yet more severe than those which had been drawn up.

About this time, the Sovereign Pontiff, accompanied by the Roman prelates, came solemnly to Clairvaux, to contemplate, with his own eyes, this living temple of the majesty of God. The annalist of Citeaux describes this visit in his own simple language:—

"The poor of Jesus Christ received the Pontiff with extreme affection. They did not go to meet him adorned with purple and silk, nor carrying church books inlaid with gold and silver; but simply clothed in their rough habits, bearing a wooden cross, and manifesting their joy, not with the clangor of sounding trumpets, nor with cries of tumultuous rejoicing, but with the sweet and modest chanting of sacred hymns. The bishops wept; the Pope, likewise, shed tears; all admired the mild gravity and the humble and mortified demeanor of this band of holy monks. The magnificence of the reception which they gave to the Head of the Church did not consist in great banquets, but in great virtues. Their bread, instead of being of pure wheaten flour, was made of flour from which the bran had not been separated; there was plain wine (petit vin) instead of sweet wine;** herbs instead of meat; and vegetables were served in place of any other kind of

---

\* *Sapa pro careno.* The word *sapa* rather means an extract of herbs than wine, from whence, probably, is derived our term *soup.* It is also translated by *petit vin.*

food. But if, by chance, there was some fish, it was placed before the Pope, rather to be seen than to be eaten."

Innocent, after having spent some days in this holy solitude, set out on his journey, and continued his visits to the principal churches and abbeys in France, exciting everywhere feelings of filial gratitude by the blessings which he bestowed on the people. At Paris he was received with great magnificence. The Jews themselves, says the chronicler, came forth to meet him, full of joy, and offered him a roll of their law, covered with a veil. The Pope received them with great interest, and said to them, as he accepted their gift: *"Auferat Deus omnipotens velamen a condibus vestris* (may the Almighty remove the veil from your hearts)!" He remained, during the Easter festival, at the Abbey of St. Denis, where he celebrated the office of Good Friday and Holy Saturday, *watching all night, and wearing on his head an embroidered tiara with a golden circlet.*

Meanwhile, the visit to Clairvaux was not slow in producing its results. Two important matters had been decided: the departure of St. Bernard to Aquitaine, and the convocation of a General Council at Rheims.

The mission to Aquitaine which was intrusted to St Bernard, and Joscelin, Bishop of Soissons, were both perilous and delicate. This vast province, which at that time extended from the frontiers of Picardy to the mountains of Navarre, was under the dominion of the young Prince William, whom we have already mentioned in the preceding chapter, but his history is sufficiently remarkable to call for some details.

William X, who was afterwards father-in-law to the Kings of France and England, and grandfather to Richard Cœur-de-Lion, belonged to the illustrious house of the Counts of Poitou, who had assumed the title of Dukes of Aquitaine. He had been brought up amid all the pomps of a splendid court; and from an early age he gave proofs of an indomitable character, and a fatal propensity to evil. But, when he became master of himself and of his father's states, by the untimely death of William IX, he found himself, while yet very young, one of the most powerful feudatory lords of France, and one of the richest princes of his time. He was a brilliant and extravagant man, of athletic proportions and gigantic height; a *good knight a arms*, says an old writer;

in his person was combined dignity and strength, and towards *all comers* he showed himself both formidable and fascinating. A chronicler says, "that at one meal he was hardly satisfied with what would have sufficed for eight robust persons in the prime of life. He could not live without fighting, and even when his provinces were at peace, he went always armed, and obliged his vassals, *bon égre, mal égre, to* fight against one another. In fact, he was another Nimrod in his passion for warfare; another god Bel in the quantity of meats which he consumed; another King Herod in his crimes and incests; for he kept, by violence, his brother's wife for three years, and boasted, like the Sodomites, of his crimes and misdemeanors."

Such was the head of the schismatical party in Aquitaine; such was the man to whom it was thought fit to send St. Bernard.

But what rendered this mission still more difficult was the unlimited credit which Gerard enjoyed with this prince, doubtless on account of his toleration of William's scandalous life. But these terrible obstacles did not damp the zeal of the Abbot of Clairvaux. Towards the end of the year 1131, he arrived in the territory of the Duke of Aquitaine, and went, with the Bishop of Soissons, to a monastery of his order at Chatelliers, near Poictiers. Without losing a moment, he considered the means of obtaining an interview with the sovereign. He disdained all underhand ways, and trusting in the omnipotence of grace, he went straight to his end by sending a message to the duke, requesting him to come to the monastery at Chatelliers. This bold proceeding astonished the monks; but William had no sooner read the letter from the Abbot of Clairvaux than, to the surprise of all, he went alone to the monastery, and remained seven entire days with the man of God. Wonderful event! The heart of this prince, harder than stone, was melted like wax under the vivifying influence of the apostolic word, and he did not leave the saint until he had promised to make amends for his crimes and do penance. However, the moment had not yet come for the decided triumph of divine grace. Hardly had William entered his palace, when his courage failed him, and he lent a ready ear to the perfidious words of the Bishop of Angoulême. The latter succeeded in turning him from the salutary resolutions which St. Bernard had suggested to him; and, as it frequently happens, his last state became worse than the first. He abandoned himself anew to his passions, with so much the more fury as he sought to close the wound which the saint's words, like a fiery dart, had made in his heart; and, to stifle his remorse, he gave himself up with fresh ardor to the delirium of crime. From that time the schism seemed triumphant, and there were no bounds to its violence. Gerard took possession of the vacant Archbishopric of Bordeaux, and retained, at the same time, the Bishopric of Angoulême; and not satisfied, as long as he saw a single orthodox bishop remaining in Aquitaine, he banished from the episcopal see the venerable Bishop of Poictiers—the last of the bishops in that province who had remained firm in the faith and loyal to the legitimate Pope.

Bernard being summoned to the Council of Rheims was unable to remain in Aquitaine to conclude the work he had begun. His presence in William's dominions had caused so much uneasiness to Gerard's adherents that all his movements were watched, and he was even threatened with death if he left his monastery. A certain time was necessary for this torrent of passions to subside. St. Bernard was aware of this, and leaving to Providence the care of ordering events and disposing the minds of men, he left the land of schism and went to Rheims, in obedience to the commands of the Sovereign Pontiff.

After an interval of four years had elapsed, the Abbot of Clairvaux perceived, by various providential indications, the issue of affairs in Aquitaine.

He was at that time in Brittany, in the territories of the Countess Ermengarde, where he was about to found a new monastery. The legate of Pope Innocent joined him there, and having taken leave of this worthy daughter of the servant of God, they both proceeded to visit Aquitaine. They informed Duke William that they had undertaken this journey to consult with him as to the means of restoring peace to the Church and remedying the evils which afflicted her. It was represented to the duke that he ought not to refuse an audience to the man of God, who had come so far to solicit it, as by his intervention it would, perhaps, be possible to pacify men's minds. The essential point was to obtain a conference, and in this St. Bernard succeeded. He represented to the duke the horrors of schisms in the Catholic Church; and using threats and prayers in turn, with that power which instantaneously subdued all hearts, he exhorted William to put an end to the revolt and to yield obedience to Pope Innocent. William, although troubled and deeply moved, would only give a partial consent to the counsels of the minister of peace. He promised obedience to the lawful Pope without, however, consenting to the restoration of those bishops who had been dispossessed of their sees, saying that he could not consent to this, because he had sworn never to be reconciled to them.

St. Bernard was not satisfied with a partial victory. *He ceased to act as man,* says a contemparary biographer, and left God Himself to act. On the day that the conference was to be continued, he was officiating at the altar, when, all at once, he stopped in the midst of celebrating the holy mysteries; he laid the Sacred Host on the patten, and then, with a kindling countenance and flashing eye, he left the altar, and approaching the astonished prince with a firm step, "We have long made use of entreaties," he said, "and you have despised us; several servants of God have united their supplications to ours, and you have made no account of them. Behold, now, the Virgin's Son, who cometh to thee, He whom thou persecutest, the Head and the Lord of the Church, the Judge at whose name every knee bows in heaven—on earth—and in hell! Into His hands—into the hands of the Just Avenger of crime—the soul which lives within thee will fall. Wilt thou despise Him also? Wilt thou treat the Master as thou hast treated His servants?"

Here St. Bernard was silent; the awe-struck people held their peace; the tears and confusion of those present betrayed their terror; all awaited in anguish the result of this unheard of act, which seemed to be the presage of a sudden manifestation of divine power. The terrified William could not utter a single word; his knees trembled under him; he fell to the ground; and when his guards raised him up he fell down again, uttering horrible cries.

Then the servant of God touched him, and commanding him by a sign to arise, he continued thus: "Go," he said, with a calm and solemn voice, "go immediately and be reconciled with the Bishop of Poictiers, whom you have driven from his see; give him the kiss of peace in token of a new alliance; conduct him yourself to his church, and render him an honor equal to the injuries you have heaped on him; recall to Catholic unity all those who have fallen away by discord or schism, and submit to Innocent as the Pontiff whom God has raised to the chair of St. Peter." The duke, subdued by the power of the Holy Ghost, which flowed from the lips, the eyes, and the sublime gesture of the man of God, was now only a passive instrument of the Divine will. He went immediately and executed punctually the orders he had received; he made his reconciliation with the Bishop of Poictiers, gave him the kiss of peace, conducted him to his church, rendered homage to Pope Innocent, and then returned to the church where St. Bernard continued to celebrate the sacrifice of the altar. Amidst the public joy and admiration caused by this event, one man alone resisted the Holy Spirit of God. That man was Gerard. More hardened than ever in his obstinacy, he only awaited St. Bernard's departure to renew his guilty intrigues; but his hour was come. He was carried off by a sudden death, without having time to acknowledge his errors. His nephews, whom he had enriched with the goods of the Church, found him one morning expiring on his bed, horribly swollen, and, in the attitude of a criminal, cursing and blaspheming. As for William, the ray of heavenly grace which had humbled him to the ground, wrought in him the wonderful phenomenon of a complete transformation. He was no longer the same man, since divine light had triumphed over his darkness. Absorbed in the contemplation of that light to which he had so long been a stranger, racked with remorse, bathed in tears, and eager to do penance, he resolved to finish his mortal career by the expiation of a holy death; and generously renouncing riches, power, and honors, he buried himself in solitude, where his life, like a torrent which conceals itself in the cavities of the earth, disappeared from the eyes of the world, without leaving any traces which historians could collect.

William was only thirty-eight years of age. Before he left his domains forever, wishing to settle the inheritance of his vast estates, he summoned the Bishop of Poictiers, whom he had formerly outraged so cruelly, and who had now acquired all his esteem. He intrusted to him his last will, which has been preserved by the annalist of Citeaux. This document deserves a place here; but its length only permits us to extract the most interesting portions. "In the name of the holy and undivided Trinity, one only God! This is my Testament. I, William, by the grace of

God, in the presence of William, Bishop of Poictiers, in honor of the Saviour of the world, of the holy martyrs, confessors, virgins, and, above all, of the Virgin Mary. Penetrated with sorrow for the innumerable sins which I have committed with inconceivable audacity, through the suggestion of the devil; and filled with a fear of the last judgment; considering, moreover, that the goods which we enjoy here below perish in our hands like unto smoke which disappears in the air; that we can hardly pass an hour without sinning; that the time of our life is very short; that those things of which we fancy ourselves the masters are frail and perishable, and that they only cause us pain and disquietude; I abandon myself into the hands of Jesus Christ, whom I desire to follow, in renouncing all for His love. I place my daughters under the protection of my lord, the king; and as to Eleanor, I give him her hand in marriage, if it is agreeable to my relations, and I bequeath to her Aquitaine and Poitou."

Thus this magnificent prince, who governed as a sovereign the whole of Western France, gave to his age the admirable example of an edifying conversion; and, at the same time, he bequeathed to the king's son, the young Louis VII, together with his daughter Eleanor, states even more considerable than those of the crown of France. These two great events, of which St. Bernard was the original cause, came to pass in the year 1136.*

But in order to take up the chronological order of events, it may be remembered that the Abbot of Clairvaux, after his first visit to Aquitaine, went to the Council of Rheims, which took place in October, 1131. All the bishops of France, England, Spain, and the Low Countries, and a great number of German prelates, composed this august assembly, over which the Pope presided in person. The king, and the most illustrious lords of the kingdom, were associated in this assembly with the princes of the Church.

---

\* It is well known that Eleanor, too celebrated by her adventures in the East, at the time of the Crusade, left Louis VII to ascend the English throne with Henry II., son of Geoffrey Plantagenet, to whom she brought her dowry, which was nearly one third part of France. Henry II, by this honest but impolitic restitution, became King of England, Duke of Normandy and Aquitaine, Count of Anjou, Poitou, Touraine, and Maine. Suger had strenuously opposed this fatal divorce, which dismembered the monarchy, introduced an enemy into the heart of the country, and gave rise to the great wars which England fought against France by the hands of Frenchmen.

"For," says Abbot Suger, "we were apprehensive lest the king's continual infirmities might deprive us of him suddenly; and as he honored us with his confidence, we advised him to crown his young son, Prince Louis, in order to avoid the dissensions which might afterwards arise on this matter. He followed our advice, and went to Rheims, accompanied by his son, the queen, and all the grandees of the kingdom." "The king, Louis-le-Gros," says another contemporary historian, "when he arrived in the midst of the venerable assembly, ascended the tribune where the Pope was seated, and kissed his feet: then, taking his place by his side, he spoke, in moving terms, of the death of his eldest son, Philip; and his words drew tears from all present. The Pope, in reply, exhorted him to raise his thoughts to the King of kings, and to submit to his decrees. 'He has taken away your eldest son,' he said, 'in his innocence, to make him reign henceforth in heaven, leaving you other sons to reign here below in your place. Therefore, you ought rather to comfort us, sire; for, as to us, we are exiles; and, truly, the generous hospitality which you have shown to us, will merit for you an eternal reward.'"

After these preliminaries, the Pope proceeded to the coronation of the young king, Louis VII, "anointing him with the oil with which St. Remigius anointed King Clovis at his baptism, and which he had received from the hands of an angel."

The council sat for fifteen days, and, thanks to the activity of St. Bernard, to whom the Pope and the prelates confided the arrangement of almost all their affairs, canons of great importance to the Church and State were promulgated.

Nearly all these canons, to the number of seventeen, were repeated in the general Council of Lateran; they formed part of the vast system conceived by Gregory VII, and the reforms which were begun under that great Pontiff. The morals of the clergy and the faithful became the subject of most wise regulations; and the manner of administering the sacred functions, as well as public affairs, the rights of war, negotiations, and civil relations, were determined in this council, according to the rules of Christian moderation.*

---

\* See the Acts of the Second General Council of Lateran. On the subject of the councils over which Pope Innocent presided during his journeys, Professor Nean-

The assembly, after having done all that the unhappy state of the times would allow for the improvement of the moral state of the people, concluded their deliberations, and were about to separate, when good tidings came, which filled the Pope and cardinals with joy. The venerable Norbert, Archbishop of Magdeburg, arrived at Rheims, and, in full council, presented to the Pontiff letters from the King of Germany, by which Lotharius renewed his homage, and announced that he was ready to open the campaign in Italy with all the forces of his empire.

der, of Berlin, renders a homage to the Sovereign Pontiffs, which we love to quote from the mouth of a Protestant. We translate literally: " It is worthy of admiration," he writes, " to find the Popes ever attentive to the moral and religious wants of their people, even when they are banished from their See, and obliged to go to war to regain it. Their journeys, which were often caused by disturbances in Rome, turned to the advantage of those states through which they passed, as they learned thus to know the state of the various Churches and people, and by their presence they lent weight and authority to the synods which were called together to remedy existing evils."—Neander Bern. und sein Zeitalter, p. 107, note 12. Abbe Fleury, on the contrary, in his Ecclesiastical History (vol. xiv., liv. lxviii., p. 425), expresses the following vile sentiment on the subject of Pope Innocent's journeys: "The Pope continued to visit the churches of France, supplying his wants from their abundance, which was a great burden to them." I should answer him with Christ— "The poor you have always with you, but me you have not always."

# CHAPTER XX

THE EXPEDITION OF LOTHARIUS TO ITALY—ST. BERNARD RESTORES PEACE TO THE ITALIAN REPUBLICS, AND RECONCILES THE FAMILY OF THE HOHENSTAUFFEN WITH LOTHARIUS—COUNCIL OF PISA.

THE critical state of affairs in Germany was far from justifying the ostentatious promises of Lotharius. Obstacles arose on every side to the Italian campaign; and the state of affairs was so complicated that Lotharius was obliged, more than once, to abandon his projects, or defer them to some other time. He had to overcome the supineness of the princes of the empire, who were not disposed to lend him the assistance of their arms, and his own secret repugnance to the Roman Pontiff. He owed his elevation to the throne,

It is true, to the suffrages of the princes of the empire, but he had not gained their esteem, and when he required their concurrence for the pacification of Italy, they remained shut up in their capitals, in displeasure at the decay of the German empire, and thus testifying their disapprobation of an enterprise which they considered to be ill-timed, and above the power of Lotharius to accomplish. The most formidable of these princes, Frederic of Hohenstauffen, the brother of Conrad, who had been crowned King of Italy, had assumed a threatening attitude, in revenge for the rigor with which he had been treated, and he seemed to be only awaiting the departure of Lotharius, in order to rally his numerous adherents around him.

In the meanwhile, Lotharius persisted in his resolution, in spite of all these difficulties. He was aware that the imperial crown alone would be able to strengthen his tottering authority in Germany, and enhance the majesty of the throne in the eyes of the German princes. It was necessary that he should receive this crown at Rome, from the hands of the Pope. He, therefore, pursued his plan; and, trusting in Providence, he exposed himself to the chances of this perilous expedition.

His vassals having refused him their assistance, he succeeded, with infinite difficulty, in collecting an army of from fifteen hundred to two thousand men, and he set out on his expedition under the most gloomy auspices. When he arrived in the city of Augsburg, which was devoted to the family of Hohenstauffen, the citizens received the royal troops with contempt; bloody quarrels arose between them and this ancient city was soon almost entirely consumed by flames. Lotharius, with his troops, hastily quitted the burning city, and continued his march, notwithstanding the fresh difficulties caused by this catastrophe. During this long interval, Innocent II and St. Bernard went to Italy, where, as had been agreed, they awaited the army which was to open the way to Rome. They did not remain inactive in this unfortunate country, which had been so long a prey to the sad consequences of schism and anarchy. Their unexpected arrival, added to the news of the expedition of Lotharius, made a deep impression on the Italians; and, whilst the adherents of Conrad and Anacletus maintained a prudent reserve—awaiting the issue of events, without compromising themselves—the partisans of Innocent and Lotharius took fresh courage, and revived their hopes.

This state of affairs seemed providentially designed to facilitate the restoration of Catholic unity in Christendom; and St. Bernard was the instrument, in God's hands, for the accomplishment of this great work. In the principal cities of Italy through which he passed, he preached peace, and endeavored to reconcile the hostile parties with one another. Amongst these, the people of Pisa and Genoa were distinguished by their implacable animosities. Fresh grievances were added to the long-standing rivalry of these two maritime powers, and they almost daily attacked each other with fire and sword, without regard to the rights of war, and sparing neither prisoners nor property. Milan, Pavia, Cremona,

Placentia, and nearly all the cities of Lombardy, suffered from the fatal effects of civil war, envenomed by religious dissensions. In the meanwhile, St. Bernard appeared amongst these armed multitudes, in obedience to the Pontiff's orders. He announced peace in the midst of war, and his words, like a ray of light, pierced through the gloomiest clouds. At his voice the Genoese, intoxicated with their recent success, laid down their arms; they liberated their slaves, set free their prisoners, and signed a treaty of peace which the saint presented to them. Pisa, no less moved by the preaching of the man of God, gave up all thoughts of reprisals, and agreed to all the conditions of a sincere reconciliation. Other cities followed their touching example; and, under the footsteps of St. Bernard, as the prophet expresses it, "The valleys were filled, the mountains were brought low, the ways were made plain, and the crooked ways straight." The man of God had now the hearts of these people, and he desired to make them all one heart and soul. This was his constant thought, and in all his labors and missions, whatever might be their object, his only aim was to unite Christians, by the living bonds of the Gospel, applying, as much as possible, to social constitutions, the harmonious laws under which monastic republics flourished. Love was the inexhaustible subject of his discourses; and, by the divine power of the evangelical word, he made cities tremble, and took their people captive. They were as eager to hear him as he was desirous to nourish them with the word. He never took any rest. From morning to night he applied himself incessantly to preaching, or particular conferences; he made himself all things to all men, like the Apostle of the Gentiles, and won all hearts to himself. The fruits of this mission of peace were beyond all expression. So great was the admiration which he excited in Genoa, that the archbishop himself offered to resign his pastoral charge to St. Bernard; but the humble monk was not to be moved either by the desires of the people or the entreaties of their pastor.*

Nothing can better enable us to appreciate the wonderful changes wrought in these republics, than the very words of St. Bernard, taken from his letters:—

---

\* This was the second time he refused the Archbishopric of Genoa.

"To the consuls, the magistrates, and all the people of the city of Genoa. Oh, what consolation I experienced," he writes, "during the short-time I abode amongst you!* Faithful people, never will I forget you! I announced the Divine word to you, and, morning and evening, you flocked to hear it. I brought peace with me, and, as you are children of peace, peace rested on you. I sowed the seed, and as it fell on a good soil, it produced a hundred-fold. My stay was short, because I was pressed for time; but I met with no obstacles or delays. I had the happiness of sewing and reaping almost in one day; and, as the fruit of my mission, I brought hope to those who were exiled, liberty to captives, terror to our enemies, confusion to schismatics, glory to the Church, and joy to the Christian world!. . . What now remains, my dearly beloved, but to excite you to perseverance? This is the crown of all the other virtues, and the characteristic of heroes. Without it, the warrior cannot triumph. By it, he becomes great, and attains to glory. It is the sister of patience, and the daughter of magnanimity; the friend of peace, the companion of holy affections, the bond of concord, and the pledge of perfection. In a word, if we would be saved—it is a small thing to begin—we must persevere unto the end."

To Peter, Bishop of Pavia, who had loaded him with praises, he answered thus: "The fruit of good seed, which has been sown on a good soil, belongs to Him who provides the seed, who makes the earth fertile, who causes the grain to grow, and ripens the fruit. In all this, what can I attribute to myself? Woe to me, if I usurp the glory due to Jesus Christ! *He* it is who changes hearts; not I. The beauty of a handwriting is not the work of the pen, but of the hand which guides it; and all I ought to say is, that my tongue has served as a pen to a skilful writer. I opened my month, but

---

* The affection of the Genoese for St. Bernard has been transmitted from age to age; and these beautiful words, "*Faithful people, never will I forget you!*" remained graven on their memory, and were realized in the course of time. The annalist of Citeaux relates that, in 1625, in the author's lifetime, the republic of Genoa was ravaged by the Duke of Savoy, and the city was on the point of being taken by assault. In this extremity the inhabitants, mindful of St. Bernard's promise, made a solemn vow to the saint; and their confidence was not misplaced. On the eve of his feast, a Spanish fleet arrived, unexpectedly, to deliver them, and saved the republic from destruction. In grateful acknowledgment of this visible intervention, Genoa placed itself under the patronage of St. Bernard, and vowed a filial homage to him.

you, worthy prelate, you opened your heart; and since you have labored better than I, you will have a greater reward."

He wrote to Innocent II to acquaint him with these facts; and this letter, like the rest, breathes a heavenly humility. "Continual adversity," he writes, "would cast us into despondency, and a long course of prosperity would inflate us with pride; therefore, Divine Wisdom has disposed all things so well, that our life is a continual succession of good and evil; so that evils, far from depressing us, should enable us better to appreciate the good which follows them; and the prospect of the good which we hope for, softens the evils which we endure. Let us thank God for having wiped away our tears, and poured oil on our wounds."

It is with regret that we abridge the edifying correspondence contained in the precious documents of this epoch of St. Bernard's life. His apostolic labors in Lombardy were more successful than a large army in removing the obstacles which detained Lotharius on the other side of the Alps. In the spring of the year 1133, the German troops entered Italy, surprised that they met with no enemies to oppose them.

The size of this army was, however, so disproportioned to the magnitude of his design, that it excited the scorn of the Italians; and although all parties prudently awaited the issue, yet none augured success to Lotharius. Even St. Bernard was on the point of losing courage; and while deliberations were pending, as to the best means of accomplishing this expedition, he wrote to recommend Pope Innocent's cause to the English king, conjuring him to send reinforcements to the German troops.

In the meanwhile, the pacification of the principal cities of Upper Italy had contributed wonderfully to pave the way to success; and the friends of Lotharius had now only reason to fear Roger, the new King of Sicily. But their fears being soon dissipated, the negotiations with the King of England became unnecessary.

Roger, who had not only usurped the crown of Sicily, but likewise styled himself King of Italy,* had to encounter so many personal enemies, that he made no account in this matter of his

---

* From the time of his coronation, Roger had signed all his decrees with the title of *Rogerius Dei gratia Sicilias et Italiae Rex.*

engagements with the antipope. The princely families of Italy were stung to the quick at the assumption of the royal dignity by the Norman house, and their resentment being aggravated by Roger's brutal conduct, terrible storms were raised against him. He had employed his forces unsuccessfully to re-establish his authority in Italy; and his army being routed, he was obliged to retire to Sicily in order to repair his losses. This opportunity, so favorable to the cause of Innocent II, enabled Lotharius to continue his march, and he encamped his army before the gates of Rome. The Romans, struck with consternation, and destitute of succor, were unable to defend themselves; and, in their perplexity, they listened to the counsels of prudence, which warned them to gain time, and prepare the way for reconciliation. To this effect they sent an embassy of peace to Lotharius to disarm his vengeance, and offer him admission into their city. This was all that he required. With his handful of soldiers he did not aspire to make himself master of Rome, nor was his interest in Innocent's cause sufficiently conscientious to prompt him to re-establish him firmly in his see. His greatest concern was to gain the imperial crown, and he was successful in obtaining it.

On the 29th of August, 1133,* Lotharius entered Rome without meeting any opposition. He concentrated his troops on Mount Aventine, while the Pope took up his abode in the palace of Lateran. The cities of Pisa and Genoa sent him some subsidies by sea; and Rome remained a tranquil spectator of this extraordinary invasion.

As for the antipope, he did not hazard an attempt at resistance. He retired to the Castle of St. Angelo with his adherents, and remained master of the quarter of St. Peter, which he had surrounded with fortifications and barricades, risking no undertaking against an enemy who was too weak to attack him.

On account of these obstacles, the coronation could not take place in St. Peter's Church. In the ancient metropolitan Church of St. John Lateran, this ceremony was performed, which had been

---

* This date does not coincide with that given by Otto of Frisengen. According to that historian, this event took place towards the end of May. It is probably the mistake of a copyist—for there are several discrepancies on this point, whilst there is none in the different accounts of historians.

brought about with so much labor, and was so visibly favored by Divine Providence. There was no display of pomp on the occasion; but when once the ceremony had taken place, the relations of the Church and the empire were completely changed. In fact, by this solemn act, the two powers were consolidated anew in the eyes of the world. The Pontiff, in placing the crown on the head of Lotharius, consecrated his own prerogatives by those which he conferred on the emperor; and the latter, ascending the throne of Germany under the double auspices of religion and victory, restored to the empire its true solidity and its ancient splendor.

Anacletus perceived, to its full extent, the check which his cause had received. He manifested a desire of entering into a negotiation with the emperor; and the latter, in concert with the Pope, sent to him St. Bernard and the Archbishop St. Norbert.* But the two servants of God found the antipope so hardened in pride that they soon gave up any effort at reconciliation. "The schismatics, without any regard to what has already been settled," writes the Abbot of Clairvaux, "call for a council to decide whether Innocent or Anacletus is the lawful successor of St. Peter. But this is only a malicious pretext. God Himself has already decided a matter which they wish to judge again. There is no counsel above the counsel of God; His Word runneth swiftly, and it has united kings and people in obedience to Pope Innocent. Who shall dare to appeal against His judgment? God has manifested His justice; it shines forth so brightly, that they must be blind who are not struck by its rays. But to the blind light and darkness are one and the same thing."

St. Bernard thus indignantly repelled the subterfuges of the schismatics, and having broken off all negotiations, Lotharius left Rome with his troops, and hastily recrossed the Alps, in order to set the glorious advantages he had gained before the eyes of the princes of the empire. On the 8th of September, he reached Wurtzburg, where the sovereigns of Germany, who were in astonishment at the almost miraculous success of his intrepid undertaking, encircled him with their homage. Fortune having favored

---

* This latter, in his quality of Archbishop of Magdeburg, fulfilled the functions of chancellor of the kingdom of Italy, while the see of Cologne was vacant, to which this title was attached. In this capacity he accompanied Lotharius to Rome.

his arms, they all magnified his valor; and his most implacable enemies dared not to disturb this unanimous concert of applause.

But matters were in a very different state in Italy. The hasty retreat of Lotharius had left Rome in a most alarming situation. The contending hostile parties, now left to themselves, were on the point of coming to blows; and Anacletus, who was become more implacable than ever, left the fortress *like a furious lion,* says a chronicler, *breathing only threats and vengeance;* while Innocent, although he was supported by the subsidies from Genoa and Pisa, and by the soundest portion of the Roman citizens, was unwilling that his presence in Rome should be an occasion of disturbance; and to avoid bloodshed, he left the city and retired to Pisa, in which town he provisionally established the apostolic see.

In the meanwhile, the watchful Pontiff, who still detained St. Bernard near his person, heard that Lotharius was holding his court at Bamberg, where he was to receive, as emperor, the oath of fealty from the great vassals of Germany. In this noble assembly, a great act of reconciliation was about to take place. Frederic and Conrad, the proud heirs of the Hohenstauffen, whose rebellion had been the cause of so many evils to the empire, had made advances towards Lotharius, and demanded to be received into favor. Lotharius had accepted their offer, but he attached very hard conditions to his pardon, and in order to humble the pride of that sovereign house he required that the two brothers should come in the garb of penitents, and prostrate themselves at the foot of the throne, in presence of all the grandees of the empire. On this condition, the emperor promised to receive them into favor, and to restore their domains, of which they had been deprived. The two princes, who were sprung from the blood of the ancient emperors, felt an insurmountable repugnance to give this satisfaction to their victorious enemy, and they drew back from their engagement at the very moment when Lotharius, seated on his throne, and surrounded by all the insignia of pomp, awaited the performance of their homage.

At this conjuncture, St. Bernard, who was deputed by the Sovereign Pontiff to the assembly of Bamberg, presented himself, in the name of the God of peace, amongst these implacable princes. He spoke, and they were unable to resist the unction of his words; all animosity vanished; their dissensions were appeased, and the holy monk effected a solemn reconciliation between the heirs of Hohenstauffen and the emperor. The latter restored their estates in Suabia, and in return obtained a promise that they would lend him efficacious assistance for a fresh expedition to Italy. St. Bernard, in making these stipulations, foresaw all the advantages that would result therefrom to the Church; for besides the apprehensions which the projected expedition would raise among the ranks of the schismatics, they would lose, in Conrad, their political chief, and Anacletus had now no other protector except Roger of Sicily.

This latter judged that the absence of the Abbot of Clairvaux was a fitting opportunity for a movement in favor of the antipope, to whom he owed his crown. He began by endeavoring to corrupt the Pisans by alternate threats and promises. But when St. Bernard heard of these proceedings, he hastened back to Italy; his anxious solicitude preceded him; for, a few days previous to his arrival, the Pisans received a letter burning with apostolic zeal.

"To the Consuls, Senators, and all the Citizens of the city of Pisa. You have been specially chosen by God as His inheritance. The Lord has made Pisa another Rome— the seat of the Head of the Church. This choice is not the effect of chance or policy; it is an ordinance of heaven—a special favor from God. As He loves those who love Him, He has inspired his vicar, Innocent, to abide among you, in order to crown you with blessings. You are as intrepid as the tyrant of Sicily is violent. You will remain unmoved by his threats, insensible to his presents, and firm against his machinations. Blessed people! I congratulate you on the graces with which the Lord has favored you. What city is not jealous of your happiness? Watch, therefore, vigilantly, over the treasure which is confided to you. Respect your Father and the common Father of all Christians. . . I have said enough for such a wise and enlightened people."

This letter comforted the Pisans, and strengthened them in their constancy. Shortly afterwards, St. Bernard re-appeared amongst them, on his return to rejoin the Pope, early in the year 1134. A new council was to be held at Pisa, about this time.

It was not without great difficulty that St. Bernard reached the city. The populations of the various cities on his road had detained him in order to hear and see him, and to enjoy the blessing of his presence. The Milanese, in particular, had recourse to his assistance and his counsels. Conrad, whom they had acknowledged as king, had now deserted them; and, encouraged by the example of the neighboring republics, they desired to be reconciled to the Pope, and to submit to Lotharius. To St. Bernard they intrusted this double mission. But he was obliged to delay his journey to Milan, on account of the approaching council, and he wrote the following letter to them:—

"You have expressed by your embassy the sentiments of esteem which you entertain towards me. As I am quite undeserving of them, I feel assured that they are an inspiration from God. I am deeply touched by this kindness from a powerful and illustrious city and I especially appreciate it at a time when her citizens manifest an intention of renouncing the schism, and returning to the bosom of their Mother Church . . . After all, if it be an honor to me, a vile and abject mortal, to be chosen by a famous city, as the arbitrator of that peace which she desires, I make bold to say that it is also honorable to her to make use of my mediation. . . I hasten, therefore, to the council; afterwards I will return amongst you, and I shall be able to ascertain whether I really enjoy that esteem with which you flatter me; and, if so, may God, from whom it comes, bring it to a favorable issue."

The opening of the council was, however, delayed, for some motive which has not been assigned by history. A misunderstanding arose between Innocent and the French king; and the latter forbade the French bishops to go to Pisa. Mutual recriminations gave rise to new difficulties; and it devolved on St. Bernard to end the conflict. "Empires and the sovereigns who rule over them," he wrote to Louis-le-Gros, "only prosper in proportion as they are subordinate to the power of God. Wherefore, then, does your majesty resist the elect of the Lord, whom you have acknowledged as your Father, and who is the Samuel of your son.* Suffer him who is the least of your subjects in rank, though not in fidelity, to declare to you, that it is not to your advantage to put any obstacle to a necessary good. I have solid reasons for saying this to your majesty; and I should mention them here, if I did not know that

---

* In allusion to the coronation of Louis-le-Jeune, son of Louis VI, who was anointed king by Innocent II.

a simple warning is sufficient for a wise man. For the rest, if you are dissatisfied with the rigorous conduct of the Holy See towards you, the agents of France who will be present at the council, will obtain the revocation of whatever can be revoked; and I, on my part, will exert myself in your behalf, if I have any influence."

St. Bernard's simple warning had its effect. The French bishops joined a considerable number of the prelates of the west, and the council was opened in 1134, under the presidency of the Sovereign Pontiff. The principal object of the assembly was to strengthen the authority of the Holy See, and to labor in eradicating the abuses which incessantly arose after so many reforms. The ministers of the Church, like the ancient prophets of Jerusalem, spoke the severe language of truth, without ceasing, to both kings and people. By the dint of perseverance, by repeating always the same truths, and renewing the same acts, they succeeded in insuring the triumph of justice over the disorder of human passions; and the dictates of religion made their way by degrees into laws and social customs.

The Council of Pisa added fresh weight to those canons which had been sanctioned at Rheims, in the preceding year; and it was the third council, not to mention that of Troyes, in which all was regulated by the counsels of St. Bernard. "The holy abbot was present at all the deliberations," writes a learned monk who was himself present at the council. "He was revered by all, and the door of his house was incessantly besieged by ecclesiastics, who desired to speak with him. Not that he was rendered inaccessible by pomp and vanity, but it was difficult to see him on account of the number who sought an interview with him. As soon as one left him another went in; so that this humble man, who assumed none of these honors to himself, seemed to be not only called to secular business but to the plenitude of power. It would be too long to detail all that took place in the council; the most important matter was the excommunication of Peter di Leone, and the perpetual and irrevocable degradation of all his adherents; which decree was observed, and has remained in force until the present day."

After the conclusion of the council, the Pope sent St. Bernard to Milan to bring back that rebellious city to obedience to the Holy See and the Emperor.

But how can we follow the indefatigable apostle in the new career which now opened before him? How shall we enumerate all the astonishing and wondrous deeds which signalized his presence in the capital of Lombardy?

O admirable power of the word of the saints! Wherever it is heard it touches, strikes, and breaks hearts; tears flow, animosities cease, injustices are repaired, piety revives; and, under its auspices, order, peace, and prosperity flourish! Nothing can resist its divine power, and everything yields and bends before the extraordinary man who kindles the fire of heaven on earth.

But we must let contemporary authors speak; we should be fearful of altering their recital by weakening the effect of their simple language.

# CHAPTER XXI

LABORS OF ST. BERNARD IN MILAN—MIRACLES—
EFFUSIONS OF HIS SOUL.

THE ancient Church of Milan deserved the reproaches addressed to one of the Seven Churches in the Apocalypse. *She had the name of being alive, and she was dead;* for she had broken the sacred bond which united her to the mother Church, the centre of living unity. The suggestions of her proud archbishop had rendered her indocile; and, not content with the illustrious rank she had always held in the Catholic world, she aimed at independence, and coveted the primacy—sacrificing the holiest laws of the Christian world to satisfy her ambition. Her first error had been in refusing to acknowledge the lawful Pope; and by this fatal schism, which degraded her in proportion as it inflated her pride, she became engaged in the interests of human policy, subject to all its complications and vicissitudes.

The Archbishop Anselm had taken no notice of the excommunication which two Popes had pronounced against him. He had been among the first to acknowledge Anacletus, and, emboldened further by Conrad's success in Italy, he excited the Milanese to support the pretensions of the antipope, and to undertake the defence of Conrad's cause. From thence resulted a political and religious collusion which rendered Milan the most powerful bulwark of Anacletus' party. All the malcontents and the enemies of Lotharius and Innocent found a sure protection in Anselm; and they augmented by their numbers the forces which were already at his disposal; but as soon as the cause of the schism had reached its highest point, it began to decline rapidly. The schismatics were successively disappointed of their resources and their hopes; and when they heard of the triumph of the German troops, the coronation of Lotharius, the submission of Conrad, and, above all, of the peace which St. Bernard had established in the neighboring cities, they turned against Anselm, and reproached him as the cause of the evils which threatened them. The unfaithful archbishop sought to escape from the resentment of his clergy by resigning his jurisdiction into the hands of the metropolitan bishop; and the latter took advantage of this state of the people's mind to prepare the way for St. Bernard.

At this favorable moment the holy monk arrived in Lombardy, accompanied by two cardinals and the venerable Bishop of Chartres. "They had hardly descended the Apenines," write the authors of that time, "when all Milan went forth to meet the man of God—nobles and citizens—the former on horseback, the latter on foot; and rich and poor left their houses as if they had deserted the town. They went out in crowds, with inconceivable reverence, to meet the servant of Christ, and, transported with joy on beholding him, they esteemed themselves happy in hearing the sound of his voice. They kissed his feet; and, although he did his utmost to prevent it, he could not hinder them from throwing themselves at his feet, and prostrating themselves before him; they tore the threads out of his garments to serve as remedies for their diseases, in the persuasion that whatever had touched him was holy, and would contribute to their sanctification. The multitudes who preceded and followed him filled the air with cries of joy and continued acclamations, until he entered the city, where he was detained for a long time by the immense crowd before he could reach the honorable lodging which had been prepared for him.

"But when they came to discuss in public the affair which had brought the servant of God and the cardinals to Milan, ¿he whole city, forgetting its animosities and former pretensions, submitted so completely to the holy abbot, that these verses of a poet might justly be applied to him:—

'Jussa sequi tam velle mihi,
Quam posse necesse est.'

"Peace was soon restored, the parties in the Church reconciled, and concord re-established among the dissentient parties by a solemn treaty. But when these matters were arranged, there arose others of a different kind.

"The devil exercised his fury in some possessed persons, the standard of Jesus Christ was opposed to him; and, at the command of the man of God, the evil spirits, affrighted and trembling, fled from the abodes they had made for themselves, being driven out by a superior power. This was a new employment for this holy legate, who had received no orders from the Roman Court on this subject; but, according to the Divine law and the rule of the faith, he produced, as proof of his mission, letters written with the blood of Christ, and sealed with the seal of the cross, before whose form and character all the powers of earth and hell must bow.

"We have never heard, in the present day, of a faith like that of this great people, or a virtue to be compared to that of this great saint. An humble and religious strife arose between them. The saint attributed the glory of these miracles to the lively faith of the people, and the people referred all the glory to the eminent sanctity of the servant of God; all, however, were firmly persuaded that he obtained whatever he asked from God.

"With this assurance they brought to him, amongst others, a woman well known to all, who had been tormented by an impure spirit for seven years. They entreated him to deliver the unfortunate woman, and to command the devil to leave her body. The holy man began to pray; he received power from heaven, and commanded the evil one, in the name of Christ; the woman was immediately cured, and restored to peace and tranquillity.

"Another time, a very aged lady, of high rank, was brought to him, in the church of St. Ambrose, in the presence of a great number of persons. The devil, which had long possessed her, had suffocated her to such an extent that she had lost sight, hearing, and speech; and gnashing her teeth, and stretching out her tongue like an elephant's trunk, she resembled a monster rather than a woman. Her hideous and fearful countenance, and her horrible breath, bore witness to the impurity of the spirit which possessed her body.

"When the servant of God beheld her, he knew that the devil was closely bound to, and, as it were, incarnate in her, and that it would not be easy to dislodge him from an abode where he had so long been master.

"Therefore, turning towards the people, who had flocked in crowds to the church, he recommended them to pray fervently to God; and, surrounded by the priests and religious who were near him, at the foot of the altar, he ordered that the woman should be brought before him, and firmly held. The miserable creature resisted; and, animated by a diabolical and superhuman power, she struggled, in horrible convulsions, amidst those who held her, striking them, and kicking the servant of God himself, who remained calm and unmoved, without being disturbed by the audacity of the demon. He humbly ascended the altar, and began the celebration of the holy sacrifice.

"But every time that he made the sign of the cross on the sacred host, he turned towards the woman, and applied the virtue of the same sign to her; the devil, at these times, testified that he felt the power of this mighty sign, by redoubling his fury, and manifesting fresh rage and anguish.

"After the 'Pater Noster' the saint descended the steps of the altar, to come to close combat with the enemy of God. He held in his venerable hands the chalice, and the paten on which was the sacred host; then, elevating them over the woman's head, he spoke as follows:—

"'Evil spirit, behold thy Judge; behold the Almighty. Resist now, if thou canst; if thou darest to resist Him, who, when about to die for our salvation, spoke these words—"The time is come, when the prince of this world shall be cast out! Behold that sacred body which was formed in the womb of a Virgin, which hung upon the wood of the cross, was laid in the sepulchre, rose from the dead, and ascended into heaven in the sight of his disciples! By the dread power of this adorable Majesty, I command thee, infernal spirit, to go out of the body of this servant of God, and never to re-enter it!"

"The devil being forced, in spite of himself, to obey, and let go his hold, displayed all the violence of his fury during the few moments that remained to him, and tormented the victim with redoubled atrocity. The holy abbot, returning to the altar, proceeded to the fraction of the saving host, and gave the pax to the deacon, that he might transmit it to the people; and, at the same moment, the woman was restored to peace and health. Thus did Satan bear witness, not by his free testimony, but by his forced flight, to the virtue and efficacy of the divine mysteries!

"The woman, who had recovered the use of her reason and her senses, returned thanks publicly to God, and threw herself at the feet of the holy abbot, whom she regarded as her deliverer. The church resounded with acclamations; the faithful, of every age and sex, expressed their admiration by cries of joy and hymns of gladness. The bells were rung; the Lord was blessed with one unanimous voice; and the whole city, transported with love for St. Bernard, rendered him an honor, if we may be permitted to say it, beyond what was due to a mortal man.

"The news of the events at Milan were soon spread abroad, and the reputation of the holy man was diffused through Italy. It was everywhere announced that a great prophet had arisen, powerful in works and words, who healed the sick, and delivered the possessed, by the power of Jesus Christ.

"But as the crowd which thronged around his doors from morning till night seriously inconvenienced and almost stifled him, he appeared from the window of his house, and from thence he raised his hands to bless the people. Many persons had come in from the neighboring towns and villages; and all, strangers no less than citizens, followed the man of God wherever he went, eager to see and hear him, and to witness his miracles.

"One day, when he was in a vast hall amidst a number of persons who crowded around him, a man of distinguished dress and appearance made strenuous efforts to approach him, but without success. At length, by alternately crawling on his hands and feet, and climbing on the shoulders of those who were before him, he succeeded in opening a way through the crowd, and falling at the knees of the man of God, he covered them with kisses. The venerable Rainald, who was standing by (and I have this fact from his lips), tried to put an end to this scene, knowing that such demonstrations were very painful to Bernard; but the man, who remained prostrate, turned to him, and said in a loud voice: 'Suffer me to contemplate and touch this servant of God, this truly apostolic man; for I say unto you, and I affirm it on the faith of a Christian, that I have seen this apostle in the midst of the apostles of Christ.' Rainald was struck with astonishment, and he would have inquired further about this vision, but refrained out of respect for St. Bernard's presence. It may be conceived what an effect was produced on the multitude by this incident."

"The saint," writes another chronicler, "*had no longer any repose, because all who were troubled found their rest in his labor amd weariness.* Those who left his presence, met other visitors who came to see him; and there was an uninterrupted succession of persons who came to ask favors of him. He restored a number of persons to health; he cured some by giving them holy water to drink; others by his touch alone; and, in the same city, in presence of various witnesses, he obtained from the Father of lights the power of restoring sight to the blind, by making the sign of the cross upon them.

"Amongst the numerous persons who came from all quarters to Milan, a noble knight brought a little girl to the servant of God, who had such a horror of the daylight that, although she always kept her eyelids closed, she also held her hands over her eyes, fearing lest the smallest ray mightstrike on them; for the light penetrated even to her brain, and caused her to utter fearful cries. Bernard blessed the child, and making the sign of the cross upon her, he sent her away in a more tranquil state; but whilst they were carrying her home, she opened her eyes, and continued her journey on foot, without needing any assistance."

Amidst the unwonted honors which were heaped upon him, this great man, who was an object of unexampled veneration, who commanded kings and people, and bore, alone, all the burden of his age, remained, as it were, dead and motionless on the moving scene to which he gave life, and never raised himself above the simplicity of his state. So that, if there was anything in him which was more admirable than his works, it was that profound humility with which he exercised the kind of omnipotence which God had conferred on him for the edification of the Church. He seemed completely indifferent to the glory, honor, and reverence which he received on all sides; deaf and insensible to the praises of the world. He was also continually subject to acute bodily sufferings; these pains were very dear to him, because they reminded him constantly of the common fate of all mortals; and he knew, by the experience of the great apostle, that virtue is made perfect in infirmity. But his soul suffered still more than his body from the strange kind of life which circumstances had imposed upon him. He sighed for the repose of the cloister; and his greatest sacrifice was to be obliged to leave the peaceful abode which he had made for himself in the desert "My life," he says in one of his letters, "is something quite monstrous; my conscience is in a continual state of alarm. I am a kind of chimera in the present age, neither priest nor layman; wearing a monk's habit, and observing none of the rules."

In order to give a more perfect idea of the interior of this great soul, we shall insert here a letter which he wrote to the monks of Clairvaux. Long as it is, we do not attempt to curtail it; for his whole soul is laid open in these intimate and spontaneous effusions of the most humble and tender sentiments:—

"I grieve at my separation from you; and I shall be inconsolable until I am once more in the midst of you. Are you not, in fact, my only consolation here below, during the sorrowful days of my pilgrimage? Whithersoever I go, I bear with me the sweet remembrance of my brethren; but the more sweet the remembrance, the more bitter is the pain of absence Alas! must my exile, then, be so long! Not that exile alone which detains us all so far from our true country, but that which separates me from you. Oh, how weary and painful it is to be so long subject to the dominion of vanity, under which all creatures are oppressed; to be confined in the horrible prison of this body of clay; to be in the bonds of sin and death, deprived of the sight of Jesus Christ, and subject to an infinite number of miseries! God gave me no other consolation than that of beholding in you His living temple, until He should manifest Himself more fully in His glory. It seemed to me that it would be easier for me to pass from this temple to that other temple for which the Psalmist sighed—'One thing I have asked of the Lord; that I may dwell in His house all the days of my life, that I may see His temple and taste of His delights.'

"Alas! what shall I say? How often has this consolation been taken away from me? If I mistake not, this is the third time that I have been torn away from my very self. My children have been weaned before the time; after giving them birth, I have not even been able to nourish them. I am obliged to abandon the care of my dearest interests to attend to those of others; and I know not-which afflicts me the most, to be taken away from the former, or to be occupied by the latter. O sweet Jesus! is my life to be thus consumed in sadness and weariness? It is better for me to die than to live; but I should wish to die in the arms of my brethren, my companions, and my intimate friends. I should have more comfort there, more helps, and greater safety. I even dare to say, Lord, it befits Thy goodness to let me breathe a little, before I depart from this world. Suffer my children to close the eyes of their father, even though I am unworthy to bear this name. May they assist him at the hour of death; may they receive his last sighs; may they comfort him in that last passage. By their prayers may they raise his soul, if Thou judge him worthy, to the abode of the blessed. May they, in fine, inter a poor man in the midst of his poor brethren. If I have found favor in Thy sight, I conjure Thee to grant me this grace; and to grant it through the prayers and merits of the same brethren with whom I desire to be united in the grave. Nevertheless, Thy will be done, and not mine; for I desire not to live or to die for myself.

"But since I have confided my sorrows to you, my dearly beloved, I must also tell you my consolations. In the first place, I presume to say that, in all my labors and fatigues, my only motive has been Him for whom all things ought to subsist. Whether I will or not, I owe my life to Him who gave his life for me; and I have devoted it to the merciful Judge, who will one day repay me for all I have suffered for His sake. If I only serve Him from necessity, I may, indeed, execute his commands; but I shall, nevertheless, be an unfaithful servant; but if I serve Him with all my heart, I shall have some glory. This, my dear brethren, is the first consideration which soothes me in my troubles. The second is, that God blesses my weak labors with success, and does not leave me quite useless in his Church. I have experienced this on more than one occasion, and you have sometimes heard of it. If there was not some pride in saying so, I would tell you, for your consolation, how efficaciously the Church has been served this time by so contemptible an instrument as I am; but it is better that these things should come to your knowledge from other lips than mine. At present the urgent solicitations of the emperor, the express command of the Pope, and the entreaties of the Church and the Christian princes, oblige me to go to Apulia, contrary to my inclination, all sick and languishing as I am, and bearing in my countenance the fearful tokens of approaching death. Pray for the peace of the Church; pray for my health; pray that I may have the consolation of seeing you once more, that I may live and die in your arms; and merit this grace for me by the holiness of your lives. My sufferings have hardly left me an interval of repose to dictate this letter, and I have done so with many tears and sobs. Baldwin, our most dear brother, has lent me the assistance of his hand to write to you. . Pray for the Pope, who testifies to me, and to our whole congregation, a truly paternal tenderness; pray for his chancellor, who has a mother's love for me; pray for those who are with him—for Luke, Chrysogones, and Ivo, who regard me as their own brother. Bruno and Gerard, the two religious who are with me, salute you, and recommend themselves earnestly to your prayers."

A wonderful thing indeed! This great saint, from the time he entered the monastic state, was always on the point of death; and each of his actions seemed to be the last effort of expiring nature. Divine Providence made use of this frail, languishing, and exhausted body, which was miraculously animated, as it were, by the divine breath, to rule the destinies of the Church and of the empires of the world.

Notwithstanding his visible infirmities, St. Bernard had to refuse the desires of a whole people at Milan, as at Genoa and Rheims, who conjured him to accept the pastoral charge.

One day all the faithful and the magistrates, headed by the clergy, came in procession to his abode, to conduct him by force to the archiepiscopal throne. On this occasion, resistance was vain; he, therefore, made use of an expedient. "Tomorrow," he said, "I shall mount my horse, and abandon myself to Divine Providence. If the horse takes me outside the walls of the city, I shall consider myself free from any engagement; but if he remains within the city, I will be your archbishop."

The next morning he mounted on horseback, and, riding at full speed, he departed in haste from the walls of Milan.

# CHAPTER XXII

CONTINUATION OF THE ABODE OF BERNARD IN LOMBARDY—FRESH MIRACLES—DEATH OF ST. STEPHEN, THE FOUNDER OF THE ORDER OF CITEAUX—DEATH OF ST. NORBERT.

MIRACLES are striking indications of the restoration of man to his preternatural state; they remind us of the power which he received from the beginning over nature, which he was called to command in the name of his Creator. This power, this high prerogative, may be regained by all men;* for all, by virtue of the creating word, bear within them the power which rules the elements, governs creatures, and commands the earth. But this power is latent, degenerated, and confined; and the noble master of all creation, the dethroned king of all earthly beings, has fallen by original sin to a level with those creatures whom he had been appointed to govern, and into dependence even upon those whom he had been appointed to set free. Hence, as St. Paul says, the groaning of all creatures who were sighing after their deliverance, and waiting for the manifestation of the children of God;† hence, the wearisome labor of liberation and purification which man has to accomplish in each; and in proportion as he raises

---

\* For every nature of beasts, and of birds, and of serpents, and of the rest, is tamed, and has been tamed by the nature of man.—Epistle of St. James, chap, iii., v. 7.
† For the expectation of the creature waiteth for the revelation of the sons of God; because the creature itself shall be delivered from the servitude of corruption into the liberty of the children of God. For we know that every creature groaneth and travaileth in pain even fill now.—Rom. viii., verses 21, 22.

himself to a restored harmony with his eternal head, he recovers, with the gift of God, his glorious prerogatives, and enters again into a participation of the Divine omnipotence. O sublime destiny of man! As soon as Divine love is born again in his soul, he finds in this love all knowledge, all virtue, all power! The kingly sceptre is restored to him; and, encircled with a crown of light, he exercises, with full and invincible authority, the high functions of pontiff and ambassador of the Most High. Such was St. Bernard: the world obeyed him, and the spirits of this world trembled at his words; the angels themselves, those who fell together with the prince of pride, bore witness to his sanctity, and feared him as one of the judges who shall come with the Sovereign Judge to carry out the sentence of the last day.

The contemporary biographers of St. Bernard relate a number of facts which attest this supreme authority. We cannot repeat them all; we shall confine ourselves to two examples, which may, perhaps, excite a smile in some incredulous reader, on account of the contrast these facts present to modern opinion; but this consideration will not hinder us. To what would science itself be reduced, if curtailed of all facts which overpass the bounds of human reason?

St. Bernard had just escaped with difficulty from the entreaties of the Milanese, who had made use of some degree of force to place him upon the archiepiscopal chair; but upon leaving Milan, he was not able to avoid the demonstrations of respect and joy which were poured out in all directions on his road. He had hardly reached Pavia, when his house was besieged by the people; the report of his miracles had filled all Italy; and from all parts he was solicited in favor of the sick. His touch, his prayer, his mere presence worked wonders; but, above all, the possessed recovered at his word the use of their understanding, and their liberty. Amongst these there was a woman of whose cure many curious particulars are related. "The husband of this woman," says an old historian, "brought her to the feet of the saint. The devil immediately began to make this unhappy person speak with contempt of the Abbot of Clairvaux; and she said, in a mocking tone: 'This devourer of roots and cabbages will never send away my little dog. She spoke many similar words, blaspheming the man of God, in order to irritate him, and lower him in the estimation of the people. But the saint recognized the artifices of Satan, and mocked at the mocker. He desired that the possessed woman should be conducted to the principal church in Pavia, dedicated to St. Syrus, that he might leave to this saint the honor of her cure. But the devil continuing his mockeries, said again: 'Syrulus shall not send me away, and Bernardalus shall not either.' The saint replied: 'It will be neither Syrus nor Bernard who will send you away; it will be the Lord Jesus Christ!' Upon which he began his prayers, and implored the help of God for the deliverance of this unfortunate female At this instant, the malignant spirit changed his tone and language. 'Oh, how gladly would I go out of this miserable creature,' said he; 'Oh, would that I could escape from the suffering which I endure in this body! But I cannot.' On being asked why he could not, he replied, 'Because the great Lord would not allow it yet.' 'Who, then, is this great Lord?' replied St. Bernard. The devil continued, 'It is Jesus of Nazareth.' 'You know the Lord Jesus, then? Have you seen Him?' 'I have seen Him,' said the spirit. 'Where did you see Him?' 'I have seen Him in glory.' 'Then,' said the man of God, 'thou hast been in glory?' 'Yes, I was in glory.' 'And how didst thou lose it?' 'We fell in great number, with Lucifer,' replied the devil.

"He pronounced these words by the mouth of the woman, with a melancholy tone; and all who were present heard it distinctly. The holy abbot then said: 'Wouldst thou not desire to be restored to this glory and to thy ancient state of happiness?' To this question the devil replied, with a very remarkable expression of voice, 'That is deferred.'* After these latter words, she kept silence, and spoke not another word. But the man of God, having returned to his prayers, cast out the infernal spirit, and the woman departed quite cured.

"All those," continues the historian, "who heard the details of this cure, expressed an exceeding joy at it; but this joy did not last long; for, at the very moment that the woman entered her house, the demon returned into her body, and agitated her with

---

\* Hoc, inquit, tardatum est. We have not been able to understand the meaning of these words. It is of faith that the devils are for ever excluded from glory. So if these words were to mean anything else, let us never forget that they were spoken by the spirit of lies.

convulsions which exceeded in violence all that she had suffered before. Her sorrowing husband did not know what to resolve upon; for, on oneside, it was a misery to him to live with a possessed woman; and, on the other, he feared to commit an act of impiety were he to abandon her. In this state of perplexity he determined to return to Pavia (for he did not live in the city), carrying his wife with him. But he did not find the saint at that place, so he followed him to Cremona, where, having rejoined him, he related his misfortune, and shed many tears. St. Bernard, touched with compassion, entered a church towards evening, and passed the whole night in prayer. The next morning he again delivered this woman from her enemy; and, fearing that the devil might gain access to her again, he made her hang round her neck a note, on which he had written these words—'Satan, I command thee, in the name of our Lord Jesus Christ, never to be so bold as to approach this woman again.' After this she remained in peace, having been entirely cured."

"There was in the same city," relates the monk Ernold, "a demoniac, whose strange howlings were a subject of mirth to many persons, but inspired serious and charitable men with lively compassion. This miserable being barked when desired to speak; and, if you had heard him without seeing him, you would have taken him for a dog. At the sight of St. Bernard, this man uttered cries like those of a ferocious dog when he is beaten with a stick. But the servant of God threatened the devil, and cast him out, in the name of Jesus Christ. Then, having desired the man to speak, the latter returned thanks to God, went into the church, assisted at the divine mysteries, and continued to fulfil all the duties of a reasonable and grateful man."

But St. Bernard, after having gone, according to the Pope's commands, through the different cities of Lombardy, at length returned to Milan. He had everywhere succeeded in appeasing resentment and cementing peace, except at Cremona, where his mediation was not accepted. This city, puffed up by its material prosperity, did not appreciate blessings of a superior order offered to it by the man of God, and he hastened to quit the place. There were serious reasons, also, for his return to Milan. The Archbishop Anselm had submitted, and offered to purge himself from the condemnation which he had incurred: it was necessary to reconcile him with the Pope, who had excommunicated him, and with the people, whose most just animadversions he had drawn upon himself. St. Bernard, seeing his repentance, made use of as much charity to defend him against his numerous adversaries as he had before shown zeal in opposing him, and obtained, by his tact and prudence, his restoration to his august functions. This complete settlement of things at Milan permitted him to remain some time there, to found a work at which he could now labor with the more liberty of spirit, as he had no longer to fear importunate solicitations to accept the archiepiscopal chair. Besides the public reforms which his labors produced at Milan, his preaching had aroused in many souls more rare and hidden fruit, thoughts of retirement, and heavenly desires after perfection; and it was to such elect souls that the holy abbot felt himself especially devoted. We have already said the involuntary share which he took in the temporal and political interests of his age was, in his eyes, only an accidental and transitory passage in his life: he underwent it from obedience; but found no consolation therein, except when it concurred towards the especial object of his vocation. This object was to make known the interior life, to establish houses for prayer, to re-unite into one single body those souls which were burning with the same desire, the same love; in short, to accomplish, by this holy union, the deepest desire of Jesus Christ—*Sint unum*. He founded, therefore, in the neighborhood of Milan, in the midst of a beautiful country, a house of his order, to which he gave the name of Claravalle, because it was so dear to his heart. He summoned monks from Clairvaux to govern it; and this new monastery, worthy of its name, was soon peopled with a considerable number of fervent souls, whose prayers and austere penances were a sure pledge to the Church of Milan of grace and benediction.

This was about the middle of the year 1134. At this time the Order of Citeaux suffered a grievous loss, which no one felt more deeply than Bernard. The blessed Stephen, one of the founders of this order, and the first guide of him who was one day to be the guide of his age—Stephen, the new Esdras, as the biographers term him, who rebuilt the walls of the terrestrial Jerusalem—the new St. Benedict, who, hoping against hope, had seen the feeble seed of the desert multiply itself so prodigiously, and overshadow the whole world with its branches of grace—Stephen, the patriarch of Citeaux, ascended to heaven, whilst Bernard, his disciple and his spiritual son, brought forth a second Clairvaux in Italy. He had felt the approaches of death, and worthily prepared himself for it. As early as the year 1133, he had declared in an assembly of all the abbots of the order, that though his strength, not his heart, was unequal to continue the functions of his weighty charge, he entreated, with his eyes bathed in tears, that they would lighten the load under which he was sinking, and requested some time of rest before descending into the tomb. In the absence of St. Bernard, another monk, named Raynard, became superior-general of the Order of Citeaux, instead of Stephen; and the latter was not long after his retirement before he terminated his fruitful career by the blessed death of the just. The exordium of Citeaux relates, in the following words, the edifying circumstances attending it: "The time had arrived when the holy old man was to receive the reward of the many labors which he had accomplished in the service of Jesus Christ, and to pass from the poor and humble state which he had chosen, according to the precepts of the Saviour, to the feast of the heavenly householder. Then the abbots of his order, to the number of twenty, met together at Citeaux, that they might be present at his blessed passage, and aid with their prayers and dutiful care the holy patriarch, who was leaving them to return to his true country. When he was, then, in his agony, and seemed almost to have expired, they were speaking together of his great merit, and expressing how happy they considered him to be, that, after having procured so much good for the Church, he might depart to God in perfect security. At these words, which St. Stephen had overheard, he roused himself, and, collecting all his strength, 'What do you say?' sighed he. 'I protest, my brethren, that I go to God with as much fear as if I had never done any good; for if my meanness has, by the help of Jesus Christ, brought forth any fruit, I dread at this moment, lest I should not have received His grace with the humility which I ought, and should not have corresponded to it with sufficient fidelity and gratitude.' Upon this," continues the narrator, "the holy abbot, breathing forth his last sigh, passed victoriously amidst the powers of the air, and reached the kingdom of peace, which had always been the only object of his desires."

In this same year, and almost at the same time, the 6th of June, 1134, another friend of St. Bernard expired, in the full vigor of his age—his faithful fellow-laborer in Italy, the venerable Norbert, founder of the Premonstratensian Order. His various and intimate relations with the Abbot of Clairvaux, the great congregation of which he laid the first stone, and, lastly, the edification which he afforded to his age, by his sanctity, his learning, and his labors, oblige us to enter into some details in this place concerning this great man.

Illustrious for his birth, as well as for his vast and perfectly cultivated mind, Norbert had received in his youth the clerical tonsure and a worldly education. His relations intended him for ecclesiastical honors; but his tastes, his thoughts, his heart, belonged to the world, and sought after its pleasures. Amidst the illusions of the imperial Court, he wasted his youth; no doubt disregarding the sting of conscience, and stifling the last gleams of interior light, amidst the torrent of passing pleasures.

The voice of the heart, when it is disregarded, is sometimes fearfully re-echoed from without upon the hardened ear. Norbert, as well as St. Paul, had experience of this truth. One day he was riding, with a single servant, to a village of Westphalia. He ambled along gently across an immense plain, when suddenly the thunder growled, and the lightning broke above his head in fearful flashes. Far from all shelter and full of terror, he allowed his horse to gallop as fast as possible, to seek a refuge; but at this moment the claps of thunder redoubled, and the fiery heavens sent down a stroke which overthrew at one blow the horse and its rider. Norbert remained during a whole hour extended on the ground, without motion, almost without life; but at length he came to himself: a spark of more intense and quickening fire had fallen from the clouds upon the darkness of his soul; and, like the apostle of the nations, he cried out, "Lord, what wouldst Thou have me to do?" "Do good, and fly from evil," replied an interior voice; "seek peace, and employ all your strength to acquire it."

From this moment Norbert became a new man. Hating what he had hitherto loved, and seeking what he had always shunned, his soul, burning with apostolic zeal, placed no limits to his penance, and aspired after nothing but the service of Him whom he had so long disregarded. The Archbishop of Cologne ordained him deacon and priest on the same day; and the Abbot Coron, celebrated for his piety, prepared him, by a retreat of forty days, for the celebration of the holy mysteries. Norbert was in the thirtieth year of his age. The whole remainder of his life was a literal verification of another sentence of St. Paul: "*I will show him how much hi will have to suffer for my name.*"\* His exemplary conduct, the courageous remonstrances which he made against the irregularities of the clergy, his eloquent and practical preaching, drew upon him the pursuit of envy and calumny. He was long considered as an innovator, and was denounced as such before the tribunal of the Holy See. Persecuted on all sides, misunderstood and deserted by his best friends, he lived in retirement, and formed an intimate communion with three other servants of God, which consoled him in his disgrace. But these three disciples were also torn from him by death; and he remained alone, useless to all, forgotten, like a grain of wheat which a careless laborer neglects to hide in the bosom of the earth. This seed must lose its own life before it can produce a new life; and when it seems to be dry and dead, a ray of divine light penetrates even to its depth, and causes it to send up stems of inexhaustible fecundity. Many devoted men came successively to place themselves around St. Norbert; they united together at Premontré, a little estate in the diocese of Laon, which had been left to St. Bernard as a legacy, and which he generously gave up to the companions of St. Norbert.† They formed themselves, conformably to the rule of St. Augustine, into an order of priests, who, under the name of canons regular, lead a common life; they practised, at the same time, the monastic excercises and the priestly functions; enjoying, at the same time, the delights of contemplation and the consolations of the sacred ministry.

This useful institution, closely allied to that of Citeaux, arose with almost equal rapidity. Bernard and Norbert, attentive to the needs of their time, mutually supported each other in their common efforts to supply them. Both, united in the pure desire of good, labored at the re-establishment of religion in the various

---

\* Acts ix 16.
† The lands of Premontré were a part of the forest of Coucy; they gave name to the congregation which had been cradled there.

councils at which they assisted together. They had recently joined together to extinguish the schism in Italy, and they had both resisted the pretensions of the antipope. Lotharius had just raised the Abbot of Premontré to the archiépiscopal chair of Magdeburg. In this place, new persecutions reanimated ancient hatred; and St. Norbert nearly paid with his life for the dangerous honor which he had so justly dreaded. He nobly pardoned those who had attacked his life; and, at length, satiated with suffering, and full of good works, he expired ripe for heaven. He died on his return from Rome, in the fifty-third year of his age.*

This great servant of God presents, notwithstanding, an example of the illusions by which certain private revelations sometimes deceive the wisest minds. St. Norbert believed, and loudly proclaimed, that Antichrist would appear upon earth during the lifetime of the men of his age; he founded this belief upon indications which he had received, and which appeared to him unquestionable. Bernard was the person who undeceived him; and we find the following passage on the subject, in a letter from the holy Abbot of Clairvaux, addressed to the Bishop of Chartres: "You ask me whether the venerable Norbert is going to make a journey to the Holy Land. I know not. A few days ago I had the consolation of seeing him, and of hearing from his month, as from an organ of the Holy Spirit, a number of edifying things; but he said nothing to me of his project. He told me then, that he knew to a certainty that Antichrist would manifest himself in our day upon earth, and would appear during the lifetime of men of our age. But the foundations upon which he supported this certainty appeared to me to be anything but solid, and his explanations did not obtain my assent. He asserts that there will be, at least, before his death, a general persecution of the Church."

The death of Norbert, whose labors in Germany and Italy had so perfectly seconded the mission of the Abbot of Clairvaux—and, still more, the death of St. Stephen—grievously affected the

---

* See Father Helyot's History of Religious Orders, vol. ii. p. 164. In the time of this author, the Order of Premontré counted thirteen hundred houses of men, and four hundred monasteries of women. In England, where there were thirty-nine of their houses, those religious were commonly called White Canons. At length, this order, too much enriched by temporal gifts, fell into spiritual poverty; and the Popes have several times judged it desirable to reform its discipline.

heart of St. Bernard, and, at length, made the burden of his long absence utterly insupportable. The public veneration, of which he so unceasingly received testimonies as numerous as they were vehement, overwhelmed his humility; and he had, for a long time, been soliciting of the Supreme Pontiff permission to return to Clairvaux, and to repose, once more, in the shadow of his cloister. But his day of rest was not yet arrived, and the Pope seemed as if he could not do without the holy monk, whom he considered as the support of the papacy, and the soul of the whole Church.

Continuing, then, his labors in Italy, he contented himself with mourning in silence over the obligation which detained him from the children whom God had given him. "I am obliged," writes he to them, "to labor at business which tears from me my sweet retirement. Pity my grief, and do not blame an absence to which the necessities of the Church oblige me, but in which my will has no share. I hope that my absence will not be much longer; pray to God that it may not be without fruit. . . Let us not discourage each other; God is with us and I am with you in Him. However far distant I seem, those amongst you who are punctual to their duties, humble, fearing God, diligent in prayer, charitable towards their brethren, may rest assured that I am always with them. How should it be otherwise, being, as I am, one heart and one soul with you? whilst if there be, on the contrary, one monk who is unruly, discontended, reckless, intemperate, idle, intractable, even if I were present with him in body, he would be as far from my heart as he would be from that of God, through the disorder of his life. But, my brethren, serve the Lord now with fear, that you may one day serve him without fear. . . As for me, I serve him freely, because I serve him with love, and it is to the practice of this love I exhort you all, my dear and tenderly beloved children; serve God with love, with that great love which banishes fear, which feels not the burden of the day, which considers not wages, which seeks not reward, and which yet causes us to act with more energy than any other motive. . . May God grant, my brethren, that this love, this celestial charity, may unite me inseparably with you, and make me always present with you in spirit, above all, at your prayers."

This tender and loving pastor, after having remained almost a year in Lombardy, at length obtained permission to return to

Clairvaux. In the spring of 1135, he took leave of the Sovereign Pontiff; he departed joyfully, leaving peace and prosperity to the country which he had watered with his words, and enriched with his benedictions.

# Fourth Period

### SCIENTIFIC LIFE OF ST. BERNARD, FROM HIS DISPUTES WITH THE HERETICS TO THE PREACHING OF THE SECOND CRUSADE. (1140~1145)

# CHAPTER XXIII

RETURN TO CLAIRVAUX—ST. BERNARD'S SPIRIT OF
PROPHECY—HE OPPOSES THE ABUSE OF APPEALS—HE
EXCITES LOTHARIUS TO A NEW EXPEDITION AGAINST THE
SCHISMATICS—HE IS RECALLED TO ITALY.

ST. BERNARD's journey through the north of Italy, Switzerland, and France, resembled a royal progress. The homage paid to crowned heads can bear no comparison to those spontaneous marks of respect, those testimonies of admiration and gratitude, which this holy monk received on his road; though his forehead shone not with the insignia of a borrowed dignity, but with the glory of true royalty, and immortal brightness. The man of God was not able to conceal his journey from a people burning with impatience to behold him. His route seemed to be known beforehand, like those stars whose influence is felt even before they appear upon the horizon. He was unable, notwithstanding all his precaution, to escape the honors which everywhere awaited him; and the humility with which he concealed himself, only made the fame of his sanctity spread the further.

At the gates of Placentia, he found the bishop and the clergy, who received him and brought him into the city in procession. A similar reception awaited him at Florence. In Switzerland, the shepherds descended from their mountains to join his company; and the pastors of the Alps, quitting their flocks, came to throw themselves at his feet, or, uttering their peculiar sharp cry from the height of their rocks, demanded his blessing.* He arrived, at length, at Besançon, whence he was conducted solemnly to Langres; and there, not far from the city, he met his monks, who had come to meet him, at the news of his approach. "All," says the chronicler, "threw themselves on their knees, and embraced him; each addressing him in his turn; and, full of joy, they conducted him to Clairvaux."

As soon as the saint had crossed the threshold of his monastery, he went and returned thanks in the church, and assembled his children in chapter, where he made them an exhortation, which, on account of his extreme fatigue, was short, but most tender and affecting. It was a consolation to him to find everything in that perfect order which he had established before his long absence. "This house of God," relates the chronicler, already quoted, "had not been disturbed in any degree; nothing had been able to affect the sanctity of the humble monks. They were all animated by the same spirit, burning with paternal love; and they lived in peace, climbing together the steps of Jacob's ladder, and hastening to arrive at the blessedness of heaven, the abode of eternal joy."

"As to the holy abbot," continues the same narrator, "he remembered Him who said, '*I saw Satan fall like lightning from heaven*;'† and he was so much the more humble and submissive to the Divine Majesty, as he found Him more and more favorable to all his desires. He did not take glory to himself that the devils were subject to him; but he rejoiced in the Lord to see the names of his brethren written in heaven, as he beheld them united on earth by the bonds of unbroken and holy charity."

But his return to Clairvaux was the signal for general renovation in the monastery. The buildings were not sufficient for the community; and as they were situated in the space between the

---

* Is it to our saint that we must attribute the names of Great and Little St. Bernard, which distinguish the two high mountains of the Vallais? Our devotion might lead us to believe this; but historical impartiality obliges us to think differently; for, in the year 996, says the legend, a servant of God of the same name, the blessed Bernard de Menthon, Archdeacon of Aoste, in Piedmont, overthrew an idol of Jupiter, which had been placed upon one of these mountains, and built on the spot a monastery destined to be an asylum for travellers. Thence the origin of the celebrated houses, which, for so many ages, have been one of the greatest marvels of Christian charity.
† Luke x.

two mountains, it was necessary to pull them down entirely, in order to rebuild them on a much larger plan.

St. Bernard consented, with great repugnance, to a removal so expensive, and long resisted the entreaties of his brothers. "Consider," said he to them, "how much labor and expense this house has cost. It was with unheard-of pains that we contrived to build aqueducts to carry water to the offices and places of labor. What opinion will be held of us now, if we destroy what we have made? We shall be accused of folly, with all the more reason as we have no money; and, besides, let us not forget these words of the Gospel, 'That he that would build a tower should first calculate what it will cost him.'" His brothers replied to him, "You must either reject those whom God has sent to you, or you must build rooms to lodge them in; for woe to us if, for fear of expense, we should put a stop to the development of any work of God."

These representations touched the holy abbot, and he yielded to the just desires of his brethren. The works, thanks to the unexpected aid which poured in on all sides, advanced with marvellous rapidity; *and the new-born Church grew, as if it had been animated with a living soul capable of motion.*

These new buildings seemed so much the more necessary, as more than 100 novices, recently admitted, had arrived to increase the number of the monks. The greater part of these came from the borders of the Rhine, where St. Bernard had preached the preceding year, when on his journey into Germany. Such was the efficacy of his words, that, amidst a crowd of hearers, there were always some who, more deeply struck than the others, abandoned the world, and took refuge in the cloister, that they might devote themselves irrevocably to the one thing needful.

Amidst the novices thus converted, there is one who deserves especial mention. "The servant of God," reports a contemporary historian, "having arrived in Germany to cement the peace between Lotharius and his nephew, the Emperor Henry, the venerable Albert, Archbishop of Mayence, dispatched to him a worthy ecclesiastic, named Masce- lin, who told the holy abbot that his lord had sent him to offer to him his services. But the man of God, after looking fixedly at him, said, 'Another Lord has sent you here to serve Him.' The German ecclesiastic, very much surprised, and not knowing what these words meant, repeated that he only came on the part of his lord, the Archbishop of Mayence. 'You deceive yourself,' replied St. Bernard; 'He who sends you here is greater than your lord—it is Jesus Christ.' At these words the ecclesiastic, guessing the thought of the abbot, said, 'Perhaps you think that I wish to be a monk? God foribid; I have never had a thought of such a thing.' St. Bernard, without insisting any longer, merely repeated that the will of God would be accomplished very shortly; and, in fact, Mascelin came soon afterwards to join St. Bernard at Clairvaux, and became one of his most generous disciples."

The spirit of prophecy, which had more than once before spoken by the mouth of the servant of God, suggested to him, at this time, a sad prediction concerning his brother Guido, which he pronounced courageously, notwithstanding the pain it must have cost him.

A monk of Clairvaux had fallen sick, in Normandy, whither the holy abbot had sent him on a mission. Full of tender care for each of his children, he proposed to have him sent for, that he might have, at least, the consolation of finishing his days at Clairvaux. But Guido, who administered the temporal affairs of his monastery, feared the expense which this long journey must occasion, and made a remark upon it to St. Bernard. "What!" exclaimed the latter, with an accent of painful surprise, 'do you think more of horses and silver than of one of your brothers? Since, then, you will not have this brother rest with us in this valley, you shall not lie there yourself."

This prediction was not long unfulfilled, for Guido, having gone to Pontigny on the affairs of the order, after a short illness died and was buried there.

The affliction of St. Bernard, at the death of a brother whom he had so much loved, was very deep; but it did not lessen his vigor, as is sometimes the case in this sort of trial; his grief did not interrupt his austerities for a single day, nor did it hinder him from joining in the exercises of the community, or fulfilling the duties of his position. Each day he broke the bread of the word to his children; and knowing that, of all food, the sweetest and most nutritious is that of love, he drew the holy subject of his discourses from the Canticle of Canticles, which furnished him with the most sublime inspirations for himself and his children.

It was his delight to retire to a little hut which he had constructed in the depth of the most solitary part of the valley, there to live amidst invisible things, and to pass peaceful hours absorbed in the contemplation of the eternal beauty. But he did not allow himself these pure enjoyments at the expense of the labor which his charge imposed upon him. He was constantly accessible to all the souls which lived on his life; and besides the cares which he bestowed on all in common, he directed, in an especial manner, the tottering steps of the novices at all times. Neither these multiplied cares, nor his daily preaching, nor the chanting of psalms, nor the difficulties which the rebuilding of the monastery had brought on him, appeared to have any effect on his mind; he was constantly calm and serene; in temper, equal and sweet; and, whilst giving himself entirely to others, he did not neglect his own progress nor forget the great need of the Church. The Church, the Holy Roman and Catholic Church, the mystical spouse, the beloved of Jesus Christ, was the incessant object of his thoughts, of his love, of his warmest solicitude. There was at this time an abuse in jurisdiction, against which he energetically raised his voice. In all parts of the world appeals were made from the local ecclesiastical tribunals to Rome. These appeals were founded on the primacy of St. Peter, which no one, in all Christendom, thought of contesting; and they offered the immense advantage of opening a way to the oppressed of all countries, whilst they imposed a check upon oppressors of all ranks. This practice was in its first institution what it has been through all ages, and which it is in our days, the highest and most salutary guarantee of justice which is possible in this world. But on account of this advantage itself, it had been used to excess and abused; such is the lot of the most excellent things when they are mingled with earthly interests and human passions. Hence arose frequent conflicts, which did injury to the episcopal authority; the bishops loudly complained of this, and St. Bernard lent them the aid of his influence to demand the maintenance of their rights within the limits laid down by the canons. The Archbishop of Treves, whose mild authority had just been intruded upon by an unfounded appeal, charged the holy abbot to write to the Pope, and thus furnished him with an opportunity of explaining the matter with a noble boldness. We may judge of this by the opening of his letter to

Innocent. "I speak freely," said he, "because my love is sincere, and it would not be so if a scrupulous delicacy or timid fear were to close my mouth. The complaint of the Archbishop of Treves is not peculiar to him, it is shared by many prelates, and even by your most devoted friends. All the provincial pastors, who have at heart the salvation of souls, cry out with one voice that they have no longer any jurisdiction in the Church, that its heads have become useless, that episcopal authority is annihilated, since no bishop has power to avenge the insults committed against God, or to punish crime in his diocese. The fault is, naturally, thrown upon you and upon the Court of Rome. You destroy, say they, the good which they do, and you restore again the evil which they had destroyed." After having maintained the rights of the bishops against those who disregarded their lawful authority, he expresses himself with not less warmth against the bishops themselves, who, through another abuse, exercised an arbitrary authority. "Many persons," adds St. Bernard, "are scandalized to see such prelates protected, supported, favored by the Holy See. . . I say it with shame, and you will hear it no doubt with grief. I agree to their not being deposed, since nobody denounces them; but are bishops of evil report worthy to be supported by the Holy See? The frankness with which I speak to you would make me fear to appear presuming if I had not the advantage of knowing and of being known by you. But I know your natural goodness, and you know, my dearly beloved Father, what is my love and the motive which causes my temerity."

This letter did not procure a reply prompt enough to satisfy the zeal of the servant of God. He wrote another, some little time after, in which, referring to the affair of the Archbishop of Treves, he says to the Holy Father: "The Apostolic See has this peculiarity, that it makes no scruple of revoking anything which has been extorted by fraud and lying whenever it perceives that such has been the case. It is also according to equity, and to the dignity cf the holy and supreme See, that no impostor shall be suffered to profit by his imposture."

It was thus that the holy monk from the depth of his cell extended the exercise of his indefatigable care over the whole Church; no interest, no vice, no abuse escaped his zeal; and the whole episcopate, as well as the Sovereign Pontiff, found in his words light to direct their conduct.

This powerful influence was not less felt in political than in religious affairs. The peace which St. Bernard had established between Lotharius and the princes of the ancient imperial house had borne fruit in Germany. The emperor might now think of reconquering Italy, and of making good his rights over Sicily. The abbot of Clairvaux had not lost sight of this plan, which he had himself laid before Lotharius; and he wrote thus to the latter in the cause of religion: "I bless the Lord," said he, "that he has elected your emperor, that you may be the defender of His name, the restorer of the empire, the protector of the Church, the pacificator of Christendom. It is to Him alone that you owe that high renown, which increases daily, and renders your name illustrious. You owe also to Him the happy issue of the perilous journey which you have undertaken for the peace of the world and the deliverance of the Church. You came to Rome to receive the imperial crown; and the more to signalize your valor and piety, you came almost without troops. If, then, at the sight of a handful of men, the affrighted people dared not defend themselves, with what terror will not your enemies be seized, when you bring down upon them the whole force of your arm? You are engaged to this by a motive of honor. . . I am, it may seem, departing from my character in thus rousing you to war; but I have no scruple in declaring that, in quality of protector of the Church, you ought to defend it against the fury of schism; and, farther, that in the quality of emperor, you ought to tear Sicily from the hands of the usurper."

Lotharius, influenced at once by the motives of conscience and the interests of his throne, decided, without delay, upon a new expedition, and opened the campaign the same year that St. Bernard spent at Clairvaux. In the spring of 1136, he began his march, at the head of a considerable army, supported by almost all the German princes. On his side, Roger prepared himself for a vigorous resistance; and the moment had arrived when the two armies were to meet to decide the fate of Rome and of all Italy. In this serious emergency it was impossible for the Pope to leave within the shade of the cloister the man who had been the principal mover in these great enterprises. At the beginning of 1137, when all questions were on the point of being decided before the gates of Rome, St. Bernard received an order to set out instantly for Italy; and he was obliged to obey it, notwithstanding his regret, notwithstanding his repugnance to reappear upon the scene of public affairs. Offering then to God the sacrifice of his repose and his spiritual consolations, he assembled his children around him, to bid them adieu, and delivered the following discourse to them, which was frequently interrupted by tears and sighs:—

"You behold, my brethren, how much the Church is agitated by troubles and affliction. The party of Peter di Leone is, by the grace of God, broken both in Italy and Guienne, and the evils which it still excites are rather imperfect abortions, cast forth in fury and despair, than perfect formations. The defenders of the schism are disarmed in those provinces. A large party of Roman knights have attached themselves to Innocent, and many of the faithful are devoted to his cause; but they still fear the violence of a hasty populace, and fear, therefore, to declare publicly the consent which they have given to his election. Peter has for his accomplices and well-wishers the villains and wretches whom he has gained over by money; and having made himself master of their fortresses, he does not imitate the faith and simplicity of Simon Peter, but rather the enchantments and malpractices of Simon Magus.

"The west having been conquered, there only remains one nation to contend with. Jericho will fall to ruins by the power of your prayers and sacred canticles; and when you shall have raised your hands to heaven with Moses, Amalek will be defeated and take to flight.

"Thus, whilst we are fighting, come you to our help, and implore the assistance of God by very humble prayer. Continue to do as you are doing; keep yourselves firm in the state in which God has placed you; and though you know not yourselves to be guilty of anything, yet never believe yourselves just; because God alone judges those whom he justifies, and the most perfect are unable to measure the depths of his judgments. Be not anxious about man's judgment; and without depending either upon your own judgment or that of others, walk on in the fear of the Lord, so that you may never exalt yourselves by comparing yourselves with your neighbors, nor be ever discouraged or cast down by comparison; but try, in all points, to do your duty, always looking upon yourselves as unprofitable servants. As for me, I must go whither obedience calls me; and, full of confidence in Him for whom I embrace these toils and dangers, I place in His hands the care of this house, and the keeping of your souls as in the hands of Him who is its true and first Father."

After having pronounced these words, he gave his paternal benediction to the assembled children of God, and departed, leaving them all plunged in grief. But he appointed his brother Gerard to accompany him in his journey.

# CHAPTER XXIV

STATE OF AFFAIRS IN HALT—ST. BERNARD AT ROME—
CONFERENCE OF SALERNO—END OF THE SCHISM

THE part of Italy placed more immediately under the influence of Roger of Sicily, did not profit by the advantages which the north and south of that turbulent country had reaped from St. Bernard's mediation. The spirit of independence which animated these states, the rivalries which had long divided them, and, more than all, the jealousy excited by the prodigious exaltation of Venice, produced a continual and violent fermentation, which the influence of religion had not yet been able to subdue. The cities which had been pacified by St. Bernard, and which had returned to the emperor's obedience, felt the shock of these political convulsions, and could not remain entirely neuter, in the midst of pretensions maintained by each hostile state, sword in hand. The Roman schism contributed but too powerfully to perpetuate these disorders; and, notwithstanding the happy turn taken by the affairs of Innocent, the antipope could still count upon resources sufficient to enable him to maintain himself at Rome, and confront the lawful Pope. The latter could depend upon the empire, France, upon nearly all the Catholic powers; but Anacletus had possession of Rome; he was, in fact, seated upon the throne of St. Peter, and availed himself of the prerogatives and preponderance which belonged to that imposing name. The immediate vassals of the Holy See also lent him their arms; and, among the latter, Roger of Sicily showed himself the more devoted to him, that his interest was bound up with the cause of the antipope.

Roger, after his first defeats, had returned to Italy at thehead of a numerous army, which he had raised in Sicily, among the Saracens, Lombards, and Normans; and, in order to animate them to war, he had promised them devastation and pillage. Unheard-of cruelties signalized the appearance of the King of Sicily; and all the country traversed by him was ravaged with fire and sword. A providential stroke was needed to stay the course of these disasters for a moment, and give the Emperor of Germany time to accomplish his designs. Roger's wife, Alberia, was a woman of noble character. She alone possessed some influence over his implacable spirit; and she had more than once ameliorated the fate of the vanquished. But Alberia died suddenly; and her death plunged the king into the deepest melancholy. Disgusted with the world, and even with his own exploits, he shut himself up alone with his grief, and left his army without a leader or an object. His long retirement gave rise to a report of his death; and at this rumor his adversaries gave themselves up to the most sanguinary reprisals Roger, infuriated by grief, took upon himself to give the lie to this report, and to prove, at the same time, that he sought no other glory than deadly vengeance upon his enemies. He rallied the remainder of his troops around him, and rekindled the war with redoubled fury. No besieged town found mercy with him; all had to submit to his cruel conditions, and through blood and havoc the conqueror marched to Rome.

Such was the deplorable state of things when the emperor, urged by St. Bernard and Innocent, appeared in Italy, at the head of the German army. He had met with no obstacle in Lombardy. The Italian cities, though they had no sympathy with German rule, opened their gates at Lotharius' approach, and gave him free passage, without lending him any other assistance. The resistance began at Bologna, and became stronger and more serious as the army approached Rome. Bologna capitulated, but Ancona stood firm; and the emperor, relinquishing the siege, and leaving Rome on his right, proceeded towards Apulia, where he hoped to effect a junction with the Neapolitans, who had promised him their assistance. The King of Sicily was there at the time, but being inferior in numbers, he avoided an encounter, and contented himself with harassing the German troops on different sides at once.

Meanwhile, the emperor regained several towns which had been taken by Roger; and, still victorious, he dislodged him successively from Capua, Monte Cassino, and pursued him to Salerno. Salerno was the central point of the King of Sicily's operations, and contained the considerable force which he had concentrated there. The united fleets of Pisa and Genoa came to aid the German army in the reduction of this town, on which was to depend the fate of all the south of Italy. But just as a decisive attack was about to be made, the inhabitants offered to capitulate; and, notwithstanding the disappointment of those who had hoped for pillage, Lotharius, in obedience to the representations of the Pope, spared the effusion of blood, and granted advantageous terms. Salerno surrendered; and the emperor, after having invested Duke Ranulf with the government of Apulia and the command of the German troops, returned with Innocent to Rome.

It was at this time that St. Bernard appeared before Salerno.

He had been detained at Yiterbo by the sudden illness of his brother Gerard, whose counsel and assistance were very precious to him. Seeing him to be dying, and even already at the gates of death, he turned to God and conjured Him to spare his brother to him, at least, till his return to Clairvaux. This cry of his heart was heard in heaven, and Gerard was soon sufficiently recovered to be able to resume his journey. Having been a soldier, accustomed to camps and to the ways of the world, Gerard possessed a degree of experience to which his illustrious brother did not disdain to have recourse. On their departure from Viterbo, they both went first to Monte Cassino to put an end to the schism which wasted it, and bring back the misled religious to the obedience of Innocent. This mission was fully successful; but St. Bernard's strength was exhausted. In his turn, he fell dangerously ill, and thought he was condemned to end his days far from his children, in a foreign land. In this persuasion, he wrote a touching letter to the abbots of the Order of Citeaux; and said to them, among other things: "I beseech the Holy Spirit, in whose name you are assembled, to unite me to you, by the bonds of the heart; I ask Him to render your hearts sensible to the evils which I endure, and to make you feel, by the sympathy of fraternal charity, the sorrows which overwhelm me. It is my weakness, human weakness, which speaks thus, and makes me sigh and wish that God would delay to call me to Himself, in order to re-unite me to you, that I may die in the midst of you."

God, who, to use the words of Baronius, would confound the mightiest things of this world by a weak and infirm man, granted the desires of his servant, and preserved a life thus wholly consecrated to the service of the Church. St Bernard, miraculously restored, went to Rome to join the emperor and the Sovereign Pontiff. The antipope, separated from Roger, and discouraged by the rumor of his defeat, had shut himself up again in the Castle of St. Angelo, where he still ruled over a great part of Rome. But St. Bernard renewed, in the very centre of the schism, the miracles which he had wrought two years before in Lombardy. He withstood revolt and insubordination by the sweetness of his words, by the wisdom of his remonstrances, by the sanctity of his life. His irresistible influence was, at first, successful only over some individual partisans of the antipope; but it soon insinuated itself into the masses, and triumphed over the most obstinate spirits. Some members even of the family of Peter di Leone yielded to the urgency of the Abbot of Clairvaux; and from that time forward the speedy extinction of the schism might be predicted. But a fatal circumstance occurred which seemed to blight all these hopes and re-open the whole question again.

Lotharius fell sick at Rome. Exhausted with fatigue, and already far advanced in years, he thought of nothing farther than to return and end his days in Germany. But he could with difficulty be removed as far as Trent; from thence, still impatient to see his own country once more, he tried to pass the Alps; but his strength failed him on the way, and he died in a shepherd's hut among the mountains. The various impressions made by this event, the news of which spread rapidly through Germany and Italy, may be easily conceived. In the critical position of the Church, the death of a monarch who had so nobly aided her, might be expected to produce most disastrous consequences. The most hostile factions now broke forth, and the King of Sicily was especially busy in lighting up the beacon of war in various parts of Italy.

In the midst of all these discouraging events, St. Bernard, strong in the help of God, was not discouraged. With the consent of the Pope, he set out for Rome, in order, if possible, to persuade Roger to put an end to the calamities which desolated Italy.

The mission was one of danger; the troops of Roger and Ranulf were on the very eve of battle.

St. Bernard arrived at the camp of the King of Sicily. He came to him with words of peace, and invited him to lay down his arms. But Roger, deaf to all remonstrance, would not listen to any proposition. The saint withdrew, announcing to him in the name of the Lord of Hosts, that he should suffer a shameful defeat. This prediction was immediately realized. The armies met in battle; and, after a short and murderous conflict, Ranulf, with his handful of soldiers, cut the Sicilian army in pieces. It is related that, after the victory, this devout soldier knelt down upon the field of battle, and exclaimed, in a transport of gratitude, "I return thanks to God and to His faithful servant; and I confess that this victory is due to his faith and his prayers." Then, remounting his horse, he pursued his enemy, and forced him to an ignominious flight.

St. Bernard had remained during the battle like Moses on the mountain, with his hands raised up to heaven; and the fervor of his prayer inflamed the courage of those who fought for justice.

Meanwhile, the King of Sicily, who was not devoid of religious faith—though a strong worldly interest kept him in schism—could not but be struck by the providential triumph of Innocent's cause. Shaken, both by the words of St. Bernard and by the defeat of his army, he consented to receive proposals of peace; and, first of all, evinced a desire to understand more perfectly the matters relating to the election of the Pope. To this end, he asked for deputies from Innocent and Anacletus, and fixed the conference at Palermo. He wished to be present at their discussions, and to decide according to the light of his conscience. Innocent charged the Abbot of Clairvaux to be his spokesman in this assembly, and associated the Cardinals Heimery and Gerard with him. Anacletus, on his side, chose three cardinals of his party—Matthew, Gregory, and Peter of Pisa—to defend his interests. The latter was renowned for his eloquence, his prodigious learning, and his skill in dialectics and jurisprudence. Roger had named him with the express intention of confounding the holy Abbot of Clairvaux.

At the opening of the conference, Peter of Pisa made a pompous discourse in favor of Anacletus, and proved the validity of his election by historical facts and precedents from the Canon Law. He refuted, beforehand, the objections of his adversaries, and attacked the foundations of Innocent's claim.

St. Bernard spoke next. "I know," said he to Peter of Pisa, "that you are a man of science and erudition; and would to God that your talents were consecrated to the good cause! For assuredly, if you were to employ your eloquence in behalf of what is just and lawful, nothing could resist you; and, therefore, we, simple and rustic men, better fitted to till the earth than to maintain disputations, would keep the silence to which our profession obliges us, were it not that the cause of the faith urges us to speak. And how can we be silent when we see Anacletus, protected by the prince who hears us, rend and tear in pieces the robe of Jesus Christ, which neither heathen nor Jew dared to rend at the hour of His passion?

"There is but one faith, one Lord, one baptism; we recognize neither a double faith, nor two baptisms, nor two Lords; and to go back to the earliest period of history, there was but one ark at the time of the deluge, wherein eight persons were saved, while all who were without it perished miserably. That ark was a figure of the Church. Now, in our days, a new ark has been constructed; and since there are now two, of necessity one of the two must be destined to perdition. If, then, the ark of Anacletus be the ark of God, the ark of Innocent must perish; and then all the Churches of the east and west will perish; France will perish; Germany, England, Spain, the most distant countries, will be involved in the same perdition; and, further, the Orders of the Camaldolese, the Carthusians of Grandmont, Premontre, Citeaux, and an infinite number of other servants and handmaids of God, will be lost in the same wreck; with bishops, abbots, and Christian princes, all will perish, all, save Roger! Roger alone shall be saved! No; God forbid! Religion shall not perish throughout the earth; and the ambitious Anacletus shall not be the sole possessor of that heavenly kingdom whence the ambitious are excluded!"

These words, animated by the penetrating grace imparted by the Spirit of God, forcibly struck the prince and the rest of the audience. Peter of Pisa himself ventured not to reply, and remained silent. Then St. Bernard grasped his hand, saying: "Trust me, let us take refuge together in the same ark, and we shall dwell therein in full security." He finished the work of conviction in private, and both set out together for Rome, where Peter of Pisa made his submission to Innocent. As to the King of Sicily, notwithstanding the unquestionable result of the conference, he dared not yet take a decided part; self-interest prevailed, in his mind, over right and justice; and, fascinated by the policy which attached him to the cause of the antipope, he turned away, like Pilate, after having asked what is truth, that he might not hear it.

But this long crisis at last approached its close. Anacletus, full of grief and disappointment, fell sick. He had been gradually deprived of all his resources, and abandoned by his most zealous partisans. These reverses, far from making him look into himself, embittered him the more, and plunged him into a state of despair, which consumed the remainder of his life. He died early in the year 1138. The schism did not, however, die with him. The cardinals of his party were too deeply compromised in this deplorable matter to submit to Innocent; and, in order to please the King of Sicily, and advance his interests, they hastened to elect a Pope in the place of Anacletus; their choice fell upon Cardinal Gregory, who took the name of Victor.

New dismemberments, incalculable misfortunes, might result from this new schism; and St. Bernard, who exceedingly feared them, used all his influence to preserve the Church from the calamities which threatened her. He succeeded in dispersing the storm, more by the power of his prayers than even by the energy of his words. Victor, the new antipope, was touched by grace; and, a few days after his election, came by night to the Abbot of Clairvaux, with all the tokens of a sincere repentance.

The happy Bernard received him with exceeding charity and joy; he led him to the feet of Innocent, to make his submission to the legitimate Pope, against whom neither arms, nor schism, nor heresy, nor all the efforts of hell, had been able to prevail. Vehement rejoicings burst forth at Rome, at the tidings of the re-establishment of peace and union. The news spread rapidly throughout all Catholic countries, and blessings were everywhere poured forth upon the Abbot of Clairvaux. He had his own part in the universal joy; it was given to him, after seven years of persevering toil and straggle, to see the proud schismatic, against whom he had struck the first blow, humbled to the earth. We read his own account of the happy conclusion of this matter, in a letter written by him to the Prior of Clairvaux: "On the very day of the octave of Pentecost, we received from the Lord the fulfilment of our prayers, in the restoration of peace to Rome, and union to the whole Church. The partisans of Peter di Leone came that day to prostrate themselves at the feet of the Sovereign Pontiff, and pay him liege homage and the oath of fealty. The clergy of the antipope also humbled themselves before the Pontiff, together with the idol whom they had themselves raised to the throne; and all have now returned to obedience. This joyful event has caused universal gladness. If I had not had a kind of presentiment of this conclusion, I should, long ago, have returned to you. Now I have nothing more to detain me here; and, instead of saying, as formerly, I will come—I say, I come. Yes; I come immediately; and bring, as the reward of my struggles, the triumph of Jesus Christ, and the peace of the Church.

"The bearer of this letter will only precede me by a few days. Here are good tidings! But the reality is better still. I come, charged with the fruits of peace. The man must be mad or impious, who rejoices not thereat. Adieu."

# CHAPTER XXV

RETURN FROM ROME TO CLAIRVAUX—FOUNDATION OF
NEW MONASTERIES—DEATH OF ST. BERNARD'S BROTHER,
GERARD—FUNERAL ORATION.

St. Bernard had excited an enthusiasm in Rome which even surpassed that which marked his progress throughout Lombardy. "When he appeared in the streets," says a contemporary biographer, "the nobles formed his train, the people uttered acclamations, the ladies followed him, and all men crowded around him with the liveliest demonstrations of respect and deference. But how long," cries the same author, "had he to endure this glory? How long a rest did he enjoy after such lengthened toil? He did not even take a day of relaxation for each year of labor; and he who had spent seven years in stemming disorder, re-establishing peace, cementing union, could not resolve, even at the entreaty of his friends, to stay more than five days in Rome, after the extinction of the schism."

The servant of God hurried away from the applause of the world to seek a sweet repose in solitude, in the society of his brethren, and in the midst of the children whom God had given him, and whose affections mingled with his in the same flame of love.

On his return to Clairvaux, about the end of the year 1138, he set himself to distribute the overflowing streams from his monastery into a number of different channels, which were to carry afar, into all parts of Europe, the fertilizing waters of grace and Christian piety.

Germany, Sweden, England, Ireland, Spain, Portugal, Italy, Switzerland, even Asia, sent to France for apostles from the school which, from that time forward, flourished for the edification of the world. The mere catalogue of these foundations would fill a volume. But we will say one word concerning the monastery which, at the desire of Innocent II, St. Bernard established at Rome. That Pontiff, who desired to see at the centre of Christendom religious, whose lives should be a perfect model of sanctity, offered them the empty buildings of St. Anastatius, near the Savian waters—hence called the Abbey of the Three Fountains.* St. Bernard, according to his custom, sent twelve monks thither, under the direction of Bernard of Pisa, a disciple and worthy son of him whose name he bore. A glorious destiny was reserved for him. He became Pope under the name of Eugenius III., and we shall read the edifying details of his history hereafter. But besides this Pontiff, who, from the humblest rank among the monks of Clairvaux, was raised to the highest dignity in the world, a number of apostolic men were formed in the same school, who successively issued from the cloister to fill the most eminent seats of the episcopate. The private secretary of St. Bernard, named Baldwin, whom Innocent II. had detained at Rome, became Cardinal and Archbishop of Pisa. Stephen and Hugh, two other monks of Clairvaux, were, at the same time, invested with the Roman purple, and received in charge the two famous Churches of Ostia and Palestrina. The dioceses of Lausanne, Leon, Langres, Ausane, Nantes, Beauvais, Tournay, York (in England), several cities in Germany, two in Ireland, asked and obtained as their bishops, disciples of St. Bernard, who enhanced the glory of the episcopate by the sanctity of their lives.

But the great soul which, like a fruitful and happy mother, had brought forth so many illustrious prelates—the prophet of God, whose disciples illustrated all grades of the Church's hierarchy—the humble Bernard, remained inflexibly on the lowest step; nor

---

* The annalist relates that this edifice, one of the most ancient in Christendom, was built on the spot where St. Paul was beheaded. It was called the Three Fountains, because from the spots touched by the apostle's head, as it bounded three times on the ground, sprang three fountains.

would he ever exchange for any worldly advantage the privilege of being the servant of the least of his brethren.

The holy abbot, notwithstanding the cares centred upon him by all these new foundations, had resumed, since his return to Clairvaux, his daily exposition of the Canticle of Canticles. In these ever-flowing discourses, he was never wearied with considering the infinite love borne by Jesus Christ to the children of men; and his burning and redundant eloquence shed over the souls of others the heavenly life and blessedness which inundated his own.

But he had scarcely recommenced this wonderful course of instructions, when his brother Gerard fell suddenly sick. He immediately called to mind the prayer which he had offered to God for him while still at Yiterbo: he had asked his brother's life only until his return to Clairvaux. The saint had forgotten this limitation of his petition; but, alas! he perceived that the moment was come when he was to be parted from a brother to whom he was bound by all the ties of grace and nature. Gerard himself tranquilly awaited his last hour, and yielded his latest breath as he finished chanting a psalm, happy to die in the arms of a brother who was also his father in Jesus Christ. On this occasion St. Bernard astonished the whole community by the wonderful firmness which he displayed and the victory which he gained over himself. Like the royal prophet, he had given way to his grief while Gerard was sick and dying; but as soon as he was dead, he became inflexible, and seemed to have stifled every complaint, every sigh, every token of sensibility. He himself arranged the funeral, he directed the office; and, during the whole of the funeral ceremonial, his calmness, his impassibility, struck the numerous choir of monks so much the more, as it contrasted with their own affliction, which burst forth in irrepressible sighs and tears. St. Bernard, till that day, had never lost a religious without weeping for him with a mother's tenderness; and how was it that now he had not a tear to give to a brother so singularly beloved, to a soul united to his own by such intense sympathy and love?

Let us hear the explanation of this strange fact, from his own mouth. On the very day of the funeral, the saint, to omit none of his duties, ascended the pulpit, and continued his exposition of the Canticle of Canticles. But he suddenly stopped; his voice was drowned in tears; grief choked him; his breast heaved and struggled with sobs. At last he threw himself, as it were, upon the bosom of his brethren, and pronounced the admirable discourse which is here subjoined. We transcribe it almost entire, notwithstanding its length, for the consolation of those who weep; and in order to communicate to them the sweet emotions we have ourselves experienced on reading this piece of Christian eloquence:—

"My affliction and the grief which overwhelms me compel me to break off this discourse. Why should I dissemble what I feel? The fire which I conceal in my bosom consumes and devours me; the more I strive to keep it within me the more does its violence increase. How, then, can I unfold this song of gladness, while my soul is sad and in heaviness? The excess of my grief takes from me all liberty of spirit, and the blow which has fallen upon me has quenched all the light of my soul. Hitherto I have striven, I have been able to master myself, fearing lest the sentiments of nature should overpower those of faith. You observed it, no doubt; I followed the sad procession without shedding a tear, while all around me wept abundantly; I stood with dry eyes by that grave, the sight whereof wrung my heart. In my priestly vestments, I said the prayers of the Church over the deceased; I cast with my own hands, as the custom is, the earth upon the body of my dearly loved, which shall soon be reduced to dust. You marvelled that I melted not into tears, you who wept less for the deceased than for me. What heart, indeed, were it of bronze, but must be touched to see me survive Gerard? It was because I collected within myself all the motives fitted to sustain my courage, to withstand my weakness.

"But I have not been able to command my feelings as I have repressed my tears—as it is written, '*I was afflicted and I kept silence.*'* I wished to concentrate my sorrows within myself; and they became only more intense and acute. Now, I confess myself vanquished; my sufferings must needs come forth, and be seen by others. Let them, then, appear before the eyes of my children, that they may have compassion on me, and may the more tenderly console me. You know, my children, what deep cause I have of sorrow; for you knew that faithful companion who has now left

---

* Ps. 76.

me alone in the path wherein we walked together; you knew the services he rendered to me; the care which he took of all things; the diligence with which he performed all his actions; the sweetness which characterized all his conduct. Who can be to me what he was? Who has ever loved me as he did? He was my brother by the ties of blood; but he was far more my brother by the bond of religion. Pity my lot, you who know all this. I was weak in body, and he supported me; I was timid, and he encouraged me; I was slow, and he excited me to action; I was wanting in memory and foresight, and he reminded me. O my brother, wherefore hast thou been torn from me? O my well beloved, why didst thou leave thy brother? O man according to my own heart, why has death parted us, who were so closely bound together during life? No; death alone could have made this cruel separation. What else but death, implacable death, the enemy of all things sweet, could have broken this link of love so gentle, so tender, so lively, so intense? Cruel death! by taking away one, thou hast killed two at once; for the life which is left to me is heavier than death. Yes, my Gerard, it would have been better for me to die than to lose thee. Thy zeal animated me in all my duties; thy fidelity was my comfort at all times; thy prudence accompanied all my steps.

"We rejoiced together in our fraternal union; our mutual converse was dear to us both; but I alone have lost this happiness, for thou hast found far greater consolations; thou dost enjoy the immortal presence of Jesus Christ and the company of angels; but what have I to fill the void which thou hast left? Ah! I would fain know what are thy feelings now towards the brother who was thine only beloved—if, now that thou art plunged in the floods of divine light, and inebriated with eternal bliss, thou art yet permitted to think of our miseries, to concern thyself about our sorrows; for, perhaps, although thou hast known us according to the flesh, thou knowest us no more. *He who is attached to God is but one spirit with Him.* He has no longer any thought or care but for God and the things of God, because he is wholly filled with God. *Now, God is love;* and the more closely a soul is united with God the fuller it is of love. It is true, that God is impassible; but He is not insensible; for the quality most proper to Him is to have compassion, and to forgive. Therefore, thou must needs be merciful who art united to the source of mercy; and although thou art delivered from misery, thou hast not ceased to compassionate our sufferings; and thy affection is not diminished by being transformed. Thou hast laid aside thy infirmities, but not thy charity; for *charity abideth,* says the apostle. Ah, no, thou wilt not forget us throughout eternity!

"Alas! whom shall I now consult in my sorrows? To whom shall I have recourse in my difficulties? Who will bear with me the burden of my woes? Who will defend me from the perils which surround me? It was the eye of my Gerard which guided my steps. Thy heart, O my brother, was more laden, more burdened than mine with the cares which overwhelm me; with thy words of sweetness and unction thou wert wont to supply my place, and set me free from secular conversations to enjoy the silence which I love. He stayed the flood of visits, and would not suffer all persons to come without distinction, and absorb my leisure; he took upon himself to receive them, and brought to me only such as he judged it fitting I should see. O prudent man! O faithful friend! He fulfilled, at once, the duties of friendship and of charity. It was not that his taste led him to these troublesome offices, but he undertook them to spare me, to assist me, believing my repose to be more advantageous to the monastery than his own. Thus, at the approach of death, 'Thou knowest,' said he, 'O my God, that for myself I have always desired retirement, and to be occupied with Thee alone; but Thy service, the will of my brethren, the duty of obedience, and especially the love of that brother who is both my father and my superior, have engaged me in the temporal affairs of the monastery. Oh, yes, it is true, to Gerard I owe whatever progress I have been able to make in my spiritual exercises. Thou wert in the midst of the embarrassment of business whilst I was recollected in my Saviour, or occupied in the instruction of my children; and, assuredly, I could repose in all security whilst thou wert acting for me as my right hand; as the light of my eyes; as my heart and my tongue. Thy hand was indefatigable, thine eye single, thy heart pure, and thy tongue judicious, according as it is written, '*The just man meditates wisdom, and his tongue speaks prudently*—Ps. 36. Gerard was useful to me in all things—great and small, public and private, internal and external. I depended, indeed, upon him, for he was wholly mine, and left me only the name and honor of my office, of which he alone bore the burden.

I was called abbot; but he fulfilled all the painful functions of my charge; and thus, by his self-devotion, he gained for me the necessary time for my exercises, my prayers, my studies, my preaching, my interior practices.

"Flow, then, my tears, flow, since you must needs fall; let the fountains of my eyes open, and let the waters pour forth abundantly to wash away the faults which have brought this chastisement upon me.

"I mourn, but I murmur not. The divine justice hath dealt rightly with us both; one has been justly punished, the other deservedly crowned. I will say, then—the Lord hath shown himself equally just and merciful; He gave him to us; He hath taken him away; and if we are made desolate by the loss, let us not forget the gift we so long enjoyed. I beseech you bear patiently with my complaints. Doubtless we see every day the dead weeping for the dead. But what do they? There is much noise and little fruit in such sorrow. Those who weep after this sort are themselves worthy of tears. For my part, I regret not the things of this world, but I regret Gerard. My soul was so bound up in his that the two made but one. Doubtless the ties of blood contributed to this attachment; but our chief bond was the union of hearts, the conformity of thought, will, and sentiment. And as we were in truth but one heart, the sword of death pierced both at once, and cut us in two parts—one is in heaven, the other is left in the dust of this world. Someone will, perhaps, tell me—your grief is carnal. I deny not that it is human, as I deny not that I am a man. Nay, more, I will grant that it is carnal, since I myself am carnal—the slave of sin, destined to die, subject to misery. What! Gerard is taken from me—my brother in blood, my son in religion, my father in his care of me, my only beloved in his affection, my very soul in his love—he is taken from me, and must I not feel it? Ah! I am wounded —wounded grievously! Forgive me, my children—or, rather, since you are my children, compassionate the sorrow of your father. No; I murmur not against the judgments of God! He renders to every man according to his works: to Gerard the crown which he has won; to me the anguish which is good for me. God grant, my Gerard, that I may not have lost thee, but that thou mayest only precede me, and that I may follow thee whither thou art gone! For, assuredly, thou art gone to join those whom thou didst call upon to praise God with thee, when in the middle of that last night, to the astonishment of all present, thou didst suddenly intone, with a calm countenance, and voice of gladness, that verse of the psalm—'Praise the Lord all ye in heaven; praise Him in the highest heaven.'—Ps 148. At that moment, O my brother, it was already day with thee, notwithstanding the darkness of our night; and that night was full of light to thee. They called me to witness this miracle, to see a man rejoicing in death. O death, where is thy victim! O death, where is thy sting! To him thou art no sting, but a song of jubilee! This man dies singing, and sings as he is dying! And death, that mother of sorrow, becomes to him a source of joy! I had no sooner reached the bedside of the dying man, than I heard him pronounce aloud these words of the psalmist: 'Father, into thy hands I commend my spirit.' Then repeating that same verse, and dwelling on the words, 'Father! Father!' he turned towards me, and said, with a smile: 'Oh, what goodness in God to be the Father of men; and what glory for men to be the children of God!' Thus died he whom we all deplore; and I confess that it almost changed my affliction into rejoicing, so did his happiness make me forget my misery!

"O Lord, I remember the covenant that I made with thee, and thy great mercies, that Thou mayest be justified in Thy words, and mayest triumph over our judgments! When we were at Yiterbo, last year, on the business of the Church, Gerard fell sick; and his illness becoming daily more and more dangerous, I thought the time was come when God would call him to Himself. I could not then make up my mind to lose, in a strange land, this dear companion of my journey; and ardently desiring to restore him to the hands which had intrusted him to me (for every one loved him, and he desired to be loved by every one), I began to pray and sigh, and I said to the Lord: 'Lord, wait till my return! Wait till I have restored him to his friends, to his brethren; after that take him, if such be Thy will, and I will not complain.'

"Thou heardest me then, and didst heal him! We finished the work with which Thou hadst intrusted us, and returned together with joy, bringing with us the fruits of peace. Alas! I had well nigh forgotten my promises, but Thou, O Lord, didst remember them, and I am ashamed of these tears, which testify my unfaithfulness. What more shall I say? Thou hast recalled what belonged to Thee; Thou hast resumed what was Thine own. My tears compel me to stop.

"Lord, I beseech thee stay these tears, and moderate my grief!"

## CHAPTER XXVI

HAPPY CONSEQUENCES OF THE EXTINCTION OF THE
SCHISM—REPONDERANCE OF THE PAPACY IN ITALY,
GERMANY, AND FRANCE—DISPUTES OF LOUIS VII WITH THE
COUNT OF CHAMPAGNE—MEDIATION OF ST. BERNARD—
VISIT OF ST. MALACHI.

THE sorrow depicted upon the countenance of St. Bernard, his altered features, and the deep grief which wasted his frame, discovered still more plainly than his words the deep wound in his heart. Yet he did not sink down in the day of affliction; and the cross, to which he remained faithfully attached, communicated a masculine and generous virtue to his soul.

Italy was then enjoying the fruit of his labors. Innocent II applied himself to cure the evils of war, and to extend to all Christendom branches from the tree of peace, which was now flourishing at Rome. He held a council in the capital of the Catholic world, at which more than a thousand bishops were assembled under his auspices. They labored for the establishment of discipline; and, in order to impress upon tHe minds of the schismatics the heinousness of their fault, the council deprived the cardinals and prelates who had embraced the cause of Anacletus of all their functions and dignities.

This rigorous measure touched, among others, Cardinal Peter of Pisa, who, having been at first the chief mover in the schism, had yielded to St. Bernard's arguments, and abjured his error in the hands of the Pope. Not considering himself, therefore, worthy of a punishment from which the Abbot of Clairvaux had promised to secure him, he applied to him, complaining of the hard measure dealt to him, and claiming his plighted promise.

St. Bernard acknowledged the justice of his cause, and took it warmly to heart. He wrote several times to Innocent in favor of the cardinal, without obtaining any satisfactory reply; he even displeased the Pope by his importunity on the same subject; but his great soul, hungering after justice, could not resolve to sacrifice the cardinal's legitimate rights. He addressed fresh letters to the Pope, at the risk of entirely losing his favor; and the expressions which he uses are remarkable. "Who, then," says he to the Sovereign Pontiff, "will do me justice against you? If I had a judge before whom I could cite you, I would show you after what manner you deserve that I should act on this occasion. There is the tribunal of Jesus Christ; I know it well. But, God forbid that I should accuse you before that tribunal, where, on the contrary, I would fain defend you! Therefore it is that I have recourse to him who has received commission to do justice to all; I appeal from you to yourself."

The effect of these energetic measures has not been related by contemporary authors; but Manriquez asserts that the Pope yielded to the representations of the saint, and that he re-established Peter of Pisa in his high dignities. Innocent II had regained, in Rome and in all other Christian states, the plenitude of his authority; he established it permanently, and used it successfully. Under his influence the German princes, assembled at Mayence, five months after the death of Lotharius, placed Duke Conrad, of Hohenstauffen, upon the imperial throne, who, under the preceding reign, had caused himself to be proclaimed King of Italy. Conrad had given unequivocal marks of loyalty and devotion to the Holy See; and, during the late campaigns, had proved himself as valiant as faithful. His election, obtained to the prejudice of Lotharius's son-in-law, Henry the Proud, entailed most serious consequences upon Germany, and rekindled the never-ending feud between the Guelphs and Ghibellines. But, notwithstanding violent opposition, Conrad III was crowned at Aix-la-Chapelle, by a legate of the Pope, the 6th of March, 1138.

The pontifical authority, now everywhere triumphant, had, by dint of patience, overthrown one by one all the obstacles which impeded the central action of Christian life and civilization.

That august power, the mediatrix between kings and people, had resumed its preponderance in the affairs of the world, and pursued, with marvellous success, the accelerated movement given to it by Gregory VII. One single enemy now remained to the Holy See; and that enemy, whose interest was to foment new schisms, dwelt in the heart of Italy. Roger of Sicily had concealed his resentment while Ranulf held him in check before Salerno; but no sooner was the latter dead, and old pretensions renewed, by the changes which had taken place in Germany, than Roger resumed his arms, and again menaced the Roman States. The Pope, alarmed at the rapidity of his progress, did not think fit to await the assistance of foreign troops; he raised an army himself, and marched in person against the King of Sicily. His zeal, and the pressing danger, filled him with courageous resolutions; it was necessary, he thought, to deal boldly with an intractable enemy. A battle was fought; but, if the issue was to the advantage of the Pope, it was not brought about by the glory of his arms, but, on the contrary, by the humiliation of his person. The two armies had scarcely met, when Roger, by a skilful manoeuvre, surrounded the Pope with the greater number of his troops, and kept him prisoner. This event happened on the 22d of July, 1138. The Pope was led to Roger's camp; but, touched with reverence at the sight of the common father of the faithful, he fell at his prisoner's feet, and showed him all the respect which Christian piety suggests. Innocent himself, moved by the conqueror's demeanor, showed a disposition to yield something on his side; and both resolved to put an end to hostilities, by a treaty of ailiance. The basis of this covenant was the confirmation of the prerogatives which the antipope had conferred upon the King of Sicily. Roger consented to receive the investiture of his possessions from the hand of the Pope; and, on this condition, he obtained the crown a second time, as a vassal of the Holy See. Thus was Sicily definitively erected into a kingdom, and peace secured to the different republics of Italy. The temporal advantage remained with the house of Roger, but the Holy See reaped all the spiritual benefits of this alliance. Innocent II, victorious even in his defeat, knew how to make use of these fortunate circumstances to add to the spiritual power all of which he had deprived the temporal. On both sides, doubtless, there was an excess; but, in the absence of a mature state of civilization, the middle age needed a firm hand to keep even the balance of political rights. Innocent had evinced great zeal and vigor, when banished from Rome and destitute of all human help; when restored to the throne of St. Peter, and victorious over all his enemies, his firmness sometimes took the form of obstinacy, and he opposed himself, as an immovable rock, to the arbitrary will of sovereigns.

At the very time of the conclusion of the Italian war, a new contest, which ended in bloodshed, arose between the Pope and the King of France. The part which St. Bernard took in this matter, obliges us to relate it at some length.

The benefices of the Church, the constant subject in dispute between the spiritual and temporal powers, had excited the cupidity of Louis VII. This young prince, jealous of the exercise of his authority over the provinces lately united to France, by his marriage with Eleanor, disputed the right of election, and curtailed other ecclesiastical liberties enjoyed by them. Serious disturbances arose, on several occasions, in consequence of these reciprocal pretensions; but when the see of Bourges, the capital of Aquitaine, became vacant, Louis VII wished to overrule the election of the chapter, and appoint one of his own creatures. The chapter resisted; and the Pope cut short all discussion, by naming, on his own authority, Peter Lachatre to the Archbishopric of Bourges.

This energetic intervention was regarded by Louis le Jeune as an infringement and usurpation on the rights of the crown; he swore, in his anger, that he would never permit Lachatre to take possession of his see; and, joining deeds to words, he persecuted the archbishop, who took refuge with Thibaud, Count of Champagne.

Thibaud, who was already at feud with the king, on account of a personal offence, took up arms and repulsed the royal troops; but he was overpowered by superior numbers, and his domains invaded, and ravaged with fire and sword. Innocent II could not look on with indifference at the revenge of Louis le Jeune, and addressed severe menaces to him. St. Bernard himself, the friend of Thibaud, and the director of his conscience, had taken part in this matter, in order to avert its fatal consequences. "I fear," he wrote to the young king, "that your highness renders my labors fruitless. You seem to regard wise counsels too lightly, while you listen, on the other hand, to the suggestions of the demon who urges you to fire and sword. Your highness, by a secret judgment of God, is permitted to entertain a false idea of things; you regard that which is honorable to you as an affront, and that which is disgraceful to you as an honor; you may be accused of loving your enemies and hating your friends. If you continue thus to act, I dare prophesy to you that your sin will not remain long unpunished. I exhort you, with the zeal of a faithful servant, to put an end to this course, to be converted, after the example of the King of Nineveh, and to stay the hand of God, which is already raised to strike you. Remember those words—'*The wovmds of a friend are better than the kisses of an enemy.*'"

Such warnings seldom failed of their effect; but the mind of the young prince was too much exasperated against the Pope, too much excited against those who had resisted his authority, to listen to the words of the man of God. He seemed even to brave the anathema which the Sovereign Pontiff pronounced against him; and hating alike Peter de Lachatre and those who had protected him, he continued his ravages in Champagne, stirred up powerful enemies against Thibaud, and gave free course to his unjust resentment. His anger was at last exhausted by its own excess. He had given orders to attack Vitry, which he was besieging; it was soon taken, and, at his command, set on fire. The flames unfortunately reached the principal church, in which most of the inhabitants had taken refuge; and Louis VII beheld, with horror, the fatal effects of his vengeance. More than 1,300 of the inhabitants, men, women, and children, perished frightfully in this conflagration; their fearful cries went to the king's heart, and struck him with terror; remorse brought down his pride; he became at once docile to tbe Pope, and wishing to be re-admitted to the communion of the Church, he conjured St. Bernard to solicit his absolution. Strange to say, he thought himself bound to continue in arms, because of his oath to Peter de Lachatre, and he asked, at the same time, absolution from Rome for his crimes, and for the oath which had led him to commit them. "You know, doubtless," wrote St. Bernard, on this occasion, to the Sovereign Pontiff, "that it is counted a dishonorable act among Frenchmen to break even a rash oath, although every man of sense acknowledges that no one is obliged to keep unlawful engagements."

This affair was delayed because of the interests of Count Ralph of Vermandois, which were interwoven with those of the Count of Champagne; and Thibaud, meanwhile, was left in the most deplorable condition. This virtuous prince, whom all historians combine to praise, was doomed to endure the most distressing vicissitudes in his old age. Almost all his vassals, emboldened by his reverses, declared against him, and aided the aggressions of the King of France. Forsaken by his friends, and without troops for his defence, he sent for the Abbot of Clairvaux, in order to derive from the bosom of religion the strength necessary to sustain such cruel trials. The servant of God set before his eyes the great models of the Christian life, and exhorted him to suffer with constancy in order to merit true glory. He represented to him, by the example of the apostle, that God chastises those whom He admits into the number of His children, and that *virtue is perfected in weakness;* because prosperity in this life makes us cowardly and indolent, while adversity strengthens great souls, and raises them to heaven by detaching them from earth.

The holy abbot succeeded at last in appeasing these differences. He effected so perfect a reconciliation between the Count of Champagne and the King of France, that the latter, upon the death of his second wife, married the daughter of Thibaud, whose son, Philip Augustus, succeeded him on the throne

St. Bernard, during the whole course of his public life, had never, perhaps, a more painful affair to settle than that which he had now brought to so happy a termination. The particular friendship which he bore to the Count of Champagne, and the immense benefits conferred on the Order of Citeaux by that virtuous prince, had imposed on him an obligation to maintain his rights and espouse his cause. But so many passions had been aroused in this quarrel, so many eminent persons had taken part in it, that it was difficult for him to interfere without raising to himself most formidable enemies. At one time, he was the object of keen resentment, not only to the King of France but to the Sovereign Pontiff himself, who, wearied with the importunity of the Abbot of Clairvaux, shut his heart against him, and even went so far as to accuse him of a want of probity. But nothing could move the saint's patience or the generous devotion he had vowed to his friend. He had never rested till he had entirely set this matter at rest.

In the midst, however, of the tribulations which, in these sad circumstances, afflicted the community of Clairvaux, St. Bernard experienced consolations of another kind, and delighted in repeating that song of the Psalmist, *"According to the multitude of the sorrows m my heart, Thy consolations have gladdened my soul."*—Ps. 73.

One of the sweetest pleasures granted to him, of which he speaks with unceasing gratitude, was that afforded by the visit of St. Malachi, Bishop and Metropolitan of Ireland. He had long known him by name, or, to speak the more Christian language of the chroniclers, he had long known and seen him in God. These two great saints, mysteriously attracted towards each other, ardently desired to meet. In the year 1139 their wish was accomplished. St. Malachi, being obliged to go to Rome, passed through France, and came to Clairvaux, where his soul was knit to that of St. Bernard as the iron is drawn to the loadstone. Enchanted with the angelic scene presented to him by the desert of Clairvaux, and insatiably desirous to see and hear the extraordinary man who had given to earth this work of heaven, he cried, with the Queen of Saba, "What I see with my eyes surpasses all that has been told me of the sanctity of this monastery. Happy are those who belong to you. Happy your children who always enjoy your presence, and listen to the words of wisdom which flow from your mouth!"

The emotion of the holy bishop was so deep that, unable to tear himself from Clairvaux, he wished to end his days there. But Bernard, although he gave him the habit of the order, would not consent to admit him among the religious; he obliged him, on the contrary, to continue his journey and his episcopal functions. St. Malachi, on his return from Rome, took back several monks from Clairvaux; he founded a monastery of the order, which soon gave birth to four other houses in Ireland, and contributed mightily to the Christian civilization of that interesting country. In the course of a second journey to Rome, however, St. Malachi returned once more to Clairvaux; and there, according to his own desire and prediction, he died in the arms of St. Bernard, and was buried in the church of the monastery.

The life and death of this humble Apostle of Ireland, afforded so much light and consolation to his age, that Bernard himself undertook to write his history. He published it, as he says in the preface, in order- to rekindle the lukewarmness of Christians by the example of the virtues which rendered St. Malachi illustrious.

Thus did the Abbot of Clairvaux employ, for the edification of the faithful, the leisure left him by public affairs, and the functions of his office. Other works issued from his pen at the same period. We will notice here his memorable letter to the Chapter of Lyons, on the subject of the feast, then recently instituted, of the Immaculate Conception of Mary. As the vigilant sentinel of the Church, he opposed this feast, which was not yet consecrated by the Holy See. At a time when all kinds of novelties were seizing upon men's imaginations, he thought it his duty to point out to the Pope a solemnity, the subject of which had not yet been positively pronounced on by the Church. "The Royal Virgin," said he, in his letter, "is crowned with so many high prerogatives, that she needs not this new homage. Praise her as the Virgin named by angels, desired by nations, known to patriarchs and prophets, elect of God, chosen among all; praise her as the channel of divine graces, as the mediatrix of salvation, as the restorer of the world; celebrate, in short, by all kinds of homage, her who is exalted above the angels; for thus sings the Church, and thus has she taught me to sing. But I have a scruple in admitting that which she does not teach me. For the rest," says he, in conclusion, "I defer on this point, as on all others, to the judgment and authority of the Roman Church; and I declare that I am ready to retract, if I have advanced anything contrary to the decision which shall be made by her."

This letter, according to the writers of the time, called forth some other works on the same subject; but the discussion did not occupy public attention. Questions of more immediate interest arose at that period: They absorbed the attention of the Roman Court, and opened a new sphere of action to St. Bernard's zeal; a career wholly scientific, in which his high mission was not less gloriously manifested than in that of politics. The material schism had been stifled, but fatal divisions still subsisted in the minds of men, and the same tendency which led nations to shake off the yoke of political power urged human reason to free itself from spiritual authority. Hence, a new phase in the life of St. Bernard, which we shall see develop and increase in the following chapters.

# CHAPTER XXVII

PRELIMINARY CONSIDERATIONS—INTELLECTUAL
MOVEMENT OF THE MIDDLE AGE.

PHILOSOPHICAL disputes, when they deeply agitate the minds of men, are never isolated contests; they attest the intellectual life of an age, and characterize its tendency. Thus, the mere enunciation of the questions raised in St. Bernard's time gives the lie to the long-cherished opinion, that the middle age was a time of ignorance and barbarism. The many and rich monuments which that age has left to our own, testify, on the contrary, its intellectual vigor; and the twelfth century especially is distinguished by its subtlety of thought as well as by the sublimity of its leading idea. The philosophical and profoundly Christian idea which ruled all the science of the middle age, was faith as the source of light. Faith was the common centre of all branches of human knowledge; and from this living source the waves of light and truth were seen to flow in harmony and order.

But the development of this idea coincided with the most critical period of the development of the human mind. The nations of Christendom had arrived at that era when imagination, exhausted by prodigious efforts, begins to fade away before positive reason—an age of maturity which has its perils as well in the intellectual as in the physical order. The man who has just attained the full use of reason acquires the consciousness of his freedom together with the sense of his dignity; he judges, compares, foresees, rests on himself, boasts of his strength, and bears impatiently the yoke of law. Hence, the aberrations, not of undisciplined imagination only, but of reason itself, which stirs up the will to revolt against authority. In the twelfth century this double tendency—that of the Christian idea which sought to enlighten science by faith, and that of the rationalizing idea which sought to explain faith by human arguments—was clearly brought out, and formed two distinct schools—the one, impersonated in St. Bernard; the other, represented by the too celebrated Abelard.

These two schools have, at all times, and in different forms, divided the scientific world. By the side of the sacred dogmas which taught the traditions of heaven and earth arose doctrines subversive of them—rationalistic systems by which the human mind attempted to reform science at its will, and to strip it of its mysteries. Hence, the antagonism between science founded on the eternal principles of revelation, and science based upon the variable premises of human thought. In fact, according as man opens himself to the Divine influence to receive light from on high, or shuts himself up within himself to enkindle it by his own efforts, so will science differ both in its tendency and its results; and from these two modes of proceeding will flow two opposite schools of teaching, to which all philosophical systems may be referred.

It will not be irrelevant to the subject before us to offer some considerations regarding these two schools, especially as they spring forth naturally from the disputes in which St. Bernard was compelled to take so prominent a part, and as they will serve, at the same time, to throw some light upon the intellectual state of the age in which he lived.

The germ of true philosophy, which is at once science and wisdom, is to be found in the sacred Scriptures. It reveals the mysteries of God, of man, and of the world, as well as the relation of man with the world and God. It tells of the fall, the dispersion of mankind, the development of evil, side by side with good, that the human will may choose between them; and of the Divine scheme for the restoration of man, and the re-establishment of harmony between heaven and earth. These truths are the foundation of all science; they were propagated, pure and unadulterated, in one of the families of Shem, from one generation to another, corrupted and degraded, more or less, among the other descendants of Noah. Moses, initiated in the secrets of God, and consecrated by a vocation from on high, engraved these Divine revelations upon tables of stone, and gave them, as a sacred deposit, to a people miraculously chosen out of all the nations of the earth. This nation handed them on to the Church, and she publishes them to the universe.

Thus has been, and still is, preserved, the knowledge of things human and divine, the science of mysteries, the true philosophy.

"This science," says a Christian philosopher, whose disciples we are proud to be,* "this science of God and of His Word, by whom all things were made; this science of the necessary relation of God with man, and of the free relation of man with God, was professed by the first Christian philosophers; some of whom, having been born in paganism, were Platonists; others, having been born in the bosom of the Church, but instructed in the arts and literature of Greece, referred all their knowledge to the centre of unity, and drew the principles and the sanction of their teaching from the Divine Word. Thus did St. Justin, St. Clement of Alexandria, Origen, St. Athanasius, and many others, seek to lead minds to the source of true science, whose object is eternal law and eternal truth, and whose result is not the mere delight of admiration and contemplation, but the love and practice of good."

The teaching of these philosophers was not argumentative; on the contrary, they laid down the doctrine in a simple, positive, and dogmatic manner, making the Word of God, not the thought of man, the foundation of science. Thus arose Catholic philosophy, a glory around the head of theology. Resting upon the rock of the Church, she applied the test of those revealed dogmas to science, and admitted the investigations of reason only when they started from the principles of faith.

Now, the rigor of these principles is a constraint upon the pride of reason; and the craving of its self-willed activity, the presumption of its self-conceit, has built, by the side of the science according to God, a science according to man. The first proceeds from the love of Divine wisdom, whence comes her noble name, philosophy; the second is a fruit of human wisdom, which covets truth, and usurps her name. According to her, philosophy is

---

* M. Bantain Phil du Christ.

not the love of truth, but the search after truth, according to the rules of dialectics— that is, to use St. Bernard's words, it is the art of always seeking it without ever finding it. It is that pagan science, boasting Aristotle for its father, which, at every period of its rational development, sets itself up as a rival to true science; and attempts, by the way of syllogism, to explore the most sublime paths of truth. "Sophistry," continues the author already quoted, "takes possession of the facts of the Gospel, to subject them to criticism; lays hold of sacred texts, of articles of faith, in order to judge them; and, as she cannot understand them, but takes them, as the apostle says, for foolishness, she turns them into ridicule or blasphemy."

As long as the art of dialectics was exercised legitimately, and in dependence upon faith, it did no injury to the teaching of the Church, but proved, on the contrary, a powerful ally; but, now become the accomplice of reason in its insurrection against faith, it degenerated into rationalism—into sophistical and puerile argumentations, which compromise the sacredness of the doctrine, even in the attempt to maintain it. Thus, in the 12th century, rationalism broke out into open warfare with positive theology; but it had, long before, given tokens of revolt. The schools founded by Charlemagne were already the exponents of this tendency. What Charlemagne undertook in the west, the celebrated Caliph Haroun Al Raschid had done in the east. Institutions arose on all sides, intended to assist the development of human intellect. Meanwhile, Aristotle had arrested the attention of the Arabs. This people, which was gifted with a strong and active intellect, delighted in his ill-translated works; and, through the medium of the Jews in Spain, the west enjoyed the fruit of their labors.

From this period, philosophy, which, among the Christian teachers, had been always kept in subordination to faith, began to deviate, and expatiate in a distinct sphere.* The impulse which

---

* The Jews played a great part in the transmission of Arabian science to the west. In the twelfth century there were brilliant schools in Spain, as well as in France, in which Aben, Ezra, Jonas, &c., shone. From these vain rationalists and bold interpreters of Aristotle, Judaism received its modem form; and the same disputations which had given rise to the semi-religious and semi-rationalistic work of the Talmud, threatened to seize on books of theological interpretation. More than one book was

Charlemagne had given to study, the excitement which he had given to reason, by laying a host of curious questions before it, occasioned disputations, adapted rather to obscure and perplex, than to further the progress of science. Thus, a woman pretended to have found the precise date of the end of the world in the Apocalypse; she alleged proofs, and found partisans. A monk of Corbie, grounding his theory upon St. Augustine, taught that all men were animated by one and the same soul. Other writers disputed as to the manner in which the Blessed Virgin gave birth to the Divine Messiah. Every kind of question, grave or puerile, became in turn the object of scholastic investigation.

As early as the middle of the eleventh century, the authority of Aristotle had attained such a preponderance that he was quoted with the same reverence as the Fathers of the Church; and neither popes nor councils could resist the influence he exerted over the Christian schools. These schools degenerated into public arenas, where truth became the sport of reason, armed with syllogisms.

Towards the end of the same century, and at the beginning of the twelfth, rationalism, fully developed, threw down the gauntlet before the theologians of the dogmatic school, to whom they gave the name of superannuated doctors; while they, on the other hand, treated the partisans of Aristotle as innovators (*doctores novi*).

One of the ancient theologians, who was looked upon as a sophist (*John the Sophist*) because he attacked rationalism at its foundation, maintained triumphantly that the abstractions of reason could not replace the reality of ideas, and that science ought not to be founded upon words which express only the notions of the mind. Around this thesis arose a vehement and celebrated dispute, which completed the schism of the doctors of the two opposite factions. John Roscelin, Canon of Compiegne, maintained that ideas were nothing but words (*flatus vocis*), by means of which we designate the notions of reason; he, and his school, received the name of *nominalists,* in opposition to the *realist* school, which regarded ideas as real things. Both schools, though they set out from opposite points, defended themselves

---

written animated by the spirit of Maimonides, composed of questions and solutions worthy of the Jewish Talmud.

by syllogistic arguments. Henceforth, rationalism ruled the spirit of the age.

It was Abelard who, representing this spirit in his own person, placed himself at the head of the movement, and popularized, in some sort, these scientific questions. Passionately fond of glory, and full of confidence in his unquestionable talent, he undertook, with a freedom unheard of till his time, to establish the truth of the dogmas of faith on the basis of reason, and to apply dialectics to the sublimest mysteries of theology. He made the attempt; and without shrinking from the consequences of so audacious a method, he dogmatized upon all questions of faith and morals. Abelard remained obedient to the Church; but his disciples, bolder and less pious than himself, pushed the new method to its utmost limits, and achieved the total separation of theology and Christian philosophy.

Such novelties, which were soon to invade all the schools, could not remain long in exercise without engendering errors and fatal heresies. The exaltation of individual reason now knew no bounds; the sanctuary of science was thrown open to every kind of doctrine; and ancient errors re-appeared, and mingled with modem subtleties.

Among the false doctrines whose germs had more than once produced their poisonous fruits, since the infancy of the Church, that of the Manicheans was one of the most remarkable, which revived in the twelfth century. It would not be easy to offer an analysis of this formidable heresy, which united, under a common denomination, all the various sects of the ancient Gnostics. Admitting two co-eternal principles, the author of good and the author of evil, the reformers of Manicheism gradually modified their system, and endeavored, more or less, to harmonize it with Christian doctrine. The result was a whimsical medley of sensuality and austerity, of misbelief and superstition, of eclecticism and pantheism, which ended in absurd theories and infamous practices.

As early as the fourth and fifth centuries, the Roman emperors had resorted to rigorous measures to exterminate these sects, whose secret assemblies and odious principles disturbed authority and revolted all honest hearts. They succeeded only in compelling them to silence, and the world seemed to be rid of them, when, about the year 660, a woman, intoxicated with the Manichean errors, strove to revive them. Her son Paul gave himself out as the apostle of a purified Christianity; and beginning by a rupture with the Catholic hierarchy, he dogmatized without mission, and sought in the Sacred Scriptures a new symbol of faith, exclusive of tradition. His disciples, the Paulicians, worthy ancestors of the heresiarchs of whom we are about to speak, the fathers of the Waldenses and Albigenses, and precursors of the heretics of the sixteenth century, would have no religion but according to the written text of the Gospel, and subjected that text to the free interpretation of their own judgment, which, in their opinion, was always enlightened by the Holy Spirit. Consistently with these principles, they successively denied, as we shall see hereafter, the dogmas and mysteries which their reason could not comprehend; and when the literal sense of Scripture too positively contradicted their arbitrary interpretations, they took refuge in the vast labyrinths of figure and allegory.

In the ninth century these sectaries, exasperated by the severity with which they had been treated, and emboldened by their numbers, mingled politics with their religious belief, and manifested very decided hostility against all government. Their conduct agreed logically with their principles; emancipated from all authority in the spiritual order, they were not slow in throwing off also the yoke of temporal authority. Such will ever be the progress of the human mind!* Asia was overwhelmed for more than thirty years by the consequences of these insurrections; and the numerous sects of Manicheism lived on in spite of obstacles, through horrible persecutions, and penetrated gradually into the west, where they formed, here and there, associations, the avowed object of which was the reformation of Church and State. The degeneracy of a vast portion of the clergy, the ignorance of the people, and the depravity of morals, were the principal causes which favored the success of these sectaries. All the elements of passion and false principle which time had matured, which

---

\* M. Guizot, in one of his lectures, has this remarkable expression: "Reform is to call things by their right name, an insurrection of the human mind against absolute power in the spiritual order." It would, indeed, be difficult to call things by a name more exact.

self-interest had multiplied, and which political circumstances had left so long to ferment, were at last to burst forth; and it was in the time of St. Bernard that the thunder-cloud came to darken the horizon of the Church. An infinite number of sects, differing in name and doctrine, were united in one common hatred against Catholicism; and the barrier once passed they stopped short at no audacious extravagance, either in doctrine or morals. Rationalism alone was in itself a sufficient calamity to the Church, but the concurrence of so many other causes of error and disorder seemed to overwhelm Christianity, and to require a superhuman power to resist it

But He who watches over the Church, and has promised her His eternal aid, did not leave her now without the help she needed. St. Bernard was there as an impregnable tower against the assaults of the enemies of truth. Let us not be surprised, then, after this gloomy picture of the dangers of the Church, at the fire, at the fury almost, with which we shall see him fight. He had giants of pride to contend with. Abelard and Guilbert de la Porree attacked, under the banner of reason, the ancient mode of theological instruction; Peter de Bruys and the monk Henry stirred up the people against the Holy See; Herbert and Tanchelm forbade marriage, and denied the efficacy of the sacraments; the Cathari or Puritans rejected the Old Testament, and the writings of the ancient Fathers; Arnold of Brescia, more vehement than all, insisted on the abolition of the ecclesiastical hierarchy; Eon de l'Etoile passed himself off for Jesus Christ; a host of other sects, surpassing each other in extravagance, preached everywhere openly the downfall of Catholicism. Nothing less than the might of St. Bernard was required to stop this inundation.

# CHAPTER XXVIII

PETER ABELARD—VIEW OF HIS DOCTRINES, HIS LIFE,
AND MISFORTUNES.

Peter Abelard, a man as extraordinary for the splendor of his erudition as for the romance of his life—the father of the sophistry of the middle age, and the patriarch of modern rationalism—seems to have been judiciously characterized by one of the writers of our day: "Abelard is in theology what he is in philosophy—neither quite heretical nor quite orthodox; but much nearer to heresy than to orthodoxy." The history of his misfortunes, written by himself, and the history of his doctrines, controverted by St. Bernard, form the great episode of the twelfth century—an episode now become vulgar by dint of repetition in the schools and in the world, and which for six hundred years has agitated science and fed romance.

There is, doubtless, nothing more common in the spectacle of human misery than to see reason and passion go astray together; and in this point of view, the adventures of Abelard and Heloise would not assuredly have been found worthy of the notice of history. But when a man thus enslaved by passion has been justly proclaimed the profoundest thinker of his age; when this man declares himself the apostle of human reason, and affects to lay the foundations of faith thereupon, it may be well to consider the solidity of such a basis, and to try it by the tests of practical life. The speculative powers of the human mind, compared with its weaknesses, present one of those significant lessons which ought not to escape the wisdom of the world!

Abelard was born in 1079, at Palais, near Nantes, in Brittany. It is said, that with a presentiment of his future eloquence, his parents gave him a name borrowed from that of the bee (*abeille*). He seemed to justify this augury. His easy elocution, joined to a marvellous subtilty of intellect, and an erudition which rendered him familiar with both sacred and profane authors, gave him the first place among the most renowned masters of his time. The external advantages of his person added, also, to the power of his talents; his figure was tall, his eye expressive, his bearing high and noble, his countenance manly and pleasing.

He had studied successively under two famous masters—Roscelin, the nominalist, and William de Champeaux, the realist. The explanation of these two systems, with their many shades of difference, would hardly fall within our limits, and would form, besides, but a mouotonous picture. It will suffice to give the leading idea, which distinguished from each other the two schools, whose controversies filled the middle age. *Realism* answered to the Platonic doctrine, which admits the *reality* of ideas—that is to say, the objective and permanent existence of the ideals, which correspond to them. *Nominalism,* on the contrary, following in the track of Aristotle, and confounding ideas with abstract notions, denied the existence of ideals, and declared that they were only words.* The question, reduced to its most simple form, was then to ascertain whether invisible things, contemplated by the eye of the mind, really exist under an ideal form, or are merely abstractions, notions of our mind, expressions of our language. This question, it will be seen, is not insignificant; it raises the most difficult problem of philosophy, it affects the whole of religion, and from its solution, when carried to the farthest term, will result either spiritualism or materialism. It is true that the consequences of this problem are not always carried to their utmost extent; its terms vary with time, and according to various turns of mind; but it will always be the pivot, around which the investigations of human science revolve. Thus, it was neither with Roscelin, nor William of Champagne, that this controversy, properly speaking, began. Its origin was in the very cradle of the human race; its root

---

* The maxim of the realists was—"*Rem de re praedicari non posse, sed ideam de ideis.*" The nominalists said—"*Entia non sunt multiplicanda praeter necessitatem.*"

in the heart of fallen man: and it appears in the first stage of childhood, in the first question asked by the child—"Is that true?" The child inquires as to the truth of what you are saying; he wants to know if your story is true; if your words correspond to an object really existing, or to a picture of your mind; he seeks truth. He is, therefore, a philosopher; and his question, eminently philosophical, is the same, when raised to a higher level, as that which was agitated, under various forms, between Plato and Aristotle, between Solomon and the Academy, between St. Paul and the Areopagus, between the realists and nominalists, between the science which proceeds from man and the science revealed by God, between the rationalistic philosophy, which sets out from below to ascend on high, and the Divine philosophy, which descends from on high to illuminate things below.

Philosophers, in all ages, have taken part in this dispute, and all continue the discussion, notwithstanding the solution of the problem, given eighteen centuries ago, by the sublimest of teachers. "We look not at the things which are seen," says St. Paul, "but at the things which are not seen. For the things which are seen are temporal; but the things which are not seen are eternal."—2 Cor. iv. 18.

This doctrine is the basis of Christian philosophy; and everything that tends to shake it is, consequently, heterodox. But it requires the submission of men to the Divine Word; and against this, the pride of science has always revolted. The fundamental difference which separates the two philosophical schools is, however, easily discerned; and if this were the place for such a discussion, we could point out the same difference in all the branches of science and art, in morals, politics, legislation, in all orders of things; for all the productions of man, as well as man himself, may be considered as reflections of heaven, or phenomena of earth. But our present subject permits us only to show the decisive part taken by Abelard in this memorable debate, and the movement which he gave to it.

Abelard having been matured both in the Platonic doctrines of William de Champeaux, and the peripatetic teaching of Roscelin, undertook, after having controverted both his masters, to conciliate their opposite doctrines, and to amalgamate them, so to speak, into a kind of intermediate theory. This attempt seemed opportune and desirable, for confusion reigned on all sides. The realists and nominalists did not understand each other. The first had, in the heat of the discussion, lost sight of the *idea,* which, in fact, escapes amid the vanity of disputation; the second, playing upon words, confounded the artificial abstractions of the mind with true and natural notions. Both were, at the same time, right and wrong, according to the different points of sight which they had taken. If Abelard had clearly and lucidly distinguished *notions* from *ideas;* if, in his doctrine of notions, he had recognized the difference which exists between those which have their root in the idea, and those which are only generalizations, elaborations more or less arbitrary of our own, he might have brought the doctors, if not the doctrines, in accordance; and, without trenching upon truths of a higher order, he might have concluded the *realism* of natural notions and the *nominalism* of artificial notions.* But this Abelard did not, and his intermediary system, called *conceptualism,* was but a new baseless opinion offered to the polemics of the middle age. Abelard, like most of the philosophers of his day, admitted but one kind of notions, and taught, with an apparent irony, that they were neither things nor words. What are they then? asked both nominalists and realists at once. Abelard replied by words, not by things. He said that notions were *conceptions* existing only in the forms of our reason: a solution evidently analogous to the doctrine of the nominalists. All the works of Abelard, moreover, attest this tendency. Abelard is a nominalist, and he it is who, by his talent and the new form which he gave to the system of Aristotle, made the science of words to prevail over the science of things. Thus, without shrinking from any of the necessary consequences of nominalism, he made the art of reasoning the great pivot of philosophy; reduced the search after truth to

---

* We call those *natural notions* which correspond to the natural order of things, and are spontaneously formed in our mind—as the notions of horse, tree, &c., general terms, all the characters of a genus, or generality of individuals. *Artificial notions,* on the contrary, are those which have no type in things above or things below; such are the technical classifiactions of certain modern sciences, which subsist only in nomenclatures, and constitute a mere nominalism more or less arbitrary: thus, in botany, for example, there is a certain class of monocotyledons which comprehends at once the lily, the palm, the asparagus, &c.; the family of cats, in zoology, comprehends the lion, the panther, the leopard, &c. These, if ever there were such, are *artificial notions.*

an exercise of dialectic skill—a kind of rationalistic mechanics applied to science—by means of which he aimed at the construction of a general system of human knowledge. He did more; not content with maintaining the principles of Roscelin and bringing them into fashion under a new name, he introduced them into the domain of theology, and undertook to explain the dogmas of faith by the mere force of logic. In the system of Abelard, faith was but an *estimation* (*aestimatio* is the word he uses)—that is to say, a provisional opinion; and it was the office of reason to justify this opinion, and prove its truth. Thus, discussing all dogmas, collecting texts and passages from Scripture and the Fathers, for or against (*sic et non*) all theological questions, he reduced matters of faith to problems, in order to resolve them by syllogisms and to invest them with a logical sanction. This attempt, conducted with consummate ability, roused all orthodox theologians, and especially St. Bernard, against him. All affirmed the Divine objects of faith to be above and independent of the judgments of reason; and they maintained that rationalistic solutions added nothing to the sanction which the Divine Word bears within itself (*justificata in semetipsa*).

We ask, on reading these dry discussions, how matters so arduous, especially in philosophy, could possibly move so many minds, and draw together so many disciples? For contemporary writers testify that an incredible number of hearers—of all countries, ages, and ranks—followed the celebrated professor and hung enraptured on his teaching; thousands of scholars followed him successively to Melun, Corbeil, St. Victor de Paris, St. Denis, into the faubourgs, the deserts, and mountain of St. Genevieve.\*
No difficulty could stop them; the hostelries could hardly contain them. It was not only the inhabitants of Paris who crowded to hear him; a number of English, Romans, Italians, Germans, Swedes and Danes were among the number, many of them men of the highest consideration, all fascinated by the teaching of the audacious master. Whence arose this popularity? How came questions of subtle dialects to excite so general a sympathy, so passionate an

---

\* The mountain of St. Genevieve was not then included within the enclosures raised by Louis le Gros around the faubourgs of Paris. It is curious to read the details of the immense popularity of Abelard's lectures. See his own history.

enthusiasm? The riddle is not hard to read; it is explained by the propensities of human nature. Abelard was the man of his age; he represented one of the features of his century—the spirit of independence—which, under various forms, was working in the multitude, loosening the yoke of a superior law. Abelard desired progress by means of human power; St. Bernard desired it by means of the power of God. It was opening an attractive way to the presumption of science to dispense with believing before understanding; and human pride found satisfaction in calling the dogmas of religion before the tribunal of human reason to be judged and approved.

It is true that Abelard always professed a sincere respect for the Church, and counterbalanced the fatal consequences of his method by a lively and docile faith: his errors were rather in his language than his mind; and the heterodox propositions which he gave forth sprang less from his personal opinions than his logical deductions. Thus, he has been accused of all heresies at once, and justified upon every point in particular; but his inexcusable fault was the application of the principles of free examination to dogmatic truths. It was this which, whether he was conscious of it or not, constituted both the charm and the danger of his teaching. Abelard, by applying such a test to theology, laid down the principle of rationalism, which, in its first development, exercised the same kind of fascination over the impassioned multitude, which was produced three centuries later by Protestantism, and which liberalism has renewed in our days with no less brilliant success.

The spirit of independence, in whatever form and under whatever name it appears, will always excite the sympathies of our fallen nature; and every doctrine which favors the triumph of self-will over divine authority (a doctrine following from the first word of independence which perverted man in the beginning), will be sure of an enthusiastic reception from the blind and insensate multitude.

Abelard was at the height of his renown, and his doctrine spreading wider and wider, when he struck upon two rocks which stood in the midst of his gigantic career—he fell upon one, and was broken; the other crushed him by its weight. Heloise robbed him of his name as a philosopher; Bernard deprived him of his reputation as a theologian.

# Fifth Period

## APOSTOLIC LIFE OF ST. BERNARD, FROM THE PREACHING OF THE CRUSADE UNTIL HIS DEATH. (1145-1158)

# CHAPTER XXIX

CONTINUATION OF THE PRECEDING CHAPTER—CONTEST OF ST. BERNARD WITH ABELARD—COUNCIL OF SENS—CONVERSION AND EDIFYING DEATH OF ABELARD.

IN THE years 1121, Abelard had been cited before a council, assembled at Soissons, under the Archbishop of Rheims, to hear the condemnation of his book on the Trinity, which he had composed according to the rules of Aristotle, and which contained manifest errors. He submitted to the sentence, and himself burnt his work; but the method which he had introduced into theological instruction made him constantly waver and fall into new errors. On one side, the boldness of his method and the unhesitating way in which he applied it to the solution of the most abstruse questions, continually drew around him a crowd of his old auditors, who pressed him to resume his public lectures and demanded of him, as he says himself, "philosophical arguments satisfactory to reason."

He was a professed monk of St. Denis; but his restless spirit would not suffer him to remain in that monastery. He left it to settle in the diocese of Troyes, where the generosity of his friends had bestowed on him a large tract of land, which was soon peopled by his numerous disciples. He built an oratory there, to which he gave the name of the Paraclete; and there, surrounded by young men who flocked to him from all parts of France, he discoursed upon the nature of God, on the mysteries of man, and on all questions of morals and metaphysics, like the Stagyrite of old in the gardens of Academus. Great was the exulting joy of Abelard at the view of his success; he expresses it with great sincerity in one of his letters: "While my body," says he, "is confined to this place, fame carries my name over the universe; all the places by which it passes are so many echoes which repeat it." But this triumph did not last long.

Already had St. Bernard, the watchful sentinel of the Church who had long observed the tendency of the new doctrines, pointed it out to the bishops and uttered a cry of warning. Abelard eluded by subterfuges and remonstrances of the powerful Abbot of Clairvaux; and, to escape the storm which threatened him, he abandoned his position at the Paraclete and accepted the Abbey of St. Gildas, which was offered him in Brittany. It is true that motives of another kind also impelled him to this sacrifice. The nuns of the Convent of Argenteuil had been dispersed, and the unfortunate Heloise was without a shelter. Abelard hesitated not a moment; he offered her the Paraclete, and she went to establish herself there with several of her companions. The Bishop of Troyes ratified this donation, and Pope Innocent II conferred on Heloise the title of abbess of the new community.

Abelard languished at St. Gildas, and though sick in body and constantly devoured by tumultuous passions, he was impatient to appear again in the world, and also to return to the neighborhood of the Paraclete, whither he was continually recalled by most pressing letters from Heloise. He had already quitted his retreat and resumed his oral lectures when St. Bernard came to seek him, in order to open his eyes, and by gentle means to bring him back to truth. Abelard, according to the account of Geoffrey of Auxerre, seemed touched by the Christian conduct of the holy Abbot of Clairvaux, and promised him to modify his doctrines; but new writings, some of which were secretly circulated in the schools, belied this promise, and showed even greater audacity than before. He also changed his tone towards Bernard; and, emboldened by the zeal of his disciples, complained of him in his turn, and accused him of calumny.

It was then that the servant of God broke silence, and pursued the innovator with his invincible energy. The letters which he addressed to the bishops, the cardinals, and the Pope himself evince his alarm, and deserve to be preserved. We give some remarkable extracts from them:

"Brother Bernard, Abbot of Clairvaux, presents his most humble duty to Pope Innocent, his much beloved Father.

"It is to you, most holy Father, that we must turn when the kingdom of God is in danger, or suffers any scandal, especially in what touches the Faith. This is the privilege of the Apostolic See, since to Peter alone it was said, '*I have prayed for thee that thy faith fail not.*' We must claim, then, of the successor of St. Peter, the fulfillment of the words which follow: '*When thou shalt be converted, strengthen thy brethren.*' Now this is the time to fulfill these words, to exercise your primacy, to signalize your zeal, and to do honor to your ministry. A man hath arisen in France, who, from an ancient doctor, is turned into a modern theologian; who, after having sported from his youth up with the art of dialectics, now, in his old age, gives forth to us his reveries on Holy Scripture; who, accounting himself to be ignorant of nothing which is in heaven or on earth, decides all questions without hesitation; who, ready to give a reason for everything, pretends, against all the rules of faith, and of reason itself, to explain even that which is above reason. This is the sense which he gives to these words of the Wise Man: '*He who believes lightly is a fool.*' He says, that to believe lightly is to put faith before reasoning; although the wise man is speaking not of the faith we owe to God, but of the too-easy credence we give to the words of men. After all, Pope Gregory taught that Divine faith loses all merit when it is based upon human reason. Mary is praised because she prevented reason by faith; Zachary is punished for having sought in reason for a support of faith. Our theologian speaks quite differently. In the very first lines of his extravagant theology, he defines faith to be an opinion (*aestimatio*); as if the mysteries of our faith depended upon human reason, instead of being supported, as they are, on the immutable foundations of truth! What! do you propose to me as doubtful that which is of all things most certain? St. Augustine did not speak thus. 'Faith,' said he, 'is not a conjecture or opinion formed within us by the labor of our reflections; it is an interior conviction, and an evident demonstration.' Let us, then, leave these problematical opinions to the peripatetic philosophers who make it a rule to doubt of everything, and who, in fact, know nothing. But let us hold to the definition of the Doctor of the Gentiles. '*Faith,*' says that apostle, '*is the foundation of the things* we hope for, and a certain proof of those we see not.' It is, then, a foundation, and not an opinion—not a deduction of our vain thoughts; it is a certainty and not an estimation."

In another letter, which he wrote to Cardinal Haiberic, Chancellor of the Roman Court, he expresses no less anxiety:

"I have seen," says he, "with my own eyes, what I had before heard of the books and teaching of Peter Abelard. I have weighed his expressions, and discovered the pernicious sense which they contain. This corrupter of the faithful, this contagious spirit, skilful to mislead simple souls, pretends to subject that to his reason which can only be laid hold of by a lively and docile faith. The true believer believes without arguments; but this innovator, not content with having God for the guarantee of his faith, must needs call in his own reason as the arbiter. Unlike the prophet, who says, '*Unless you believe you shall not persevere,*' our doctor accuses the faith which comes from the heart of lightness, perverting that passage of Solomon which says, '*He who believes lightly is a fool.*'"

"Peter Abelard," he writes again to Pope Innocent, "labors to destroy the merit of faith, and imagines that he can comprehend, by his own thought, all that God is. He mounts up to heaven, he descends into the abyss; there is nothing above or below which can escape his knowledge. He is a man great in his own eyes, disputing of faith against itself, inflated with his own wisdom, intruding himself into the secrets of God, and forgiving heresies for us."

"I sent you," said he to Cardinal Gregory, "the writings of Peter Abelard, that you may know the spirit of this doctor. You see that like Arius, he introduces degrees into the Trinity; like Pelagius, he exalts free will above grace: like Nestorius, he divides Jesus Christ. What, then; after having escaped from the lion's jaw,* must we not beware of the poisonous breath of the dragon? The first could not carry his rage beyond the tomb; the last will perpetuate his pernicious doctrines throughout ages to come."

The persevering activity displayed by St. Bernard soon arrested the rationalistic doctor in his successful course. But Abelard, who was in good faith, and full of confidence in his orthodoxy, and who relied also on the number and influence of his friends,

---

* An allusion to the antipope, Peter di Leone.

protested against the accusations of the Abbot of Clairvaux, and loudly declared his intention of defending himself in full council.

In the same year, 1140, on the octave of Pentecost, a great assembly of bishops and theologians was to meet in the town of Sens. Abelard wrote to the archbishop of that metropolitan see, to declare that he was ready to justify his doctrines before all the world; and he earnestly prayed him to summon the Abbot of Clairvaux, in order to put an end, by a public discussion, to the unjust accusations by which he was pursued. The archbishop desired nothing better than to submit the questions in debate to the judgment of the council; and St. Bernard was invited to go thither to meet Abelard; but, at first, he excused himself. "The Archbishop of Sens," he wrote to Rome, "sends for me, who am the least of all, to fight, hand to hand, with Abelard; and he fixes a day on which this doctor is to maintain, before the assembly of bishops, the impious assertions against which I have ventured to raise my voice. I decline to appear there, because, in good truth, I am but a child; because my adversary is a veteran in this warfare; and, besides, I think shame to submit to the subtleties of human reasonings the authority of the Faith founded upon truth itself. Therefore, I reply that he needs no other accuser than his own writings. Besides, this affair does not affect me personally; it belongs to the bishops, who are the judges and interpreters of doctrine."

Nevertheless, the bare announcement of a solemn controversy between the two most celebrated personages of the time excited the most extraordinary interest throughout France. It was to be, in fact, a passage at arms, not only between two men remarkable for their captivating eloquence, but between the leaders of two schools which personified the two contrary tendencies of their age; the one representing the principle of Divine authority, the other proclaiming the pre-eminence of human reason; both combatting in the cause of God—one, by the wisdom of heaven; the other, by the science of earth. Such a conflict promised an extraordinary spectacle. The king himself and the nobles of the court desired to witness it; and on the appointed day all that was most illustrious in the State as well as in the Church hurried to Sens, and joined the prelates and Fathers of the council within the sacred precincts.

Let us hear St. Bernard's own account:

"I was obliged to yield to the entreaties of my friends. They saw, in fact, that everyone was preparing for this conference as for a kind of public spectacle, and they feared lest my absence should be a stumbling block to the weak, and an occasion of triumph to error. I went thither, therefore, though reluctantly, and with tears in my eyes, without any other preparation than that recommended in the Gospel: '*Do not meditate beforehand what you shall answer; it shall be given you in the same hour*'\*, and those other words, '*The Lord is my helper, what shall I fear?*'"†

"It was with these arms," says a pious chronicler, "that the new David came to battle against Abelard—that Goliath, sheathed in the heavy armor of human science, and loaded with the formidable apparel of scholastic arguments."

The two champions presented themselves before the august assembly; all eyes were fixed upon them. The papers were produced, the heads of accusation enumerated; then was a mournful silence; the council waited till Abelard should clear himself, and defend his doctrines.

But, O confusion! he tries to speak, and words fail him; he is struck dumb at the sight of St. Bernard. The servant of God will not pursue his advantage; he refuses to trample upon an already vanquished enemy; he simply points out the most glaring errors in the writings of Abelard, and leaves him the choice either to retract or defend them. But the rationalistic philosopher remains speechless. At last, he left the council, declaring that he appealed to the Pope.

This unexpected issue struck all minds with deep amazement. The judgment of God Himself seemed to dictate the sentence of the council. Thus, notwithstanding his appeal to Rome, Abelard's condemnation was pronounced unanimously. "I have seen," cried St. Bernard with David—"I have seen the impious exalted like the cedar of Lebanon; I passed by, and he was no more." But this splendid triumph, far from exalting the humble monk of Clairvaux, drew from him deep sighs over the miseries of human life; and, in a letter to the Pope, which we would gladly transcribe

---

\* Matt. x. 19.
† Psalm cxvii. 6.

entire, he expresses himself in this touching manner: "It is necessary that scandals come; but it is a very sad necessity. Thus the prophet exclaims, '*Who will give me the wings of a dove that I may fly away and be at rest?* I would be out of the world, so crushed and overwhelmed am I with sorrow. Fool that I was! I hoped for some repose after the fury of the lion had been tamed, and the Church restored to peace. She, indeed, enjoys peace, but I enjoy it not. I remember not that I inhabit a valley of tears, a barren land, fruitful only in briars and thorns, which grow up as fast as they are cut down. Alas, charity grows cold, and iniquity abounds daily more and more." The acts of the council were referred to Rome, and Innocent, after maturely examining the censured propositions, confirmed the judgment of Sens and condemned their author to eternal silence.

Abelard was now on the threshold of two diverging paths, of which one leads to life, the other to death. He might, by a humble submission to the authority of the Church, write his name for all eternity in the book of life; or, by a proud resistance, enroll it among those haughty spirits who imitate the old rebellion of the prince of darkness. Grace triumphed in the heart of Abelard. Humiliation had made a large opening in that sick heart; a new feeling, an emotion like to a vast earthquake took possession of that gigantic mind, and the victorious light of the Holy Spirit descended into the depths of his soul.

Abelard published an apology, of which we subjoin a few fragments:

"To all the children of Holy Church, Peter Abelard, the least of all.

"It is a common maxim, that the best things may be corrupted; and thus, according to the account of St. Jerome, to write many books is to attract many censors. In comparison with the works of others, mine are of little account; yet I have not escaped criticism; though in my books, God knows, I find not my faults, and I pretend not to defend them, if there they be found. Perhaps I have erred in writing certain things otherwise than I should have done; but I call God to witness, who judges the thoughts of my heart, that I have said nothing in malice, or of a perverse will. I have spoken much, in different public schools, and I have never given my instructions as hidden bread or stolen waters. If, in the multitude of my words, some dangerous assertions have glided in, according as it is written, that 'in much speaking we cannot avoid sin,' the care of obstinately defending myself has never driven me into heresy; and I have been always ready, for the satisfaction of all men, to modify, or wholly to retract, whatever I have said amiss. Such are my sentiments, and I will never entertain any others."

This act was but the first step in his sincere return into the holy paths of salvation. He had intended to go to Rome, to the feet of the Sovereign Pontiff, when, docile to the inspiration of God, he went first to open his conscience to Peter the Venerable, the learned Abbot of Cluny. He became attached to the spot where he had regained his peace; he asked an asylum there; and, wearied with the disputations of the schools, disgusted with the vain applause which had inflated his pride, he seriously turned his attention from the things of earth, to have his conversation, like St. Paul, in heaven. Peter of Cluny, whose tender and delicate charity had greatly contributed to the work of this conversion, brought Albelard to St. Bernard, and set the seal to his evangelical mediation by reconciling these two great men, who thenceforward gave mutual proofs of affection and esteem. Abelard, happy in the peace which religion had restored to him, lived two years longer, "during which," says the chronicle of Cluny, "something divine appeared to him, in his spirit, his words, his actions." Death found him prepared, by his deep and salutary penitence; for humility, ever victorious in the struggles of this life, ever efficacious in healing the wounds of the heart, had at last delivered him from the evils which his exaltation had brought upon him.*

---

* Abelard died April 21, 1142, at the age of sixty-three. His body was removed, by the care of the Abbot of Cluny, to the Paraclete, where Heloise herself was buried, May 17, 1164. The united remains of these two celebrated persons underwent several removals, and the vicissitudes of their lives seemed to be prolonged after their deaths. Their remains were brought to Paris in 1800, and they now repose in the same tomb, in the cemetery of Père la Chaise.

# CHAPTER XXX

APPLICATION OF THE DOCTRINES OF RATIONALISM TO POLITICS—ARNOLD OF BRESCIA—REVOLUTION AT ROME.

IT IS a certain truth, attested by the history of the world, that every new idea deposited in the human mind manifests itself sooner or later, like the seeds of the earth, by good or evil fruit; and the thoughtful man, who contemplates his own times, may, by a penetrating glance at the germs contained in its predominant idea, foresee and foretell such events as, in a more or less distant futurity, will be successively produced in all the circles of social life. This foresight, when exalted to a supernatural degree, constitutes the *seer*, or prophet; God illuminates his interior sight and discovers to him, within the bosom of a principle, the series of consequences which it contains, and which will be manifested in their time. But, when the idea has once been embodied in a philosophical system, its necessary consequences may be perceived by the unassisted sight of the intellect; and reason herself, by the help of a strictly logical process, becomes capable of foreseeing the positive results and distant applications which must spring from it. It was thus that St. Bernard, endowed at once with the prophetic vision and the gift of human foresight, protested from the first against the doctrines of Abelard and predicted, with a confidence which seemed exaggerated from its very intensity, the heresies and revolutions which they should bring forth in ages to come. Some of St. Bernard's contemporaries reproached him for excessive rigor; later centuries, and especially our own, have accused him of having attacked Abelard with a bitterness unworthy of a noble and holy soul; but history has justified his conduct; and, besides, is it not the common lot of those who watch upon the mountain, to be misunderstood and misconstrued by those who sleep in the shadow of the valley below?

Between the revolutions, however, of the twelfth century and the principles which give them birth, no long interval elapsed; and the condemnation of Abelard was hardly pronounced when his disciples, bolder than their master, already began to introduce into political questions the method of free inquiry which he had brought from the domain of philosophy into that of religion; rationalism, both theoretical and practical, offered a strange fascination to unquiet and discontented minds; it cast a doubt upon the principles of social order, as it had already done upon the principles of science; and, at the same moment that the spirit of independence revolted against the authority of the faith, an analogous movement appeared in politics and threatened to shake the very foundations of society. It was at Rome itself, around the loftiest seat of human authority, that the new doctrines were first put in agitation. Men of influence, though as yet few in number, claimed for reason the right to do, in politics, what she had attempted in religion; and, playing upon the passions of the multitude, they exalted liberty at the expense of power. From Rome, this spirit of emancipation spread over the rest of Italy, into most of the cities of Germany, and into many provinces of France. It was a sort of universal revolution, arising from one single impulse which, doubtless in the designs of Providence was to have developed itself according to the slow and regular course of events; but which, pushed beyond all bounds and separated from the eternal principles of order and duration, threatened to miss its end by a violent and premature birth. The era of political liberty had begun; it could not be, it ought not to have been, repressed; but the Church, the heavenly guide of nations, would have directed its impulse and determined its limits. The great *communes* were formed in France; the clergy seconded this movement towards liberty, when it wrought in the way of unity and under the influence of authority; they opposed it, on the other hand, when the self-impelled activity of man, impatient of the delays of Providence, anticipated the maturity of nations and claimed the exercise of new rights by ways of rebellion and violence. The moment was critical and extremely serious. The unity of the Church was to be preserved in the diversity of political constitutions, and liberty was to be consecrated without overturning authority. This was the delicate problem which, in theory as well as practice, monopolized the thought of that century, and which events were now to resolve. At Rome, more than anywhere else, the minds of men were prepared to carry out the doctrines of rationalism. The wars of Italy, the long struggle between the papacy and the empire, the schism which, even after its extinction, still lived on in the minds of men; all these elements of strife and opposition were but waiting for a positive doctrine to make them effervesce. Political questions, more than once cut short by the fate of arms, remained speculatively undecided; they gave back a fearful echo when human reason offered to resolve them. It was Arnold of Brescia, a zealous follower of the theories of Abelard, who gave birth to the political rationalism, whose principles again agitated the world in the sixteenth century and took a distinct form, under the name of liberalism, in the nineteenth. Modern history may have exaggerated the part played by Arnold in the events of his time; but he is, nevertheless, a very remarkable person, inasmuch as he attached himself to the philosophical movement begun by Abelard; and, being passionately given to logic, carried it out to its extremest consequences.

Arnold of Brescia was a monk, whose origin and early history are unknown; he had studied under Abelard, and witnessed his defeat at the Council of Sens. Of a rash and enthusiastic spirit, a heated imagination and obstinate will, he nourished an unbounded pride under the appearance of austere piety. The vices of his age hardened his heart; the condemnation of his master sharpened his zeal; rancor, passion, the spirit of opposition, kindled his eloquence. Like another Oza, he attempted to support the Church with his feeble hand; because, as Holy Scripture says, "the oxen which drew the ark of the Lord kicked, and made it lean aside." He did not confine himself to pointing out abuses; he took in hand to prosecute and stigmatize them; and to this end he excited the animosity of the people against riches and power. Like those imprudent laborers whose zeal was rebuked by our Saviour, he did not hesitate to pluck up the good grain with the cockle, in order to clear the ground of the householder;

and rather than let alone a single abuse, he attacked the most sacred institutions to which it might be attached; in short, his idea—beautiful, indeed, in theory, but impracticable and therefore, senseless—was to restore the Church to its primitive state, to the conditions and proportions, that is, of its infancy: and to that end he wanted to make a level ground, to overthrow what centuries had formed, to recommence the work of the apostles, to reconstruct the Christian commonwealth on the plan of its first commencement: in short, ignoring all the laws of progress and the steps already made; endeavoring, as it were, to force the tree back into its germ, he preached a reform of discipline which tended to little short of replacing the Church in the swathing bands of infancy. This attempt failed not to meet with the fate of all premature revolutions. Arnold preached, at first, in his own country; he demanded that the clergy should be reduced to poverty, that the bishops should not be allowed to have lands, that the Pope himself should renounce his possessions and his temporal sovereignty. The first effect of this theory was a revolt of the people of Brescia against the bishop of the province. Arnold took refuge at Rome, and there found a wider sphere for the dissemination of his principles. He declaimed against the vices and luxury of the clergy, against the degradation of the pontificate, against the cupidity of the great, to which he attributed the enthrallment of the people. In these eloquent discourses, the stormy apostle quoted, in turn, the maxims of Titus Severus and of St. Paul, the names of Cato, Fabius, and the Fathers of the Church; he reminded the Romans of their ancient liberty, the glories of the republic, the dignity of old Rome. By dint of flattering men's passions, he succeeded in forming a numerous party; but being sought after, by command of the Pope, he was obliged to escape pursuit, to leave Italy; and sowing, on the way, the fatal seeds of his doctrines, he traversed France and Switzerland and at last settled at Zurich, where he remained a long time in full security. But, while the episcopate seemed tranquil as to the ulterior enterprises of Arnold, there was one man who, from the depths of his solitude, uttered a cry of alarm. That man was St. Bernard. "Know you not," wrote he to the Bishop of Constance, "that the robber hath come in by night, not into your house, but into the house of the Lord, of which you are the guardian? Is it possible that you do not know what is passing close to you, when the noise of it has spread even to us, who are so far distant? Do you still doubt of whom I speak? I would that Arnold's doctrine were as sound as his life is austere. He is a man who eats not, drinks not, thirsts not, but, like the devil, for the blood of souls: he is of the number of those of whom the Apostle speaks, who have the form of godliness, without its spirit; of those, concerning whom the Lord Himself said: '*They shall come to you in sheep's clothing; but inwardly they are ravening wolves.*'\* Wheresoever this man hath dwelt, he hath left such frightful traces of his sojourning that he hath never dared to appear there again. His own country, agitated by his presence, has been constrained to banish him. Exiled from France, he maintains, among your people, the errors of Abelard, with a heat and an obstinacy surpassing that of his master. Alas! if Holy Scripture would have us '*take the little foxes, which waste the vineyard of the Lord,*'† far more ought we to bind and chain a cruel wolf, ready to fall upon the fold of Jesus Christ."

This letter, and the fear in which the authority of the Abbot of Clairvaux was held, put an end to the preachings at Zurich; but the innovator, persecuted in Switzerland, found a secure asylum with the papal legate himself, who had been, like Arnold, one of the hearers of Abelard. It was St. Bernard again who, by his energetic warnings, came to disturb him in this new retreat. He addressed the apostolic legate directly, and without preamble. "Arnold of Brescia," he writes, "is a man of a sweet and seductive conversation, but his doctrine is poisonous; he has the head of a dove, and the tail of a scorpion—a monster produced, or rather vomited forth, by the town of Brescia; which Rome has rejected, which France has repulsed, which Germany detests, which Italy refuses to receive; and it is said that you are sheltering him! Take heed, I conjure you, lest your protection encourage him to do still greater evil.

"How do you not see, in every place he has passed by, the fatal traces of his passage? Was it without a reason that the Holy See compelled him to fly beyond the Alps? To protect such a man is to be unfaithful to the Pope, or, rather, to God Himself."

---

\* Matt. viii. 15.
† Cant. ii. 15.

The severe and active vigilance of St. Bernard pursued Arnold into all his hiding places. But while he escaped from the condemnations pronounced against him, his doctrines, repeated by numberless echoes, reverberated on all sides and produced a vehement effervescence, especially at Rome.

The people of Rome and Tivoli were at this time carrying on a furious contest; their mutual rivalry had reached such a point of exasperation in the strife that the Pope himself, after having defeated those of Tivoli, was obliged to defend them against the fury of the Romans, to avert a general massacre and prevent the town from being sacked. The clemency of the Pontiff offended the Romans and gave occasion to an insurrection. At a given signal the multitude fell upon the ancient capital; and forgetting that they retained nothing of the old Romans but their degenerate name, they leagued together and swore to re-establish the ancient republic. They began by forming a senate—a body which had disappeared from the city since the time of Charlemagne; they invested it with the government of all temporal matters, leaving to the Pope the care of things spiritual alone. This sudden revolution was not effected without bloodshed; the people, emboldened by their triumph and ungovernable in their outbreaks, stained the first acts of their emancipation by murder and pillage; several buildings were pulled down; a cardinal was killed in the street. Innocent II, already far advanced in years and worn down by the toils of the Pontificate, had met the popular exigency by conciliation alone; but now, consumed by grief, his sorrows aggravated by these public calamities, he died, full of bitterness of heart, on September 22, 1143. The next day a new Pontiff, Celestine II, was raised to the apostolic chair; but a few months after his elevation, he also found rest in the tomb; and his successor, Lucius II, mounted the throne of St. Peter but to pay with his life for the zeal which he displayed against the excesses of his frantic people.\*

These sinister events gave fresh anxiety to St. Bernard and redoubled the energy with which he consecrated all his powers to the service of the Church.† He viewed Arnold of Brescia as

---

\* Baronius relates that this Pope was killed by a stone, in an insurrection.
† It was on this occasion that St. Bernard wrote his epistle to the Romans, in which he said to them, among other things: "In the time of your fathers, the universe was

the author of all these evils and earnestly recommended that he should be imprisoned, and so prevented from fanning the flame which he had lighted. "Alas!" cried he, "is there no one, then, zealous enough to do this good office to the Church?" But Arnold, issuing forth from the darkness in which St. Bernard's vigilance had forced him to hide, went secretly to Rome, and showing himself unexpectedly in the midst of the people, whose idol he was, he rekindled by his burning words the passions of the multitude, and personally directed the execution of his own plans. He caused a patrician to be nominated from among the senators to administer public affairs; revived the ancient forms, the republican laws and functions, and parodied, as far as possible, the institutions of ancient Rome. In the delirium of these vain reminiscences, they went so far as to restore the order of Roman knights, and rebuilt the Capitol; as if the mere name of that illustrious ruin could restore the glory and majesty of Rome. The presence of Arnold had lent a mighty energy to this movement. It was principally directed against the temporal sovereignty of the Holy See; but that sovereignty was a necessary auxiliary to the papacy, especially in the middle age—a fact too living, too inherent in the manners, the belief, the necessities, the institutions of Christendom to be seriously contested; and it was a monstrous attempt to attack the double power which held people and kings in equilibrium, and, at the same time, presided over the religious unity and the civilization of the world. Thus this attempt, like all others of the kind, could not escape that kind of reprobation from God which seems to strike with impotence every enterprise whose aim is to shake the supreme dignity of the See of St. Peter.

The revolution of Arnold, thus wrought out of the order of Providence, could have neither duration nor consistency; and, as usually happens, those who had embraced it with the greatest ardor were soonest disgusted with it, and became its first victims. The populace itself got tired of ransacking the eternal city; and no one could take delight in seeing things sacred and profane involved in the same destruction. Zeal began gradually to cool;

---

subject to you; and now you make your city the laughingstock of the universe. Cardinals, bishops, sacred ministers have, by your hands, been driven out of the city, and despoiled of their goods," etc.

and before the arrival of Conrad, who had succeeded the Emperor Lotharius, the gates of Rome were thrown open to the Sovereign Pontiff, and the reins of government replaced in his hands.

By the year 1145, this short but bloody revolution was appeased. But the troubles consequent upon it, and the spirit from which they arose, were propagated far and wide. The new doctrines had disenchanted those only who had experienced their sad results; they still numbered many partisans who persisted in regarding them as the purest dictates of reason.

Arnold of Brescia withdrew into Tuscany. He did not abandon his projects, but pursued them with a caution which regard for his own safety required. It was not till 1153, ten years after the seditions in Italy, that the emperor seized him and brought him prisoner in Rome. He was condemned to die on a scaffold, and suffered his punishment before the eyes of a populace which, having extolled him as an apostle, exulted at his death.

# CHAPTER XXXI

NEW ANXIETIES OF ST. BERNARD ON ACCOUNT OF THE ELECTION OF EUGENIUS III—BOOK OF THE CONSIDERATION.

THE HOLY SPIRIT, who watches over the doctrines of the Church, seems in certain great vicissitudes to wait till all human resources are exhausted before He testifies, by a visible interposition, His never-ceasing aid. It is especially in the choice of the Sovereign Pontiffs that this supernatural intervention is sometimes manifested in a most marvelous manner; and very often, when things are come to an extremity and hope itself is gone, the man suddenly appears who is commissioned by God to rule the tempest and accomplish what the course of events requires. At the period of which we write, Christendom was strongly convulsed by schisms, errors, passions, interests, abuses, vices of all kinds, which worked within her and enfolded her without like an unclean garment. Her state was the more critical, as in the midst of the Roman revolution she had lost three popes in succession; and thus, while attacked in the very principle of her hierarchy, she was also deprived of the visible head which impersonated that principle. In those dark days, it would seem, humanly speaking, that the head of the Church should have been a man mighty in word and deed, a splendid name, fitted to awe the world—one of those war-chariots, to use the words of Holy Scripture, which have teeth and points of iron, to break in pieces mountains and hills. But in the ways of Providence, help often comes from the quarter whence it is least expected; and, to animate faith and confound presumptuous reason, the Spirit of God chooses the weak to overcome the mighty—a man, a child, a peasant, without name, birth, learning, or authority, is oftentimes drawn from the retirement of a cloister to direct nations and march at the head of kings.

The history of all ages is full of these examples—but that presented by the exaltation of Eugenius III is particularly remarkable.

Pope Lucius died on February 25, 1145, at the moment when the populace of Rome, in the intoxication of its triumph, was overthrowing everything that offended it. The senators attempted to dictate the choice of a new Pontiff; the cardinals, now dispersed abroad, could with difficulty communicate together; the ambition of some of them, and the intrigues of some of the most influential, complicated the embarrassment. Any delay, however, might endanger a new schism and rekindle civil and religious war.

At this fatal crisis, a monk of Clairvaux is suddenly informed that the cardinals have unanimously raised him to the chair of St. Peter! This monk belonged neither to the episcopal body nor to the college of cardinals—he was the timid Bernard of Pisa, a disciple of St. Bernard who had been sent by him, five years before, to Rome to found the monastery of St. Anastasius. Even this mission seemed beyond his powers, for his function at Clairvaux had been *to feed the stove and make a fire for the religious, who were benumbed with cold after matins because of the scantiness of their clothing.* Being placed, then, against his will over the convent of St. Anastasius, he had to suffer so many vexations and calumnies from a false brother that he was in danger of becoming, according to his own words, the laughing stock and derision of the whole city. In his distress he had earnestly entreated to be recalled to Clairvaux. "O my father," he wrote to St. Bernard, "since I have been away from you, my life has been consumed with sorrow and my days passed in sighing. Unhappy that I am! I no longer hear that sweet voice which so deliciously charmed my ears; I see no more that face so loved and so longed for. What shall I do, then, overburdened as I am? Suffer me, O Reverend Father, suffer me to go and seek some repose. Would to God that the world might reject us, and oblige us, by its persecutions, to retire into solitudes, and take refuge in mountains and caves of the earth!"

It was this monk, so weak and so humble as to be overwhelmed by the charge of a single monastery, who beheld himself suddenly raised to the highest pinnacle of Catholicity. "But," says the annalist of Citeaux, "by an extraordinary grace from Him who had called him to so eminent a station, the Abbot of St. Anastasius experienced a change like that which passed upon the apostle whom Jesus Christ chose to be head of the Church; for as that apostle, before the effusion of the Holy Spirit, had neither wisdom nor illumination, but received, on the holy feast of Pentecost, all the gifts needful for his high vocation, so the pious abbot received, in a moment, such abundant grace that he was changed, like the first of the apostles, into a new man; so that everyone was astonished from the very first at the exalted wisdom and firmness of his conduct."

Immediately after his election, the cardinals came to fetch him from his cell and led him in all haste to the Lateran Palace, where, according to the usage of the Apostolic See, the new Pontiff was acknowledged, and proclaimed under the name of Eugenius III.

At these unexpected tidings Rome was in an uproar; the people assembled and remonstrated; but Eugenius, accompanied by the cardinals, quitted the city by night and retired into a fortified monastery, where he received episcopal consecration, the 24th of March, of the same year.

These events had passed so rapidly and spontaneously that Christendom remained a long time in amazement, but when the news reached the desert of Clairvaux, St. Bernard, struck with astonishment, felt all the anxiety of a disconsolate mother. He dreaded the dazzling elevation for his spiritual son; and, in the first moment of his anxiety, he wrote a letter to the cardinals, the disordered style of which expresses the various sentiments which agitated his soul. He begins, without preface:

"God forgive you! What have you done? You have brought back among men one who was already in the grave; you have embarrassed with cares and business one who desired neither business nor care; and you have compelled him to mingle among men, and to appear upon the stage of the world! You have forced him into the first place who desired but to be the last; and this last state is more perilous to him than the first. You constrain a man, who is crucified to the world, to live again in the world; and after he had chosen to be below all in the house of his God, you have chosen him out to place him above all! Wherefore have you overturned the designs of the poor? Whence came it into your minds to surround his path with thorns and briars, to turn him aside out of the way and hinder his goings? Who induced you to seize suddenly on a man so simple and unlearned; to drag him from his cloister, and place him on the throne of St. Peter? What! were there no wise men among you? Was there no one more capable than Eugenius of the functions of the papacy? Assuredly it is a thing altogether absurd to take a poor little man, covered with rags, and make him the master of princes, bishops, and empires! But what do I say when I say it is absurd! Is it not rather admirable? Certainly it is either one or the other; I deny it not. I do not reject the thought that this may have been the work of God, who alone doeth wonderful things: but I fear for our Eugenius; for he is very tender and delicate, full of reserve and modesty, and accustomed rather to silence and contemplation than to the management of business; so that I fear lest he want the qualities necessary for the high office in which you have placed him. What think you must be the feelings of a man, passing thus, without preparation, from the solitude of the heart and the secrets of interior prayer, to the tumult of the world, like a child torn from the breast of its mother? Alas! unless the Lord hold him by the hand, he needs must fall; and he will be crushed under the weight of a burden too heavy for his strength."

This letter characterizes, at once, both Bernard and Eugenius. But here is another, addressed to Eugenius himself, in which the mingled tones of respect, tenderness, and humility make sweet harmony:

"Bernard, Abbot of Clairvaux, offers his most humble reverence to his well-beloved Father and Lord, Eugenius, by the grace of God, Sovereign Pontiff.

"The tidings of your elevation have reached this country. Attentive to all that I heard, I delayed to congratulate you, thinking that you would inform me of it yourself; I waited till some messenger should come from you to tell me what had passed; I hoped that one of my children would come to assuage my grief—saying, '*Joseph, thy son, is in good health, and ruler over all the land of Egypt.*' I am writing, then, against my will. But since I have begun, I will speak to my Lord. I dare no longer call you my son; you have been so, but now you are my father. You are above me;

but it is through me that you are. Yes, I must say it, *I have begotten thee by the Gospel*; you are my hope, my joy, and my crown before God; '*A wise son is the glory of his father.*' True, I shall no more call you my son; '*The Lord hath given thee a new name.*' The hand of the Most High has made this change. Abram was called Abraham; Jacob, Israel; and, to speak only of your predecessors, Simon was called Peter; Saul received the name of Paul. Thus, by a change which I presume to be useful to the Church, my son Bernard is named Eugenius, and becomes my father.

"After this change it remains for you to change the name of the Church which God confides to you, that instead of Sarai she may be called Sarah. Understand this enigma; may God give you the knowledge of it. If you are the friend of the bridegroom, call not his spouse *your princess* but *the princess*. Instead of appropriating to yourself what is hers, be ready to give her what is yours—your own life. Shall I be the only one who joys not in your exaltation? Yes, I do rejoice; but my joy, I acknowledge it, is tempered with fear; my heart is torn by the conflicting sentiments. Though I have lost the title of your father, I have still a father's tenderness of heart; I contemplate your elevation, and I tremble lest you fall. I am dazzled by the splendor of your dignity, and I shudder at the perils which surround you. It is the place of St. Peter, of the prince of the apostles, of him whom the Lord appointed head and master of His household. His ashes will rise against you, if you follow not his spirit and his example. His hands were pure, his heart disinterested. He said, with confidence, '*I have neither gold nor silver.*' I will say no more. You are set over nations and empires, to pluck up and to destroy, to plant and to build. Yet, remember that you are but man. Lose not sight of God, who overthrows the mighty of the earth. How many popes have died within a short time before our eyes! Their reign was very short; it will be the same with yours. Amid the pomps of a transitory glory, meditate incessantly on your last end; and bethink you that you will soon rejoin in the grave those whose place you now occupy on the apostolic throne."

Eugenius went, after his consecration, to reside at Viterbo, until peace should be restored to Rome. He was still there when he received a deputation from the Bishops of Armenia, who came to submit their differences with the Greeks to his decision. One of these bishops declared before the Roman Court that he had seen, during the celebration of the Holy Sacrifice, two doves, surrounded with light, over the head of the Pontiff. In fact, during the eight years he occupied the Holy See, Eugenius III displayed such vigor and energy in his whole conduct, that all enmities, as well as all material obstacles, melted away before his word. He offered a needful occupation to impetuous spirits, by exciting them to undertake a new crusade; and while he turned European activity towards the east, he worked in the very heart of Christendom at salutary reforms, and prepared the way for a general renovation. True, Eugenius had St. Bernard for his guide; he was his light; and it was the merit and the glory of this great Pope that he faithfully followed such a guidance.

The written instructions which the holy Abbot of Clairvaux sent him, at different periods, composed the celebrated book, known under the name of the "*Book of Consideration*;" a sublime work, which, placing us with the Pope at the very center of the edifice of Catholicism, shows us, under every possible point of view, the immense plan of the Church, and its vast dimensions. The idea of this work is that of the reformation of the Church, by the development of the internal and quickening powers of the papacy. St. Bernard understood well all the resources which this divine institution contains, to heal, repair, restore the languishing forms of Christendom; and, under the corruption of these forms, in the very bosom of death, he perceived the ever-living principles and indestructible germ of a new and immortal existence. Thus, according to St. Bernard, the celestial healing of the Church was to begin and end with the Pope. "Your *Consideration*," said he, "must begin with you and end with you. You must first consider yourself; then what is below you; next, what is around you; lastly, what is above you."

These four great perspectives embrace, as we see, the whole universe, and they indicate the principal divisions of the work. We will cast a glance over them.

In the first part, St. Bernard, viewing the person of the Pope, clearly distinguishes between the man and the Pontiff. "What are you? You are what you were; and the dignity with which you have been invested has not stripped you of your nature. You are a man, and though you have been made a bishop, you are still a man.

Lift the veil which envelops you, and you will find a man naked, poor, miserable, born for labor, not for honor; born of a woman and conceived in sin.

"But now become Pope, who are you? What rank do you hold in the Church of God?

"You are," replies St. Bernard, "the High Priest and Sovereign Pontiff, the Prince of Bishops and Successor of the Apostles; you have the primacy of Abel, the government of Noah, the patriarchate of Abraham, the orders of Aaron, the authority of Moses, the jurisdiction of Samuel, the power of Peter, the unction of Jesus Christ. You are he to whom the keys have been given, to whom the sheep have been confided. There are others who are door-keepers of heaven, others who are pastors of flocks; but you are both door-keeper and pastor in a far more glorious measure, as you have received this double title in a different manner from others. Each of them has but a portion of the flock; but the whole flock together has been committed to your care. You are pastor, not only of the sheep, but of the pastors; the others share your toil; to you belongs the plenitude of the power.

"Their authority is restrained within certain limits; yours extends even over those who have received power over others. Behold what you are!"

But after this magnificent enunciation of the prerogatives of the successor of St. Peter, Bernard draws a parallel between the two elements, divine and human, which constitute the Pontiff, and draws out their different relations.

"A madman upon the throne is but an ape upon the housetop. Listen to what I have to say upon this subject. It is a monstrous thing to see supreme dignity and a narrow mind; an eminent position and ignorant behavior; a diffuse tongue and a useless hand; an eloquent speech and barren actions; a grave face and light conduct; sovereign authority and vain and changeable resolves. I hold up the mirror before you, that you may recognize your defects, that you may acquire what is wanting to you; all is wanting to him who thinks he wants nothing. Seek to perfect what is wanting, and be not ashamed to confess your wants."

From this consideration St. Bernard passes on to the second, which refers to what is below the Pope—that is, to the whole world confided to the Sovereign Pontiff, not that he may domineer over it, or possess it, but that he may govern it with wisdom. "For," said he, "there is neither poison nor steel which I dread so much for you as the passion for dominion." He desires that the Pope should extend his care over all, without respect to persons, because he belongs to all—to the wise and to the unwise, to the faithful and to infidels, to Jews, to Greeks, to Gentiles. It is a part of his ministry to labor for the conversion of those who have not the faith, to hinder those who have the faith from losing it. The saint then proceeds to probe the wounds of the Church. He deplores the want of zeal in some, the oversharpness of zeal in others; he points out ambition and avarice as the two most frightful of these wounds—the sources of the most deplorable abuses; above all, he demands a reform of the abuse of too frequent and easy appeals. "You are appealed to from all parts of the world; it is a witness of your primacy. What can, in fact, be more beautiful than to see the weak shielded from oppression as soon as they take shelter under your name? But what an evil, on the other hand, to see him who has done the wrong rejoice in its protection? Awake, O Man of God, when these things come to pass." Having concluded in favor of the right of appeals, so that the abuse of a too frequent recourse to them be avoided, St. Bernard touched upon another evil which troubled the hierarchy—that of exemptions. "It is a general grievance of all churches," he says; "they complain that they are mutilated and dismembered. You ask why? Because abbots are exempted from the jurisdiction of bishops; bishops from that of their archbishops and patriarchs. Is this orderly? Is it excusable? You do it because you can do it; but the question is whether you ought to do it." Here the holy writer points out the means most fitted to reanimate the circulation of the vital sap through all parts of the Church; he desires that the Pope should take care that everyone should remain at his post, and fulfill the duties of his state; that subordination should be revived among the clergy, discipline in the monasteries, good order in the various ranks of society; and thus, while respecting the instructions born of Christian piety, he desired to free them from the bonds which hindered their development, and to reform the customs which had fallen into desuetude.

In the third part, St. Bernard proposes to the Pope the consideration of the things around him—that is to say, the pontifical court, the cardinals, the clergy, and the Roman people. The saint evinces some embarrassment in entering upon subjects so delicate, on which custom would be pleaded against him; and upon which, whatever he might say, although practiced in former times, would be regarded as new, and would give displeasure to "*the satraps with whom majesty suits better than truth.*" Yet, said he to Eugenius, there have been pastors before you who gave themselves entirely to the care of the flock. Pastors both in name and truth, who regarded nothing as unworthy of them, except what might be against the salvation of their sheep; who gave to them their labor, their goods, their existence, and had no other end before them but to form a people perfect before God. "What is become of this custom?" cries St. Bernard; "you see all the zeal of certain ecclesiastics centered upon the preservation of their own dignity. They give all to honor, and little or nothing to sanctity. If some circumstance calls upon you to humble yourself, to make yourself more accessible, they tell you at once that this does not befit your dignity, that this does not befit your rank, your character. The last thing spoken of is what is due to God."

The saint reviews and stigmatizes energetically the excesses which, in his time, stained the Roman Court. He then returns to the Pope, and addresses him in this bold apostrophe: "What, then, will you not awake amid the bands of death which surround you? I feel a holy jealousy for you; and God grant that it may be as profitable to you as it is ardent in me! I know your dwelling place; infidels and flatterers are of your company. They are wolves and not sheep; and yet you are their pastor. You cannot deny it; or he whose place you hold would deny you—I speak of St. Peter; but do we hear that he ever appeared in public laden with gold and jewels, clothed in silk, borne upon a white litter, surrounded by soldiers, and followed by a pompous train? Assuredly, Peter believed himself able, without all this paraphernalia, to fulfill the Lord's command, '*Feed my lambs, feed my sheep.*' Indeed, in all this splendor which surrounds you, one would take you for the successor of Constantine rather than for the successor of Peter; yet I counsel you to endure these things for a time, but not to require them as of absolute necessity." This simple counsel, which concludes his description of Roman pomp, is characteristic of the prudence of the man of God; and, at the same time, marks out the boundary which separates him from the modern reformers, whose uncommissioned zeal makes war upon needful, though temporary forms; like madmen, who would cut down the tree to free it from the insects which cleave to its leaves and bark, they would purify the Church by destroying the papacy. It is not by abuses that we can correct abuses; and evil will never yield to a greater evil. It is by good, on the contrary, according to the words of Holy Scripture, that we must overcome evil. Thus, after a severe investigation into all the vices which had glided, together with human passions and weaknesses, into the holiest institutions of the Church, St. Bernard points out the contrary virtues as the truest and only antidotes of vice; and he sums up, most admirably, those which ought to adorn the Pontiff of Rome. "Consider, before all things," says he, "that the Roman Church, of which God has made you the head, is the mother, and not the sovereign of other Churches; that you are, not the sovereign of bishops, but one among them—the brother of those who love God, and the companion of those who fear Him. Consider that you ought to be a living rule of justice, a mirror of sanctity, a model of devotion, the preserver of the truth, the defender of the faith, the teacher of nations, the protector of Christians, the friend of the Bridegroom, the guide of the Bride, the pastor of nations, the preceptor of the ignorant, the refuge of the oppressed, the advocate of the poor, the hope of the unfortunate, the guardian of the orphan, the stay of the widow, the eye of the blind, the tongue of the dumb, the staff of the aged, the avenger of crime, the terror of the wicked, the glory of the just, the rod of the mighty, the scourge of tyrants, the father of kings, the moderator of laws, the dispenser of canons, the salt of the earth, the light of the world, the priest of the Most High, the vicar of the Saviour, the anointed of the Lord, the God of Pharaoh!"

This the idea of the papacy! Is there anything more sublime among human realities?

# CHAPTER XXXII

CONTINUATION OF THE PRECEDING—GENERAL IDEA OF THE PHILOSOPHY AND MYSTICAL THEOLOGY OF ST. BERNARD.

In the "Book of the Consideration," as in all his other writings, St. Bernard views simultaneously, and never apart, the active and the contemplative life—faith and works, love and its fruits, charity and its marvels. The final end of his teaching and of his life is the same—union with God by contemplation and love; union with men by action and charity. Thus, in the instructions addressed to Eugenius, after having determined the Pontiff's relations with the things of this world, he transports him into the invisible world, into the sphere of divine ideals, and initiates him into the science which is acquired, not by the activity of the mind, but by the contemplation of a purified intelligence.

Here St. Bernard soars, as it were, by a sublime flight, into the celestial spheres. He first considers the angels—he explains their names, their hierarchies, their prerogatives, their different functions; next, approaching the most exalted objects of theology, he contemplates the Divine Majesty, and develops that dogma, so fruitful in applications, of the union of the Divine Word with human nature.

Bernard, like all ascetic teachers, founds science upon love, and seeks to raise man to eternal truth, far less by abstract speculations than by purity of heart and the practice of Christian virtues. "The things which are above us," said he, "are not taught by words; they are revealed by the Spirit. Now, contemplation must seek; prayer, ask; sanctity, merit; purity, obtain what words cannot express."

Blessed are the pure in heart, for they shall see God! Now, God is truth itself. To contemplate truth, then, in that mysterious and ineffable abyss, we must pass through a purgative way, which strips us of all that intervenes between us and truth, between our darkened eyes and the light of heaven.

By this profoundly Christian character we recognize the school of practical philosophy to which St. Bernard, as well as Hugh and Richard of St. Victor, belonged—a school which, despising the vain abstractions of dialectics, brought science into relation with the inmost necessities of the soul. In the works of St. Bernard we find no complete system of scientific doctrines, but scattered ideas, sublime rays of light, which enlighten and regulate the whole range of philosophy.

Setting out from love as the source of wisdom, he proves that purity of heart, the condition of pure wisdom, comes from the love of divine things; as impurity of heart, the cause of all error, arises from the love of earthly and carnal things. Hence the various kinds of love, which, according to their degree of purity, bring man near to God. St. Bernard traces the ascending scale. The soul must pass at once from virtue to virtue, and from light to light. In proportion as she is dilated by the fire of love, her vision becomes wider and brighter. She loves and contemplates: she contemplates what she loves; and these two acts, the act of will which loves, and the act of the intelligence which contemplates, will be blended in eternity into one and the same act, uniting man with God; for, when our mind shall see God as He is, our will shall be united to His, and work, in union with Him, *the works of God.*

The end of man is to know and love; and he who loves most purely knows most perfectly. Now, in order to know the eternal object of love, the soul must be sufficiently purified to be capable of feeling the divine agency and the presence of God. This sentiment is, as it were, the aurora of the spiritual sun, which rises upon the soul, and unveils before it the sublime horizon of the invisible world—a solemn moment, whose undefinable mystery cannot be expressed in words. "Even if I had myself experienced it," says St. Bernard, in his humility, "do you think that I could speak of what is unspeakable? It is not the tongue, it is the unction of grace which teaches these things; they are hidden from the great and the wise of this world, but God reveals them to babes."

Yet the sensible and certain token of the interior awakening is the new force by which the heart is carried on to the practice of virtue, and a certain knowledge of self which precedes more lofty contemplations. St. Bernard explains this by his own experience. "You ask me how I came to know that the Word was near? Would you know this? Because He is living and efficacious; and, at the moment that He entered into my soul, He awakened it out of sleep; He moved, softened, wounded my hard, sick, and stony heart. He began to pluck up and to destroy, to build and to plant, to water my dryness, to enlighten my darkness, to open what was closed, to enkindle what was frozen. The Spouse—the Word—from the time of His entrance into the interior of my soul, has never made His presence known by any extraordinary tokens, either by voice or visible appearance. I have felt His agency only by the movement of my heart; and I have experienced His active power by the amendment of my vices, by the mortification of carnal passions, by the penitent view of my faults, by the renewal of my life, by the enlarged vision of all things which show forth His greatness."

The soul which aspires after this divine light must, therefore, seek first, and in all possible ways, to please Him who reigns in the celestial city. She must tarry a long time in the darkness of faith, bringing forth in gradual development generous deeds and fruits of love. Then, concentrating herself, and attracting the light, by the ardor of her desires, into her inmost cell, it is converted into a furnace of sacred fire; the soul becomes all luminous, and expands before God by the internal heat of ardent charity. "Then," says St. Bernard, "the soul is constrained to manifest itself outwardly, like a lamp which was once under a bushel, but can no longer remain hidden. The body even, the image of the soul, partakes of this light, and diffuses it by all its organs; it shines in its actions, words, looks, movements, in its ever sweet and gentle smile. The visible beauty of virtue is a token of the soul's maturity, and of her fitness for the spiritual marriage bond with the Divine Word."

This marriage, this heavenly alliance, is, as we have seen, the point to which all St. Bernard's lessons tend; this union of the soul with God is the grand object of the ascetic life and of Christian philosophy; it begins in this life, and is consummated in eternity. The holy doctor returns unwearied to this one idea; he views it on all sides, and applies himself to free it from all that might tarnish its perfection. He first shows the possibility of this alliance: "Let it not be thought," says he, "that the inequality of the two terms renders the union imperfect, or impedes its consummation. Love supplies all, fills all voids, bridges over all gulfs; it forms an indissoluble bond and renders the spiritual marriage perfect."

He explains this marriage, and unveils its glorious mysteries: "It is a chaste and holy love, sweet and strong, intense and lively, which of two makes but one, according to the testimony of St. Paul: 'He who adheres to God is but one spirit with Him.' Happy the soul which is bound by such a love! And how shall the bride of Love fail to love her Bridegroom? How shall the Bridegroom, who is Love, fail to be loved by His bride?"

The possibility, the means, and the conditions of this union being laid down, St. Bernard approaches another point of no less delicacy. He admits, with all ascetic writers, the transformation of men into God; but he carefully avoids all pantheistic identification, by the clear and precise distinction of the two substances, the created and the uncreated which can never be confounded; and he thus avoids the rock on which so many philosophers have struck. The 71st sermon on the Canticle of Canticles contains the formal doctrine of St. Bernard on this important question: "The union of man with God consists," says he, "not in a confusion of natures, but in a conformity of wills. Between the three Divine Persons, there is an unity of essence and of substance; between the soul and God there is an unity of affection and of sentiment." This same truth is repeated elsewhere in a more didactic form: "God," said he, grappling at once with the question of pantheism, "God is the being of all things; not that all things are the same things with Him, but they are of Him, in Him, and by Him. He, therefore, who created all things is the very being of the things which He created; but He is the being of beings in such sort that He is the principle and not the material of them."

St. Bernard, in his discussions with Abelard and Gilbert de la Porree, attaches the highest importance to the pure exposition of the doctrine of the Holy Trinity, which, with all the Fathers of the Church, he regards as the basis and safeguard of Christian philosophy. This dogma, by distinguishing three distinct persons in the absolute One, gives the complete idea of the Divinity. In fact, God may be considered, according to Scripture, as Being, Light, and Love.

As *Being*, the Father is the infinite and absolute abyss of all being; the Son, the infinite and absolute manifestation of being; the Holy Ghost, the infinite and absolute life of being. Considered as *Light*, the Father is the object eternally knowing; the Son is the subject eternally known; the Holy Ghost is the living and eternal relation between the object and the subject. Lastly, the Father, considered as eternal *Love*, loves eternally; the Son is the term eternally loved, and who, from all eternity, has responded to this love; the Holy Ghost is the substantial relation between the Father and the Son, the love proceeding from both. Thus the dogma of the Trinity, revealing the perfect fulness of God, if we may so express ourselves, excludes by this very revelation the idea of the *necessity* of creation to complete or develop the Deity; it consequently avoids all subtle confusion between the finite and the infinite. Beyond the orthodox limits of this sacred dogma, creation is indistinguishable in the eyes of philosophers from the uncreated Substance—and hence the ancient and modern errors of dualism, pantheism, and polytheism. St. Bernard, stayed upon this immutable mystery, fears not to sound all depths connected with the origin of created things. He interprets the thoughts of St. Augustine upon these deep questions, admitting with him, and with most mystical theologians, the pre-existence of the creature in the Divine Wisdom. "Where shall we place the reason of things," says St. Augustine, "but in the intelligence of the Creator Himself? For there was nothing to contemplate out of Himself from which to copy creation. Now, there is nothing in the Divine intelligence but what is eternal and unchangeable. Therefore, those reasons or principles of things, which Plato calls ideas, are not only ideas, but their being is the true being, because they are unchangeable and eternal, and all that is, whatever the manner of its being, exists only by participation of them."

"The reason of all things," says Origen, "existing in the Wisdom by whom all were made, it follows that there also has always existed a world as much more beautiful, more highly adorned, more magnificent than the sensible world, as pure reason excels materialized realities."

This is exactly the doctrine of St. Bernard. He finds on high the prototypes of things below; and he contemplates from on high, after a far more sublime manner than Plato, the celestial ideals which pre-exist in the Divine wisdom. "Those who are in heaven," says he, "have always before their eyes the mirror in which they see all things clearly. They see the Word, and in the Word all things which were made by Him; so that they have no need to borrow from creatures the knowledge of the Creator. They have no need to descend among creatures even to attain the knowledge of them; for they see them in this mirror in a far more excellent manner than in themselves."

The holy doctor gives the name of predestination to the pre-existence of these ideas. "Predestination," says he, "did not begin with the birth of the Church; nor even with the creation of the world, nor with any period of time whatever; it preceded all ages. The assembly of the elect has been always in God, by predestination; it has been always present to Him, always beloved by Him. For," adds he, borrowing the words of St. Paul, "God hath blessed us with spiritual blessings in heavenly places, in Christ, as he chose us in him before the foundation of the world, that we should be holy and unspotted in his sight in charity." (Eph. 1:3, 4). St. Bernard then viewed man at once in the real and in the ideal world; between these two worlds, he admitted necessary relations and communications, and it was in this sense that he said, "That the same things which are within us by the subtlety of their spiritual nature, are also above us by the sublimity of their being."

With the mysteries of creation he connects the work of the Incarnation of Jesus Christ. These two primordial ideas have but one explanation—love. Both were conceived in the Divine wisdom; the end of both is the realization of the spiritual marriage of the creature with the Word. Hence, the mysteries of love admirably symbolized in the Canticle of Canticles; they express the different degrees by which the soul enkindled, transfigured by the Word, is, in some sort, *deified* with Him. St. Bernard develops this sublime view by natural analogies, and deduces from it all the principles of the ascetic life. "As a little drop of water," says he, "when it falls into a vessel full of wine, seems to cease to be what it was, and takes the color and form of wine; as iron, heated by fire, losing its own form, reddens and becomes like to the fire itself; as the air, penetrated by the light of the sun, is, in some sort, transformed, and becomes luminous like that body, so in the saints all human affection melts, ceases to be itself, is ineffably transformed, and totally engulfed in the Will of God. The human substance will, in truth, subsist, but under another form, with another glory, with another power."

The restoration of humanity, wrought by the incarnation of the Word, supposes its fall. Here we encounter the problem of the origin of evil, its co-existence with the Sovereign Good, its propagation in the world, and the manner of its transmission. St. Bernard, without especially treating on these deep questions, touches upon them in several of his writings. His doctrine is that of the Fathers of the Church.

He establishes, especially in his work on grace and free will, that evil, both in its origin, and in all the acts which reproduce and perpetuate it, is always the effect of the liberty of the created being. And this sentiment is so energetically expressed by the holy Doctor, that in his opinion the persistence in evil, even of the devil himself, results from his constantly perverted self-will. "It is not," says he, "a foreign and violent force, but a wilful obstinacy and obstinate will of the devil which fixes him in evil, and prevents his turning towards good."*

As to the nature of evil, it is hard to lay hold of; for, according to St. Bernard, as well as St. Augustine, all that *is* is good, and evil can have no proper substance. "If evil were a substance, that substance would be good." "That which is evil," says the holy Bishop of Hippo, "is the diminution or privation of good."†

---

\* This truth, which throws such great light on the dogma of eternal punishment, has been fully developed by M. Bautain, in the 87th letter of *La Phil du Christian*. "The angel of darkness," says he, "preferred to live of himself, and he will always prefer independence to subordination. It was he himself, who chose that state of violence so contrary to the law of his own nature. He is in torments; but the cause of his torments is in himself, not in God; it is the energy of his opposition, the ardor of his self-will; and his torments will last so long as he shall will that which is contrary to the law of his being; and he *will* will it always, because infinite love cannot force him to renounce his pride and acknowledge his dependence.

† "Evil," says M. Bautain, "has no substance, no being; it is but a negation, or the

Another very mysterious question connected with the preceding is that of the transmission of evil through human generation. St. Bernard expresses a very positive opinion on this subject: "The carnal birth," says he, "destroys; it is the spiritual birth which saves me."

"Sin," adds he, "is communicated to us by the way of generation, and redemption comes to us through our own spiritual generation, by the cross and death of Jesus Christ." He develops this thought in another work: "We have all justly," says he, "contracted the sin of Adam, because we have all sinned in him, inasmuch as we were all in him when he sinned, and as we have all been born of his flesh by the *concupiscence of the flesh itself.* But who doubts that the spiritual birth, which we derive from God, is far more real than what we derive from Adam, according to the flesh? considering, above all, that we were in Jesus Christ, according to that Spirit, long before we were in Adam, according to the flesh."

Thus, in all philosophical questions, Bernard returns to the primitive ideal of things. He looks upon that ideal in the double point of view of science and of practice. Science, if it be true, must produce its reflection on the character. The real life or practice must, in like manner, be governed by this divine ideal, which is at once the model and the living law of man.

Applying these views to the entire work of redemption, he finds there the realization of one and the same idea, which contains in germ the whole development of the world and of humanity. This plan of divine wisdom has three phases; and St. Bernard seems to connect them with the personal action of the three terms of the Holy Trinity. The triple knot of the covenant, contracted between God and man, is thus explained: the first covenant was made by the Father; the second, wrought by the Son, was the complement of the first; a third covenant, consecrated by the Holy Ghost, will be the perfection of the other two. The first was engraved on tables of stone, that it might be, as it were, set before man; the second was implanted in man himself, to unite him substantially with the Son; the third is to be expressed by its manifestation in the life of the elect.

---

refusal, by the creature, to admit the truth and the virtue of being."

"The creation and the reconciliation," says he, "relate to the present time; but the confirmation relates to the world to come. The Father created the world in the beginning of time; the Son reconciled it in the fulness of time; the Holy Spirit will perfect it after the end of time.

"The Son said of the Father, 'My Father worketh until now;' and He adds, speaking of Himself, 'and I work.' —John v. But the Holy Ghost may say, until the consummation of ages, 'The Father and the Son have worked until now, and I begin to work;' that is to say, when He shall have made our body spiritual, then our body shall be united to the spirit, and the spirit to God. The Old Testament tells us of the creation of the world, and promises its reconciliation; the New reveals to us this reconciliation, and promises its perfect fulfillment."

We will conclude this chapter, in which we have only been able to indicate briefly the partial elements of a sublime philosophy, by remarking the truly apostolic freedom with which St. Bernard handles the most interesting questions of Christian science. The contemplative or mystical school to which he belonged, had faith for its basis and love for its end; between these two boundaries philosophy might speculate freely under the ever-open eye of the Church. The authority which watches over the deposit of sacred traditions desires not to hinder the production of these fruits of light which Christian doctrine brings forth; like the householder who brings out of his treasure things new and old, according to the needs which change with changing time, the Church tolerates, animates, and encourages all the efforts of genius, all the labors of intellect, all the investigations of human thought. But she keeps them to the path traced out by the Divine Word; and she shows herself as inexorable and inflexible to the proud spirits whom pride drives out of the road of orthodoxy, as she is liberal in her trust and confidence towards the talent which remains faithful to her.

The following chapter will show us the necessity of this severe vigilance.

# CHAPTER XXXIII

A GLANCE AT THE HERESIES OF ST. BERNARD'S TIME.

THERE is no error too absurd to be embraced by the human mind, when disdaining the guidance of the sacred traditions; it follows its own light in the search after truth. It would be a useless, and, perhaps, an impossible task, to retrace all the aberrations of thought; the diversities of logical error would be found, perhaps, to equal the infinite variety of moral vices; and these, in their turn, viewed in a psychological and physiological point of view, would, doubtless, find their degraded types in the multiplicity of corporal maladies. This triple manifestation of evil springs originally from the same source; and each, according to its kind, issues in a fruit of death. It is a remarkable fact, that a period of immorality ordinarily brings on a period of error, and that again is followed by the scourge of corporal maladies. These three series of evils are far more closely connected than is generally thought, and they produce one another; morals regulate the mind, and the mind rules the body; and public health actually depends upon doctrines, as doctrines depend upon morality. It would, perhaps, be an interesting study, setting out from this point of view, to characterize each century by the nature of its predominant evil, and trace the successive influences which have ruled the world. But, without wishing to insist on this observation, and confining ourselves to the time of which we are treating, it is manifest that the twelfth century is distinguished by the aberration of human reason, and by the heterodox tendency of intellectual speculations. The predominance of barbarous manners in the preceding century had prepared the way for this tendency; it was followed, a century later, by physical calamities of all kinds, and a period of frightful mortality.*

We shall here content ourselves with exposing the principal heresies of St. Bernard's time; we shall hereafter see him in conflict with them.

The method of Aristotle was, as we have seen in the preceding chapter, the great instrument by the aid of which the innovators undertook to justify their eccentric doctrines. The species of fanaticism to which the study of the Greek philosophers had given rise in the Christian schools had carried the rationalistic theologians into absurdities. Some, carried away by the seductions of Manicheism, supposed a primitive nature, co-existent with God, co-eternal with Him; subject, in its development, like God Himself, to necessary and absolute laws. Others, reviving the reveries of the Indians and the Gymnosophists, viewed creation as the eternal object of the divine love, and thus considered all created beings as consubstantial with God; a gross pantheism, which confounded God, man, and nature together.† Others again—and this was the most general aberration of the spirit of the age—carried the taste for disputation, and the spirit of curiosity, made more subtle by dialectics, into Christian theology; so that, in their discussion of dogmas, they mutilated them, as it were, in order to adapt them to scholastic categories and subject them to the narrow conceptions of reason. Lastly, impetuous and austere innovators, under pretext of purifying morals, undertook the task of reforming doctrine and uprooting heavenly and earthly plants together from the field of the Church; they composed a new Christianity, which broke into a thousand fragments and subdivided into as many sects. These various heresies, which had been long hatching in darkness, displayed their symbols openly at the period when Arnold of Brescia flattered himself that he had struck down the head of the Church. The first propaganda was organized in Languedoc; Provence, and several dioceses of southern France were soon infected. These countries seemed more

---

\* The numerous and strange maladies which broke out at the end of the 13th century are well known. It was especially under the race of Valois that nations were decimated by them.

† German pantheism, especially the school of Hegel, seems to be an offspring of these old errors.

accessible than others to the enterprises of innovators. Besides, the kind of charm which oriental mysticism exercised over lively imaginations, the gross manners and ignorance of the clergy and the vices and public scandals of which too many among them offered a revolting spectacle, lent but too powerful an aid to the preachers of the new doctrines. These men at first confined their attacks to the clergy; but from the clergy they passed on to the ecclesiastical hierarchy; from the hierarchy, to the authority of the Church; and, this barrier once broken through, errors poured in floods into the schismatical schools. Each of these schools gave itself out as the one only true Church, under a name borrowed either from its head, or from the city where it had just sprung up.*

Thus arose, almost simultaneously, the different Manichean sects, which favored by Roger, Count of Albi, became afterwards so formidable under their new name of Albigenses. They had been preceded by the Petrobusians, disciples of Peter of Bruys. They again divided; and from the midst of them issued forth the Henricians, more violent than their predecessors. Tanchelme and his partisans, known in the twelfth century under the name of the heretics of Cologne, mitigated the doctrines of the monk Henry and propagated them in Flanders, Cologne, Utrecht, and Holland. The Apostolicals of Perigueux, the Cathari of Italy, the Patarins or Perfect of Germany, the "Passagiens," the "Bonshommes," the Arnoldists, the Publicans, and a host of others, signalized themselves by the singularity of their dogmas, and by their common revolt against the center of Catholic authority. The Manicheism of the Albigenses, as contemporary chronicles testify, was not the same as that of Manes. They taught that God had created Lucifer, who, having revolted against God, was driven from heaven with his angels; and that, having been banished from the invisible regions, he had produced the visible world, over which he ruled. God, to re-establish order, then created Christ, who was thus, like Lucifer, only a *creature of God*. It was in this last point that the Albigenses agreed with the Arians. These sectaries,

---

* As we retrace these facts, we seem to be writing a history of the Reformation in the sixteenth century; so true is it that the same errors always lead to the same results.

full of resentment against the clergy, because of the severity with which they had been treated, directed their chief assaults against everything in religion which was connected with the priesthood. They rejected the doctrine of the Sacraments, the ceremonies of the Church, the prerogatives of the pontiffs, condemned tithes, and stigmatized ecclesiastics who possessed property. It was this which gave them especial influence, and drew all discontented spirits and avaricious nobles, impatient to invade the domains of the Church, to their side. St. Bernard, who was called upon to combat them, draws a hideous picture of the sects who professed some of the dogmas of this formidable heresy. He accused them of leading a dissolute life, under deceitful appearances; and brings forward, in particular, their teaching concerning marriage, infant Baptism, abstinence, Purgatory, and prayer for the dead. Among these heresiarchs, Peter de Bruys distinguished himself by his audacity. He dogmatized in Languedoc and Provence, while his disciple, Henry, preached at Lausanne, and played the apostle in several other parts of France. The first was a layman; the second a renegade monk. Both taught that children not yet come to the use of reason were incapable of receiving Baptism effectually; and acting on that opinion, they rebaptized adults whom they received into their sect. Besides this heresy, they professed many others, more or less pernicious, which the venerable Abbot of Cluny reduces to five heads: 1) They condemned the use of sacred buildings, temples, and altars, and overthrew them. 2) They rejected the worship of the cross. 3) They forbade the celebration of the Holy Sacrifice, regarding the Mass as useless or superstitious. 4) They taught that neither prayer nor good works, any more than the Mass, can avail to the relief of the departed. 5) They cut out of the canon of Holy Scripture several books of the Old and New Testaments.

These novelties had captivated many minds, and fomented lamentable disorders. Nothing was to be seen in Provence but Christians rebaptized, temples profaned, altars overthrown, crosses burnt. "The churches are deserted," cried St. Bernard, as he viewed, on the very spot, the ravages of heresy; "the churches are deserted, the basilicas without worshippers, the people without priests, the priests exposed to contempt, and Christians without Christ! They strip our temples as bare as synagogues, they rob our Sacrament of all that is sacred, they deprive our solemn days of their august solemnity! Men die in their sins; and their souls alas! pass from this life to the dread tribunal of God, without having been reconciled by the Sacrament of Penance, or fortified by Holy Communion!* Little children are excluded from life because the grace of Baptism is refused to them, and they are hindered from approaching Him who, nevertheless, has said, plainly enough, 'Suffer the little children to come to me.'"

Oh, how well does this language express a true solicitude for the salvation of souls! St. Bernard, on this occasion, does not lose his time in refuting doctrines; he is too eager to save souls. He views the doctrines only in the fatal effect they exercise upon souls; he touches them to the quick; he points out their fatal consequences, and we shall soon see him hastening, not to dispute or discuss, but to instruct and heal.

Meanwhile, the Henricians fortified themselves at Toulouse, whither the Abbot of Clairvaux instantly repaired. Other heretics, stilled by the Tanchelme, propagated errors more dangerous and extravagant still, at Cologne, and in a part of Holland. Tanchelme, or Tanchelin, was, like Peter de Bruys, a mere layman. He pretended to have received a mission to reform the discipline and teaching of the Church. Like all the other reformers of his time, he declaimed first against the Pope, the episcopate, the usurpations of the clergy; he soon interpreted, after his own fashion, the Sacrament of the Altar; and these first attempts were but the preliminaries of his insane doctrines. Meanwhile, these doctrines found partisans. Tanchelme, elated by the success of his preaching, believed himself not only an apostle, but represented himself as the Son of God, maintaining that Jesus Christ was God only because the Holy Spirit rested upon Him; that thus having received, like Jesus Christ, the plenitude of the Holy Spirit, he was not inferior to Him. The people believed him; and Tanchelme was honored as a *divine man*. It is even asserted, on the testimony of Abelard and others, that he permitted a temple to be built in his honor, while he overthrew the temples consecrated to Jesus

---

* St. Bernard stayed the outbreak of heresy in the 12th century. What would have happened if there had been a St. Bernard in the 16th century? What if we had a St. Bernard now?

Christ. This heresiarch had begun his career by denouncing the disorderly lives of the clergy; he ended by sanctioning the same disorders, and gave example of scandals far more monstrous than those against which he had protested. Such was the infatuation of his disciples that they boasted of the infamous favors which the *divine man* had granted to their wives and daughters.

Some other sects, derived from these of Cologne, had arrived by another road, if not at the same extravagances, at least to a sort of Christianity no less devoid of life and truth. "They taught," writes the Provost of Cologne to St. Bernard, "that the perfect alone compose the true Church, and that all other Christians are abandoned to superstition and error." Their stumbling block had been the dogma of Purgatory; they rejected it, and maintained that souls on leaving the body passed immediately to their place either in heaven or hell. "Ask them, then," cries St. Bernard, "ask them to explain to you what Jesus Christ means when He speaks of a sin which shall not be remitted either in this world or the other. Why did Jesus Christ speak thus, if neither remission or Purgatory be possible in the other world?"

By the breaking of this one link in the chain of revelation these heretics lost the whole of the Christian doctrine. After having denied Purgatory, as a consequence of their negative principle, they denied the efficacy of prayer for the dead. But this was one of the most ancient usages consecrated by tradition; to escape it, tradition must be denied; but again, this custom is supported by certain books of Holy Scripture; these books, therefore, must be rejected. Lastly, the Fathers of the first centuries, and especially St. Augustine, prayed for the dead, and the Church, in all ages, has commemorated them in her offices. Therefore, replied the heretics, St. Augustine and the Fathers followed on this point the reveries of paganism, and the whole Church, from the very first centuries, has fallen into superstition and error. Thus, every column of Christian antiquity fell under the axe of this fatal logic.

This pseudo-Christianity, stripped of its fundamental dogmas, of its traditions, its worship, its secular monuments, and all the guarantees of its integrity, was not long before it began to mingle with the doctrines of a false mysticism, which, rejecting all forms in order to preserve the spirit alone, abandons man to his own vain imaginations. The Cathari, so called from the testimony they bore to themselves, as forming the Church of indefectible purity, opened the door to the strangest superstitions, while they closed it against the teaching of the Church. According to these heretics, the devil is the creator of material elements, it was he who formed the body of Adam of the slime of the earth, in which an angel of light was inclosed; he afterwards made the woman; and having cohabited with her, Cain was the fruit of their union. Eve, in her turn, seduced the man; and the forbidden fruit of which Scripture speaks, is nothing else but the symbol of their commerce. "They taught besides," says a grave author, "that the sun is the devil, that the moon is Eve, that the stars are demons, and, lastly that no man can be saved out of their sect." This same author speaks of another sect who went to the contrary extreme from those who rejected the Holy Scriptures.

The Passagiens aspired to a pharisaic sanctity, by the literal observance of the ancient law. They maintained that Jesus Christ had never abolished that law, and that it was necessary to salvation to return to the Sabbath, circumcision, and other observances of the synagogue.

Lastly, the Arnoldists, disciples of Arnold of Brescia, had, after their rupture with the Church, framed a mitigated Christianity of their own. Their preaching was directed principally against the Pope; and they recognized the Church everywhere, except where its visible head resides. Thirty of these fanatics crossed over to England to disseminate their doctrine; but they were cut off at the very beginning of their enterprise. History assigns to them but one single conversion; one old woman only assisted the innovators and received the seed of heresy.* William of Newbury, an almost contemporary historian, relates their examination and punishment; all protested, to their last breath, against the authority of the Pope and the teaching of the Church.

There was another fanatic, at this time, whom we will just mention here to complete the sad picture.

---

\* I look upon this woman of the 12th century as the mother of Anglicanism; at least, that which she conceived in her womb another woman brought forth some centuries later. With doctrines the time of gestation is sometimes longer, sometimes shorter; and centuries may elapse between the laying down of a principle and the realization of its consequences.

He was a noble Breton, Eon de l'Etoile, who, in the delirium of his enthusiasm, announced himself as the messenger from God, sent to judge the living and the dead. Eon had, it is said, been struck with the concluding words of some prayers of the Church which he did not understand: *Per eum qui venturus es judicare vivos et mortuos.* He fancied that he was pointed out in these words, and persuaded others of the same. His pretended revelations about the end of the world and the Last Judgment made an impression on the people; and he was not arrested without a formidable resistance. Pope Eugenius treated his doctrine as folly and not heresy.* He caused the insane preacher to be confined; but his disciples, madder than himself, chose to suffer burning rather than renounce the worship of their master.

Such were the sects which arose in the 12th century and organized an immense conspiracy against the Church, which called forth a long cry from all Christendom.

We do not speak here of the errors of Bishop Gilbert de la Porree, to which we shall have to revert hereafter. Those errors arose rather from an abuse of logic in doctrinal matters than from willful opposition to the teaching of the Church. Gilbert de la Porree dared not maintain the proposition which he had hazarded in the presence of St. Bernard, and he hastened to sign the profession of faith composed by him.

It was necessary, according to the words of the Gospel, that the seeds of all these errors should show forth their fruits, before the plants which had not been planted by the heavenly Father could be known and rooted up. Those fruits were ripe; and the Abbot of Clairvaux, being charged by the Sovereign Pontiff with the preaching of the Crusade, made this high mission serve to the extirpation of heresy; it was by the holy folly of the cross that he was destined to confound the doctrines of men.

The chronological order of this double series of facts forms a new period in the life of St. Bernard, which will form the subject of the last part of this work.

---

* Eon, in Greek, signifies Being. The Gnostics gave the name of Eons to the pretended incarnations of the Supreme Being, who, according to them, manifested themselves, from time to time, upon earth. It is probable that some vague tradition of this kind mingled with the folly of Eon de l'Etoile.

# CHAPTER XXXIV

### IDEA OF THE CRUSADES—STATE OF CHRISTIANITY IN THE EAST.

Hail, Holy Land! Land of human sorrows and divine mercies! Land of prophecy, country of God and man, our eyes now turn towards thee. At thy very name we feel an irresistible emotion, and the depths of our souls re-echo the accents of the royal psalmist: "O Jerusalem, may my right hand perish, if ever I forget thee!"

But if we would speak worthily of Jerusalem, we must borrow the language of St. Bernard: "Hail, then, holy city, city of the Son of God; chosen and sanctified to be the source of our salvation! Hail to thee, dwelling place of the Great King, whence have emanated all the wonders of ancient and modern times which have rejoiced the world! Queen of nations, capital of empires, see of patriarchs, mother of prophets and apostles, first cradle of our faith, glory and honor of Christianity! Hail, promised land, once flowing with milk and honey for thy first children, thou hast produced the food of life and the medicine of immortality for all future ages. Yes, city of God, great things have been spoken of thee!"

Although now dead and withered, Jerusalem, like the prophet's bones, seems still to possess the virtue of giving life to the dead who touch her ancient remains. Her name, like the name of God whence it is derived, is invested with a hidden power, which at certain periods manifests itself like the electric spark and diffuses a sacred emotion throughout every land; and when the world goes astray, when it becomes exhausted, or slumbers in the shadow of death, this life-giving name awakens it, and the angel who descends into the pool of the holy city stirs the springs of life, and pours the heavenly sap once more through the veins of the human race.

There has never been any great idea, or first principle, or heavenly inspiration, which has not arisen in the Holy Land before its diffusion throughout the world. There, in the beginning, flowed the tears and the blood of sinful man; there, under the mount of skulls,* are laid the remains of Adam and those of the mother of the living. Melchisedek came there to offer the sacrifice of future reconciliation; and under that high-priest's footsteps, according to the eternal decree, arose Salem, the city of peace. The three races of mankind—the descendants of Shem, Ham, and Japheth—each in its turn mingled their ashes with those of the father of all men; and thus around the first human grave, the primitive altar of mercy, was found the sacred field of the dead—that vast cemetery of the sons of men, which gradually enlarged its limits into the uttermost parts of the earth. On this mystical altar flowed the blood of beasts, the blood of man, and the blood of God; and from the summit of this altar, on the Holy Mount, where Christ consummated His sacrifice, Divine grace flowed forth upon the dead and watered the dust of man, which will one day revive again.

All the nations of the world appear to have laid claim to the Holy Land; for it has been possessed, or occupied in turns, by the principal people of ancient and modern times. From time to time it has been inhabited by new tribes, and it is by the flux and reflux of their blood that Jerusalem, the very heart of the earth, nourishes the pulses of her mysterious existence. There can be no doubt that the Crusades, which are the great drama of modern history, form a link in this long chain of mysteries. To see in these wars nothing but the enthusiasm of a few warriors rushing to the deliverance of a sepulchre, would be to strip their history of its leading idea, and to overlook in the plan of Providence one of the most magnificent developments of the work of Christianity.

---

* Calvary, "the place of skulls," on which was raised the Cross of Christ, is said to contain the ashes of Adam and Eve. This assertion is by no means authentic, but is founded on pious tradition which the Church has never condemned.

We have already said that in the history of man there is an order of invisible things in which the origin and last consequences of events often escape our investigations. While we are in this life we can only perceive the reflections and secondary effects of hidden causes; and, according to the apostle's doctrine, Christian science should be exercised rather on great and permanent realities than on passing phenomena; yet, were we only to judge of the Crusades by their visible results, we must allow that they were the expression of a sublime idea, and a kind of Divine necessity in some sort, which alone could have produced such great results.

It is not our object to enter into the details of this phase of our history. Other historians have recounted the exploits, the labors, the conquests, and the striking vicissitudes of the Christian heroes of that age; but it is fitting that, on entering upon this province of history, we should bear witness to the spirit which animated the Holy Wars, and the immense influence which they exercised upon Christian civilization.

In the first place, the question decided by the Crusades was not whether the Holy Sepulchre should belong to the disciples of Christ or the disciples of Mahomet; but the dispute was as to which of these two religions should possess the sovereignty of the world; this question was carried before the tribunal of the Holy City.

The formidable race of the Turks had established their empire over all the East, and from thence they threatened an invasion of the West. The nations of Europe, weakened by the dismemberment of their territories and their civil dissensions, trembled at the approach of the waves of this impetuous torrent. How could its onward progress be arrested otherwise than by the union of all the people of Christendom in one universal barrier? But, like all great undertakings, such a concourse and general stirring of nations could only be effected under the influence of a religious idea. The divine breath of religion only possesses the power of inspiring all men with one common sentiment, uniting them in one thought, and kindling among them a universal flame of generous enthusiasm.

The human mind at that period was doubtless unable to comprehend the sublime and vast ramifications of this great idea; man is almost always the blind instrument of a work which surpasses his understanding; the seed that he has sown can only be revealed by its fruit. The Crusaders, in their warlike ardor, aimed only at the deliverance of a sepulchre, and they were the deliverers of the world. But it was fitting that the essential idea of the Crusades should be displayed in all its simplicity, in order to be received and understood by the intellect of the age. The object in view was to rescue from the devil that sacred land above which the heavens had opened to give testimony to the Son of God. This was clear to the capacity of all, and the magical influence of this divine idea captivated the whole of Christendom, and revived its faith. The first result of this movement was a spirit of union among the nations and a wonderful harmony of sentiments, thoughts and interests, which unexpectedly put an end to all religious dissensions, political disturbances and civil wars. In the next place, as a natural consequence, followed the exaltation of the Papacy, which always resumes its place at the head of human affairs when the spirit of concord is to be revived among the nations. The Crusades alone gave to the Holy See more weight and influence in the affairs of the world than any doctrine, theory, or triumph by sword or word, before or since; and this central influence and great preponderance which it possessed was the mainspring of the development of the middle ages, and of the civilization of future times.

How can we but admire the power which thus called together a hundred nations and united them in one common brotherhood? Only a century before this time it was a difficult matter to collect an army of five or six thousand men. It was in the heart of this great Christian army that the influence of the Head of the Church resumed its ascendency over Catholic unity; add to this consideration the magnanimous virtue to which the Holy Wars gave birth; and if we even look at the matter from another point of view and reflect on the number of idle and degenerate Christians which the nations of the West poured forth into the East and the universal purification of the Church which ensued, we shall discover in the Crusades a new series of inestimable advantages.

This purification of the Church was not only moral and material, but it was chiefly manifested in the sphere of the intellect. In the preceding chapters we have seen how great was the fermentation of the public mind; the exuberance of human thought overflowed on every side; and if, at that period, the energetic activity of reason had not been subdued by a higher attraction, it would have swallowed up civilization in its infancy, and Europe would have relapsed into the darkness of barbarism. And from the intellectual point of view we may see one of the most extraordinary and immediate effects of the Crusades. The name of Christ, preached everywhere with the authority of faith, imposed silence on the discursive exercises of human reason. The remembrance of the holy places, where the mysteries of divine love had been accomplished, revived Christian piety in the minds of men; fruitless discussions gave place to tears of compunction, and to the vain disputes of feebler times succeeded a spirit of active energy, the distinguishing characteristic of the ages of faith. It would be difficult to conceive what the fate of Europe might have been if the Holy Wars had not opened a new course to the development of the human mind. The progress of civilization was much more endangered by the errors of reason than by the invasion of barbarians; and we are unable to determine which would have been the greatest misfortune for the Catholic world, the triumph of Mahometanism or that of heresy. The Church had to encounter the united attacks of these two adversaries at the same time; the efforts of both were defeated by the Crusades; and the preachers of the Holy Wars were so filled with the consciousness of the double mission they had to perform, that their words were equally directed against heretics and infidels; the Crusaders themselves spontaneously turned their arms against both these enemies.

It is certainly true that the soldiers of the cross were not always guided by the spirit of God, or influenced by justice, charity, and truth; we do not pretend to deny the monstrous abuses which too often disgraced their enterprises. But, in this place, the only important point for consideration is the great idea which predominates over all these questions; and it is rather by this idea than by the facts which resulted therefrom that we must judge of the man whose fiery eloquence aroused the spirit of the Crusades.

Half a century had hardly elapsed since the conquest of the Holy Land by Godfrey de Bouillon; and the preservation of this new kingdom by a mere handful of Christians seemed to be even more miraculous than the conquest itself; in fact, all the efforts of the many formidable enemies who surrounded them had proved unable to dislodge them. The Franks of the East, trusting in their acquired rights and full of faith in the future, lived on from day to day, without anxiety as to the hostile preparations which were then being made in the Saracen camp. It seemed to them that it was, humanly speaking, impossible to lose that beloved land, which had been purchased by so many labors, and, as it were, consecrated by an effusion of Christian blood. But towards the close of the year 1144, a fatal disaster disturbed their security and overthrew all their hopes. The city of Edessa, the chief bulwark of Eastern Christendom, fell again into the hands of the Mussulmans. Edessa, according to an ancient tradition, was the first Christian city, for it was said that its king had been converted by Jesus Christ Himself. The fall of Edessa made Antioch tremble, and Jerusalem, at that time governed by a woman, was left desolate and defenceless.* At this perilous juncture, a cry of distress arose from the East which resounded throughout western Christendom. The misfortunes of the Holy Land excited a universal sorrow—but nowhere did they meet with more deep sympathy than in France. The new kingdom had been conquered and founded by the arms of France; French princes were its feudatory possessors; a Frenchman was seated on the throne of Jerusalem; and although every Christian state was interested in the preservation of this eastern colony, on account of the immense resources which it offered for the piety of pilgrims as well as for the purposes of commerce and navigation, yet the honor of France in some sort depended thereon, as that country was more closely allied to the Holy Land, through the French princes who were its rulers. The news of the capture of Edessa reached France about the beginning of the year 1145; and the idea of hastening to the assistance of the eastern Christians forthwith took possession of the mind of Louis VII. The young king, who suffered from an uneasy conscience, hoped that so holy an enterprise would blot out his errors and afford him, at the same time, an opportunity of displaying his valor. The remembrance of his unjust quarrels with

---

\* The city of Edessa was the capital of the principality founded in Mesopotamia by Baldwin, brother of Godfrey de Bouillon. It was taken, after a horrible massacre, by the Sultan of Baghdad, in 1144. At that time the throne of Jerusalem was occupied by Melisinda, widow of Falk of Anjou, and regent during the minority of her son, Baldwin III.

the Holy See, the remorse he felt for his exactions in Champagne, and above all, for the horrible catastrophe of Vitry-le-Brule, weighed heavily on his soul; and to these powerful motives was added his desire of fulfilling the vow made by his elder brother, who had died before he was able to accomplish his resolution of making a pilgrimage to the Holy Land.

Notwithstanding these considerations, however, Louis VII did not fulfill his generous intentions; and whether the difficulties of the undertaking appeared to him insurmountable, or whether his ardor was cooled by the remonstrances of his minister, Suger, many months elapsed, during which the sympathy of the country was only expressed by tears and fruitless lamentations. It belonged to the Roman Pontiff, the common father of the Eastern and Western Christians, to give an active impulse to the interest universally excited by the fate of Jerusalem. He turned his eyes towards France, the country of those illustrious heroes, who, forty years before, had delivered the Holy Sepulchre. He exhorted their sons to defend this glorious conquest of their fathers, and he offered the honor of the initiative in the undertaking to Louis VII.* The words of the Holy Pontiff met with a powerful echo in the king's conscience, who now only awaited some solemn occasion to publish his pious intentions.

"In the year of the Incarnate Word 1145, on the feast of the Nativity," says the chronicler, "Louis, King of France and Duke of Aquitaine, held his full court at Bourges, to which he more especially summoned the bishops and lords of his kingdom, and confided to them the secret intentions of his heart.

"After him, Godfrey, Bishop of Langres, a man of great piety, spoke, in moving terms, of the destruction of the city of Edessa, and the disgraceful yoke which the infidels had imposed on the Christians. His words, on this sad subject, drew tears from all present; he then invited the assembly of nobles to unite with the king in rendering assistance to their brethren.

---

* The letter of Eugene III is not only addressed to the king, but to all the French people: "*Dilectos Filios, principes et universos Dei fideles per Galliam constitutos.*"—Otto Frising. Degesta Frid. Lib. 1, gap. 35.

"Nevertheless, the bishop's words and the king's example only sowed a seed, the harvest of which was gathered at a later period. It was decided that a larger assembly should be called together at Vézelay, in the country of Nivernais (in Burgundy), at Eastertide, so that on the very feast of the Lord's Resurrection, all those who were touched by His grace might concur in the exaltation of the Cross of Christ.

"The king, who was very solicitous for the success of his design, sent deputies to Pope Eugenius, to inform him of these matters. The ambassadors were received joyfully and dismissed with apostolic letters, enjoining obedience to the king on all who should engage in the holy war; regulating the fashion of the arms and clothing of the soldiers of the cross; and promising unto those who should bear the sweet yoke of Christ, the remission of their sins, and protection

It was accordingly resolved that a new Crusade should be undertaken; but public opinion was not agreed as to the expediency of so arduous an enterprise. No one had presumed openly to oppose the king's resolution; but the ardor of enthusiasm was dampened by political troubles, and the dangers of such a distant expedition. The spark was still wanting which was to kindle the materials for so vast a conflagration. The state of affairs was no longer the same as at the time of the first Crusade; the ardor of the Knights of the Cross was very much cooled by their knowledge of the places and of the obstacles to be encountered, the remembrance of the sufferings which Godfrey's companions had endured, and the experience of their old warriors. Suger, above all, the prudent counsellor of Louis VII, who entertained a very positive view on political matters, did not approve of the project of the Holy War, and he endeavored, though unsuccessfully, to turn the king's mind from this design. With reason and conscience on his side, he did not hesitate to trust the decision of this matter to the wisdom of the holy Abbot of Clairvaux. The latter was, therefore, summoned to Bourges; and Suger, in submitting this important question to his consideration, was far from supposing that St. Bernard himself would ardently embrace the idea of a Crusade, and renew, throughout Christendom, the wonders of the age of Peter the Hermit.

Bernard, however, refused to pronounce his opinion before the arrival of the apostolic brief. Many historians even say that it was by his advice Louis VII sent ambassadors to Rome. But the private letters which St. Bernard wrote to Eugenius III, on this occasion, afford evidence of his personal views, which he imparted to the Holy See. "The great news of the day," he writes, "cannot be a matter of indifference to anyone; it is a sad and serious affair, and our enemies alone can rejoice at it. That which is the common cause of Christendom ought likewise to be a subject of universal sorrow. . . I have read somewhere that a valiant man finds his courage augmented in proportion as his difficulties increase; and I add, that the just man also grows greater in adversity. Jesus Christ is cruelly persecuted; He is struck, if I may dare so to speak, in the very apple of His eye; He suffers in the very places where He suffered formerly. Holy Father, the time is come to unsheath your two swords! Who may do this, but you, who are the successor of him to whom they were entrusted? Both those swords belong to Peter; they must be drawn from the scabbard when necessity requires it; one must be drawn by your order, the other by your own hand.

"It was said to St. Peter, '*Put up thy sword into the scabbard.*' — John xviii. This sword, therefore, belonged to him, as well as the other sword; only, he was not to use it with his own hand.

"And now, I say, the time is come when you must use both these swords; on this occasion, you should imitate the zeal of him whose place you hold. I hear a voice crying out, 'I am going to Jerusalem, there to be crucified anew!' Some may be deaf to this voice; others may hear it with indifference; but you, the successor of St. Peter, who cannot close your ears, you should exclaim, '*Though all should be scandalized in Thee, yet will I never be scandalized.*' Let us not be discouraged by past reverses, but rather let us endeavor to repair them. Because God does what He wills, is man, therefore, dispensed from doing what he ought?

"It is true that, according to the words of Scripture, we have eaten the bread of sorrow, we have been drunk with a bitter wine; but why shouldst thou be discouraged, O friend of the bridegroom? It may be that God is touched with compassion for our miseries, and will henceforth show us more mercy. This, you know, is His ordinary way of dealing with man; and His most signal graces are oftentimes purchased at the price of some great misfortune. The danger is imminent, and calls for speedy succor. The zeal which inflames me has made me speak with boldness."

These burning words excited the solicitude of the Holy See; but, as we are about to relate, the result was far otherwise than St. Bernard had foreseen.

# CHAPTER XXXV

### ST. BERNARD IS COMMISSIONED TO PREACH THE CRUSADE—DIFFICULTIES OF THIS MISSION—ASSEMBLY AT VEZELAY.

EUGENIUS III had the interests of the Eastern Church so much at heart that he would have wished, like Pope Urban II, to go to France, that according to his own expression, he might himself sound the trumpet of the Gospel, to summon all the brave and intrepid warriors of the French kingdom to defend the Holy Land. But the late revolution at Rome detained him beyond the Alps, and he was unable to preside, in person, at the assembly of Vézelay. To fulfill this apostolic mission he sent, as his delegate, the man whose authority surpassed, in some sort, that of the Pontiff himself; and when St. Bernard received the commission to preach the Crusade, its success was already ensured beforehand.

The humble monk of Clairvaux was overwhelmed with fear by the orders of the Holy See. He was at that time in the fifty-fourth year of his age; but his fragile and languid frame was so attenuated and weakened by austerities, and so exhausted by long sufferings, that his life seemed to be prolonged by a miracle. It was with difficulty that he could support himself on his feet and for three years he had not left his monastery except when obliged by the most important affairs of his order; and even on these occasions, he was frequently compelled to excuse himself; for, as an old chronicler says, "he was almost dead, and you would have thought he was about to breathe his last. And yet, this frail and emaciated body was animated by a superhuman strength when it became the organ of the Spirit of God." "At such times," writes one of his contemporaries, "he gradually became animated, and his sweet and burning words flowed from his lips, like a river of milk and honey, which sprang from his heart as from a furnace of divine love."

The monk Wilbold, Abbot of Monte Cassino, who had seen St. Bernard a few years before and had been struck with his eloquence, writes as follows on this subject: "This venerable man is exceedingly pale, being attenuated by the fasts and excessive austerities of the desert; he bears the deepest traces of humility, compunction, and penance; he breathes such perfect sanctity, that his very appearance has a persuasive eloquence, even when he does not open his lips. He is endowed with great genius and wonderful talents; he speaks with simplicity; his enunciation is clear, powerful, and full of unction; his action is always easy and natural; his manner full of grace and truth. The sight of this great man is a most moving sermon; his discourses edify, and his example incites to virtue."

The Sovereign Pontiff, therefore, knowing the high endowments and supernatural gifts of St. Bernard, had well nigh forgotten the corporal infirmities of him who was his father in Christ. He solemnly charged him to preach the holy war, and named some other distinguished men to share in his ministry: "But," adds the chronicle of William of Tyre, "amongst those who were chosen to fulfill this mission, so pleasing to the Lord, the first and principal delegate was Sieur Bernard, Abbot of Clairvaux, a man of most holy life, who deserves to be universally held in immortal remembrance." The formally expressed will of the Holy See prevailed over all excuses; and Bernard, full of zeal for the Church and deference towards its Head, courageously accepted the weighty burden of this apostolic mission.

But when the Abbot of Clairvaux appeared amongst the men of the age, to draw them from their hearths and precipitate them upon Asia, he did not find them in that favorable state of mind which had so wonderfully conduced to facilitate the preaching of Peter the Hermit. We have already noticed that several causes had tended to change the dispositions of men's minds. We must not omit to mention another cause, which would seem to have been one of the principal obstacles that St. Bernard had to encounter.

At the period of the second Crusade, the fervor of Christian piety was displayed in another manner, and by works which accorded, at that time, with the dictates of conscience. The great object of popular devotion was to erect holy basilicas to the glory of God and the honor of the Blessed Virgin. Several vast confraternities, in which there was a community of property and labor, were established in different places to pay their debt of gratitude towards the Church, and to leave a monument of their piety during their pilgrimage through this land of exile. These confraternities were admirably organized, and men and women, rich and poor, gentle and simple, aspired to the honor of becoming members of these associations, to which no one was admitted unless he first made his peace with God by a humble confession of his sins and had made a vow to obey the superior of the congregation, and to assist his sick brethren according to the rules of Christian charity. Nothing could be more edifying than the religious discipline by which so many were united together in good works. They went, with their banner unfurled, through mountains and valleys, under the guidance of a priest, and marched together as one man. On this subject we may read some curious details, in a letter written in 1145 by the superior of a monastery in Normandy, who had seen a magnificent cathedral arise in the place of his modest church. "Who ever before saw," says the Abbot of St. Pierre, "princes and powerful lords, warriors and delicate women, bowing their necks under the yoke to which they suffer themselves to be attached, in order to carry weighty loads, as if they were beasts of burden? They are to be met in thousands, drawing one heavy machine and carrying, to a great distance, wheat, wine, oil, limestones, and other materials for the workmen! Neither mountains, valleys, nor rivers can impede their progress; they journey on, as the people of God in former times; but the greatest wonder is, that these countless multitudes march without any disorder or disturbance. They raise their voices only at a given signal, and then they sing hymns, or implore mercy for their sins . . . When the associates arrive at their destination, they halt near the church; then they watch by their wagons, like soldiers in a camp; when, at nightfall, they light their tapers, prayers are intoned and an offering is made over the holy relics; then the priests, the clerks, and the faithful return to their homes, greatly edified, walking in their order, praying and singing psalms for the sick and the afflicted."

Such was the popular expression of Catholic piety in the twelfth century; tending to fix the active imagination of the middle ages, while it cooperated efficiently with the internal work of the spirit of Christianity, which under every form unites men in one common task. And it was thus that those immortal masterpieces of modern times arose on the soil of Catholicity as monuments to all future ages of the power of associations which are animated by the spirit of religion!

It may, however, be supposed that these labors of love were so many obstacles to the heralds of the holy war. It cost many a struggle to leave the sacred edifice incomplete, in order to run all the risks of a distant expedition, when, without quitting their hearths, men could labor for the glory of the Church and share in the numerous indulgences granted by the Sovereign Pontiffs to the works of Christian confraternities. These reasonable considerations, joined to the apprehensions of human prudence as to the doubtful issue of a Crusade, paralyzed all warlike enthusiasm; and the resolutions made at Bourges lost their ascendency over the public mind. But when it became known that St. Bernard had embraced the cause and was about to preach it to the world, all further reasoning was silenced, and the people only awaited the oracle of the man of God.

The assembly of Vézelay had been adjourned to the holy week of the year 1146, at which time St. Bernard was to begin his mission. But in the meanwhile he did not remain inactive, for his letters remain a proof of the zeal which consumed him, and his written words may give us an idea of those burning discourses which he so frequently pronounced; but unfortunately, no traces of them are to be found in contemporary histories.

Desirous above all things to lay the sure foundation which attracts heavenly graces, he addressed a letter to the Patriarch of Jerusalem, to recommend him the virtue of humility, without which every other virtue is useless and which alone fills the place of all the rest. This letter is full of a serious and moving unction. "When it pleased the Most High," he writes, "to discover His profound decrees concerning the salvation of the human race, He manifested His love towards men so far as to give them His uncreated Son; and that Son being made man to serve mankind, called those whom He chose, and chose those whom He preferred. But amongst them was one whom He specially loved; this was the beloved of all the beloved—the elect of the elect; and He confided to him, in the last hour of His sacrifice, His own mother, the Virgin Mary . . . Wherefore do I make this preamble? To what point am I coming? Listen attentively. The Lord has chosen many whom He has invested with the sacerdotal dignity; He has established many princes over His people; but among all the bishops in the world, you alone are constituted over the house of David; to you alone has been confided that blessed land where arose the fruit of life, where was born the mystic flower, the lily of the valley. . . 'Take off thy shoes,' the Lord once said to Moses, 'for the place where thou now art is holy.'* And you, too, who dwell in this same place, divest yourself of all earthly attachments . . . Oh, how terrible is this place, where the father went out to meet his prodigal son, and, throwing his arms around his neck, clothed him with a robe of glory; where the Saviour of mankind, so mild and so loving, poured out oil and wine on our wounds; where the God of all consolation has made with us the covenant of an eternal alliance. . . O holy, sacred place, into which our divine Redeemer entered not only with water, but with water and blood;† where He deigned to live and die!. . . Who can be found worthy to follow Him? He alone who has learned from Christ to be meek and humble of heart. Without humility we run the risk of being lost here. Would you lean upon a solid, unshaken foundation, be grounded in humility, which alone will render you worthy of the position you occupy and will draw upon you the favors of God; who, albeit He is so great, looks upon all that is most lowly in heaven and on earth." Those ties of friendship, formed and multiplied by Divine Providence, which the saint had cultivated for many years with the most illustrious men of his time, became of great importance when the Crusade was announced. He made them conduce to the success of his ministry in a wonderful manner; and thus, before he aroused all the western nations by the power of his words, he influenced the

---

\* Exodus iii. 5.
† 1 John v.6.

highest grades of society in many different directions, by a less visible but more penetrative force. He directed the consciences of kings and pontiffs; and through them he was the director of his age. Amongst those souls whom he led in the ways of God, and who, more than any others, at this moment needed the light of the servant of God, we may mention the Queen of Jerusalem. Notwithstanding the distance which separated them, Melisinda had long kept up a close correspondence with St. Bernard.* She was a widow, and a queen-regent, and these two titles gave her a special claim on his solicitude. But St. Bernard, who wrote letters of twelve pages to the least of the poor, and the meanest monk, sent but few lines in answer to the kings and great ones of the world. "Accept," he writes to Melisinda, "accept these few words which I send you as seeds from a distant country, that they may produce a rich harvest in your heart.

"You have lost the king, your husband; and your son, the present king, is as yet too young to bear the weight of a crown. All eyes are turned upon you. Arm yourself with courage in the present circumstances; display, as a woman, all the vigor of a man; regulate all your affairs with so much moderation and prudence that none of your subjects may have to regret the loss of their king, or to draw any comparison between the sovereign they have lost, and the sovereign who fills his place. You will say, 'I cannot do this; it is beyond my capacity and strength; I am only a weak, timid woman, and a novice in the art of governing.' Yes, my daughter, these are real difficulties, and I know them very well. But though the waves of the sea are terrific, God has almighty power to calm them; nothing can resist His power." In another letter, he addresses her in the following beautiful words: "That you may reign worthily over men, it is necessary, my daughter, that God should reign over you. The Queen of the South came to

---

* This assertion is founded on the following passage from a letter of St. Bernard to Melisinda: "I am the first to renew our former correspondence, in the hope of receiving a speedy answer," etc. Ep. 239. See also the Ep. 204, 351, and 352, the only letters to be found in the collection; but they afford evidence of other letters which no longer exist. They are all in the style of a father writing familiarly to his spiritual daughter.

Jerusalem to hear the wisdom of Solomon; she desired to become the scholar of that great prince, that she might learn how to govern her states. But the master whom I propose to you is greater than Solomon—it is Jesus Christ Himself, Jesus Christ crucified. Learn in His school, in your state of widowhood, to be meek and humble of heart; and in your capacity of queen, learn to love justice and protect innocence."

It was thus that, by his letters and his apostolic missions, the servant of God prepared the way for the new Crusade, and neglected to endeavor to excite the zeal of both princes and people. At length the Easter festival of the year 1146 came round. The fame of the sacred orator had drawn immense numbers to Vézelay. The king and his great vassals, Queen Eleanor, and several prelates, knights, and men of all ranks, met together on the brow of a hill, which had been chosen for the sitting of parliament, for want of a larger space. "For," writes the contemporary chronicler, "neither the large church, nor the public square, nor the castle could contain the vast multitudes which flocked together from all sides; therefore, a wooden machine (*vastam machinam*, says Odo de Denil—doubtless a kind of pulpit) was constructed on the side of the mountain, from whence the Abbot of Clairvaux might address the assembled people.

"St. Bernard, *fortified by apostolic authority and his own sanctity*, ascended the platform, having by his side the young king, Louis VII, who already wore his cross; and when the heavenly orator began, according to his custom, to diffuse the dew of the Divine Word, he was interrupted by an universal cry of 'The cross! the cross!'"

The preacher was unable to finish reading the Pope's encyclical letter. Raising his voice on high, he gave utterance to the plaintive accents of the holy city, and conjured the French princes and the Christian people to arm for the defence of the sepulchre of Christ!

"It is the will of God! it is the will of God!" the whole multitude cried out with one voice. The king, deeply moved, cast himself at St. Bernard's feet, in the presence of all the people, and solemnly pledged himself to march to the assistance of the Holy Land. Armed with the sacred sign of salvation, he spoke in his turn, and declaring to the people the happy resolution with which God had inspired him, he convoked these brave warriors, and represented to them, in moving terms, the opprobrium and blasphemy cast by the impious Philistine on the house of David. The words of the pious monarch, interrupted only by his sobs, electrified all hearts. The whole of that vast audience burst into tears, and the surrounding hills echoed the shouts of the multitude. The queen, following the example of Louis VII, asked, and received from the Abbot of Clairvaux, the pilgrim's cross; several bishops in their turn took the cross likewise; after them an immense number of lords and barons crowded round the platform and asked to receive the cross. Among the most illustrious, history mentions the brave Robert Le Dreux, the king's brother; Henry, son of the Count of Champagne; Theodoric d'Alsace, who at an advanced age preserved the intrepid vigor of youth; the chivalrous Enguerrand de Coucy; Archambauld, Lord of Bourbon; Hugh de Lusignan, a *number of other valiant warriors, knights, and men of low degree.* The supply of crosses was not sufficient for the great number of pilgrims; and St. Bernard tore his own garments, to make crosses of the fragments, in order to satisfy their pious impatience; and thus, in tattered garments, he remained until the evening, occupied in *sowing* rather *than distributing* these glorious symbols of Christian faith. During the following days the enthusiasm of the multitude, far from decreasing, was more and more augmented. The holy joy of the Crusaders was rapidly diffused on all sides, and the influence of example contributed to the success of the sacred word. The movement had begun in earnest, and the Spirit of God had prevailed and triumphed. At the prospect of a new Crusade all private animosities were forgotten. The Christian princes sealed their reconciliation by treaties of peace, and laid down their arms to reserve them for more worthy exploits. Louis VII, docile to the advice of St. Bernard, took all the necessary measures for the success of his undertaking; he sent ambassadors to Roger, King of Sicily, to obtain provisions and vessels; he wrote to the Emperor Conrad and the King of Hungary to ask of them a free passage through Germany and Hungary; and finally, with a solicitude becoming him as head of the undertaking, he sent deputies to Manuel Comnenus, Emperor of Constantinople; and after these preliminaries had been arranged, he fixed the time of departure for the ensuing Spring, and dismissed the assembly.

"Then," writes the chronicler, "all returned joyfully to their homes; and as to the Abbot of Clairvaux, he went about preaching in all quarters, and in a very short time the number of the Crusaders was multiplied beyond measure."

# CHAPTER XXXVI

PERSECUTION OF THE JEWS IN GERMANY AT THE TIME OF THE CRUSADE—ST. BERNARD UNDERTAKES THEIR DEFENCE—HIS LETTER TO THE PEOPLE OF GERMANY.

AFTER the assembly of Vézelay, St. Bernard visited the principal towns of Burgundy and the neighboring provinces, in order to enroll soldiers under the standard of the cross. The success of his preaching was everywhere enhanced by the fame of his miracles; and in a short time the whole of France was set on fire by the words of the man of God. He was revered as a second Moses sent by heaven to lead God's people to the promised land.

At Laon and Chartres, and in several other towns, meetings were held to hasten the preparations for the Crusade and consult for the interest of the pilgrims. St. Bernard was present at all the most important of these assemblies; and when he was unable to attend in person, he sent letters or deputed as his representatives monks who were animated with his spirit, and able to re-echo his words. At Chartres, the assembly deliberated on the choice of a general whose prudence and sagacity should fit him for the command of the whole army. "But," writes an annalist, "all will doubtless be astonished to learn that, by universal consent, the Abbot Bernard was promoted to the command of the expedition, to march at the head of the officers and soldiers.

Bernard refused this formidable honor; but, as he was urgently pressed to accept it, he referred his cause to the Pope, and besought of him not to abandon him to the *caprice of man*. "I know not," he writes, "on what grounds this assembly has chosen me to be the head and the prince of the army. For my part, I protest that I never wished, desired, or contemplated the possibility of such an event. As far as I can judge of my own strength, I do not think I should ever reach such distant regions; and, moreover, who am I, that I should range an army in order of battle, or march at the head of the troops? What could be more contrary to my profession, even though I possessed sufficient strength, and were not wanting in experience?" The Crusaders, when they gave their votes for St. Bernard, believed they should thus become invulnerable, so great was the confidence they reposed in him. They expected that victory would attend their steps, if the army were confided to the care of a man who seemed to share in the omnipotence of God. But he persisted in his first refusal, and the Pope approved his determination.

Whilst the holy Abbot of Clairvaux was thus occupied in preaching throughout France, Germany was troubled with violent disorders, which excited his solicitude to the utmost degree. Popular enthusiasm almost always oversteps the prescribed bounds, even when it proceeds from a good motive; it is a difficult matter to preserve it from the influence of human passions; and the people, blinded by frenzy, become cruel, and call for victims to satisfy their fury. At the time of the first Crusade, the impetuous zeal of the soldiers of the cross had been kindled against the Jews, under the pretext of not leaving at home those enemies of Christ whom they were going to attack in a distant land. Upon the occasion of every new expedition fresh scenes of carnage took place; and the second Crusade had no sooner been announced, than a persecution of this kind was declared in all the towns bordering on the Rhine. A German monk named Rodolph left the cell of his monastery to summon the people to exterminate both Jews and Saracens. His vehement words met with a too ready sympathy in all the provinces which he visited. At Cologne, Mentz, Worms, Spires, and Strasbourg, the cries of death to the Jews were mingled with the war-cries of the Crusaders; and the holy cause of Christian chivalry was very nearly compromised by the most culpable excesses.

The accounts of these disorders were sorrowful tidings to all the servants of God, who were animated by the spirit of the Gospel; but, in these circumstances, none equalled St. Bernard in the exercise of the most lively compassion and mighty charity. He immediately wrote letters to Germany, to put a stop to the preaching of the fanatical apostle; and owing to his interference, the Jews found protectors on all sides. The bishops, above all, undertook their defence. Henry, the Archbishop of Mayence, sheltered them in his own house; but notwithstanding this asylum, they could not all escape from the fury of their persecutors and some were massacred at the very feet of the prelate.

There is still extant an interesting chronicle written by a contemporary Jew, who was desirous of transmitting to posterity the remembrance of the woes of Israel and the gratitude of his nation towards St. Bernard. The writer was thirteen years of age when the Crusade was preached in 1146. While he was yet a child, he was present at the tragic scenes which he relates; and his interesting narrative is so nearly connected with our present subject, we cannot do better than give some extracts in this place. It begins thus: "I, Joshua Ben-Meir, was born in the month Tebeth, 5257. My family belongs to the sacerdotal race; and when my father was banished from Spain, he settled in the city of Avignon, in Provence, watered by the Rhone. From thence we went to Genoa, where we have ever since remained.

"When the western people learned that the Turks had retaken Edessa and some other provinces in Judea, formerly conquered by the uncircumcised, Pope Eugenius sent deputies to all parts, to say to the kings and people—What do you here? We are overwhelmed by calamities, and you are unmoved. Take courage! March to the land of Israel; exterminate the Turks, and cut them off from the number of the nations! Then the priest Bernard went from town to town, carrying everywhere the complaints of the uncircumcised people of the East.

"But this was a time of desolation and mourning for the house of Jacob, which was oppressed with extreme sorrow and covered with wounds; her knees failed; groans of sorrow proceeded from her entrails; her face became pale with anguish and fear: for a priest, named Rodolph, came to preach in Germany and to mark with a particular seal all those who were about to fight for Jerusalem. This wicked man excited the people, by vehement discourses, to exterminate those amongst us who had been spared in the first persecutions. He said to them, 'Come, the hour has arrived for this people; we must put an end to them; they must be massacred to the last man!'

"This priest then went to many towns, seducing the Christian dogs, and representing to them that they must first massacre the Jews, and then follow him to Palestine. The Jews suffered anguish, like unto that of a woman in the throes of childbirth. They trembled and shuddered, finding no refuge nor hope anywhere. Then they cried unto God—'O God, Adonai,' they said, 'look on us with pity! It is not fifty years since our blood was poured out like water, and we were put to death for confessing Thy holy name; and, behold, we receive new chastisements! Hast Thou then cast us off forever? Wilt Thou do nothing more in our favor for the glory of Thy powerful and terrible name?'

"The Lord God was moved by the groans of His people; He remembered His covenant, and returned to His great mercies. He raised up against this cruel Belial the wise Bernard of Clairvaux, a town in France. This priest (according to their way of speaking) calmed them, and said: 'March towards Zion; defend the tomb of our Christ! But touch ye not the Jews; speak to them with mildness: for they are of the flesh and bones of the Messiah; and, if you molest them, you will run the risk of touching the very apple of the Lord's eye! No; the disciple Rodolph has not preached according to the truth; for Truth has said, by the mouth of the Psalmist, 'Slay them not, lest at any time my people forget.' (Ps. lviii.12).

"Thus spoke this wise man, and his words were powerful; for he was loved and respected by all. They listened to him, and the fire of their anger was cooled, and they did not accomplish all the evil they had intended to do. The priest Bernard had not, however, received either money or ransom from the Jews; it was his heart which led him to love them, and suggested to him to speak good words for Israel. I bless Thee, O my God; for we had roused Thine anger, and Thou hast spared us and consoled us by raising up this just man, without whom none of our lives would have been saved. Thanks be to Him who saves and comforts us! Amen."

The writer, after this preamble, relates numerous cruel actions which were perpetrated, even when the persecution had ceased to be general. In many places, the Jews were obliged to leave their homes and seek an asylum in the caves and mountains. At Cologne, the archbishop shut them up in the fortress of Falkenberg to save them from the pursuit of their enemies. Two young Israelites, who had left the castle, were assassinated on the mountain; their wretched father braved every danger to discover the murderer; he found him and dragged him by force to the archbishop's house, crying out with tears for justice and vengeance. The culprit was condemned to lose his eyes, and he died after this torture. "May all the enemies of the name of Israel perish thus!" writes the chronicler. At Wurtzburg, a report was suddenly spread that a Christian had been drowned in the river. The Jews were accused of this crime; and the populace rose against them, and massacred them in great numbers. "Rabbi Isaac," says the same writer, "was killed while at his book, together with twenty-one of his disciples, who surrounded him. A young girl, their sister, was taken and dragged, in spite of her lamentations, to the *house of lies*, and as she had the courage to spit upon the idol, she was ill-treated with blows, and was left senseless on the marble pavement. She feigned to be dead, for fear of receiving fresh outrages, and *stirred neither hand nor foot*. But, towards midnight, when she was left alone, a Christian woman who found her there took compassion on her, and afterwards restored her to her father. May the name of God be eternally blessed. Amen."

These and many other such occurrences which daily took place troubled the holy joy and hope which St. Bernard felt in the cause of the Crusade. The servant of God wrote forthwith to the Archbishop of Mentz; and in his letter he breaks forth into a torrent of indignation against the conduct of Rodolph: "I remember well that sentence uttered by the Lord Himself—'*It must needs be that scandals come; but nevertheless, woe to that man by whom the scandal cometh.*' The man of whom you speak has received his mission neither from God nor from men, nor by men. If he pretends that he has a right to preach, because he is a monk or hermit, teach him that a monk's office is not to speak but to weep; and that to a hermit the whole world ought to be a prison, and the desert a paradise; but he, on the contrary, regards his solitude as a prison, and the world as a paradise! O heartless man! O shameless man, whose foolishness is set on a candlestick that it may appear before the eyes of all men! I have three things to reproach him with: First, he has usurped the ministry of the Word; secondly, he has braved the authority of the bishops; thirdly, he has sanctioned homicide... What then? Will not the Church triumph much more gloriously over the Jews by persuading them, and leading them back to God, than by immolating them at the point of the sword? Does she then ask in vain, by incessant prayer, that the Lord our God will deliver that perfidious nation from the veil which covers its understanding, and deprives it of the light of truth? This prayer of the Church would have no meaning, if she despaired of reclaiming infidels to the faith. She prays, because she knows the merciful designs of Him who returns good for evil, love for hatred. What do the Scriptures say? '*Slay them not.*' And again, '*When the fulness of the Gentiles shall come in, all Israel shall be saved.*' And again, '*When the Lord buildeth up Jerusalem, he will gather together the dispersed of Israel.*' This is what the Scriptures proclaim: 'And thou, thou dost make liars of the prophets and apostles, and renderest of no avail the treasures of Christ's mercy and love.' No, the doctrine which thou dost preach, is not thine own; it is the doctrine of the spirit of error, of the father of lies, who hast sent thee; thou dost repeat the lessons of thy master, *who was a murderer from the beginning*; who loved falsehood, and performed lying works. O detestable doctrine! O monstrous and infernal wisdom, contrary to that of the apostles and prophets, and the enemy of all grace and piety. Sacrilegious doctrine, which was conceived by impiety, and can only bring forth iniquity... I limit myself to these words; I cannot say any more on the subject."

The crimes which were perpetrated in Germany were not our saint's only subject of sorrow. He had to deplore the general condition of that country, which, for many years, had been a prey to violent political convulsions. The quarrels between the empire and the papacy had weakened the authority of both these powers, and their influence over the people was almost entirely paralyzed. The implacable animosities of the Guelphs and Ghibellines were the cause of incessant trouble to the reigning power; and Conrad III, who had but lately succeeded to the throne of Lotharius, could only keep the balance even by repeated concessions.

In this state of things, Germany and other nations of Christendom stood in need of some powerful motive which should restore harmony, and heal all divisions, at least for a time, by summoning all to labor for one common end. The holy war seemed likely to insure the fulfillment of this object, and such was the conviction of St. Bernard. The Germans, as a nation, had taken no part in the first Crusade; they had been left outside of the expansive and progressive movement of civilization; besides this, the hostile spirit which they cherished towards the Head of the Church had deprived them of that principle of unity which is the governing power of all Christian constitutions; from the concurrence of these various causes arose the discords which then prevailed in Germany. The empire was tottering under the weight of its ancient power; and its subjects, who were divided amongst themselves, vainly strove to overcome the interior and exterior obstacles which tended to the dissolution of their national spirit, or rather hindered it from taking form and consistency. A great work remained, therefore, to be done in Germany, and it was by St. Bernard that the idea of it was conceived. He had already conferred with the Pope on the subject; and the persecution of the Jews afforded him an opportunity of manifesting his intentions publicly. He resolved, therefore, to visit Germany; but before undertaking so arduous a journey, he addressed a memorable epistle to the Christian people of Germany, in which, more than in any other act, he exposed his views relative to the Crusades. All the historians of the time have inserted this important document in their annals; we do not fear to prolong the subject by extracting the principal passages of this epistle:

"To our lords and most dear fathers, the archbishops, bishops, all the clergy, and Frank people of Germany and Bavaria, Bernard, Abbot of Clairvaux, wishing they may abound in the Holy Ghost.

"The subject on which I address you relates to Jesus Christ and our common salvation. Pardon, then, the unworthiness of him who speaks to you, in consideration of Him whose interpreter he is. It is true, I am myself of little account; but the zeal with which Christ inspires me for your good is not a matter of little account. My brethren, this is an acceptable time, a time of grace and salvation. The Christian world is disturbed; the whole earth is troubled; for the God of heaven has begun to destroy the country where He once made Himself visible to men, and conversed among them for more than thirty years—that country, rendered illustrious by His miracles, consecrated by His Blood, and vivified by the first fruits of the Resurrection; and now, because of our sins, that promised land is devastated by a sacrilegious people, the enemies of the cross. Alas! if we do not vigorously resist their fury, soon will the Holy City be ruined, the sacred memorials of our redemption and those places where the Blood of the Immaculate Lamb was shed, will be delivered up to profanation and sacrilege. What do you, brave soldiers? and you, O servants of the Cross? Will you abandon the Holy One to the dogs, will you suffer your pearls to be trampled under foot by swine? How many sinners, after confessing their sins with tears, have visited those places to implore the Divine mercy, since the time when all impiety was banished therefrom by the religious valor of our fathers? The enemy has seen all this, and he trembled with fury; he gnashes his teeth and pines away with envy. He incites his ministers, the children of perdition, to ruin this land and destroy all vestiges of religion. This irreparable loss would be a subject of eternal sorrow for future ages; and it would stamp our own age with endless opprobrium and disgrace. Sinners! admire the infinite resources and the depth of God's goodness! In fact, what opportunity of salvation more worthy of Divine wisdom could he offer to Christians buried in all sorts of crimes, who have been murderers, ravishers, adulterers, and perjurers, than by deigning to make them ministers and cooperators in His designs. This is a great subject of confidence for you. O sinners! If He desired to punish you, He would reject your services, whereas He now claims them. I repeat it once more, think seriously on the treasure of His mercies. He disposes of events in such a manner, that He would seem to ask your assistance solely to have an occasion of assisting you Himself. He desires to be regarded as your debtor, that He may repay you, and grant you His forgiveness and eternal glory. Hasten, then, to display your zeal, and take up arms in defence of the Christian name, you whose provinces are teeming with young and valiant warriors, if I may believe public report. Renew the ranks of your soldiers, and banish from among you that malice which has hitherto armed you against one another, and caused you to perish by your own hands. What madness to stain your sword with the blood of your brother, and to deprive him, by one blow, of the life of both soul and body. Oh, what misery! your victory is fatal to yourself, you fall under the wound which you have dealt against your brother. No, that is not courage, it is neither magnanimity nor bravery; it is a frenzy, a madness, which makes you run such risks. I offer to you, warlike nation, a more worthy occasion of fighting without danger, of conquering with glory, and of dying happily. Blessed is he who raises the standard of the cross! Blessed is he who hastens to arm himself with this saving sign! After all, my brethren, I advise you, in the apostle's name, not to believe every spirit . . . I rejoice to hear of your zeal for religion; but it must be tempered by knowledge. Far from ill-treating the Jews, you ought to spare them; you are even forbidden by the Scriptures to banish them from your land. Hear what the Church says by the mouth of the prophet: '*God hath made known to me concerning his enemies: slay them not, lest at any time my people forget.*' —Ps. lix.

"The Jews are, as it were, the figures and living memorials of the passion and sufferings of our Saviour. They are dispersed throughout the world, that the just punishment of their crimes may be the witness of our redemption. Wherefore the Church says, in the same Psalm, '*Scatter them by thy power; and bring them down, O Lord, my protector.*' —Ps. lix.

"These words have been literally fulfilled; they are dispersed, humbled, and reduced to a hard servitude. However, they will one day be converted, and God will look down on them with mercy. 'When the fulness of the nations shall have received the Gospel, then all Israel shall be saved.' On the other hand, if the Jewish people were exterminated, the hope of their conversion would be vain. Even if they were idolaters, they ought to be tolerated, and not massacred. If they do us any violence, we have magistrates to repress and punish them. The piety of Christians resists the rebellious; but it spares the submissive, especially those who are the depositaries of the law and the promises, '*whose are the fathers, and of whom is Christ, according to the flesh, who is over all things, God blessed for ever.*'[*] It will be necessary to entrust the command of the army to skilful and experienced captains; and all the troops should march in one body, that they may be

---

[*] Rom. ix. 4,5

better protected. You know, doubtless, the adventures of Peter the Hermit in the first Crusade. This man having placed himself at the head of the army which was entrusted to his guidance, exposed it to so many perils, that scarce one escaped from death, either by hunger or the sword. I should fear the same misfortune for you, were you to follow the same course. I pray the Lord to preserve you therefrom. Amen."

# CHAPTER XXXVII

ST. BERNARD GOES TO GERMANY—HIS INTERVIEW
WITH THE EMPEROR, CONRAD III—EXTRAORDINARY
MANIFESTATION OF HIS GIFT OF MIRACLES.

The apostolic letter of St. Bernard produced a deep impression on the warlike people of the Rhine, who were already incited by the example of the French. The numbers of the Crusaders were everywhere increased, not only in Germany, but likewise in Hungary, England, Italy, and all the countries to which the Abbot of Clairvaux addressed his pathetic epistles; but, except in France, this universal movement was ill-directed, and degenerated into merely partial agitations, where there was no head to guide and control it. The saint saw the urgent necessity of applying a remedy to this state of things; but it was difficult—nay, almost impossible—for him, at his distance from the scene of action, to establish the spirit of order and unity amongst so many heterogeneous elements. His letters to the Lombards and other people of Italy aroused their zeal, but failed in organizing their forces, or in imparting a spirit of concord to their enterprise. In England the difficulties were greater than in any other country. Never since the invasion of the Danes had that unfortunate country suffered from miseries to be compared to those which it endured under the government of the weak Stephen. That spirit of insubordination, which was fermenting in other countries, had become, as it were, naturalized in England, together with the Norman chiefs who had conquered the country. The people were slaves; but the lords, entrenched in their fortresses, aimed at independence; and, in contempt of law and order, they daily provoked each other to endless and sanguinary combats. The crown itself, which was disputed by Queen Matilda, was a brand of discord thrown amidst the passions of the populace. Such a state of affairs gave little hope of success to the preachers of the Crusade. It is true a certain isolated number of brave knights enrolled themselves under the banner of the cross; but the great mass of the nation, like the waves of the sea which surrounded their island, was a prey to such violent disturbances that it was not possible for the voice of religion to triumph over these obstacles. It was necessary that the various parties should have time to exhaust themselves by their own excesses; for a crisis of social as of individual life can only be calmed when it has begun to sink into a kind of lassitude. St. Bernard, therefore, renouncing the hope of uniting all the states of Christendom in the great idea of the Crusade, fixed his eyes on France and Germany—the two nations which, by their superiority of intelligence and power, held the first rank among the people of Europe.

It was, indeed, a vast project to unite together the Franks of Germany and the Franks of Gaul in the holy cause of the faith. However, the state of the empire appeared to offer more resources than England. The political crisis in Germany was on the decline, and the parties which still existed were less subdivided and less virulent against one another. The Germans, who naturally loved heroic adventures, displayed, moreover, a pious compassion for the misfortunes of Jerusalem, and they seemed to have long awaited a chief who should be capable and worthy of leading them forth. But such a chief was not to be found. The Emperor Conrad III, who had been elected by the influence of the Ghibellines, was held in check by the formidable party of the Guelphs. Their inveterate enmities did not, it is true, lead to an open rupture; but they cherished a mutual animosity and a morose and threatening defiance, which was never far from a breach of the peace. No German prince, were he Guelph or Ghibelline, would have dared to leave his hearth for a distant expedition, while matters were in such a state; and thus the generous ardor of the Germans was completely thwarted.

St. Bernard felt himself interiorly moved to go amongst these *valiant Teutons*, so renowned for their bravery, that he might enroll them in the service of Christ. Doubtless he foresaw that he would reap an abundant harvest; but he was not prepared for a success surpassing that which he obtained in France. His zeal allowed of no delay; he took no account of the severity of the season, nor of the fatigues of the journey, nor of his continual infirmities; and, about the end of the autumn of the same year (1146), a short time after the assembly of Chartres, he set out, accompanied by two monks of Clairvaux—Godfrey, his biographer, and Gerard.

Here begins a long series of labors and miracles, which the companions of the holy monk registered day by day and which are loudly attested by contemporary historians, which the twelfth century, with one voice, has related for the admiration of posterity, and which even the most incredulous writers have been forced to admit, though they could not comprehend them.* Godfrey, one of the secretaries of the illustrious abbot during this journey, comforted the community at Clairvaux by sending them a faithful account of the miracles wrought in Germany; and this writer, whose style is so admirable for its ingenuous simplicity, complains that his pen cannot suffice to relate so many things. "The servant of God," he writes, "works miracles more easily than we can write them." From his person seemed to flow all those virtues which once characterized the divine mission of the greatest apostles. His breath, his blessing, his touch, his prayer, his very presence, wrought prodigies of wonder. The most inveterate maladies disappeared suddenly at the voice of the man of God;

---

* Among the many authoritative testimonies which we might quote here, we shall only avail ourselves of one, that of a Protestant—Luden, a grave historian, who is generally ruled by the spirit of his sect, and shows little favor to St. Bernard. "It is absolutely impossible," he says, "to doubt of the authenticity of St. Bernard's miracles (*durchaus nicht in zweiful zu ziehen);* for we cannot suppose that there was any fraud, either on the part of those who relate them, or on the part of him who worked them." The German historian, after relating, in support of his assertion, the circumstances in which the saint restored speech to a man who had been deaf and dumb from his birth, concludes his note with the following judicious remark: "If the anguish of filial piety suddenly restored speech to the dumb son of Croessus, who, on beholding his father in peril, cried out, 'Man, kill not my father!'—if fear, I say, loosened the tongue of this man, why should not faith produce the same effect?"—Luden, *Gesch der Teutschen*, buch xxi., cap. 10, vol. i., nota 12. This observation is just; but would it not have been more lucid, and, above all, more Christian, to consider the power of man as a participation in the Divine omnipotence, and as a gift of God bestowed on the sanctity of regenerate man?

whose populations, in a number of different towns, published, with gratitude, the miracles they had witnessed. In every place on his journey he wrought the most astonishing and instantaneous cures; the blind recovered their sight; to the deaf and dumb hearing and speech were restored; the paralytic received the use of their limbs; the possessed, the lunatic, and the demoniac were delivered from the spirits which tormented them. But the greatest of his miracles was the conversion of hardened hearts and the penances to which public sinners submitted.*

The Abbot of Clairvaux had proceeded at once to Mentz, where the impetuous monk Rodolph was disseminating his doctrines. Moved to sorrow by the misfortunes of the Jews, he had it very much at heart to stop the guilty excesses of which they were the victims. In this matter his ministry of peace had nearly proved fatal to himself; for the hatred of the populace was implacable, and when it became known that the Abbot of Clairvaux was interfering in favor of the Jews, menacing cries were raised against him. It required no less than the authority of St. Bernard himself to quell the tumult. However, he did not run the risk of opposing himself publicly to Rodolph; for he was fearful lest the whole city might rise in sedition, so great was the influence which this man had acquired. He endeavored to accomplish by meekness what bishops and magistrates had vainly endeavored to do by force. Taking him aside, he represented to him the responsibility which he was assuming to himself, and, at the end of a short conference, he prevailed on him to retire to his cloister. Thus, at the sole presence of St. Bernard, the false prophet, who by his senseless harangues had almost compromised the noble cause of the Crusades, disappeared from the eyes of the world.

As soon as order was restored at Mentz, the servant of God set out again on his journey, to continue the course of his apostolic labors. He passed through Worms, where he enrolled a great number in the Christian militia; but what he had most at heart was to

---

* M. de Sismondi (*Hist. des Fran.*, vol. v.), being unable to refute facts so universally attested, explains them, after the manner of Voltaire, by attributing them to fanaticism. The incredulous must needs have a great amount of credulity, to believe that fanaticism can restore sight to a man born blind.

rejoin the emperor, who was at that time holding his court in the town of Frankfort-on-Maine. He was personally acquainted with Conrad III; and the latter could not have forgotten the services which he had rendered to him when, thirteen years before, he had reconciled the house of Hohenstauffen with Lotharius. He therefore hoped, in the present conjuncture, to exercise a salutary influence on the monarch's mind, and to interest him seriously in the great object of his journey. He met with a distinguished reception at Frankfort, it is true; but nothing seemed to justify the hope he had conceived. None of the German princes showed themselves favorably disposed towards the holy expedition; and the emperor himself, with whom St. Bernard had several conferences on the subject, so far from furthering his views, refused to take any share in so doubtful an enterprise. On one occasion, indeed, the emperor replied very dryly to the repeated instances of the saint, and told him that nothing was further from his mind than the thought of a Crusade. The Abbot of Clairvaux did not press the point any more, and *mildly answered that he would be careful not to importune his royal majesty thenceforth on this subject.*

From that time he began to think of returning to Clairvaux; for his mission in Germany seemed to him to have come to a sad termination. "Besides," adds the chronicler, "he was impatient to see his own once more; *for the mother could not forget the children she had brought forth, and who, for more than a year, had been separated from their mother's bosom.*" He was, therefore, anxious to hasten his departure; but the emperor, fearing lest he might have grieved the servant of God, made every effort to detain him for some days. In reality, Conrad was very uneasy in conscience; he had never opened his mind to St. Bernard, and he was careful not to manifest any sentiments which might betray his wavering resolutions; but while he thus endeavored to deceive himself his agitation betrayed his secret uneasiness, and his conduct towards the herald of the Crusade and the marks of singular veneration which he publicly bestowed on him proved that if he had no sympathy for his mission, he had, at least, a religious fear of raising any obstacles in his way. One day an immense crowd gathered in the church to see the face of the man of God. He had suddenly cured a paralytic old man, who was known throughout the town for his bountiful alms-deeds; and this miracle, as well as many others no less striking, had been proclaimed by the chimes of the bells and the admiring cries of the multitude. The concourse was so great that no power could restrain the crowds of the people, who rushed impetuously into the vast basilica. St. Bernard, closely surrounded on all sides, would have been smothered by the crowd, had not the emperor, throwing off his mantle, raised him up in his powerful arms and borne him away to a place of safety.*

In the town, Count Adelphus, one of the nobles in the emperor's train, was desirous of trying in person the effect of the power of the Abbot of Clairvaux. He brought to him a blind and lame child, whose cure seemed to him utterly impossible. The thaumaturgus blessed him, and at the same moment the child recovered the use of his limbs, and his eyes were opened.

We may conceive the sensation caused by these wonders, and the weight which they added to the mission of him who performed them. The people demanded the cross; but the princes, who were restrained by political considerations, wavered in a state of anxious perplexity.

St. Bernard, from that time, foresaw what would be the happy result of his labors; however, like the wise husbandman, he thought it would be well to quit for a time the field he had cultivated, and to leave the care of ripening the seeds of the word to the power of divine grace. He prepared, therefore, to leave Frankfort and to return to Clairvaux, whither he was called by the desires and the remembrance of his brethren; but a new sacrifice was required of him, and his self-denial gained the victory once more over his desire of repose. Hermann, Bishop of Constance, earnestly entreated him to edify his vast diocese by preaching the Crusade. For a long time Bernard resisted, but at length, *overcome by the constancy of my Lord of Constance*, he embarked with him, and sailed up the Rhine. They stopped at the towns and principal villages on the banks of the river, and reaped everywhere the most abundant fruits from the preaching of the cross. This voyage was a

---

\* A chronicler relates that the emperor laid the saint at the feet of a miraculous statue of the Blessed Virgin, and that the statue, with a sweet voice, said these words in the Roman language: "*Ben venia, mi fra Bernarde!*" To which the saint replied, "*Gran merce, mi Domina.*"

kind of triumphal march. A numerous train followed St. Bernard. Besides the two monks of Clairvaux, who acted as secretaries, "we were several companions," says one of them: first, the Bishop of Constance, and his chaplain, Eberhard; the Abbot Baldwin and Frovinus, an old monk of Einsieldelen, afterwards superior of the convent of Engellery, at Untervalten; then, three secular priests, Philip, Archdeacon of Liege, who became a monk at Clairvaux;* Otto, and Franco, with whom was also the celebrated Alexander, of Cologne, who became one of the most illustrious men of the order of Citeaux. This latter was on his way to Rome, when he met the saint and was a witness of his miracles. From that time he attached himself to him and never left him. The company consisted of eleven venerable persons besides Bernard; and every evening they used to note down, in an itinerary journal, the glorious actions which they had witnessed. But they were unable to write down all: "*for it would require volumes to recount all we have seen,*" says one of them; "*but if we were silent the stones would cry out.*" Philip of Clairvaux sent to the Archbishop of Rheims an extract from his journal, which has been preserved intact; and this curious document, together with many others of that time, will enable the reader to follow the apostolic journeys of St. Bernard, step by step.

In the latter days of November, 1146, the holy company set out on their way to Constance. They spent Sunday, December 1, at Kintzingen, and the two following days at Friburg, in Brisgau. Let us hear the travellers speak:

*Bishop Hermann*—"The first day, at Friburg, there were only some poor, mean people, who asked for the cross. The holy abbot made us pray that the eyes of the rich might also be opened, and hardly was this prayer ended, *when the richest—nay, even the most hardened*—came to receive the cross from his own hand.

*Philip*—"Let us note down, likewise, the manner in which he restored sight to a blind old man; virtue had gone out of our holy

---

\* It is from the said Philip we have these details. He says, in the following ardent and simple words—"I entered the school of Christ, and bade adieu to the world for ever, and for ever and ever."

father; not from him, however, but from the word and the sign of life.

*Hermann*—"This morning, fourth feria, after Mass, I presented to him a girl who had a withered hand; he cured her on the spot.

"*Philip*—I saw him restore sight to a child deaf and dumb from his birth.

*Hermann*—"I myself spoke to the child at the moment when the Sign of the Cross was made on him, and he heard and answered me distinctly.

*The Abbot Frovinus*—"A mother brought us her little blind child; the Sign of the Cross restored his sight; but what was the mother's surprise when the child stretched out his hand to an apple which I offered to him!

*Eberhard*—"On leaving the church, an infirm and paralytic man, who could only drag himself along, recommended himself to the holy abbot. Hardly had the latter touched him with his stick, in my presence, than the man felt himself cured, and went away, leaping for joy."*

These miracles, which are noted down simply and shortly, one after another, by ocular witnesses, would form too large a volume, if we were to place them under the eyes of our readers. They were so numerous that the witnesses themselves were unable to detail them all. At Doningen, near Rheinfeld, where they spent the first Sunday of Advent, Bernard cured, in one day, nine blind persons, ten who were deaf or dumb, and eighteen lame or paralytic; on the following Wednesday, at Schafhausen, the number of his miracles was still greater. At last, on Friday, the 13th of December, they arrived at Constance. The bells of the town announced the wonders which attended the footsteps of the man of God. The people, with a thousand cries of "*Kyrie eleison!*" "*Kyrie eleison!*" "*Christ uns gnade,*" ran to meet him, giving glory to Jesus Christ. All praised God, and not one mouth was silent in the midst of these joyful manifestations. The preaching of the Crusade seemed to have become a mere accessory in this universal agitation. He spoke—or, rather, he showed himself—and, at the mere sight of the apostle, at the first sound of his voice, the people burst into

---

* Phil. de Clarav., p. 1188

tears; and the minds of his hearers became humble and docile, and answered his appeal. Thus, a long stay in each town was not only unnecessary, but even impossible, on account of the tumultuous concourse of people who flocked together, desirous to hear the saint's words, and still more anxious to see his miracles. At Constance, as at Frankfort, he was nearly suffocated. His garments were torn off, piecemeal, to make crosses, *which he found very inconvenient*; and he was frequently obliged to accept new clothes.

It was about this time that St. Bernard converted a young knight, who was *rich in earthly goods, but poor in those of heaven, and full of vice and iniquity*. His name was Henry; he had received a good education; and as he *spoke French and German*, he attached himself to the saint, to serve as his interpreter. This remarkable conversion produced a no less remarkable miracle, which we must not pass over in silence. The noble Henry was riding alongside of St. Bernard, on the highway, when he was all at once followed by one of his former squires, who attacked him with jeers and insults. *He was a man of Belial, a lover of perversity, and incredulous in all things*; he blasphemed the servant of God, and cried out with all his might, "Go, follow the devil; and may the devil take you!" While the travellers thus continued their journey in peace, the holy abbot was entreated to give his blessing to a crippled woman, whom they laid at his feet. This occurrence only served to increase the fury of the madman; but when he beheld the woman suddenly cured, he fell back, as if struck by an unseen hand, and lay stretched on the earth, without life or motion. His former master, horrified at his awful death, cast himself at St. Bernard's feet, and implored him to take pity on this soul, *which Satan had filled with malediction*. "It is on your account," he said, "it is because he blasphemed against you, that this terrible judgment has befallen him!" "God forbid," replied the saint, "that anyone should die on my account!" Then, retracing his steps, he leaned over the corpse of the squire, and slowly recited the Lord's Prayer, his voice tremulous with emotion. "Hold him by the head," he said, to the numerous standers-by. Then, anointing him with his spittle, which he frequently used as if it were a medicinal remedy, he cried out, "In the name of the Lord, arise!" And he repeated, "In the name of the Father, and of the Son, and of the

Holy Ghost, may God restore thee to life!" These words, uttered in a solemn tone amidst the mournful silence of the spectators, had hardly ceased when the dead man arose and looked up to heaven. At the sight of the corpse, erect and restored to life, the people manifested their admiration and surprise by loud acclamations. The saint, meanwhile, addressed him as follows: "Now," he said, "what are thy dispositions? what art thou about to do?" "My father, I will do all you command," replied the squire, who was completely changed. He took the cross, and enrolled himself in the ranks of the Crusaders. One of those present asked him if he had really been dead. "I was dead," he answered, "and I heard the sentence of my condemnation; for if the holy abbot had not interposed, I should now be in hell." Henry, who was more deeply struck than the rest by this extraordinary event, retired to Clairvaux, where he made his profession; and he was oftentimes wont to relate to his assembled brethren the grace which he had received, and the wonderful prodigy which he had witnessed.

Shortly after, St. Bernard left Constance with the same companions who had attended him thither, except Bishop Hermann, who gave his place to a holy priest named Wolkemar. They passed through Zurich, Rheinfelden, Basle, and Winterthur, and arrived at Strasburg on the eve of the fourth Sunday of Advent, December 22, 1146. The miracles ceased not during this memorable journey; and, to use the expression of one of his biographers, "We should fear not to say enough if we only mentioned some of his miracles; and to tell less than the truth if we related a great many. When he was preaching at Strasburg and the other German cities, it is a wonderful fact that, though he only spoke in Latin or in the Frank language, he was understood by all, and his words moved even those who knew no other tongue than German." The monk Godfrey says that these persons heard him with so much the more affection, as they were moved and touched by the very power of his words far more than by the interpretation of a learned man who explained his discourses. They proved this by the compunction with which they struck their breasts and shed tears.

Meanwhile, the day of Our Lord's nativity drew near; and the emperor had chosen that festival to hold a general diet in the city of Spires. St. Bernard had promised to be present at the assembly. He left Strasburg the evening of Sunday, December 22, and arrived at Spires on the following Tuesday, being the vigil of Christmas. The inhabitants of the different towns and villages stood on the banks of the river, waiting with impatience for the vessels to pass by, that they might receive the blessing of the man of God, and lay the sick at his feet. All had their share in the wonderful grace which God attached to every word and action of His servant.

His entrance into the imperial city of Spires has been described by a number of contemporary chroniclers. "The bishop, the clergy, and the citizens came to meet him with great solemnity, with crosses and banners; and the members of the various guilds, carrying the badges of their profession. He was conducted through the city, amid the sound of bells and sacred hymns, to the door of the cathedral, where the emperor and the German princes received him with all the honor due to the Pope's envoy. There was an immense crowd of people, some of whom had come from a great distance, to see and hear the saint, and to behold the countenance of the wonder-worker.

"The procession advanced from the great doctor of the cathedral to the choir, chanting joyfully the hymn to the Queen of Heaven, '*Salve Regina*.' Bernard, conducted by the emperor himself, walked in the middle of the procession, surrounded by crowds of people, and deeply moved on beholding the interior of the majestic basilica; but when the last accents of the hymn to the Virgin had died away through the sacred aisles, after these words, '*Filium tuum nobis post hoc exilium ostende!*' the holy abbot, transported by his enthusiasm, added a threefold aspiration, '*O clemens! O pia O dulcis Virgo Maria!*'"

These sweet and tender words, which flowed spontaneously from St. Bernard's heart, were thenceforth added to the hymn "*Salve Regina*," and completed its sublime poetry. They are still sung in all Catholic churches, at the appointed seasons; but, in the Cathedral of Spires, the "*Salve Regina*" is solemnly chanted every day in the year, in honor of St. Bernard; and this custom still exists. Plates of brass were laid down in the pavement of the church, to mark the footsteps of the man of God to posterity, and the places where he so touchingly implored the *clemency*, the *mercy*, and the *sweetness* of the Blessed Virgin Mary.

The miracles were less numerous at Spires, "because," said one of the companions of his journey, "the multitude of the curious was too great, and the glory of God does not manifest itself in favor of curiosity." The assembly at the diet was very large. The greater number of the bishops and princes met together to discuss the affairs of the empire; and in this august assembly the ceremony of the emperor's coronation increased the splendor of the religious solemnity. But St. Bernard was deeply concerned at the dispositions of these great personages. Their irreconcilable animosities rendered them deaf to any overtures of peace; and the servant of God vainly endeavored to allay their mutual grievances, and to make their personal interests give way to the cause of the Holy Sepulchre. But neither the miracles by which he proved that his mission was divine, nor the ardent and apostolic remonstrances which he addressed to the princes and to the monarch himself could overcome their supineness. Conrad, however, appeared to be more moved than the rest; and two days after Christmas, on the feast of St. John the Evangelist, after he had been urgently pressed by the Abbot of Clairvaux, he announced that he would deliberate on the matter in his council, and that, on the following day, he would give a definitive reply.

This was a critical moment. An incalculable number of events depended on the emperor's resolution. Bernard, however, did not wait until the next day. He was celebrating the Holy Sacrifice, in the presence of the court and a great number of the faithful, when, yielding to one of those inspirations which had so often produced great effects, he turned towards the people and pronounced an impassioned discourse on the woes of the Holy Land. In the midst of his oration, he addressed himself directly to the emperor; he spoke to him, *not as to a sovereign, but as to a simple individual*; he reminded him of the gifts he had received, and of the graces which had been vouchsafed to him; he reproached him with his ingratitude; and, full of Divine inspiration, he cried out, in a voice of thunder, "O man! what wilt thou answer in the day of judgment?". . . Conrad, struck with terror, and pierced, as it were, even to the marrow of his bones, interrupted the preacher, and demanded the cross of Christ. "I acknowledge," he said, with tears, "that God has given me many graces; and, with the help of the Lord, I will not render myself unworthy of them." And he added,

"I am ready to devote my life to the Lord, and to go withersoever He calls me!" The people, deeply moved and astonished at this extraordinary scene, raised their hands to heaven, and filled the basilica with prolonged acclamations; the whole city was in a state of excitement and commotion; and the earth re-echoed, afar off, the people's cries of joy and enthusiasm.

Meanwhile, the humble St. Bernard remained profoundly recollected after this miracle of miracles, and taking the sacred banner from the altar, he placed it in the emperor's hands and adorned him with the glorious symbol of the God of hosts. At the same moment all the princes, with one simultaneous impulse, knelt at the feet of the holy preacher and asked for the pilgrim's cross. Foremost amongst them was the young Frederic of Suabia, the emperor's nephew and the heir to the throne, afterwards so famous under the title of Barbarossa. He took the cross, in spite of the tears and entreaties of his aged father. The barons and knights eagerly followed the example of their lords. And not only the grandees, but the people—"*les menues gens et les gens du grand air*"—were desirous to receive the cross from St. Bernard's hands. No obstacle, no consideration could resist this unanimous impulse; the great interest of the Crusade had absorbed all other interests and feelings. Men differing in age, rank, education and descent, united together in the same cause and enrolled themselves under the same standard; and the diet which had been convoked to remedy the wrongs of Germany was now only occupied in discussing the fate of Jerusalem. This sudden change was looked upon by all as the *miracle of miracles*. Hope revived in every heart; and all, forgetting their past dissensions, roused themselves from their lethargy, to begin a new life and taste the consolations of religion. "Wonderful to tell," says a contemporary chronicler, "robbers and brigands came together from all parts to do penance, and vowed that they would shed their blood for Christ!" "Every reasonable man," adds the historian, "who witnessed the changes wrought in them beheld the finger of God, and was not the less astonished!"

Oh, who shall work such a desired revolution at the present time? Who shall unite us all in one common work? Who shall reveal into us the idea, the sentiment, which can break the bonds of egotism, enlarging the mind and kindling in the heart of man the fire of a living and life-giving faith?

# CHAPTER XXXVIII

CONTINUATION OF HIS JOURNEY AND HIS MIRACLES—
RETURN TO CLAIRVAUX.

THE MISSION upon which St. Bernard had come into Germany was almost concluded. The wonderful success of his work, the sudden and rapid advance which it had made from its very beginning, the happy transformation which had been its blessed result, demonstrate, at once, the tendency of the age, and the power of the man who gave it this direction. Such a power, whatever be its origin, never produces such great results as when it is applied to real necessities and is founded upon the spirit of the men themselves, amidst whom it manifests itself. Under this aspect, the Abbot of Clairvaux was truly the man of his age; for there exists between certain men and certain facts a reciprocal influence, a flux and reflux of life, an action and a reaction, the history of which would verify the phenomenon of which we speak. Then men receive from their age the spirit and the power by which they rule it; and the age receives from them its characteristic movement and physiognomy. Hence these great characters who appear like hieroglyphics to mark the great epochs of humanity. History shows them to us, in the center of their sphere of action, as indefatigable as those robust artisans, who by turns stir up and extinguish the fire whose brightness glares upon their sweat-stained visages, and who bend upon the anvil the iron, which scorches while it invigorates their nervous limbs. Thus we may explain the irresistible ascendancy which St. Bernard exercised over his contemporaries. He gave the impulse to the Crusades; and the movement, begun in France, was propagated from province to province, across the vast countries of Germany, from the Rhine to the Danube; all Europe was shaken, and Asia trembled to its foundation. A new era opens upon us; a complete regeneration wrought out with all the agony of a painful childbirth. The East and West are making themselves ready for the battle; and out of the bloody shock shall the modern world arise. Bernard might have hoped for a little rest after the events at Spires; and anyone but himself would have been satisfied to have raised two formidable armies, at the head of which he had placed the King of France and the Emperor of Germany. But the eagle glance of this great man knew no bounds; and in the vast horizon which it embraced, he did not forget the secondary interests which the heads of the crusading armies had generously sacrificed to the cause of God. The departure of Conrad and his companions in arms left Germany in a very dangerous situation; it afforded to the Guelphs a favorable occasion for attempting to gain the crown. One means alone would prevent new troubles; it was to enroll in the Christian army even such amongst the sovereigns of Germany as had not taken any part in the diet of Spires. St. Bernard made the attempt, and it succeeded like all his other undertakings. He wrote to Bavaria, where the principal heads of the Guelphs were assembled; and his letters, brought and read by the Abbot Adam of Eberach, produced in that place the same effect as his preaching had done elsewhere. The valiant Guelph, Duke of Bavaria, took the cross; a great number of prelates and barons followed his example, amongst others the celebrated Otho of Frisingen, a grave and determined man, who, in Germany, had at first pronounced against the Crusade, as Suger had done in France. Soon afterwards, other princes of various countries engaged themselves with the best of their men of arms in the militia of the cross: Ladislaus, Duke of Bohemia; Odoacer, Marquis of Styria; Amadius, Duke of Turin; Bernard, Count of Carinthia; Conrad, Duke of Zaeringen; and a crowd of chiefs and noblemen took the vow to fight against the infidels. The Saxons themselves, those brave warriors, so long unfortunate, yet always dreaded by the dynasty of Conrad, enrolled themselves under the sacred banner; and all parties reposed under the shadow of the cross; all, both Guelphs and Ghibellines, mingled and encamped together. "A profound silence reigned throughout the West," says

Otho of Frisingen, "and not only was there no more war, but it would have been accounted a crime to carry arms publicly."

St. Bernard spent the remainder of this memorable year at Spires, and did not resume his journey till the fourth of January, 1147. At his departure, the emperor, the princes, and the numerous battalions of Crusaders crowded around him to hear his words for the last time, and to pay him their last homage. The sacred orator addressed to them a touching exhortation; "and *his words*," says the historian, "*were not human, but divine.*" The brilliant train set forth, advancing with difficulty on account of the immense crowd which poured through the streets and along the road. Suddenly a poor, crippled child threw himself before the saint, and asked his blessing; at the same moment this child arose, perfectly cured. At the sight of this miracle, the emperor, who was riding at the side of the saint, and the whole astonished crowd, sent forth their acclamations of surprise, blessing the wonder-working saint; but he, drawing back from all this homage, turned towards Conrad, and said to him: "It is on your account that this cure has been worked, that you may know that God is with you, and that your undertaking is pleasing to Him."

Bernard and his travelling companions, having taken leave of the German court, again descended the Rhine to Cologne, in order to return into France by way of Belgium and Flanders. They rested the Monday (January 5) at Kreutznach, and the next day they went on to Bobart, a large town situated on the banks of the Rhine; they stopped at Coblentz, and at Bingen, where the man of God had serious conversations with the Abbess Saint Hildegarde, of whom we shall have to treat at some length in one of the following chapters.

In all the cities through which the servant of God passed, he renewed his preaching and his miracles; but the edification he gave was nowhere greater than at Cologne. He knew the impatience of this city to receive him; and in order to escape the honors which they were preparing for him, he made his entrance secretly, in the evening. But "glory pursued him who fled from it"; and the news of his arrival had hardly spread through the city when the inhabitants flocked in crowds to his dwelling and testified their tumultuous rejoicing throughout the whole night. "The crowd was so close and so *intolerable*," says one of his disciples, "that the holy abbot could not go out of his house. He remained at a window, from which he blessed the people; and it was only by means of a ladder placed in the street that they were able to present to his notice the sick, whom he restored to health. They dared not open the doors on account of the multitude which besieged the entrance. As to myself," says the monk Gerard, "being desirous of entering the house, I could not do so in any way; and from nine in the morning till evening, I remained in the street, without being able to reach either the door or the ladder, so completely was every avenue stopped up." The writer abandons the attempt to enumerate the number of miracles which took place at Cologne during the four days (from the ninth to the twelfth of January) they remained in the city. On the Sunday, St. Bernard celebrated Mass in the cathedral; he was preparing to break the bread of the Word, but, to satisfy the wishes of all, he preached in the marketplace, where his discourses electrified the multitude. Wonderful cures distinguished this day. A woman who had lost her reason through the bitter grief she had felt at the death of her husband was brought to him, and regained, on touching the holy man of God, her senses and her power of mind. Another woman, subject to nervous convulsions, received her health at the moment he blessed her with the holy Sign of the Cross. A woman of quality who from the age of fifteen had been deprived of the use of an eye, had lost all hope of recovery after having vainly tried every kind of remedy; she recommended herself to the servant of God, and regained her sight. Fourteen other cures are named in the journal as having taken place on the same day, "and these miracles," says one of the secretaries, "were not done in the dark, but in full day, in public, before the whole world, that all the world might glorify *God, who is wonderful in His saints*." But these sudden cures were but the smallest portion of the wonders which the servant of God performed in a less visible manner. He displayed, indeed, all the plenitude of the power which Jesus Christ gave to His Apostles of casting out evil spirits and healing every sickness and infirmity;* but his miracles, like those of the Apostles, as also those of Jesus Christ Himself, always contained something symbolical, and were but the visible signs of another species of

---

\* Matt. x. 1.

miracle, of an operation more interior, more mysterious, which was accomplished in the soul. The conversion of hearts, the triumph of light over darkness, of peace over vengeance, of justice over iniquity, of Christian piety over stupid indifference; such were the great effects arising from his indefatigable instructions.

The inveterate evils which had, for a long time, destroyed public morals, had produced a blindness, a deafness, a fatal paralysis far more fatal than any physical evil; and it was to these deep wounds that he applied all the unction of his words. Hence arose the disposition which characterized a great number of the Crusaders. The lively and vehement reaction which they manifested in favor of the holy war arose from the deep want ever experienced by the spirit of penance; for true penitence always feels itself irresistibly drawn towards some work of expiation. But this warlike enterprise, so suited to the temper of the multitude and to the popular impetuosity, could not have the same attraction for certain tender souls which, having returned to God, felt themselves drawn to an interior life and yearned for more peaceful labors—for a life of recollection and of prayer. These souls attached themselves more closely to St. Bernard; and in the neighborhood of Cologne alone there were, without reckoning women, nearly sixty who abandoned the world, most of whom retired to Clairvaux.

The Abbot of Clairvaux, accompanied by an always increasing number of his disciples, went from Cologne to Juliers, thence to Aix-la-Chapelle, where he celebrated the holy mysteries in the Chapel of Charlemagne, *the most celebrated in the whole Roman world.* "Aix," says the Chaplain Eberhard, with great naiveté, "is an agreeable abode; but more so for the senses than for the soul. The prosperity of the merchants is their death; and woe to the undisciplined house! I say not this for their ruin, but for their amendment, if at any time some of them should read these words; and, would to God, that but one among them might be converted and live." The same narrator relates the following fact, which happened at Aux-la-Chapelle: "We were at the altar of the Blessed Virgin, and I attended upon the Reverend Father, when a young girl was presented to him; he blessed her, and she was healed; but the crowd was so great that we were obliged to retire."

We will quote a few more instances from the journal of the travellers:

*Gerard*—"Today the miracles seem to have been redoubled. The crowd follows us everywhere, and the fields are as full as the towns. A mother brought a great girl, who had been deaf and dumb from her birth. The charitable Father imposed his hands on her, and instantly, in our presence, she obtained both her hearing and speech. We had scarcely proceeded a few steps when a man, quite as deaf, was suddenly healed."

*Godfrey*—"Until the occurrence of this miracle, I was before him, and preceded the crowd; but, struck with the exclamations which every moment resounded behind me, I made careful inquiries concerning all which had happened, and I ascertained the fact that, on this one day, our holy father had healed, on the road, one blind girl, three deaf persons, one cripple, and, after that, five blind men."

*Abbot Campigius*—"When we arrived in the evening at Juliers, a city which owed its origin to Julius Caesar, we found a crippled woman prostrate on the steps of the church. The saint, moved with compassion, took her by the hand, and raised her, *with so much the more ease, on account of her great faith.*"

*Gerard*—"This morning, after the celebration of Mass, a woman of considerable importance, the niece of the Count of Juliers, who was entirely deprived of the use of one eye and could see very little with the other, so that she could not walk without a guide, was instantaneously healed, by the simple Sign of the Cross. This miracle, like the others, was the subject of public rejoicing; and the people incessantly cried out, 'Christ uns gnade!' 'Christe eleison!' During the whole route, at Maestricht, at Liege, Mons, Valenciennes, Cambray, and Vaucelles, unnumerable miracles gave token of the passing of the man of God. On leaving Liege, a young man, blind from his birth, was presented to him. 'His eyes were not only sightless,' say two of the chroniclers, 'but they dried up, and the lids close shut.' The saint opened them, touched them with his venerable fingers, and immediately restored their sight. The happy young man, at seeing the light, which he had never known, felt an extraordinary emotion. 'I see,' cried he, 'I see light, I see men, and I see creatures with hair.' Then he clapped his hands, and, jumping for joy, exclaimed, 'O my God, now I shall never again hurt my feet against the stones.'"

But Bernard, notwithstanding the desire which continually urged him to go back to his cloister, thought that he ought to stay some days in Flanders, where he knew, like St. Paul at Ephesus, *that a great door was opened to him.* The words which he addressed to the population of this province had not the Crusade alone for the object; they were principally directed to morals and doctrine, which the new heretics took pains to pervert. The man of God erected a wall against the enemies of the Church; and *casting his net into the stream of the age, he drew forth an abundant draught of men of letters and noble personages.* Among the latter the annalist of Clairvaux relates a conversion, the edifying circumstances of which claim a place here.

Arnulph of Majorca was one of the wealthiest and most highly esteemed nobles of his province. He was living in pleasure and magnificence, when, on St. Bernard's journey, he listened to a sermon which caused the veil to fall from his eyes. Touched with grace and penetrated even to the depths of his soul, he resolved immediately, in imitation of the Apostles, to quit his house, his relatives, his country, and to follow Jesus Christ. But his family was numerous; his sons and his brothers, his fortune and the honor of his house, claimed his presence. He thought it best, therefore, to conceal his design till a favorable time, and not confide to anyone, not even to St. Bernard, the secret of his conscience. Time rolled on, and Arnulph, instead of disengaging himself from his worldly ties, engaged himself still more deeply in them, until one day he saw a poor shepherd arrive at his door, who threw himself at his feet, saying to him: "My lord, I pray you, by the love of Jesus Christ, to take me to Clairvaux to save my soul and yours." The noble Arnulph, struck by this mysterious event, could no longer resist the voice which urged him, and, arranging his affairs, he set off for Clairvaux with the shepherd whom God had sent to him. He there found the saint, and revealed to him, with an effusion of tears, the iniquities of a long life. But, to his great surprise, the man of God, after having exhorted him to persevere in the Order of Citeaux, only imposed on him, as a penance, a triple recital of the Lord's Prayer. "What, O most charitable father," exclaimed the penitent, "do you not take seriously the conversion of so unworthy a sinner? Assuredly, ten years of fasting and mortification would not suffice as expiation of my crimes, and you only give me three Paters." The saint replied, "Do you think you know, better than I do, what is needful for you?" "God forbid that I should be so presumptuous," replied Arnulph; "but I entreat you not to spare me in this world, that I may find my happiness in the future life." "Do as I bid you," replied the Father, "and do it with confidence; and, where you shall have laid down the burden of the flesh, you shall ascend to God without any other." The tone of inspiration and authority with which he spoke calmed the conscience of Arnulph, and gained him profound peace. But, soon after, this *soldier of God* fell sick of an inflammation of the bowels; and the illness made such rapid progress that the holy oils were administered to him. Amidst his greatest sufferings, and when the sick man seemed ready to die, he was heard to cry out suddenly, "O Lord Jesus, yes, all Thy words are true"; he repeated these words so often that one of the assistants attributed it to delirium. "No, no," cried the dying man, "what I feel is not delirium; but I attest, with my whole heart, that every word of the Lord Jesus is infallibly accomplished. He has promised in His Gospel, to those who renounce all things to follow Him, a hundredfold in this world, and eternal life in the world to come. Well, I feel at this moment the truth of these words; the spiritual consolations which I experience surpass, a hundredfold, all the joys of the world which I have left." After saying these words, *he fell asleep, sweetly and peacefully, in the Lord.* Thus were the words of the holy abbot accomplished, "When you shall have laid down the burden of the flesh, you shall depart to God without any other."

St. Bernard had been detained in Flanders till towards the end of the month of January. He passed through Laon and Rheims and arrived, on the second of February, the day of the Purification, at Chalons-sur-Marne. In this city he found the French princes assembled, and the king himself, as well as the ambassadors of Conrad III, who all, at the news of his arrival, went to meet him, and brought him in in triumph. He left Chalons on the fourth of February and rested at Barsur-Aube; and on the following Thursday, the sixth of February, he reached his peaceful retreat of Clairvaux. Like a well-watered tree which bears fruit at all seasons, he returned laden with a crown of fresh fruits. His return caused life and joy to superabound throughout his blessed abode. Thirty postulants had followed him from the neighborhood of Cologne to Clairvaux; thirty more had either set off, or were about to rejoin him immediately.

# CHAPTER XXXIX

ASSEMBLY AT ETAMPES—ARRIVAL OF POPE EUGENIUS III IN FRANCE—DEPARTURE OF THE CRUSADERS FOR THE HOLY LAND.

THE SAINT had scarcely passed a fortnight or three weeks at Clairvaux when he was obliged to quit his retreat once more, to assist at a general assembly of the barons and prelates of the kingdom which the king had convoked at Etampes. The opening of *the Parliament* took place on February 16, 1147. Louis le Jeune presided at it in person, and presented the different questions upon which he called for the attention and deliberation of the counsellors. The enthusiasm seemed somewhat cooled; but at the sight of St. Bernard, *who had just confederated together, for the army of the cross, the sovereign and the great men of the Teutonic kingdoms*, every countenance was lit up, and the whole assembly felt a thrill of joy and warlike ardor which it is hard to describe.

The first day was passed in listening to the ambassadors of Conrad, and the deputies of Geisa, King of Hungary, who came deputed by their sovereigns to promise the Crusaders a free passage through their countries. They read also the letters of the Greek Emperor, Manuel Comnenus, containing the most emphatic protestations of friendship, in reply to the notification which the King of France had made to him of the Crusades. The eastern and hyperbolical style of these missives shocked the good sense of the French. Godfrey, Bishop of Langres, taking compassion upon the king, who was blushing to hear such flattering words, and unable to endure the never-ending phrases of the reader and the interpreter, interrupted them, saying: "My brethren, be pleased not to say so much of the glory, of the virtues, and of the wisdom of the king; he knows all this, and so do we too. Tell him, then, more briefly and more plainly, what you have to say."

The next morning the assembly was employed in planning the best route by which to reach Palestine. The ambassadors of Roger, King of Sicily, proposed to go by sea, as being the surest and only way by which the whole multitude of the Crusaders could be transported, in a few weeks, to the ports of Syria. They strongly insisted on the advantages of this course and described vividly the numerous inconveniences, the perils, and inevitable vicissitudes of a long journey through barbarous countries; but the principal motive which they alleged to support their opinions was the remembrance of the old treason of the Greeks, and their perfidy at the period of the first Crusade. The wisdom of these Norman-Sicilians was not relished; and, whether the hatred which they bore to the Greeks, their aggressors, made their evidence suspected, or that navigation offered no attraction to the adventurous spirit of the French warriors, the advice of Roger, unfortunately, did not prevail in the assembly. It was determined that they should descend the valley of the Danube, in order to reach Constantinople by land. On the third day, the lords and prelates, solely occupied with the interests of France, took into consideration the care of the kingdom, and its administration during the absence of the king. "After the Abbot Bernard," says the chronicle, "had made his prayer, to invoke the light of the Holy Spirit, the King Louis, restraining his power by the fear of God, as was his usual custom, gave up the choice of the guardians of the kingdom to the prelates and the nobles. These retired to deliberate, and returned, after a short delay, having decided what was best to be done. Bernard walked at their head; and, pointing with his finger to the Abbot Suger and the Count William of Nevers, he said, 'Behold the two swords which we have chosen; they are sufficient.'"

"This double choice," continues the chronicler, "would have pleased all the world, if it had contented one of the two elected; but the Count de Nevers declared that he had made a vow to retire to the Chartreux; and, shortly after, he retired to the cloister, notwithstanding the earnest remonstrances of the king; and no entreaty could turn him from his pious resolution."

Remonstrances, no less vehement, were needed to determine the Abbot Suger to assume a dignity which presented to him a burden *rather than an honor*. He refused it a long time; but, at length, vanquished by the entreaties of the king and the *orders of the Pope himself*, he accepted the regency; and the disinterestedness and noble integrity with which he administered the affairs of the kingdom are known to posterity.

These various measures having been arranged, the meeting separated, and nothing was thought of but preparations for departure. On all sides, in France, in Germany, in almost all the countries of the West, the population was in motion. Nothing was to be seen on all sides but Crusaders; nothing to be met but pilgrims and troubadors. The heroic times seemed to be again revived; a kind of disgrace attached to those knights who had not taken the cross; and, in token of ridicule, they had a spindle and distaff sent to them.

Immediately after the dissolution of the parliament of Etampes, St. Bernard hastened to return to Clairvaux. He did not stay long there; for the interests of the Holy Land, and, perhaps, even more serious motives, of which historians furnish us with no clear idea, obliged him to take a second journey into Germany. He was at Treves on March 27; and, during the preparations for the Crusade, the annalists mention him as being sometimes at Frankfort, sometimes at Metz, at Toul, afterwards at Troyes, at Sens, at Auxerre, at Tonnerre, and at different other places. This second mission may have been occasioned by a deep political affair, which a party of German Crusaders had to accomplish. We will speak of this hereafter; and we will give the basis upon which we found our conjecture. However this may be, this second journey was neither less useful nor less rich in miracles than the former. Miracles, too numerous to be related, and astonishing conversions, were effected daily, and were the abiding traces left by the man of God on every part of his course.

"In these circumstances," says the old historian of the Crusade, "in order that there might not be wanting to this holy enterprise either blessing or grace, the Roman Pontiff, Eugenius, arrived in

France, and came to celebrate the Pasque of Our Lord in the Church of the blessed Denis."

It was in the spring of the same year, 1147, that Eugenius III desired to behold, with his own eyes, the great things which St. Bernard had done; and besides this first motive, which led him to France, he proposed to himself, whilst the Christian army was fighting the infidels in the East, to labor with the Abbot of Clairvaux for the extirpation of the heresies which were being propagated in the West.

The arrival of the Pope in France redoubled the enthusiasm of the Crusaders, and produced general rejoicing. The king, accompanied by a brilliant court, went to meet him as far as Dijon. As soon as he perceived him, he got off his horse and threw himself at the feet of the Pontiff, *covering them with kisses and tears.* Eugenius accepted, in the name of Him whose place he held, the testimonies of humility and love given by the King of France; he praised the hereditary virtues of the illustrious family of Hugh Capet, and spoke *in suitable terms* of the piety of Henry, the king's brother, who, some time previously, had embraced the monastic state of Clairvaux and distinguished himself amongst the other monks by the austerity of his life.*

After this discourse, which *exceedingly edified the faithful*, the Supreme Pontiff and the King of France took the road to St. Denis, where they arrived on the vigil of Easter. This solemnity was celebrated in the royal basilica, with all the magnificence which was suitable to the presence of the august Pontiff and the whole court of France. The principal chiefs of the Crusaders assisted at the office; and amidst them were distinguished, with just pride, the Grand Master of the Templars, and one hundred and thirty Knights of the Temple, who had come from Jerusalem to join themselves to the expedition of Louis VII. This great day was one of feasting and holy consolation, both to the king and the men-at-arms. All graces seemed poured forth upon that army; and Germany envied France the happiness of possessing in

---

* We must here recall to our minds that Eugenius had been together with Prince Henry, a simple monk at Clairvaux.

her bosom the Vicar of the Saviour of the world, the heir of the Prince of the Apostles.*

But the journey of the Pope and his long residence at Paris occasioned great expenses, which fell principally upon the richest religious communities, whence arose some murmurs; and several Gallican ecclesiastics, not satisfied with secretly protesting against the Pontifical court, aroused an opposition against it, which was manifested by a remarkable adventure. "Eugenius III," relates the Abbot Alberia, "having gone in procession, on the day of the great Litany, to St. Genevieve, the clerks of this church, armed with rods, fell upon the Pope's followers, *who were well beaten*; and the blood flowed in the street."

The Pope punished the guilty persons very severely, and replaced the clergy of St. Genevieve by regular canons from St. Victor, to whom this ancient church was granted. But the malcontents were not to be set at rest; they fomented new disorders every day, even coming during the night and making an uproar to disturb the office of matins. They conducted themselves so ill that the minister Suger, to put a stop to their proceedings, threatened them severely, *that he would have their eyes put out, and their limbs torn in pieces.*

This menace re-established order in Paris. The great difficulty of the present emergency was to find money to furnish the enormous expenses of the Crusaders. The gifts of piety were, no doubt, considerable; but they would not suffice to maintain a great army. To create new resources, Louis VII borrowed money, raised imposts, established taxes, which were approved and regulated by the Supreme Pontiff. The greater part of the higher nobility were in similar circumstances. It is true they possessed immense territorial wealth; but they had no pecuniary resources; because, living without care for the future, they habitually expended the whole of their revenues.

---

\* The Emperor Conrad sent, several times, deputations to prevail on the Pope to come into Germany. The last, composed of three illustrious prelates, entreated him to consent at least to an interview with the Emperor, at Strasbourg; but the Pontiff never accepted his invitation, for reasons of which history gives various interpretations.

We know how much this embarrassment itself, and the expedients to which it gave rise, contributed to modern civilization, by means of the franchises granted, in return for money, to the citizens and commons. Most grievous violence disgraced this period of emancipation; but political liberty found its equilibrium amidst these vicissitudes; and, as in all other instances of human progress, it was bought by dear experience.

While these events were passing, all the roads which led from Metz to Ratisbonne were successively covered with innumerable crowds of pilgrims. The first-mentioned of these cities had been pointed out as the place of reunion for the Crusaders of France; the second was the rendezvous for all those of Germany. It had been agreed between the two sovereigns that a certain interval should be left between the departure of these two expeditions; in order that, as they were to take the same road, they might not fail of procuring provisions, in the long extent of country which they would have to pass over. Conrad opened the march in the month of May; Louis the Young was to follow him in the latter end of June. The emperor, before placing himself at the head of his troops, caused to be acknowledged, as his successor on the throne, his son, Prince Henry, still a child, who, without any opposition, was crowned at Aix-la-Chapelle. This important event, so providentially brought about, completed the joy of the head of the dynasty of Hohenstauffen, by securing the German crown to his family. The young king was not yet of age to rule; his guardians and the regents of the kingdom were the venerable Archbishop of Mayence and the Abbot of Corby, who administered the Germanic states with a fidelity equal to that of the Abbot Suger. After these wise arrangements had been made, Conrad, surrounded by his brothers, Otho of Frisengen and Henry of Bavaria, and his nephew, Frederic of Suabia, as well as by the most illustrious princes of the south of Germany, came in great pomp to Ratisbonne, where an army awaited them such as had never been seen in former ages. The élite of the Teutonic knights, covered with shining armor, of gold or steel, made seventy thousand shining lances glitter in the sun; "the earth," says an old historian, "bent under the tread of their horses; and on the vast plain, in all directions, floated ensigns and colors, casques of silver, cuirasses, and bucklers." Besides the companies of nobles, the army drew after it a multitude of light horses, of foot soldiers, and pilgrims of both sexes, and in so great number that, according to the expression of Otho of Frisengen, the fleets were not enough to transport them, and the plains were not large enough to muster the battalions. The army, led by the emperor in person, directed its course across Hungary, Thrace, and Bulgaria, towards Constantinople, where it was to encamp until the arrival of the French Crusaders.

Louis VII, the Most Christian King, had prepared himself for the expedition by Christian deeds. As the moment of departure drew on, he was anxious to propitiate God, "and performed," says the chronicler, "*such things as are praiseworthy and excellent.*" He went, accompanied only by two servants, into all the religious houses, and amongst the poor, lavishing bounty upon them and carrying his abnegation so far as to visit the lepers, comforting them and serving them with his own hands.

After having thus satisfied the *devotion of his heart*, he went with his barons to the Church of St. Denis, whither his mother, Queen Adelaide, had preceded him, with his wife, Eleanora, and a numerous crowd of Crusaders. The royal basilica displayed on this occasion its most magnificent ornaments. Amongst the living reminiscences which presented themselves to the eyes of the pious monarch were the venerated images of the heroes of the first Crusade—Godfrey de Bouillon, Raynaud, Tancred, Baldwin, Hugh de Vermandois, and their immortal companions shone forth in the windows of the sanctuary, upon which were represented the fight of the Antioch, the battles of Dorylaeum and Ascalon, and the taking of Jerusalem.

Pope Eugenius, the Abbot Suger, and the clergy received King Louis in the choir, who, prostrating himself very humbly on the ground, remained long in adoration. Then the Pope and the abbot opened a little golden door and drew out, with great solemnity, a silver coffer, which contained the relics of the blessed Martyr, that the king might contemplate and kiss him whom he cherished in his heart, and become more joyful and intrepid. Then, having taken the oriflamme from the altar, he received from the hands of the Pontiff the pilgrim's staff and scrip, with the apostolic benediction. At last, the ceremony being finished, he retired into the monk's cloister to escape the eagerness of the multitude, *sleeping in their dormitory and eating in their refectory.* In the morning he embraced all around him and departed, followed by their prayers and tears. "I shall not attempt," continues the chronicler, "to describe this touching scene. The king's mother and wife fainted away and seemed about to die of grief."

To paint so painful a scene would be an undertaking as wild as impossible. The French army was neither less powerful nor less magnificent than the Teutonic. It counted not less than 100,000 Crusaders, not reckoning the foot soldiers and the pilgrims unable to bear arms. This formidable mass encamped at Metz, in the Imperial States; thence it moved towards the East. But directly after his departure, Louis VII seemed to discover the mistake he had made in taking the young queen, Eleonora, with him. This example authorized the knights to have their wives with them; and these having also *chambermaids not very modest, caused great scandal in the army.* Other elements of disorder mingled in the holy expedition. Effeminate troubadors, speculators, adventurers, drawn thither by a desire of gain or pleasure, travelled in the rear of the regular troops, greedy to devour their substance.

There was no longer time to obviate all these inconveniences. Odo de Deuil relates that Louis VII made, indeed, rules for discipline and severe regulations: "but," adds he, "*I have forgotten them; for, as they were never carried into execution, I have not retained them in my mind.*"

The army set forth on June 29, 1147—two months after the German expedition. It passed through Worms, Wurzburg, Ratisbonne, where it crossed the Danube; following most exactly the route of Conrad.

A third expedition, composed in great part of English and pilgrims from the north of Germany, had embarked, shortly before, at an English port, to reach Asia by sea. This fleet, long delayed by unfavorable events, landed on the coast of Portugal, where a brilliant passage of arms consolidated, as we shall see hereafter, the formation of this new kingdom, which had been recently founded by a count of Burgundy.*

---

* Portugal, successively occupied by the Arabs and the Moors, afterwards, in great measure, lost in the kingdom of Castille, was raised to the rank of an independent kingdom by Alphonso of Burgundy.

During the whole course of their journey, for a distance of 500 leagues, the two land armies had been received with the most generous hospitality. It was not so when they touched in the Greek territory. "Everywhere else," says Odo de Deuil, "the inhabitants sold us honestly what we required, and we dwelt in the midst of them in the most peaceful manner. The Greeks, on the contrary, shut themselves up in their cities, and sent down from the walls, by means of cords, the food we wanted. This very inconvenient mode of supplying us with provisions could not be agreeable to a crowd of pilgrims, who, tired of suffering hunger in a fertile country, began to obtain by violence and pillage what was necessary to their existence." "The Greek emperor," adds the same chronicle, "regarded the western warriors as men of iron, whose eyes darted flames, and who shed torrents of blood with as much indifference as water."

The malice of the Greek schismatics, and the disorders which were fermenting in the bosom of the Catholic armies, were but too certain presages of the terrible issue of this expedition. Our object is not to write the history of the Crusade. We must abide with the holy monk of Clairvaux on this side the sea, where episodes of a different kind, and which more especially bear upon his life, demand our attention; at the return of the Crusaders, we shall revert to the events of the holy war, that we may give a correct summary of its results.

# CHAPTER XL

ST. BERNARD COMBATS THE HERETICS IN LANGUDEOC—
HE RECEIVES TWO ILLUSTRIOUS VISITORS AT CLAIRVAUX—
THEIR HISTORY—COUNCIL OF RHEIMS.

WHILST the Frank and Mussulman armies were contending in Asia, the Sovereign Pontiff was probing the internal wounds of the Church and devoting himself to the work of expelling from it the poison of heresy. The progress of error had been already repressed at its source by the glories of the holy war, and heresy appeared to have lost the sort of charm which it had exercised over the lovers of novelty, from the moment that nobler interests had taken possession of the public sympathy.

But if the tree of the knowledge of evil no longer exhibited its proud summit in the light of day, its roots stretched all the deeper into the darkness of the earth; and its seeds, dispersed by the winds, were preparing to bring forth, at some future time, the fruits of bitterness and death.

The Pope, according to the ancient tradition of Rome, was in no hurry either to condemn or to punish; he desired to penetrate to the bottom of things; and for this purpose he waited till the noise of arms should have ceased in the West, that he might examine, amid the peaceful and universal silence, the doctrine of the innovators. He settled himself for a time at Paris, where St. Bernard, on his return from Treves, was not long before he joined him. The first point which arrested their attention was the doctrine of the Bishop of Poictiers, Gilbert de la Porée. This prelate, already very far advanced in age but still imbued with the subtleties of Abelard, had scandalized certain members of his clergy by the rationalism which he had introduced into the theological schools. The Pope perceived the pernicious errors which might proceed from this method, but he adjourned his definitive judgment to the following year, that he might leave the accused time to complete his defence, and to place his doctrine before the eyes of a more numerous council.

Another case, which could not so well endure delay, pressed very much upon the Holy Abbot of Clairvaux. It was the terrible ravages which the apostate, Henry de Bruys, had caused in the southern provinces of France. We have given an account in another place of the doctrines of this heresiarch and the disturbance occasioned by him both in churches and individual souls. Eugenius judged it fitting to send into these provinces the Cardinal Albini, Bishop of Ostia, accompanied by the learned Godfrey Bishop of Chartres, and St. Bernard himself. The latter had first dispatched a letter to Hildephonsus, the Governor of Narbonensian Gaul. He blamed him for having tolerated the preaching of the monk Henry, and set before him most energetically all the evils of which it had been the cause. "The infection which this man has spread through your states," said he, in conclusion, "is felt throughout the whole world. This is the cause of the journey which we are about to undertake. I come not amongst you of my own accord; duty calls me, charity draws me. Perhaps it may be granted to me to pluck up out of the Church this poisonous plant, with its multiplied offshoots. It is true, mine is but a feeble arm for such work, but I reckon upon the help of the holy bishops with whom I come, and on the powerful aid which I expect from you. At the head of the prelates to whom the Holy See has confided the care of this important affair is to be seen the illustrious Cardinal Bishop of Ostia, celebrated in Israel for the victories which he has obtained over the enemies of God. It belongs to you to give an honorable reception to this prince of the Church, and to second, according to the power which God has given you, a mission which has no other object but your salvation and that of your subjects."

Notwithstanding this recommendation, and perhaps against the good will of Count Hildephonsus, the legate was disrespectfully received by the city of Albi. The great majority of the inhabitants of this unhappy city had rejected, together with the dogma of the supremacy of the Pope, the greater part of the teaching of the Church; and not only did they refuse to assist at the Holy Sacrifice which the Cardinal celebrated in their Cathedral, but they evinced, by cries and sounds of discordant music, the displeasure which his visit caused them and the hatred they bore to the Holy See. "These people," writes Godfrey, "welcomed him with the braying of asses and the sound of drums; there were scarcely thirty of the faithful at his Mass."

St. Bernard arrived in the same city two days after the cardinal. "In the morning he caused the bell to ring for Mass," says the chronicler; "and, whether from curiosity to behold the most celebrated man of his day, or from the extraordinary blessing which followed wherever he went, the Albigenses flocked in such great numbers to the church that the vast nave could scarcely contain them." The servant of God, after the celebration of the Holy Mysteries, mounted the pulpit to preach the Gospel to the multitude of erring men, who were all impatient to hear him. He spoke to them with the greatest gentleness and explained to them, article by article, the different points of Catholic doctrine which the innovators had rejected or corrupted. Not satisfied with rectifying their doctrinal errors, and enlightening their minds, he applied himself especially to the task of gaining their hearts, according to the recommendation of the prophet,* "Speak to the heart of Jerusalem;" and this method was the most easy to him, because his gracious words poured forth from an inexhaustible fountain of love. A power at once sweet and penetrating, a balsam of life, insinuated itself into the depths of their rebellious hearts and softened their minds, like a soft shower which re-animates a field of corn and sinks into the dried stems, recalling sap and life. The people who heard him showed, by their tears, the feeling which he had kindled within them; and the discourse was scarcely finished, when truth triumphed. "Enter, then, into yourselves," said the holy preacher; "return, erring children, into the unity of the Church; and, that we may know who are those who have received the word of salvation, let them raise the right hand to heaven in token of their adhesion to the Catholic Faith." At this moment all

---

* Is. xi.

raised the right hand and testified, by a shout of joy, their return to the bosom of the Church.

The monk Godfrey, who regarded this touching scene as one of the most marvelous effects of the words of the man of God, describes several other miracles wrought at Bergerac, at Calais, at Vertefeuille, at Toulouse, and at other places. The most remarkable fact is that which happened at the town of Sarlat, in Périgord. "In this place," says the chronicler, "after having preached to the obstinate heretics, they presented loaves to him to bless, as he was in the habit of doing elsewhere. When he had done this here he pronounced the following words: 'You will acknowledge that we announce the truth to you, and that the innovators have seduced you from it, if your sick people recover their health by eating this bread.' At these words, as he thought too positively spoken, the pious Godfrey, Bishop of Chartres, became alarmed, and added: 'Which means that they shall be cured if they eat with a lively faith.' 'No,' replied the saint, in a tone which bespoke perfect confidence, 'I say that all those who shall eat of this bread shall be healed of their sickness, that they may recognize, by this token, that our words are according to God and His truth.' The miraculous bread produced numberless cures; and this miracle so forcibly struck the population of the neighboring towns that Bernard was obliged to change his route to escape from the *intolerable honors* of which he was the object."

At Toulouse the effects of his words were not less abundant; but the excitement and the demonstrations of respect which were showered upon him by the inhabitants of this town nearly brought a serious illness upon St. Bernard. It is said that his hands were many times so covered with kisses that they *swelled considerably*, as did also his thin and delicate arms, to such an extent that he could no longer give the benediction. But his infirmities did not lessen his zeal, and like a victim ever ready for the sacrifice, he labored for the salvation of his brethren at the expense of his own life. It is this profound abnegation which so fitted him, in the hands of God, for great things. "What dost thou expect from me, my Lord and my God?" said he one day; "these people seek for miracles, and we shall derive small profit from our words if Thou dost not confirm them by the tokens of Thy power." He pronounced these words as he left the house of the Canons Regular at Toulouse, where an ecclesiastic named Bernard was ill, having been struck with palsy. But the man of God had hardly passed the threshold of the door when the dying man sprang from his bed and ran after St. Bernard to thank him, with an effusion of gratitude, for his sudden and perfect recovery. The Canons, alarmed at this resurrection, fled with loud cries, because they believed that *the soul having already left the body, this was a phantom*; but the truth reassured them. The noise of this miracle attracted so many people together that the Saint hid himself in a cell, carefully guarding the door and all the approaches to it. "As to the ecclesiastic who had been so marvelously healed," adds a contemporary, "he went to Clairvaux, where he assumed the religious habit; and some time after, the reverend father sent him into Languedoc, near Toulouse, to place him at the head of the monastery at Valdeau, which he still governs."

St. Bernard and the pontifical legates followed the traces of the monk Henry, who fled from town to town; they purified, in every place, the churches which he had defiled, re-established the ancient worship, and pulled up all the tares in the field of the Church. "Jesus Christ be blessed! The faith triumphs; infidelity is confounded! Piety is glorified; impiety is destroyed." Such are the expressions by which the gratitude of contemporaries is expressed. No doubt scandals were sown in the earth, sooner or later to burst forth; but how many souls were saved from the wreck by the aid of the holy abbot of Clairvaux! This glorious mission being terminated, he quitted the provinces which he had evangelized, leaving to them in writing the substance of his verbal communications. His letter to the inhabitants of Toulouse displays his apostolic vigilance. "I repeat to you," said he, "my earnest recommendations never to receive amongst you any preacher who has not received a mission from the Holy See, or the approbation of your bishop. 'How shall they preach unless they are sent?' says the apostle. These foreign preachers bear the appearance of piety, but they possess not its spirit. They conceal their poison under the appearance of sweetness; and they have the art to wrap up their profane novelties in divine language. Distrust these persons as men who would poison you; and discern beneath their sheepskin the wolf which it conceals."

The cell at Clairvaux was, at all times, the dearest object of the desires of the man of God. It was there he repaired his strength, there he gained fresh light at the foot of his crucifix, and there he held the most intimate communications with the Eternal Source of Life. He was able at last to return thither, after all his toils, and enjoy some rest, whilst awaiting the opening of the council of Rheims. But his repose was never free from labor; and from the first moment that he found himself in the midst of his children, he began again to nourish them with his loving spirit, and to shed over them the sweetest outpourings of his apostolic soul. It was about this time that his renown drew upon him two visits, of which historians make particular mention.

Peter of Portugal, sent by the king his father, came to thank the Abbot of Clairvaux for the deliverance of his country, through the conquest which had been made from the Moors of a very important fortress, by the assistance of the Crusaders. He declared that his father had made a vow that if he gained this victory, he would build a monastery of the order of Clairvaux in his dominions; and he asked for some of his monks to make this foundation. The annalist of Citeaux relates that the King of Portugal had seen St. Bernard in a dream, who promised him victory. This astonishing message greatly moved the desert of Clairvaux; and the monks, penetrated with gratitude, intoned the Te Deum together in thanksgiving. But St. Bernard did not comply with the desires of the King of Portugal until he had consulted God in the depths of his heart; he then wrote a letter to the monarch, containing, amongst others, these words of prophecy: "We have been informed of the great devotion which has suggested to you the desire of founding a monastery. This obliges me to send you some of the children whom I have nourished, for Jesus Christ, with the milk of holy doctrine, that they may afford you the means of effecting your pious intentions. And, with respect to the monastery which you are going to found, I must tell you that, as long as it is preserved in its integrity, your kingdom will also remain in its integrity under the sceptre of your race; but when anything is taken away from it, your crown will be transferred to others. I pray the Saviour of the world to protect your Highness and the illustrious queen, your consort, and to bless you in your posterity, that you may see your children's children rejoicing in the possession of your dominions and estates."

It is observed by historians that this prediction was accomplished in 1580, after the death of King Sebastian, who fell in Africa in a battle against the Moors. The Cardinal Henry, his uncle, succeeded him, in default of other heirs, and being the first to violate the integrity of the monastery, he lost his crown, which passed from the race of Burgundy to the house of Castille.*

But Prince Peter of Portugal, upon leaving Clairvaux, bore away in his bosom the arrow of God's Spirit, which pierced his soul. Heavenly desires arose within him, and banished every other thought. Neither the splendor of royal greatness, nor the applauses which were bestowed on his valor, had power to efface the deep impression which St. Bernard had left on his heart. Ten years after this visit, the magnanimous prince trod under foot all those things which shine most brightly in the eyes of men, and, renouncing the world to follow Jesus Christ, made the monastic vows, and died the death of the saints, in the year 1165.

A second visit, not less memorable, was that of the King of Sardinia. The following is the relation of the exordium of Citeaux: "The King of Sardinia—a very noble and powerful prince—named Gumard, made a pilgrimage to Tours, to visit the tomb of the glorious Saint Martin. The reputation of Bernard attracted this prince to Clairvaux, to behold the man of whom he heard such great things. The servant of God received him with all the honors which were due to him; but, as he could not refrain from casting the net of the Gospel, he conversed with this prince on

---

* The historians of Citeaux give some curious details about this monastery, which was founded at Alcobaca, eighteen miles from Lisbon. The number of monks, which was at first very small, afterwards increased to more than a thousand, who succeeded each other night and day in chanting, without interruption, the praises of God. In the end this house was so greatly enriched by royal bounty that the abbot possessed at last thirty towns, among which were four seaports; he exercised civil and criminal jurisdiction over more than six thousand vassals. "It is but too well known," adds a pious historian, "how injurious such great wealth and temporal advantages are to those who by their profession, are obliged to lead a life of poverty, hidden, unknown, penitential, and disengaged from the cares of the world."

the great affair of salvation, exhorting him to put himself into a fit state to appear with confidence before God."

These words appeared to fall barren to the earth, without producing any visible effect; but the Saint, at the moment that Gurnard took leave of him, blessed him, and said these words: "I have prayed Our Lord, with many entreaties, for your conversion; but I have not yet been heard. I leave you to go away now, but know that you will come back someday." The king was much struck with this prediction, and had very soon no other thought but to devote himself to God. He resisted for a long time the power which drew him to Clairvaux; but this power was divine, and he was forced to yield to it. So, leaving to his son his sceptre and crown, he thought of nothing but following his vocation. The peace of the cloister had more charms for him than the vain pleasures of the earth; the humility of Clairvaux seemed more precious than the grandeur of the world; the society of the pious servant of God, more sweet than that of his troop of courtiers; in short, *heaven seemed to him more desirable than Sardinia.* "But God, who determined to make of this prince a new man," adds the historian of Citeaux, "did not take from him altogether the noble and loyal heart which had, as it were, a natural inclination towards royalty—he only changed the object; he made him comprehend that there is nothing greater or more worthy of a noble heart than to serve God, and that true greatness consists in governing the world and our own passions." Gurnard was forty when he retired to Clairvaux, and died in a happy old age about the year 1190.

Meanwhile, the council which the Supreme Pontiff had convoked at Rheims began its labors on March 22, 1148. At this time, Bernard went to take his seat in the midst of the prelates and abbots who composed the venerable assembly. Suger, the regent of France, was one of them, as well as eighteen cardinals and a number of bishops of Germany, Spain, and England, in addition to those of France. The council was first occupied with questions of doctrine. The Breton Eon de l'Etoile was brought before it, who gave himself out to the credulous people as the judge of the living and the dead, and failed not, notwithstanding his folly, to excite the fanaticism of a crowd of disciples. The Pope judged him more unhappy than guilty, and confided him to the vigilance of Suger, who caused him to be shut up for the rest of his days; but his disciples, more excitable and dangerous than himself, redoubled their boldness in preaching, as if they were persecuted apostles. They did not relinquish their undertaking until several of them had been given over to the flames by the secular arm.

The council afterwards turned its attention to Gilbert de la Porrée. This bishop brought several large volumes to justify his assertions by the authority of the Fathers. He had fallen into error by applying the categories of Aristotle to the Divinity; so that he made a distinction between the Divinity and God. The Pope, *tired of his long lectures*, pressed him to explain himself upon this serious subject; and Bernard, to avoid these subtle discussions, brought forward the orthodox propositions which condemned those of Gilbert. "You maintain, then," said the latter, addressing St. Bernard, "that the Divinity is God." "Yes," replied the saint; "that is my belief; and let it be written with a pen of steel, and a style of adamant!" The energy of Bernard put a stop to these recriminations; and at the clearness of his words the scholastic subtleties vanished away. The council condemned the errors of Gilbert de la Porrée; and this bishop showed himself so humbly submissive to the judgment of the Church that the Pope sent him back in peace to his diocese, where he ended his life in an edifying manner in the discharge of his episcopal functions. After the settlement of doctrine, the council renewed the canons of ecclesiastical discipline, which had been put in force under the preceding Pontiffs. The zeal of the Abbot of Clairvaux was redoubled on this occasion, and developed with intense ardor, when the question became that of the correction of the disorders and vices which had been introduced into the manners and morals of the clergy. It was to these irregularities, and above all, to the culpable facility with which holy orders were conferred, that he attributed the greatest evils of the Church. "It appears," said he, in a work published upon this subject, "that the Church has been widely extended, and that the sacred order of the clergy has been likewise extended. The number of the brethren has been multiplied to infinity; but, O my God! though Thou hast augmented the number, Thou hast not augmented the joy; for it would seem that the merits of men have diminished in proportion as their number has increased. They run discriminately into holy orders, and they embrace, without respect or consideration, that spiritual ministry which is fearful even to angels."

To remedy these abuses, which the Saint regarded as one of the most fatal sources of heresy, schism, and corruption of manners, there was no surer means than the re-establishment of the old and holy rules of the clerical life. Some great and salutary reforms had been already realized. The Council of Rheims established new laws, and gave to the ancient ones a greater sanction and authority; and thus was effected, gradually and without disturbance, that internal and external purification of the Church which was generally demanded by the conscience of Christendom.

# CHAPTER XLI

COUNCIL OF TREVES—EXAMINATION OF THE REVELATIONS OF ST. HILDEGARDE—HISTORY OF THIS PROPHETESS—HER RELATIONS WITH ST. BERNARD—GLANCE AT HER WRITINGS.

ADALBERON, Archbishop of Treves, invited the Pope and cardinals to come to his metropolitan residence, making them the generous offer of *defraying the expenses of that venerable company for three months' space.* Eugenius III accepted the proposal and went with St. Bernard and a great number of the Fathers of the Council to Treves, where they continued the important investigations which they had commenced at Rheims. A bright luminary shone at this time in a monastery on the banks of the Rhine. St. Hildegarde, Abbess of the Benedictines of Mount St. Ruppert, near Bingen, was announcing future events with the energetic accents of a prophet, and from the depths of her cell sent forth warnings and terrible threats against the pastors and their flocks.

The picture of lamentable disorders was certainly no novelty in the twelfth century. All the sectaries had begun their attacks upon the Church by similar descriptions; and heresy and schism had always supported themselves by the proud pretense of healing the evils of Christendom, and bringing her back into the way of God. The words of St. Hildegarde, then, coincided, so far, with the clamors of the heretics, as well as with the sighs of truly Christian souls. But her language, though more severe and cutting than all the rest, drew on her the serious attention of the spiritual powers, because it proceeded from a deep humility, which is inseparable from a true love of the Church. She evidently spoke with authority from on high; and far from rashly provoking the rebellion of the people, she never addressed herself but to the lawful depositaries of ecclesiastical authority. She wrote to the Pope: "Poor and worthless as I am, the Holy Spirit suggests to me those things which I should say to you. O Father of pilgrims, glorious Father, bright shield of the Church, primitive root of the spouse of Jesus Christ!. . .you, the first named after Christ, charged with the care of the whole flock, holding the place of Jesus Christ Himself . . . give, I pray you, give precepts to the masters, and rules to the disciples."* St. Hildegarde was, for a long time, regarded as a visionary—a simple and timid virgin. She dared not manifest outwardly the gifts with which her soul was enriched; but at length, from the midst of her weakness, God caused to flow forth so bright a light that contempt was followed by glory, and the princes of the earth, as well as the Pontiffs of the Church, received, with trembling, her reprimands and her counsels.

We have seen, in one of the preceding chapters, that St. Bernard, when on his journey into Germany, turned out of his road to pay a visit to the celebrated prophetess. The following is the account of this interview in the chronicle of Trithemius: "From Frankfort, the venerable abbot descended to the neighborhood of Bingen, where Hildegarde, a very devout nun and virgin of Jesus Christ, had built a monastery upon Mount St. Ruppert. It is said that he held very sweet conversation with her upon future blessedness; for this servant of God was known to Bernard by her writings, and by the reports he had received of her. On his arrival

---

* We quote these texts, amongst a thousand others, only to place them in contrast with those garbled quotations by which modern times have been much deceived. Protestantism, to legitimatize its birth in some degree, has adopted to itself the patronage, not only of all the ancient heresiarchs, but of all those great spirits of the Middle Ages who deplored the evils of their time and the weakness of the heads of the Church, and therefore put St. Hildegarde, and even St. Bernard, in requisition, to justify their recriminations against the Papacy and the Catholic Hierarchy. We hear that very recently there has appeared in Germany a book written in this hostile spirit. For this reason, we have studied, to greater extent, the works of St. Hildegarde, truly desirous that this labor may contribute to enlighten the faithful upon anti-Catholic publications.

at the convent, after the customary ceremonies, he asked for the writings of the abbess; he read them with the greatest care, as they were very differently judged by divers persons—some reverencing what they did not understand, and others condemning them as mere reveries. But Bernard, *edified beyond description*, turned towards his companions: 'These revelations,' said he, 'are not the work of man; and no mortal will understand them unless love has renewed in his soul the image and likeness of God.' However, one of those present observed that many persons, both learned and ignorant, religious and secular, daily pierced the soul of the handmaid of God by repeating that her visions were only *hallucinations of the brain*, or deceits of the devil. Upon which, St. Bernard replied: 'Let us not be surprised, my brother, that those who are sleeping in their sins should regard revelations from on high as follies, since the apostle affirms that the animal man cannot comprehend the things of the spirit. Yes, certainly, those who lie buried in pride, in impurity, or in other sins take the warnings of God for reveries; but if they were vigilant in the fear of God, they would recognize, by sure signs, the divine work. As to those who believe those visions to be the suggestions of the devil, they show that they have no deep knowledge of divine contemplation; they are like those who said of our Lord and Saviour Jesus Christ that He cast out devils through the power of Beelzebub.' Then, addressing Hildegarde herself, he said: 'For you, my daughter, fear not the words of men, since you have God for your protector. Their vain discourses will vanish like straw; but the word of God will endure forever.'"

The chronicler adds nothing to the relation of this interesting interview; but the letters which remain to us from St. Bernard and St. Hildegarde give us an idea of the intimate relation which, from this time, arose between these two great souls; a holy union, a strict and intimate bond, which does not require length of time for its formation, for it is knit in the eternal world. It is the result of a radical uniformity, a fundamental analogy, which characterizes certain Christian souls and produces sympathies far more attractive and *unitive* than exterior attractions and natural affections. This kind of union is the rare and inestimable fruits of the sublime prayer of Jesus Christ: "My Father, make them one." Once formed, these unions are indissoluble; they are contracted at the first meeting; such souls know each other, understand each other, love each other, without any human motive; and this love is consummated in Jesus Christ. Such was the spiritual bond which existed between Hildegarde and the holy Abbot of Clairvaux. We can judge of it from some passages in their letters. "I reply in great haste," writes the servant of God, "to your words of affection and pious tenderness; would to God that the overwhelming nature of my affairs would allow of my saying more to you. Blessed be God who heaps His graces upon you. But remember always, my dear daughter, that His grace is a gratuitous gift, to which you ought to correspond with love and with humility; 'for God resists the proud, and gives grace to the humble.' And, for the rest, what instructions, what lessons do you expect from me? Have you not an interior master, who teaches you all things by His unction? I know that the light of the Holy Spirit discovers to you the secrets of heaven, reveals to you that which is above the reach of common men. When, then, you are before God, in those holy seasons when your spirit is united to His, remember me and all those with whom I am spiritually united." This letter would seem to be an answer to a relation which St. Hildegarde had given him, in which she thus expresses herself:

"Venerable Father! you who, with a sublime zeal and an ardent love of God, Jesus Christ, enroll your soldiers under the banner of the Holy Cross . . . I am strongly actuated by the light which I see in spirit, and which does not make itself manifest to the eyes of my body. It is more than two years, my father, since you yourself appeared to me in this vision, like a man staying the sun. I weep on account of my weakness and pusillanimity. O my kind and very dear father, I place myself in your soul; pray for me, for I have much to suffer when I do not declare what I see and hear . . . I conjure you, by the glory of our heavenly Father, and by His admirable Word, and by the sweet unction of the Spirit of Truth, and by the holy Word by which all creation speaks, and by the Word Himself by whom the world was made, and by the majesty of the Father who sent His Word into the bosom of a virgin, where He took flesh, like honey uniting itself to a ray of light; I entreat you to receive my words into your heart, and cease not until you have arrived at God by the aspirations of your soul; for

God Himself wills that it should be so. Adieu! Adieu! Be strong and vigorous in your holy combat."

The life of St. Hildegarde affords matter for curious observation to psychologists. From her infancy, almost from the cradle, she lisped the divine mysteries and seemed, by a wondrous organization, to be able to contemplate, at the same time, spiritual beings and earthly realities. Her parents, the Count Hildebert and the pious Matilda, could not mistake the signs of precocious holiness which appeared in their child. They devoted her to Jesus Christ; and, when scarcely eight years old, the young girl entered a monastery and was trained to the ascetic life under the directions of the blessed Judith, who lavished on her the tenderness of a mother and clothed her with the holy habit. Her teaching was as simple as her life; she learned to chant the Psalms and to accompany them on the psaltery. And thus did the first half of her life flow sweetly along; and she would never have been distinguished from many other souls unknown to the world, but precious before God, if she had not been placed, against her will, upon the candlestick, to give light to the Church.

But we will let her speak for herself:

"Wisdom teaches me in the light of love, and commands me to set forth the manner of my vision. She says to me, O man, speak thus of thyself: From the first moment of my formation, when God, with His breath of life, gave me existence in the womb of my mother, He planted in me the seed of this faculty of vision. . . For in the year of the Incarnation, 1100, the doctrine of the apostles began to grow cold among Christians, and among the ministers of the Spirit. At this time I was born, and my parents, with pious prayers, consecrated me to God. When I was three years old, my soul trembled at a bright light which appeared to me. I did not then know how to speak of these visions, which were continually renewed to me, until I had attained my fifteenth year; and I wrote several of them with trembling; for I was surprised sometimes to see outwardly those things which I had never till then beheld but within myself; and having asked my nurse one day if she saw such things, she replied no. Then I suffered great perplexity, and I dared not name these visions to anybody."

The saint then relates her long sufferings, her singular maladies, which more than once left her like one dead, insomuch that once preparations were begun for her interment. The fear of man and a timid modesty prevented her from revealing the dictates of the Holy Spirit.

"I was forty-two and seven months old," says she, "when suddenly a bright ray, coming from heaven with a dazzling splendor, pierced through my whole body; it kindled my soul, illuminated my brain and my bosom, and sweetly consumed me without burning me; or rather, sweetly burned without consuming me. I felt myself instantly invested with a new light; I understood Holy Scripture; the key of David was given me; I comprehended the Psalms, the Gospels, and the other books of the Old and New Testaments; I contemplated the mysteries in them, without, however, knowing the letters which composed the text, nor the arrangements of words and syllables."

From this moment St. Hildegarde, thoroughly renewed and transformed, yielded herself to the voice of God, who commanded her to write her revelations. She obeyed, and instantly her maladies disappeared and she arose from her bed of suffering—"my veins, and the marrow of my bones, were filled again with strength and vigor." Miraculously set free from all fear, she published, like the prophet Jonas, the warnings and judgments of the Most High.

But the Bishop of Mayence, not knowing whether these extraordinary revelations were to be received or rejected, thought it best to submit them to the wisdom of the Sovereign Pontiff then presiding at the Council of Treves. Eugenius III examined this matter with the greatest care; he wished to judge himself of the writings of this celebrated abbess; "and it was the Abbot of Clairvaux, of blessed memory," says an ancient biographer, "who prevailed with the Pope not to permit so wonderful a light to be hidden under a bushel." He sent several examiners to the convent where the virgin dwelt, to make inquiries, without noise or vain curiosity, concerning everything which could afford any light to assist the Pope's judgment. When they returned to Treves, they brought back the book of the revelations of St. Hildegarde, which was read in full council. The Pope himself, deeply moved, several times took the office of reader upon himself; and all the Fathers, admiring the purity of this light, gave glory, with *heart and mouth*, to the Creator of so many marvels. The books which were presented to the council formed a large collection, entitled, "*Scivias: Know the Ways of God.*"\*

This title is, perhaps, one of those mystic words which were peculiar to the saint, and which darted sometimes out of her soul, like the words of an unknown tongue. Many expressions of this nature are untranslatable; but they are distinguished by their exceeding radical energy, and by the harmony of their formation. It would be very difficult to convey an idea of the style of St. Hildegarde. To be able to appreciate them, we need some rays of the light which made her writings so fruitful. Truth seems to repose there in all its fullness; it shines in every word—in the form of the expression as well as in the depth of the meaning. Thus, as Hildegarde herself declares, she saw in her soul the reflection of heavenly things, whilst the eyes of her body were contemplating the same truths in the phenomena of earth. Thence arose an admirable symbolism, between the facts of nature and the divine mysteries, which forms the characteristic peculiarity of her teaching. It is a simultaneous intuition into the two worlds, seized upon in their reciprocal and interpenetrating relation. The world, the universe, are transparent to the eyes of the Saint; she dives down with a lucid glance, even to the mysterious root of things, and to the central point where finite objects touched upon the infinite. Besides the visions which relate to the state of the Church and its future destinies—visions from which we will quote some remarkable fragments in the next chapter—the "*Scivias*" contains many treatises upon the nature of God and man, upon the mysteries of life, upon *sounds* and divine music, upon certain parts of medicine and natural science, upon the virtues of plants and the elements. The greater part of these treatises, or visions, follow a general view into a number of different applications. She insists upon *the primary matter of all things*, on primitive creation, uncreated Wisdom, which she calls the "Vesture of God, His dwelling, His throne." According to her, "Wisdom, the heavenly city, the Virgin, the Church," afford the closest analogy with this primitive creature. She also gives the name of the "Vesture of God" to the humanity of the uncreated Son; and she

---

\* "*Scivias Domini*: Know the Ways of God."

says, "the eternal God had, from eternity, in His idea (in His knowledge), this vesture, which is the humanity of His Son."

The following are some fragments of the visions of "Scivias":

"I saw a very pure atmosphere, in which I heard a ravishing harmony of musical sounds; harmonies of joy from on high, concords of different voices, concerts of souls, which are vigorously persevering in the love of truth; sighs and transports of souls who regain these joys after a fall; exhortations or virtues, urging each other to the salvation of people, delivered from the yoke of Satan." This vision is called "The Symphony of the Virgin Mary." She addresses herself, in these words, to the august Queen of Angels:

"Resplendent pearl, the pure light of heaven is poured into Thee! The Father, by His only Word, first created the matter which was disturbed by Eve. But in Thee, O brilliant diamond, the same Word took flesh, and brought forth again all virtues, as in the beginning, when He caused all creation to come forth from the primitive earth." The Saint often speaks of music, as of a language full of mystery. She says, in one of her letters, "The soul is a harmony"—a strong and graceful expression! She affirms that music is the voice of the Holy Spirit—a sublime language, of which earthly music is only a degraded imitation. She wishes this art, of heavenly origin, to be cultivated with piety; and she gives the name of "sages" to those who have been its organs, and have lent instruments for its use.

We love to verify the relations between the observations of the learned and the contemplations of the saints; the agreement between earthly realities and revealed truths must necessarily be brought out by true science.

St. Hildegarde, in another vision, contemplates the tower of Wisdom—a tower which is not yet completed, but which rises continually beneath the hands of fervent laborers. At the foot of the tower men are agitating themselves about speculative science; they come and go, and enter not; only practical men make their way, and seat themselves, clothed in white garments, on the different steps of the celestial edifice, ascending towards the summit, which is ever rising higher and higher.

Amidst these mystical visions are often discovered rays of light, which clear up many obscure parts of Holy Scripture. We will only give one example, which will terminate this chapter. The following difficulty was proposed to her: The Sacred Scriptures teach on one side that the Eternal Father created all things *at once*; and, on the other, the book of Genesis relates that God finished the work of creation in six days. How shall we reconcile these two passages? The Saint replies: "The Almighty God, who is Life, without beginning and without end, and who, from all eternity, conceived all things in His idea (*in scientia sua*), created, at the same time, the matter of heavenly things and the matter of earthly things—*i.e.*, heaven, luminous matter; and earth, opaque matter. Now, the luminous matter darted forth, as it were, rays of condensed light, which the opaque matter reflected; so that they were united together. And these two matters, created simultaneously, appeared as one circle. And, at the first *fiat*, the angels came forth, with their dwelling place of luminous matter; and, because God is God and man, they were created in the image of the Father; and the humanity, with which the Son was about to clothe Himself, was created in His image. Thus, at the command of God, every creature came forth, according to its species, from the opaque matter. For the six days are the six works; the beginning and the end of each of these works forms what we call a day; and, after the creation of the first matter, the Spirit of God was borne upon the waters; and, at the same instant, without any interval, God said, 'Let light be.'"

# CHAPTER XLII

CONTINUATION OF PRECEDING CHAPTER.

The wisdom of St. Hildegarde's teaching, the powerful interest connected with it, and the sanction which has been imparted to her works by the Council of Treves, little as they are known in our day, will justify us in the eyes of serious readers for the length to which part of our labor has extended. We shall give a few more extracts from her writings.

St. Hildegarde, after rebuking certain faithless pastors, rises to high contemplation, and gazes on the Catholic priesthood in its divine source:

"The Son of God laid the foundation of the Church, as in olden times Noah built the ark on the summit of the highest mountain. Into it, through the gate of faith, He introduces people and kings, princes of the earth, just men and sinners. He it was who, in the person of Abraham, consecrated obedience; and the Word having made Himself flesh, submitted Himself to obedience unto death. In the mystery of circumcision He typified baptism, by means of which the apostles, in the name of Holy Trinity, opened the gates of salvation, and overwhelmed the old enemy of mankind. A new generation came forth from these mystical waters, by the Spirit, to make amends for the barrenness of Eve; and then did Mary bring into the world a greater grace than Eve had lost.

"And the Word having become man, it pleased God to establish amongst men a hierarchy, corresponding to that of the angels—the bishops, the priests, and other orders of the Church being ordained to reproduce the divers degrees of angelic choirs;

and thus the people, regenerated according to the Spirit, received honor in the eyes of God. But in the end this same people forsook the way. They began to break the covenant with the Holy Spirit; they neglected to attend to His precepts, that they might follow their own way, and give themselves over to corruption of manners and doctrines, and yield themselves up anew to the dominion of their own passions. And from the midst of the light, I heard a voice saying to me, 'O daughter of Zion! thy children's crown of honor is obscured; it shall be taken away, and the overflowing mantle of their abundance shall be diminished. They have breasts, and they do not feed the lambs; they have throats, and they do not cry; they have hands, and they do not use them; they seek glory without merit, and merit without work. . . Let them beware lest they lose their liberty like Chanaan, who lost his blessing and became the slave of his brethren.'"

After having unveiled the schemes of Satan, regarding those men who do his works, the Saint predicts the terrible schism which has actually arisen in modern times, and reveals some of the most remarkable circumstances attending it:

"I Who Am that I Am, I say to those who listen to me—When these things shall come to pass, *a people blinded by error* and *more wicked even than those who are now going astray*, themselves deceivers, shall fall as a ruin upon the deceivers. They shall pursue you, without ever being weary, and shall bring all your iniquities into open daylight. They shall publish them aloud, and say of you, 'They are like scorpions in their lives, and reptiles in their deeds!' And, puffed up with a false zeal for the house of the Lord, they shall apply this imprecation to you: '*The way of the wicked shall perish.*' And yet these men, who, stirred up and seduced by the devil, shall thus act toward you, shall appear with pale, calm faces, and regular demeanor. They will make alliances with the princes of this world, and say to them, 'Why do you endure these impious men, who sully the earth with their crimes? They are given up to wine and licentiousness, and if you do not expel them from the Church, "her ruin is sealed."'"

"Now, the people who shall treat you thus will adopt a costume different and more rude than yours; they will cut their hair in another style, and appear before the eyes of men most holy and of irreproachable lives; for they are not misers; they heap not up treasure, but make profession of great austerity. And yet the devil is with them, concealing his poison as he did at the beginning of the world, when he occasioned the fall of Adam. By means of the spirits of the air the devil has communication with them; for the wickedness of men fills the air with this kind of spirits, which, like a plague of flies and gnats, swarm around the dwellings of the perverse."

Then the Saint points out the different forms of virtue which each of these seducers will assume. They will, at the instigation of the devil himself, practice disinterestedness, chastity, and other austere virtues. She then proceeds, carrying her prophetic glance still forward into the future:

"Those who at this time shall have become weak in faith, will be caught in the snare by this seeming piety. They will lend their servile aid to the attempts of the innovators, and will imitate them as much as possible. They will become attached to them, because they believe them to be just, and will join with them in persecuting those wiser men who persevere in the faith. Amongst these there will be very courageous soldiers; but congregations of pure life will not be seduced; for we shall see the accomplishment of the words of Elias, 'Many of the just shall be preserved'; and as they have not embraced these errors, their foundation shall not be torn up: as says the Lord, 'Iniquity shall be purged out by iniquity';. . .for it is needful that sorrow and contrition should purify the works of man; 'for it must needs be that scandals come; but, nevertheless, woe to that man by whom the scandal cometh.'

"Now, these seducers are not they of whom it is said that they shall follow Satan, when at the last day he shall rise even up to heaven, to make himself like to God, as he did at the beginning: *they will only be the bud, as it were, and the precursors of them.* But the Sun of Justice will arise at last, and better days will dawn for you. Past evils will make you more vigilant, and inspire you with the fear of God. You will shine anew like pure gold, you will strengthen yourselves in this blessed state, and you will be as firm as the angels who were confirmed in love by the fall of Lucifer. Now, then, O children of God, hear and understand what the Spirit says to you, that you lose not your inheritance. As for me, a poor and timid woman, I have been for two years vehemently urged to give you this warning; but, on account of the divisions in your Church, I have waited till this day."

The Saint seems, in these prophetic revelations, to unroll to the eyes of men the whole course of ages, until the final end of all things. She describes, in mysterious characters, the great changes of the past and the future which appeared at once before the eye of her soul; but the truths to which she most energetically calls the attention of Christians are those which bear relation to Antichrist, and the last days of the world. We will here quote some passages of those which are most remarkable, because it may do good to repeat them to an age which has but little thought of these things. The Saint thus begins: "There will come a time in which men, seduced by the son of perdition, will bring doubt upon the faith of the Church, and will say, with anxious heart—What must we believe about Jesus?

"Then the Catholic Faith will waver amongst the nations; the Gospel and the doctrine of salvation will be neglected; the relish for the Word of Life will be lost, and the ardor of love shall grow cold. O pastors! *I Who Am*, am about to reveal those things, which till now have been sealed up in Holy Scripture. For the time is appointed when the son of iniquity is to come. Strengthen yourselves and take courage, O all ye My elect, and keep guard against the snares of death. Keep close to the Divine Word, and follow His steps Who appeared on this earth, not with the pomp of gorgeous ostentation, but in the most profound humility. Hear and understand! Behold what the Spirit says to the Church concerning the time of the last error—'The son of perdition shall be thrown down, and hell will vomit its corruption upon earth, face to face, in the perdition of perdition.'

"But the head must not be without a body and without limbs. The head of the Church is the Son of God; the body and the limbs are the Church and her children. Now, the Church has not yet attained to the fulness of her stature. She will go on developing until the number of her children is fulfilled. 'Then,' says the Lord, 'I will dissolve its elements together with all that is mortal in the flesh of man . . . Already is the sixth number finished and the seventh begun; it is a time of rest.'. . .You, then, O men! who shall be alive at that time, you have got another period to pass through; and then will arise the homicide who will undertake to overturn the Catholic Faith."

St. Hildegarde here repeats the words of the Gospel, that no man can tell the moment when Antichrist shall make himself manifest to the world; the angels even know it not. But this manifestation will be, as it were, a parody of the Incarnation of the Divine Word. She goes on:

"Christ came neither at the beginning nor at the end of time. He came towards evening (*ad vesperas*), at least when the heat of the day was declining. What happened then? He opened the marrow of the law, and gave vent to the great floods of virtue. He restored to the world holy virginity in His own person, that the divine germ, impregnated by the Spirit, might take root in the heart of men. The homicide also will come suddenly; he will come at the hour of sunset, at the time when night succeeds day. O ye faithful, listen to this testimony, and preserve it in your memory as a safeguard, so that terror may not find you unprovided, nor the man of sin, taking you at unawares, drag you to perdition. Arm yourselves with the weapon of faith, and prepare yourselves for a fierce battle.

"The man of sin will be born of an impious woman, who, from her infancy, will have been initiated in profane sciences and all the artifices of the devil. She will live in the desert with men of perverse mind; and will give herself up to crimes with the more unbridled license, as believing herself authorized therein by communications from an angel. And thus, in the heat of burning concupiscence, she will conceive this son of perdition without knowing who is his father. She will then teach that fornication is permitted; she will give herself out to be a saint, and will be honored as a saint.

"But Lucifer, the old and cunning serpent, will fill the worthless fruit of her womb with his infernal breath, and will make himself entirely master of the fruit of sin; who, as soon as he shall have attained the age of manhood, will himself assume the office of master, and teach a false doctrine. Soon afterwards he will rise in insurrection against God and His saints; and will acquire so great power that, in his foolish pride, he would raise himself to the clouds, and, as in the beginning, Satan said, 'I shall be like unto the Most High,' and fell; so, in the last days he will fall, when he shall say, in the person of his son, 'I am the Saviour of the world.'

"He will make alliance with kings, princes, the rich and powerful men of the earth; he will condemn humility, and exalt every doctrine of pride. His magical art will simulate the most wonderful miracles; he will disturb the air; he will command the thunder and the tempests, and cause hail and horrid lightning; he will remove mountains, dry up rivers, and clothe with fresh verdure the barren trees of the forest. By his deeds he will exercise influence over all the elements, over dry land and water: but he will put forth his infernal power chiefly over men. He will seem to restore health, and take it away; he will drive away demons, and restore life to the dead. How shall this be? By sending some possessed soul into a corpse, there to remain a short time: but these sort of resurrections will be but of short duration.

"At the view of these things some will be overcome and believe in him; others, without giving him entire credence, will still hold to their primitive faith, whilst, at the same time, they will desire the favors of the man of perverse mind, or fear his displeasure. Thus many will be seduced amongst those who, keeping the eye of their soul closed, live habitually amidst externals; and men will say, in the general perplexity of the Church—Is the doctrine of Jesus true or false?

"At this time Enoch and Elias will appear. These two venerable men, extraordinary by their age and their stature, will bear testimony before the children of God, that the son of perdition, the minister of Satan, has come upon earth only to effect the perdition of men. They will traverse the places in which he has spread abroad his doctrines, and will perform miracles by the power of the Holy Spirit. The faithful will be strengthened, the faith revived; but the wicked will begin to tremble.*

---

* On the subject of Enoch and Elias we must remember that these two men were exempted from death. "Enoch walked with God, and was not, for God took him."

"But the man of sin will make one effort more; and, swollen with pride, he will attempt to raise himself above all things, that he may be adored. He will go up into a high mountain thence to ascend to heaven; but a clap of thunder will cast him down, and the Lord will destroy him with a breath of his mouth . . . As soon as the impious one shall be cast down, many erring souls will return to the truth, and men will make rapid progress in the way of holiness; and as David recalled his wife to whom he had been united, though stained with adultery, so the Son of Man will recall the synagogue, and make it enter into His grace.

"Then will the spouse of Christ arise strong and powerful with wonderful beauty, and her magnificence will shine with a cloudless brightness. All will acknowledge that the Lord alone is great. His name shall be made known by all creatures, and He will reign forever."

Here we will conclude this striking subject to the examination of which the Council of Treves devoted three months. A larger space than this volume affords would be required to give a more complete, adequate idea of it. The Sovereign Pontiff, after maturely examining the spirit of St. Hildegarde, wrote with his own hand these words of approbation: "Preserve," adds he, "and treasure up in your heart the grace which God has lavished upon you, and repeat not, but with the greatest prudence, what the Spirit suggests to you to say."

Hildegarde, supported by the apostolic authority, and more and more celebrated throughout the Church, continued her mysterious function of prophecy till the age of 82. The collection of her letters, at the head of which is that of the Pope, which we have just quoted, evinces the important relations which subsisted between her and the successors of Eugenius, Anastatius IV, Adrian IV, and Alexander III, as well as with the emperors, princes, and most eminent dignitaries of the Christian world.

---

—Genesis v. 24. "Elias went up to heaven in a whirlwind." —2 Kings ii. 11. The catechism of Montpelier shows, by a number of passages, quoted from Holy Scripture and the Fathers, that the conversion of the Jews will follow after the appearance of Enoch and Elias.

All received with fear and compunction of heart the words of the humble virgin. She died on September 17, 1179, the day on which the Church honors her memory.*

---

\* Papebroch relates that he had seen the body of this saint in good preservation in 1660, at the time that this precious relic was transferred from Mount St. Ruppert to the monastery of Eibengen, in the Rhingan. Her head was covered with a few locks of red hair turning to gray. In the same monastery is preserved the habit of the saint and a penknife, with a handle of jacinth, which St. Bernard had given her as a keepsake; and moreover, a very large volume of parchment, containing all her works.

# CHAPTER XLIII

VISIT OF POPE EUGENIUS III TO CLAIRVAUX—CHAPTER OF CITEAUX—GREAT CELEBRITY OF ST. BERNARD.

AFTER sitting for three months at Treves, the council being ended, Eugenius III returned to France and took the road to Clairvaux, still retaining St. Bernard with him. The great number of miracles which the servant of God performed all along his journey attracted such crowds of people to the presence of the Pontiff that he was one day nearly suffocated by it. It was with the greatest difficulty, reports the historian of Citeaux, that he extricated himself from the crowd; at length, after a slow and solemn journey, they reached Clairvaux, where the presence of Eugenius, amidst his ancient companions, caused as much edification as joy. It is thus that one of the contemporary chroniclers describes the event. He says: "After Eugenius had held the council, he visited Clairvaux, and displayed the glory of the Sovereign Pontiff to the eyes of the poor of Jesus Christ. All admired a profound humility in so exalted a station, and were astonished to see that on the summit of power he preserved with exactness the purity of the holy rule which he had adopted; so that humility being united to grandeur, it shone outwardly for the honor of the supreme dignity, without in any way diminishing the solidity of his interior virtue. He had, upon his flesh, a woolen shirt; he wore his cowl night and day; and whilst preserving the habit and interior dispositions of a religious, he appeared outwardly the Sovereign Pontiff, by the splendid ornaments he wore on his person. Thus," continues the narrator, "he did a very difficult thing, which is to represent, in one man, the life and behavior of two different persons. They carried embroidered pillows for him, and his bed was covered with rich counterpanes and elegant scarlet drapery; but, if you had lifted up these adornments, you would have found beneath a mattress of chopped straw and a woolen covering. Man sees the face and God discerns the heart; and this Pope tried to satisfy God and man. He spoke to the religious, not without shedding many tears and interrupting his discourse with sighs from the bottom of his heart. He exhorted, he consoled them, and he behaved towards them as a brother and companion, rather than a lord and master. But, as the large number of persons who accompanied him did not permit him to stay long with them, he bade them adieu and quitted them, but in the body alone; for his heart remained always in the midst of them."

On leaving Clairvaux, Eugenius went to Cluny, which was flourishing again under the hands of Peter the Venerable; he visited several other monasteries in Burgundy, and stayed at Citeaux, the mother Abbey of Clairvaux, to assist at the general chapter of the abbots of this order. He desired to take a part in their labors, not in his quality of head of the Church, "but as one of themselves, for the love he bore to Jesus Christ."

Citeaux, formerly a dark and impenetrable forest, in which a few poor religious expiated, by the macerations of penance, the luxurious lives led in some other monasteries, had become, since the vocation of St. Bernard, the metropolis of the monastic life for the whole Christian world. The convents of this order, now infinitely multiplied, had extended themselves to the extremities of Europe. It was in these mysterious abodes that the Spirit of God restored, as through the very functions, and according to the laws of natural life, the losses and backslidings which had taken place in the body of the Church. Here holiness, learning, sacred traditions, evangelical virtues, concentrated their rooms, filled with sap and life; whilst the exterior branches were withering upon the trees, and the spirit was daily withdrawing, more and more, from the lifeless forms. Rome herself was no longer to be found at Rome; she was renewing her youth in the desert; she was drawing from the hidden springs of monasticism that strength of which the papacy felt the need to reappear with fresh vigor, at the summit of human affairs, to guide the councils of kings and the progress of nations, to preside over the general civilization of the world.

The chapters of Citeaux revealed, also, the remarkable fact of a hierarchy, and a powerful organization, introduced into the vast development of the monastic life. The whole Church found itself surrounded by a living network, the threads of which were twisted around the mystic hearth of Citeaux. From this source, as from the depths of the heart, sprang forth the blood which was to restore the form and renew the whole body of the Church. It was under the immediate influence of this new spirit, and thanks to the imposing hierarchy which came forward to support the crumbling edifice of the secular clergy, that Catholic unity remained strong and unbroken, till the time when it was to be exposed to its trials.

To obtain an idea of the deep and living piety which the powerful Order of Citeaux nourished in its bosom, we must read the words which Pope Eugenius addressed to the abbots who composed the general chapter. We do not fear to weary our readers by quoting some passages well fitted to edify Christian piety. It was a year after his visit to Citeaux that Pope Eugenius addressed this letter to the chapter:

"We should have greatly desired, my very dear sons, to be able to assist again, in person, at your holy meeting; so that, being all united and bound together by one spirit, we might, also, in the same union, treat with each other of the means of improving in virtue and rendering ourselves worthy of that divine joy which the Holy Spirit sheds over souls. But being called by the order of Providence to guide the vessel of the Church amidst the ocean of the world, on which we are tossed by the waves and tempests which assail us on all sides, and the duties belonging to our state detaining us here, we are obliged to act contrary to our will, and have not the liberty of returning to you as we had desired; we can in no other way make ourselves present amongst you, but by means of our letters; or assist at your venerable assembly otherwise than by the inclination of our heart, and by the affection we bear to you; entreating and supplicating of you, in the name of charity, to unite yourselves in spirit with us, and implore for us the grace of the Almighty. For in the station in which we are placed, raised on the top of the mountain, beaten on all sides by impetuous winds, we yet hope to maintain ourselves, if we are assisted by your prayers. Never lose sight of the ancient fathers who founded your holy order; and consider how, after having quitted the world and despised all it had to offer, they left the dead to bury their dead, and retired into solitude to sit with Mary at the feet of Jesus Christ, there to receive the heavenly manna all the more abundantly as they were more distant from Egypt . . . The light and glory, which they shed on all sides, shone upon the whole body of the Church; and it was their words which filled the cruse of the widow of Sarepta with the little drop of oil which still remained therein. They, in fact, received the first fruits of the Spirit, and this divine oil which penetrated their souls has run down to us. For this cause is it that you must not degenerate from their virtues, that you may be in the branches what they were in the stem, and that having derived from them the seeds of life, you may bear the same fruit that they bore.

"You see in what manner they, who have allowed their lamps to go out, desire you to give them of your oil, and how ardently the children of the world, when they come to themselves, after grovelling like beasts in the mire, wish to put themselves under your guidance, and to be aided by your prayers. . . But as you have nothing which you have not received, preserve in yourselves a great sentiment of the goodness of God, and very low and humble ones of yourselves, that you may walk in the steps of Him who has commanded you to look upon yourselves as unprofitable servants after you have done all your duty. For if you have received the gift of tongues, the grace to heal diseases, the knowledge of things to come; if your words are full of unction; if they are more edifying and delightful than the most excellent odors; if the world respects and venerates you and runs after the odor of your perfumes; all these things are not of you, but the work of Him who said, 'My Father has not ceased from the beginning of the world to act in you and bring forth His grace in your souls.'"

We should have been glad to give, for the edification of our readers, the whole letter which St. Bernard wrote in answer, in the name of the chapter of Citeaux; but we can only quote the first few words: "The voice of the turtle was heard in our meeting, and our hearts were filled with consolation and joy. Truly the words which you addressed to us were pure, lively, wise, and all burning with that divine flame which consumes your heart; they breathe a spirit of life—an ardent spirit which thunders, which reproves, which inflames; it is the sign of the love which you bear to us—a jealous love, but of a jealousy according to God."

Oh, how well such a correspondence, at once so serious and so sweet, expresses the spirit of Christianity! It was at Citeaux that this evangelical spirit was kindled, and thence, as from a wide furnace, it spread its flames to warm the whole earth.*

Eugenius III on leaving Citeaux resumed the road to Rome, whilst St. Bernard returned to his cloister at Clairvaux. He was now at the height of his glory. Peter the Venerable, who wrote to him at this time, addresses him as the *firm and exalted pillar, not only of all religious orders, but of the whole earth*. Another holy man, the Archdeacon of Chalons, calls him the great arbiter of things divine and human, the master of Christians, the chariot of the Church and its guide. His contemporaries compare his celebrity to that of Solomon, whose face the whole world desired to behold. "It would be difficult to persuade oneself," says an ancient historian, "that the King of Israel could have so entirely gained the affection of the East by all his glory, as this holy abbot had obtained that of all the world by his humility; but, I may also add, that it is very difficult to find, in any history, a man so renowned and so generally beloved, in his own lifetime, from the rising to the setting of the sun, from the north to the south. For his reputation extended over the eastern Church and to Hibernia,

---

\* Citeaux offers, at the present time, but a melancholy spectacle. We visited this desert in the month of October, 1839, and this visit wrung our heart. Modern industry, more pitiless than the Vandals of past ages, has sought to drive from the place the slightest remembrance of the Cenobites, who civilized and sanctified it. Upon the ruins of the abbey rises a sugar manufactory of beet-root, which has since fallen into ruins; and a wretched playhouse supplies the place of the monks' library, perhaps even of their church! The cell of St. Bernard, which was still in existence twenty years ago, has also been sacrificed to the *utility* of a manufactory. They showed us its remains. A castle, or rather a villa, painted yellow, contrasted strangely with the tombstones and loose bones which we tread under our feet. We examined, with great care, old plans of the immense enclosure, which included more than 200 acres, without counting the fields, farms, the courtyards, and other dependencies of the monastery; but now it is not easy to recognize even the site—three villages have been constructed out of the remains.

where the sun sets; towards the south, and into the most distant provinces of Spain; towards the north, into the distant isles of Denmark and Sweden." He receives letters from all parts—on all sides they were sending him presents—all the world was asking his blessing; in which, like a fruitful vine, he extended his branches over the whole earth. Bernard was overwhelmed under the weight of this immense reputation, and was no longer able to dispatch all the business of all sorts which flowed into Clairvaux. To understand his wonderful activity, we must examine more than 500 letters of his which remain to us, and which, almost all, relate to affairs, either political or religious, in which he was obliged to concern himself. The nominations or deposition of bishops, the wants of all the churches, questions upon doctrine, quarrels between princes, the defence of the oppressed, the complaints of the people, the arbitration of property, the foundations of monasteries—in short, all sorts of cares, and the solution of every kind of difficulty, seemed to have been committed into the hands of this extraordinary man. He groaned at being thus overwhelmed, and complained of it to Eugenius. "Alas!" wrote he to him, "it is said that I am Pope, not you. They run to me from all parts, and oppress me with business"; and yet, he adds in another letter, "My health declines daily, and my strength diminishes more and more." The zealous servant of God spent the whole year 1149 at Clairvaux, consuming the remains of his precious life in the service of the Church; and yet, always regarding himself as a useless servant, as a poor sinner, *like an ant harnessed to a chariot.* He was then approaching his sixtieth year; and the weakness of his body, added to the celestial attraction which made him long and sigh after his heavenly country, gave him a presentiment of his approaching end. He desired, like St. Paul, the dissolution of his earthly tabernacle, that his union with Jesus Christ might be consummated.

But a great and last trial still awaited him. To make his immolation complete, it was required of him that he offer his honor as a holocaust; and that after having shed throughout the whole earth the blessings of heaven, he should reap, in return, like his divine Master, the contempt and ingratitude of men. At the very moment that his fame was shining most brilliantly, it was suddenly covered with a black cloud; and the great man, who was at once the idol of the people, the oracle of the Church, the arbiter of divine and human things, became, in the eyes of the world, an impostor and a false prophet. The unfortunate news from the Holy Land produced this sudden reverse in public opinion. The unexpected issue of the Crusade became known; and this terrible disaster fell with all its weight upon the Abbot of Clairvaux. It was he who had stirred up the holy war; he it was who had preached it, who had stood surety, as it were, for its success by wonders and miracles; it was he, therefore, who had ruined France and Germany, who had been the first cause of the destruction of the Christian armies. He was loudly accused of having betrayed the Church; and, in short, these rumors increasing daily, they applied to him the words which were spoken by the Jews against Moses: "He craftily brought them out of Egypt, that he might kill them in the desert with famine."*

This formidable murmuring of all Christendom did not disturb the interior peace of St. Bernard. His calm and serene conscience bore witness that, upon all these solemn occasions, he had never acted without the command of God and the Holy See. Into the hands of God, then, did he confidently commit the care of his person and his reputation; and we shall soon see what was his conduct amidst all the insults which he had to endure. But it was not the public scandal alone which weighed heavily on the heart of Bernard—this was only one part of the afflictions which were destined to purify his soul; other sufferings—more piercing wounds, more personal and burning woes—were mingled in his cup of bitterness. In imitation of the Man-God, in whose steps he had trodden from his infancy, he was to drink this chalice to the very dregs before his death.

---

* Exod. xxxii. 12

# CHAPTER XLIV

DISASTERS OF THE CRUSADE—SORROWS OF ST. BERNARD.

THE SAD tidings from the scene of war were but too true. The whole Western world was plunged in mourning, more especially France and Germany. Conrad had been the first victim of Greek duplicity. He had not been able, indeed, to maintain discipline in his army; and the countries which they traversed were forced to submit to every kind of insult and rapine. On this account, the Emperor of Constantinople trembled at his approach; and in order to get rid of the army more expeditiously, he urged them to cross the Bosphorus, and supplied them, under the outward show of faithful friendship, with all the means for effecting this passage. Conrad, notwithstanding previous agreements, had not waited the arrival of the King of France, to effect the junction of the two armies; he found himself entangled in the defiles of Cappadocia, where Comnenus had placed his ambuscades, when Louis VII arrived in his turn before the gates of Constantinople; for in that place a league was formed, in the councils of the Greek Emperor, against the holy enterprise, a thousand times more formidable than the Mussulman armies. The Greek historian, Nicetas, does justice on this occasion to the good faith and noble confidence of the French character, and hesitates not to condemn the cunning artifices which his countrymen, the Greeks, employed to weaken the courage of the Crusaders. But the latter were not long in discovering the dissimulation of their pretended allies; and amidst the sumptuous festivities offered them at Byzantium, they made the certain discovery that Manuel Comnenus, the worthy son-in-law of him who ruined the first Crusaders, was holding intercourse with the Turks, and revealing to them the plans of the Latins for the campaign. This treason excited just indignation in the French camp, and proposals were made to take possession of Constantinople. The Bishop of Langres supported this council with all the authority of his experienced* age. "Constantinople has been for a long time," said he, "the troublesome barrier between us and our eastern brethren. It would give us free access to Asia. The Greeks, you know, have allowed the sepulchre of Jesus Christ to fall into the hands of the infidels, as well as all the Christian cities of the East. Doubtless Constantinople itself will soon fall a prey to the Turks; and in her exceeding cowardice she will open the road on the West to these barbarians. The Emperors of Byzantium neither will defend their own states nor allow others to do so. They have always paralyzed the efforts of the Catholic warriors. Let us, then, hasten to prevent our own ruin by that of the traitors, and let us not leave behind us a city which seeks to ruin us."

Thus spoke the venerable Bishop of Langres; and under the ramparts of Constantinople, the French were not afraid to deliberate upon the fate of the Greek empire.

"To our sorrow," adds an ancient historian, "and to the sorrow of all Christians who remain faithful to the Apostle Peter, the advice of the Bishop of Langres was not listened to." Manuel Comnenus, that the French might not have time to change their resolution, hastened their departure as fast as possible by stirring up the spirit of emulation among them, by rumors of pretended victories gained by the Germans. But the army had hardly been transported to the Asiatic border of the Bosphorus when it learnt the bloody discomfiture of the Teutonic warriors. Frederic

---

\* Some philanthropic historians, amongst others M. de Sismondi, blame this advice with great vehemence as a *shameful treason* which would *have stained the honor of France*. It seems to us, on the contrary, that such a maneuver would have been a glory to France, and the safety of Constantinople. Perhaps M. Sismondi would have thought the same if he had not thought it a good opportunity to cast an ignominious epithet upon the advice given by a Catholic bishop; for it must be confessed that this melancholy sectarian spirit is but too often the moving spring of this learned historian's judgments.

Barbarossa, the nephew of the Emperor of Germany, came himself to the French camp with this astounding intelligence; and soon after, Conrad, covered with wounds and dragging along the wrecks of his almost destroyed army, came to join Louis VII, who received him with tears of compassion.

The two monarchs and their confederates renewed their oath to accompany each other into Palestine; but whilst Conrad went to Constantinople to recruit his strength, Louis pursued his march between mounts Ida and Olympus, and performed prodigies of valor on the borders of the Meander. The Crusaders crossed the river, under the eyes of the two armed bodies of Mussulmans, whom, as they emerged from the water, they attacked, sword in hand, and then formed their ranks on the borders of the stream. This was the first and the only glorious action during this formidable campaign. The pilgrims attributed it to a miraculous interposition, and believed themselves invincible. The chiefs were beguiled by presumption. Their disputes and want of regularity weakened all discipline; and before long, sickness, the effects of intemperance, began to mow down the soldiers of the cross. According to the accounts of historians, the misfortunes of the army principally arose from the dissolution of manners. The presence of women in the army enervated its powers; and such was the disorder of the camp that a captain, clothed in ridiculous finery, was seen commanding a numerous troop of Amazons. These excesses brought on others still more deplorable. Geoffrey de Rancogne, the head of the advanced guard, had received an order to occupy the crest of a mountain, to protect the march of the army across the difficult gorges of Western Phrygia. But, unfaithful to his mission, he went to encamp in a neighboring valley, and thus abandoned the army to a horrible massacre. "The day declined," relates the chronicle, "and our troops were swallowed up, one after another, in the gulf which lay between these immense rocks." The king himself was only extricated from this danger by dint of his valor and presence of mind. Separated from his knights and assailed by the Turks, he darted up the side of a rock and defended himself heroically with his bloody sword. He escaped by a miracle; and it was not till after many other misfortunes that he was able to reach Antioch, and rally the remains of his chivalry; but in that Christian city, given up to luxury and oriental manners, he discovered, with grief, the error he had committed in bringing his wife Eleanor with him. This deplorable episode to the Crusade is well-known, and the complicated disasters which it added to contemporary events.

Louis VII concealed, as long as it was possible, both the misfortunes of his army and his own dishonor; but at length the report reached Europe, and the impression it produced was deep and terrible. The minister Suger wrote to the monarch to entreat him to return without any delay to France. "As to the queen," said he, "I advise you not to evince towards her the displeasure she occasions you, till you have arrived in your own dominions, and are able to reflect upon it maturely." But the king still remained nearly a year in the Holy Land, seeking, together with Conrad, who had brought him some reinforcements, to repair the misfortunes of the campaign. He embarked, at length, in the month of July, 1149, and after a short stay at Rome, with Pope Eugenius, he landed on the coast of France. He returned with a few hundred knights; twenty-eight months previously, he had departed at the head of more than a hundred thousand men.

The return of the king confirmed all fears and renewed all sorrows. There was scarcely a family which had not some loss to deplore, and never were so many widows and orphans before seen in France. The lamentations were general; but instead of considering the faults which might have caused the fatal issue of the Crusade, public animadversion seized upon one man alone—upon him who had been the soul and mover of this great enterprise. In the first moment of stupor, even the most devoted friends of St. Bernard did not know what answer to make to these accusations, which seemed so well-founded; they beheld only the present evils; and even his miracles, which had appeared to authorize their zeal, became a subject of scandal. As to Bernard, he silently endured all the humiliations which were heaped upon him, adoring in the depths of his soul the incomprehensible judgments of God. He waited a whole year before he sent to the Pope a few words in his own defence; but during this time of sharp trial, how often must his soul have sighed over the ingratitude of men! It was one of his own disciples who struck the deepest blow.

Nicholas, a monk of Clairvaux—a man whom he had nourished with his words, and on whom he had lavished his affection—a man to whom he had confided his most intimate thoughts, his whole correspondence, and the care of his most important affairs, betrayed and compromised him in the eyes of the whole Church. Nicholas, according to the testimony of the annalist of Citeaux, was a young man, endowed with the rarest gifts of grace and nature; he was handsome, amiable, and active, with a penetrating understanding and brilliant and flowing eloquence. He had taken the Cistercian habit, and had been admitted at Clairvaux during the absence of St. Bernard. He very soon obtained the esteem of superiors; all admired him; all regarded him as one capable of great things; "*but*," says the chronicler, "*like the apostate angel, who ruined himself by the contemplation of his own charms, he appropriated to himself these gifts of God, to offer them in sacrifice to the idol which vanity had erected in his heart.*" The Abbot of Clairvaux took him for his secretary; and this employment, which brought him into relation with the most considerable personages of Christendom, swelled his pride and made him a traitor.

It was not until the year 1151 that, amidst the many other afflictions which tore his heart, Bernard discovered all the treachery of his perfidious secretary. He convicted him, in the presence of Peter the Venerable, of having made a false seal, and of having made use of it to write a number of letters in his name; of having recommended under this false title unworthy men to the Roman Court; and, in short, of having violated the most sacred laws of God and man. Nicholas, ashamed and silent, could not endure the presence of these two servants of God. He left them, like Judas, during the night, and retired to England; but, frustrated in his ambitious hopes and given over to the spirit of vengeance, he pursued his benefactor with the blackest inventions of calumny, and did his utmost to tarnish his reputation.

The great anxiety of St. Bernard was not to justify his insulted honor; he accepted this new feature of conformity with his divine Master; but he found considerable difficulty in redressing the difficulties which Nicholas had raised, and in neutralizing the fatal effects of so monstrous an abuse of confidence. Several prelates, abbots, and religious communities complained of having been injured by the Abbot of Clairvaux; and he did not know how to reply to so many grievances. He wrote to the Pope: "The monk

Nicholas has gone out from us; but he was not of us; he is gone, but has left behind him the frightful effects of the perversity of his heart. Besides books, gold, and silver, which he carried away with him, he was found in possession of three seals—his own, that of our prior, and a third which was mine. It was not the old seal, but one which I had made expressly to avoid frauds and mistakes. How shall I find out the infinite number of persons to whom he may have written unknown to me? How shall I be able to destroy all the impostures of this kind which he has sent to the Court of Rome? How shall I fully justify all those whom he has injured? I dare not defile my lips and your ears by the recital of all the crimes of which he has been guilty." Not content with this notice to the Pope, his anxiety induced him to write again, fearing that other false letters might be in circulation. "I am told," said he, "that there are many such letters addressed to the Court of Rome. To avoid all such things for the future, I have again changed my seal, and upon this which you see, I have had my figure and name engraved." The annalist of Citeaux, after having described with horror the conduct of the monk Nicholas, makes some serious reflections upon the fall of religious. "A terrible example," says he, "showing the necessity of humble and continual vigilance. The Church warns us that no man is secure; that no community, however holy it may be, is exempted from temptations and weaknesses; that the regularity of exterior practices does not always prove the uniformity of spirits and agreement of wills; in short, that holy places only sanctify a man in proportion as he himself aspires after holiness."

It would be difficult to relate, in this place, the incredible troubles which, at one and the same time, overwhelmed the holy Abbot of Clairvaux in this the latter end of his life. Everyone seemed to attack him with impunity; persons of all conditions, ecclesiastics, even prelates who had themselves been of Clairvaux, added to his sufferings, and believed they were doing some miraculous action in defaming this great man, so meek and so humble of heart; but they could never disturb his unchangeable serenity; and like the Apostle Paul, whose character and life seemed revived in his person, he showed himself faithful in all things, by great patience in "tribulations, in necessities, in distresses, in stripes, and in prisons; in seditions, in labors, in watchings, in fastings;

by chastity, by knowledge, by sweetness, by the Holy Ghost, by charity unfeigned, by the word of truth, by the power of God, by the armor of justice on the right hand and on the left, by honor and dishonor, by evil report and good report; as deceivers, and yet true; as unknown, and yet well-known; as dying, and behold we live; as chastised, and not killed; as sorrowful, yet always rejoicing; as needy, yet enriching many; as having nothing, and possessing all things."* These eminent qualities of the apostolic man never shone with a brighter lustre than in the time of his humiliation and sorrow. One of his biographers relates a characteristic anecdote on this subject. "A certain cleric," said he, "having come to Clairvaux, demanded in an imperious tone of St. Bernard, why he would not admit him into his community. 'What good is it,' said he, 'for you to recommend perfection in your books, when you will not afford it to those who are seeking for it?' adding, in an angry tone, 'If I had your books in my hands I would tear them to pieces.' 'I think,' replied the servant of God, 'that you have not read in any of those books that it is impossible for you to become perfect at home; for, if I recollect what I have said, it is a change of manners, and not a change of place, which I have advised in all my books.' On which, this man, transported with rage, struck him so rudely on the cheek that it grew red and swelled. Those who were present at this sacrilegious action, unable to contain their fury, were about to fall upon the wretched man; but the saint stopped them, and entreated them, in the name of Jesus Christ, not to touch him, but to let him depart without molestation." Another fact, and the last we shall relate, was more painful to the tender and delicate soul of St. Bernard; but, on this occasion, sin caused his charity to abound.

"Hugh, a simple monk of Clairvaux, had been called to Rome by Pope Eugenius III, who consecrated him Bishop of Ostia and invested him with the Roman purple. The new cardinal, in consequence of St. Bernard's refusal to send him a monk whom he had asked for, turned furiously against his spiritual father; *he abused him in private and in public, threatened him with violence, without even asking the reasons which had caused the refusal of Bernard.* When we consider," adds the annalist, "that the holy abbot saw

---

* 2 Cor. vi. 4.

himself thus treated by one of his own children, then a cardinal, and this for an affair in which he had no personal interest, we shall admire the unparalleled modesty which the servant of God evinced in the answer which he sent him, as follows:

"'Woe to the world because of scandals!* What, do I give you scandal? But how have I offended you? What scandal have I then given you? Who would believe it unless they were ignorant of the mutual affection in which we have hitherto lived? Sad and sudden change, which causes me the greatest pain. He who supported me once would now oppress me; he who defended me, now attacks and threatens me; he pours out maledictions and anathemas against me; he accuses me of prevarication and perfidy. Our first fathers were only condemned after they had been heard and duly convicted of the greatest crimes. You have treated me with less justice. I have been so much despised that I have not been considered worthy to be heard in my justification. I am condemned without being asked the reason of my conduct, without being called upon to repair the fault which I may have committed, without even being clearly informed of what crime I am accused, without having been granted the means of explanation or reply. Now, at least, let me pray you to have the goodness to hear me, and receive my excuse; if this be not sufficient, at least it is true and sincere.'"

After having represented the motives of his conduct, he finishes by these Christian words: "Behold what I have thought right to say in my defence. If I have acted with imprudence, you may reprove me, and even punish me; but I am certain that, in all cases, the just will reprove me with mercy and charity, and will not traduce me publicly with indignation and anger. As for the rest, I bless God for His having, before my death, deprived me of a consolation which was too sweet to me, and in which I felt, perhaps, too much pleasure—that of enjoying your favor and that of my Lord—that I might learn from my own experience to hope nothing from men."

---

* Matt. xviii. 7.

# CHAPTER XLV

### APOLOGY OF ST. BERNARD.

TIME, that great consoler of all human troubles, calmed by degrees the fierce storm which the disasters of the Crusade had raised, and at last permitted the voice of truth to be heard. The holy war had not, it is true, answered the expectations of men; its issue seemed to frustrate all hope, and to have belied the promises of God Himself. But the hand of Providence infallibly accomplishes its own work; it combines with the acts of human freewill; and from this combination results, in the end, the progress of civilization and the facts of history. These facts do not, indeed, show themselves immediately to the limited eye of reason; neither politics, nor national glory, nor military tactics derived immediate benefit from the holy expedition. But if, according to human views, no positive result can be discovered in other relations, the results to the eyes of faith were immense, and did not escape the observation of judicious minds, even in the time of St. Bernard. Even at that time, several writers, enlightened by the Spirit of God, acknowledged as a remarkable truth the grace which owed its birth to the blood of the Crusaders. This salutary grace was the purification of a great number of sinners by the voluntary acceptance of death. Death, blood, and sacrifice, fill up a large place in the chain of Christian mysteries, and must form a large part in our views of the things of this world as connected with eternity. Bernard had said this in his letter to the Germans: "Is it not a wonderful way of salvation which God opens to criminals," writes he, "when He offers to homicides, ravishers, adulterers, perjured men, and malefactors, whom the world rejects, the opportunity of dying for so holy a cause?" And these words were exactly accomplished. We will not here repeat what we have before observed; but we must remember the state of Christianity when it emerged from the barbarism of the tenth and eleventh centuries. Providence opposed the inundation of corrupt manners and false doctrines, two species of ramparts. On one side the new monastic orders—such as Citeaux, Fontevrault, Premontré, the Carthusians; on the other, the battlefield of the Holy Land—a career more vast and more accessible to the multitude, where the soldiers of the faith might offer their lives to expiate their crimes, and triumph over themselves by dying for Jesus Christ. Yes, assuredly, this manner of victory, though it may raise a smile in superficial minds, is not without glory before God, nor without fruit to man. These fruits distinguished the Crusade of St. Bernard. No doubt if these warriors had fought in obedience to him, according to the rules of Christian discipline, they would have been victorious over themselves, as well as over the enemies of God. Their passions interposed an obstacle to this double victory—they were overcome; but, in shedding their blood at the foot of the cross, in giving up their bodies to the Saracen scimitar, to the evils of war, to the torments of death, they saved the life of their souls, and procured for the Church another species of glory. We repeat this truth—Since the day when Christ, dying on the cross, illuminated the world with divine light, the Church has never developed, nor enlarged, nor spread herself, but by passing through the successive transformations of death. She never grows, nor advances, nor increases, but by this means; she is ever stripping herself to be clothed with new life, and humbling herself to be exalted.

Thus, at the beginning, her divine light seemed to be extinguished in the blood of the martyrs, and immediately afterwards we behold it again illuminating the whole earth. During the subsequent ages, she is all but overwhelmed by the irruptions of the barbarians; and again rises full of life to the surface of the wave, holding in her hand the olive, the symbol of peace. In the middle age she is about to be swallowed up in the East; but though conquered she remains mistress of the world, and victorious Mahometanism receives its death wound. In these latter times we have seen her trodden under the foot of her own children, and hell aroused against her, crying, Let us crush the wretch! She again arises, and again offers both light and salvation to the world. Such is the course of the Church; she has never come out of the way of the cross; in it she falls, and in it she rises again, as He did whose footprints she follows; and the end of this way is rest, and glory, and divine immortality.

These truths, of which profane history makes but little account, did not elude, as we have said, the pious meditations of some writers of the time of the Crusade. Those who replied to the slanderers of St. Bernard proclaimed these truths, when pointing out the unhappy cause of the misfortunes of the holy war.

We will give some interesting testimonies on this subject, gathered from one of the most ancient biographers of the Abbot of Clairvaux. Otho of Frisengen, an historian whose judgment is the less to be suspected as he tells of what he beheld with his own eyes, and frequently appears not even favorable to St. Bernard, expresses himself in these terms: "If we say that the holy abbot was inspired by the Spirit of God to animate us to this war, but that by our pride and licentiousness we have disregarded his salutary counsel, and that we have, therefore, reaped, as the harvest of our own disorders, the loss of goods and of men, by misery and the sword, we shall say nothing but what is conformable to reason, and justified by the examples of antiquity."

To this we may add the testimony of the Englishman, William of Newbridge, a conscientious writer, whom Mabillon calls "*vir bonae notae et fidei Scriptorem*"—"The emperor and the King of France" suffered from the perfidy of the Greek emperor, to whom our people had given offense by their excesses. We read in Scripture that a countless army of the people of God were infected by the crime of a single man; so that, being suddenly deprived of the divine protection, it lost its strength, and was struck with languor. And the Lord, having been consulted, replied that the people had been polluted by an anathema; and He said, 'Israel, the anathema is in the midst of thee! Thou shalt not triumph over thine enemies until the author of the crime shall be cut off.' Now, our army was so full of sins and vice, which violated, not the laws of arms only, but those of Christianity, that we have no reason to be astonished that the divine favor did not assist the enterprises of men so impure and corrupt. Our camp was not chaste, but filled with impurity. Many trusted in the multitude and power of the troops; and thus, resting with bold presumption on an arm of flesh, according to the language of Scripture, they did not recognize the power and the mercy of God, for whose cause alone, they, however, pretended that they had taken up arms."

Such confessions as these enlightened public opinion, and by degrees dissipated the clouds which had accumulated upon St. Bernard's head. The friends of the Abbot of Clairvaux, and, especially, some remarkably zealous preachers, consoled the afflicted people by the language of religion. "Those Christians," said they, "who were immolated in the East, for the Faith, were less to be pitied than such warriors as had escaped death, but who on their return home, had returned to their old iniquities, '*like the dogs which returned to their vomit.*'"They recalled to mind the advice of St. Bernard, and the "*miracles, more eloquent than words,*" by which the divine counsels had been promulgated—in short, they prevailed on Christians to weep over themselves rather than over the servant of God.

Amongst this species of consolation, which many excellent men thought it right to send to St. Bernard himself, we find a letter which, under an original form, breathes so lively a faith, and a candor and confidence so pious, that the reader will be glad to find it here. It is from John of Casa-Maria, an abbot of the Order of Citeaux, who relates to the Abbot of Clairvaux a vision which he had seen concerning the Crusade. "I am told," says he, "that you, my well-beloved father, are still grieving over this great affair—I mean the expedition to Jerusalem, which has not had the success which we desired. It is on this account that I take the liberty of humbly declaring to you what God put into my heart on the matter, when my mind was very much taken up with it; remembering that the Lord sometimes reveals to little ones those things which are hidden from the more eminent; and that Jethro, though a stranger, gave advice to Moses, who spoke face to face with God. I think, then, my very dear Father, that the Almighty has drawn much fruit from this Crusade, though not exactly in the manner which the Crusaders expected. If they had conducted themselves like Christians—that is, loyally and piously—in this war, the Saviour would have been present with them, and caused their arms to triumph; but, as they gave themselves up to all sorts of crimes, and as God, when He suggested the expedition, foresaw all the dangers into which they would fall, His providence made even these events to serve the designs of His mercy; and sent them such misfortunes and checks that, being purified by crosses, they might attain to the kingdom of heaven. Many of those who have returned from the expedition have confessed to me that they have beheld many men die rejoicing in their fate, fearing to fall back into their sins should they return to Europe. And, in order that you may feel no doubt of what I assert, I will confide to you, under the seal of confession, and as to my spiritual father, that the holy martyrs, John and Paul, the two patrons of our church, have, more than once, visited us; and having lately inquired of them what we ought to believe about the Crusades, they answered that many of the Christians who fell in the holy wars have been called to fill the places of the fallen angels. Know, also, that they spoke of you with the greatest respect and honor, and predicted your approaching end. Since, then, this enterprise has attained its end, though not according to the will of man, but of God, it becomes your wisdom to find your consolation in Him whose glory only you desire; for it was in His foresight of the salutary effects of this enterprise that He gave you the grace and power to put it into execution. May he vouchsafe now to crown your career happily; and grant to me the happiness of contemplating, with you, His Divine and Adorable Majesty in heaven."

The "*season of disgrace,*" as St. Bernard called this epoch of his life, began to grow brighter; and a visible reaction took place in favor of the Crusade. It was not till then that the saint addressed his "*Apology*" to the Pope, which he inserted in the second "Book of the Consideration." We will here quote some passages of it. "We," said he to the Pope, "announced peace, and there was no peace; we promised rest, and behold only trouble. Did we, then, act rashly, and of our own will? Did we not follow your commands, or, rather, those of God, in following yours?

"All the world knows that the judgments of God are true; but the late event is so deep an abyss, that we may well call those blessed who do not take scandal at it. But, yet, how shall human presumption dare to blame what it cannot understand? Let us call to mind the acts of Providence which have occurred in past times, that we may obtain some light on this matter . . . I speak only of a thing of which no one is ignorant, and yet no one is desirous of knowing, in these times; for the heart of man is so formed that it forgets, in time of need, certain truths, which it knows quite well when the need is not present. Moses, when he brought the people of God out of Egypt, promised them a better land; for, if he had not, would this people, who cared for nothing but earth, have followed him? He brought them out; but he did not bring them to the land which he had promised them; and yet, we cannot certainly attribute this sad and grievous event to the temerity of their leader. He did all things by the command of God, who foresaw everything, and confirmed the words of Moses by miracle." St. Bernard adds that as the sins of the tribes of Israel caused them to perish in the desert, so those of the Crusaders, who imitated them, were the cause also of their misfortunes. He next recalls what happened to the tribes of Israel, who, though they had fought by the command of God, were twice beaten by the tribe of Benjamin. "Now, how, I pray you," adds he, "would the Crusaders have treated me, if I had prevailed on them to return a second time to the battle? and if, after a second defeat, I had said to them again, 'Go back, a third time?'. . .And yet, this was actually the case of the Israelites; and it was not till the third time they obtained the victory."

The holy abbot declares that his personal justification sprang from the testimony of his conscience; and he concludes with these words: "As for myself, I am little concerned at being condemned by those who call good evil, and evil good; who take light for darkness, and darkness for light. And if needs be that one of two things should happen, I would rather that men should murmur against me than against God. . . I willingly endure the words of slander and the blasphemies of impiety, provided they are directed against me, and not against God. It is an exceeding honor for me to be, in some degree, united to Jesus Christ, when He said, the '*assaults of those who have insulted thee have fallen upon me.*'"

And thus it was that the catastrophe of the Crusade did not overwhelm the holy Abbot of Clairvaux. He never doubted the truth of his mission; and the principle of the holy wars remained pure and sacred, notwithstanding the disasters which obscured their glory; and, besides, it must be confessed that the extermination of the largest portion of the Crusaders served not only for the salvation of many, as was remarked by John of Casa-Maria; it was felt also in another sphere, especially in Germany, where the disappearance of so many warlike men and turbulent princes greatly contributed to maintain peace, or, at least, to stifle bloody quarrels. The celebrated dissensions between the Guelphs and the Ghibellines were almost extinguished by the consequences of the Crusades; and historians agree in attributing this result to the death of the principal combatants.

Before we quit this subject, let us make one last observation upon this whole chain of events. It is a remarkable fact that the whole Christian army, which St. Bernard had called out, was divided into four branches. The two first, and the most formidable, which were the French and the Germans, traversed Europe and Asia in a most magnificent array; but, too confident in their own strength and faithless to the *God of Armies*, in whose name nevertheless they had taken up arms, they perished, and their very glory only served to render their defeat more striking. But two other armies, of whom history makes very little mention, set forth, without ostentation or commotion; and they accomplished great things. We have already spoken of the brilliant exploit performed on the banks of the Tagus. It was the Crusaders of England and the maritime countries of the north, led by an unknown chief, who, by their united and generous valor snatched Portugal from the hands of the Saracen and gave a new kingdom to Christendom. The Moors of Spain had been more than once conquered by the Cid and his valiant companions. Successively driven from the provinces which they occupied, they had entrenched themselves in the fortresses of Portugal, when Providence ordained that the fleet of the Crusaders should approach these coasts. They flew to the aid of their brethren in Spain, besieged and took Lisbon, made themselves masters of several other Mussulman towns, carried off their spoils, and established a Christian throne—first occupied by a Frenchman.*

---

* Alphonso of Burgundy, grandson of King Robert.

At the same time, other Crusaders, as little noticed by the world as these, turned their arms against the idolatrous people on the shores of the Baltic. These warriors, chiefly composed of Saxons and Danes, were distinguished by the peculiar form of the cross which they wore on their breasts. It surmounted a globe, an image of the earth, the universal symbol of Jesus Christ. It was thus that the idea of the holy wars was developed and carried out. In this last expedition the material results were but inconsiderable; but very important Scriptural conquests contributed to the extension of the Church. The Saxons treated their neighbors, the Sclavonians, as they had themselves been treated by Charlemagne. They attained a similar end; for, according to the reports of those historians who most strongly disapproved this enterprise, it was nevertheless on *this occasion that Christianity was first introduced into Pomerania and Russia.*

The Saxons were, indeed, only carrying out an idea which had been suggested by the Pope. Eugenius III, according to the annals of Baronius, had conceived a two-fold plan, which the Crusaders were to execute; one relating to the infidels of the East, the other to the idolaters of the northern countries of Europe. Was it on account of this negotiation that St. Bernard made his second journey to Germany? We have not found any positive document which would enable us to affirm it; but, considering the importance of that mission, and its coincidence with the Pope's arrival in France and the journey of St. Bernard, we have hazarded the conjecture; and, besides, if we reflect on the position of the Saxon princes with respect to the Emperor of Germany, we perceive the great influence which he must have exercised in the councils of these sovereigns, to induce each of them to raise a separate army and to fight on his own account. Religion alone had sufficient power to secure the success of such a plan. Now, the irresistible organ of religion, the mighty interpretation of the will of the Church, was St. Bernard. But the work of Providence was not terminated by the second Crusade. The strife between Christianity and Mahometanism—a strife in which the Crusades themselves were but one of the most memorable episodes—continued for many ages with more or less spirit, under other forms, until the day when the Mussulman power was broken against the valor of John Sobiesky, at the gates of Vienna. Since this day, the religion of Mahomet has not issued out of its territorial limits—it remains paralyzed, and is sinking rapidly into decay. Before the period of the holy wars, and during their continuance, Mahometanism was spreading on all sides, constantly invading the Christian world in Spain, Sicily, Africa, throughout all Asia; Catholicity dared to attack it in the heart of its empire, and remained master of the world. This was the final result of the Crusades, and is a sufficient apology for St. Bernard.

# CHAPTER XLVI

DEATH OF THE MOST ILLUSTRIOUS CONTEMPORARIES OF ST. BERNARD—HIS LAST ILLNESS—HIS LAST MIRACLE.

THE ERA of renovation which had begun with the twelfth century developed widely under the visible agency of Providence; but the men who had guided the Church and the State disappeared successively from the scene, and in less than two years, Christendom was deprived of the most eminent personages of the age. This funereal catalogue began in 1152, with the death of the Abbot Suger, and ended in the following year with the death of St. Bernard.

The faithful Suger, in his old age, took very much to heart the cause of the Crusades and interested himself on the subject with an ardor the more surprising, as he had before endeavored to dissuade the King of France from taking part in them. His biographer says that the soul of the Abbot of St. Denis was daily grieved to see no glorious results of this great pilgrimage. He feared much that, in consequence of the misfortunes of the expedition, the glory of the Christian name would be extinguished in the East, and that the holy places would be trodden underfoot by the infidels; he had likewise received letters from the King of Jerusalem and the Patriarch of Antioch which entreated him to bring them aid, because Raymond, the Prince of Antioch, was dead, and the city, unless promptly succored, was on the point of falling into the hands of the infidels. Emboldened by his zeal, he did not hesitate, in concert with the Abbot of Clairvaux, to excite to another Crusade; and the pious Louis VII, a worthy progenitor of

St. Louis, was ready to raise once more the standard of the cross. A meeting was held for this purpose at Laon, to consult on the method of delivering their brethren in the East; but the courage of both knights and clergy failed, and no result followed.

But still Suger, with a perseverance which was his characteristic, did not give up his design; and he resolved on nothing less than to raise troops in his own name, and march at their head to Jerusalem. His fortune was entirely consecrated to the preparations for this undertaking; "but," says the chronicler, "while he was thinking of his departure, and sighing for the holy warfare, he was seized with a low fever; his soul, still firm and vigorous, struggled for some time against the weakness of his frame; but he was not slow to perceive that the hour was come in which he was to resign his soul to God. Feeling himself, then, called to the heavenly Jerusalem, he selected from amongst the bravest knights of the kingdom a man of courage and experience, whom he caused to take an oath upon the cross, to repair in his place to the Jerusalem which is on earth; and he charged him to pay the soldiers with the treasure which he had sent beforehand to Palestine." When St. Bernard learned that his old friend was near his end, he wrote him the following letter: "Fear not, man of God, to despoil yourself of your earthly man, the weight of which incessantly draws you down to the earth, and attracts you towards the abyss. What have you in common with the earth—you who, on leaving this world, will be crowned with glory? You cannot, O man of God, return to your God until you have put off the clay in which you are enveloped, and have given back to the earth that which the earth had lent to you. I earnestly desire to behold you at this time, and to receive your blessing; but as none of us disposes of himself, I dare not promise you positively what I doubt whether I shall be able to perform; but I will endeavor to make that possible which is not so at present. However that may be, I beg you to believe that, having loved you so long, I shall never cease to love you. I do not lose you; I only send you before me to Our Lord; my soul will remain united to yours in an eternity of love. Remember me when you shall have arrived at that place to which you go before me, that God may grant me the grace soon to follow you, and enjoy the same happiness with you; and be convinced that, notwithstanding our separation, I shall always preserve the precious remembrance of you."

The Abbot Suger—the noble type of an incorruptible minister, and justly styled by his contemporaries the *father of his country*—expired, at the age of seventy years, the thirteenth of January, 1152. His death, like his life, was an act of perfect Christian abnegation. St. Bernard, to whom he owed his glory before God and man, made his eulogium in these few words: "If," writes he to Eugenius, "there be any precious vessel adorning the palace of the King of kings, it is without doubt the soul of the venerable Suger." The tomb which opened for this just man was not long before it received the remains of others not less illustrious. History mentions at the same time the death of Geoffrey Plantagenet, whose house had so glorious a destiny in England; also that of Thibault the Great, Count of Champagne, who, during a reign of fifty years, united, invariably, in his own person, military bravery to the most sublime Christian virtues; that of Ralph, Count of Vermandois, the inseparable companion in arms of Louis VII; and, lastly, of Conrad, Emperor of Germany, who was followed very soon afterwards to the grave by his young son, Henry, who had been crowned during the lifetime of his father. Germany and France long felt the consequences of these losses. Eighteen days after the death of Conrad, on March 4, 1152, his nephew, the Duke of Suabia, too well-known under the name of Frederic Barbarossa, assumed the imperial diadem and began his celebrated reign.

St. Bernard himself approached the end of his career. For a long time past, the servant of God had been detaching his mind, as much as possible, from all the cares of this world; *his conversation was in heaven*; and, amidst business and troubles of all kinds, he lived more than ever within himself, preparing for the great passage from death to life.

From the beginning of the fatal year, 1152, he experienced a return of his old maladies and suffered from long fainting-fits, presages of his approaching dissolution; but his mind, ever calm and vigorous, commanded his enfeebled limbs, and he was still able to use them within the monastery in the service of God. He exerted himself, notwithstanding his complete exhaustion, to celebrate the Holy Sacrifice daily; saying to those who aided and supported him at the altar that no act was more efficacious towards the last passage than to offer oneself as a holocaust, in union with the adorable Victim immolated for the salvation of man. His words, more rare but more penetrating than ever, breathed forth the sweet ardor which consumed his soul; and oftentimes, after celebrating the holy mysteries, so bright a fire from heaven encircled him that no one could approach him without feeling within himself a double portion of love and fervor. His brethren, his beloved children, sorrowfully compassionated his sufferings, and detained him with all the force of prayer and by every bond of tender love; day and night the whole community asked of God, with tears, the preservation of a father so dear to them. It appeared as if so many earnest supplications were granted, for the saint recovered some strength. But he called his large family around him, and with a touching and loving accent he entreated of them to let him die. "Why," said he to them, "would you keep here on earth so wretched a man? Your prayers have gained the victory over my desires; show me greater charity, I entreat you, and let me depart to God."

Notwithstanding the acute sufferings to which he was a victim, he wrote, with a trembling hand, to one of his dearest friends, the Abbot of Bonneval. This was his last letter; it must be read: "I have received," said he, "with much gratitude, the marks of affection which you have sent me; but nothing, henceforth, can give me pleasure. What joy can a man taste who is overwhelmed with suffering? I have no moment of respite, except when I go entirely without food. I can say, with Job, that sleep has departed from me, lest the insensibility of sleep should hinder me from feeling my sufferings. My stomach can no longer endure any food, and yet it causes me pain when I leave it altogether empty. My feet and my legs are swelled with dropsy; but, that I may conceal nothing from your heart, which interests itself in all that concerns me, I must confess, though, perhaps, somewhat imprudently, that amidst all these evils, my soul sinks not; the spirit is ready in a weak frame. Pray to Our Lord, who desires not the death of sinners, to keep me at my departure out of this world, and not to delay this departure; for it is time for me to die. Aid with your prayers a man devoid of all merit; that in this momentous hour the tempter may not triumph over me. In this, my extremity, I have yet desired to write to you with my own hand, to show you how much I love you, and that when you recognize my handwriting, you may also recognize my heart; but I should have been much better pleased to have spoken than to have written."

Bernard received, six weeks before his own death, the sorrowful news of that of Pope Eugenius. This holy Pontiff, after having governed the Universal Church, for the space of eight years and a half, with the prudence and firmness of an apostle, died peacefully on July 8, 1153. He had triumphed over the most implacable enemies of the Holy See, by weapons of meekness and love; and under his pontificate, agitated as it was by a violent crisis, both political and religious, the primacy of St. Peter reassumed its vivifying influence over the affairs of the world. The Cardinal Bishop of Ostia consoled the holy Abbot of Clairvaux by a letter, concluding in the following manner:

"We who knew this great Pontiff perfectly well are convinced that he has been raised to the third heaven, without, however, leaving us orphans; for he will intercede for us before that God who has called him to share His glory. Yet do you, who are the head of that body whence he was taken to be placed upon the Apostolic chair, cease not to entreat God for him, that He may grant him an entire remission of his sins, and augment his happiness and his crown in heaven." The annalist of Citeaux bears testimony that though Eugenius III has not been canonized according to the strict forms of the Church, yet he has not failed to be beatified and canonized by the unanimous consent of Christendom.

The unexpected death of this Pope, whom Bernard loved so deeply and so tenderly, tore his heart and forced his tears to flow. This loss seemed to have taken from him his last consolation, and every day he became more and more estranged from all things which were passing around him. Godefroy, Bishop of Langres, had come to see him about this time to consult him upon some important affair; he was surprised at the little attention which the servant of God paid to his words. He guessed his thoughts, and said to him, "Do not trouble me any more, I am no longer of this world"; and, in fact, he sought only to loosen the last threads which bound him to this earthly life. All the rays which darted from his soul were concentrated in God—his love and his delight; and he had reached, on the wings of pure desire, the joys of the immortal country.

But a miracle was destined to crown the life of this great servant of God. "He was lying on his bed of anguish," relates his contemporary biographer, "and *was completing manfully the course of his earthly life*, when the Archbishop of Treves came to Clairvaux, and threw himself at the feet of the saint, entreating and conjuring him to assist the province of Metz, in which most lamentable scenes were passing. The nobles and the commonalty, who had been for some time in open hostility, were carrying on a bloody war; and already more than 2,000 of the citizens had perished in the wars."

The Archbishop of Treves, in his quality of Metropolitan of the country of Metz, had proceeded, with the pious care of a good pastor, to separate the combatants and to prevent greater misfortunes. But they did not listen to his voice—they repulsed his mediation; and the prelate, deploring his inefficiency in this frightful conjuncture, saw but one resource; this was to call the Abbot of Clairvaux to the field of battle and to commit to his hands the pacification of these intractable spirits.

At the affecting recital of these troubles, which the archbishop interrupted with his tears, Bernard felt himself interiorly urged to reply with confidence to this appeal—his zeal was reanimated, his bones seemed endued with fresh energy; for, says the chronicler, "*God held his soul between His hands, and did with it as He pleased.*"

He arose from his bed and set off for Metz! The two armies were encamped on the two banks of the Moselle—on one side, the citizens, breathing nothing but hatred and fury; on the other, the nobles and their men of war, intoxicated with a first victory and ready to commence the attack. Suddenly the man of peace, supported by some venerable monks, presents himself in the midst of the combatants—he is feeble, he cannot make himself heard, he is not even listened to; but he passes from one camp to the other, seeking to calm their passions, without, humanly speaking, perceiving the least possibility of success. His presence in the camp has only the effect of suspending for a moment the shock of arms. But Bernard does not despair; he calms the anxiety of the monks who surround him, saying, "Do not fear; for, notwithstanding the difficulties which cross our path, you will see the restoration of order." In short, in *the middle of the night*, he received a deputation from the principal nobles, declaring that they would accept his mediation. In the morning he assembled the most considerable of both parties in a *little island upon the river*, whither came a crowd of boats bringing the chiefs of the various troops. Bernard heard all their griefs and appeased them; his words triumphed over all their wicked wills: the fighting men laid down their arms, and the kiss of peace passed throughout all the ranks!

A miraculous cure signalized this memorable journey. "There arrived," says a biographer, "*by the order of Providence*, a very poor woman, who had suffered for eight years a most acute disorder, and she presented herself to the servant of God and asked his blessing. This woman was constantly agitated by convulsive tremblings, the sight of which excited as much horror as pity. Bernard began to pray, and in an instant, before the eyes of a crowd of witnesses, the woman's agitations ceased and she was restored to perfect health.

"So striking a miracle produced a sensation which it is difficult to describe; all who were present, even the most hardened men, beat their breasts and declared the wonders of the power of God. This scene lasted for about half an hour, during which," adds the historian, "tears of admiration and gratitude flowed without ceasing."

But the man of God, surrounded by an immense concourse of people and pressed upon by the crowds who threw themselves at his feet, was in danger of losing, as once before in Germany, the slight remnant of life which still animated his frame. He was very near being suffocated, and the monks were obliged to carry him away; and putting him into a little boat, they darted off precipitately. The nobles and the magistrates followed to rejoin him. "We cannot fail," said they, "to hear favorably one who we see is so loved and heard by God; and we will attend to his advice, because God has, at his prayer, done such wonders before our eyes." But the saint would not receive their praises, answering them, "It is not for me, but for you, that God has done these things." St. Bernard then went to Metz, to the bishop's house, where, by his care, all the conditions of a solid and sincere peace were concluded and signed between the belligerent parties. This work was terminated!

And it was the last which you achieved in this world, O man of God! it was the last jewel with which the God of peace enriched your brilliant crown. You may say with the patriarch Simeon, "Now may Thy servant depart in peace."

As the mariner, on returning from a long voyage, lowers and folds up his sails when he sees the port in which he is about to cast anchor, so the blessed disciple of Jesus Christ, after having finished his course, returned humbly to his holy home at Clairvaux; and there, extending himself once more on his bed of suffering, as upon a precious cross, he lay tranquilly awaiting the hour of his deliverance.

# CHAPTER XLVII

DEATH OF ST. BERNARD.

LET US now enter into the silent cloister of Clairvaux and mingle amidst the dismayed disciples who surrounded the couch of their father, contemplating, with a holy fear, the last shining of that bright star, whose light only disappeared from the horizon of the world to rise more glorious and radiant in the land of spirits.
The gentle Bernard seemed like some ripe and perfect fruit bound to this earthly life by a slight thread, which the least motion might break. He had received the Sacraments and Last Unction of the Church; and, while awaiting his last hour, he was still lovingly employed in comforting his children. How shall we paint their grief? Standing around him, they looked on him anxiously, suffering in the depth of their souls, speaking without words, praying with tears, and still hoping against hope—such is the blindness of love! Filial tenderness cannot comprehend the possibility of certain separations; it shuts its eyes to the opened tomb of a mother or a father, as the mother over the cradle of her infant. It would seem as if hearts, entwined around each other by so pure an affection, can neither live nor die without each other. No reasoning, no consolation, not even the Christian Faith, has power to destroy this last illusion; so much is it founded upon eternal truth! The Apostles themselves were unable to preserve themselves therefrom; the still carnal and human affection which they bore to their divine Master blinded their minds, and they could never understand the announcement of His death. "We have ourselves experienced," writes one of the disciples of St. Bernard, "what the

Evangelist tells us of the blessed Apostles, who, when Our Lord predicted His Passion, knew not what He was saying, and did not understand His words; it is hard for the heart to believe that which occasions it such invincible horror." Thus did the monks of Clairvaux preserve, to the last moment, a vain hope which concealed from their minds the too real prospect before them of losing their father. But he, *touched with pity in the bottom of his soul*, did all he was able to soften their sorrow and strengthen their courage. *He warmed their hearts with the sweetest consolations*, and exhorted them to abandon themselves with confidence to the divine Goodness and to persevere in heavenly charity. He promised them that, even in leaving them, he would not depart from them, but would have a care for each of them after his death; and then, with a sweetness which no words can describe, he besought them earnestly to love one another, to advance in the holy path of Christian perfection, and to remain faithful to their vocation, in the fear and love of God. Then, addressing them with the spirit of an apostle, he said, with St. Paul, "My brethren, we beg and entreat you, in the name of our Lord Jesus Christ, that, as you have learned of us to live and to please God, you would continue so to walk, that you may advance more and more in holiness; for the will of God is that you should become saints.". . . 1 Thes. iv. 1, 3. Then he called to his bedside the Superior General of the Order of Citeaux, the venerable Abbot Gozevin, and several other abbots and prelates who had arrived at Clairvaux to pay their last duties to him. Gozevin melted into tears; for though, according to the monastic hierarchy, he was placed above St. Bernard, he loved him with filial love, and acknowledged him as his master and father. The Saint thanked them all, and, with a tremulous voice, bade them farewell . . . This scene broke the hearts of his children! "O tender father, O beloved father," cried they, with sobs, "will you then leave this monastery? Have you no pity upon us, your children, whom you have nourished at your own bosom, whom you have brought up and led like a tender father? What will become of the fruits of all your labors and anxieties? What will become of the children whom you have loved so well?" These piteous exclamations moved the maternal heart of the servant of God, and he wept. "I know not," said he, casting towards heaven a glance of angelic sweetness, "I know not to which I ought to yield—the love of my children, which urges me to stay here; or to the love of my God, which draws me to Him."

These were his last words. The tolling of the bells, accompanying the funeral chants intoned by 700 monks, interrupted the deep silence of the desert, announcing to the world the death of St. Bernard. It was on the twentieth of August, 1153, at about nine in the morning. The saint was 63 years of age; he had been for 40 years consecrated to Jesus Christ in the cloister, and for 38 he had exercised the office of abbot. He left behind him 700 monks at Clairvaux, and 160 monasteries, founded in different countries of Europe and Asia.

We shall not attempt to describe here the desolation, the groans of the pious cenobites, when they were deprived of such a father. Each one went to imprint a fond farewell kiss on that sweet, calm countenance, which neither suffering nor death could deprive of its heavenly smile. They gazed on high as if they could behold the soul of Bernard, under the form of a chaste dove, rising majestically towards heaven. "O Father, O chariot of Israel!" cried one of his disciples, overpowered at once by grief, reverence, admiration, and love, "O my Father, harbor for the shipwrecked, buckler of the oppressed, eyes to the blind, support of the tottering. You were, most tender Father, the model of perfection, the mirror of holiness, the type of all Christian virtue, the glory of Israel, the joy of Jerusalem, the wonder of the age, the ornament of the world, the fruitful olive, the abundant vine, the cedar of a thousand branches, the magnificent palm tree, the vessel of election, the vessel of honor in the house of God, the holy candlestick, adorned with pearls and precious stones; the high and immovable column of holy Church, the mighty trumpet of the mouth of God, the harmonious organ of the Holy Spirit! You delighted all pious souls, you supported the weak, you cast down the impious! Your step was humble, your countenance modest, your aspect full of grace . . . O happy saint, beloved of God and of men, whose life and whose death were precious before the Lord. He has passed all the tempests of this world, and has now reached the peaceful haven of the heavenly Jerusalem. He has passed from labor to rest, from hope to reward, from the promise to the crown, from faith to light, from pilgrimage to home, from time to eternity, from the world to God! Happy passage; and sorrowful exile to those who remain weeping in the desert."

Thus sighed these pious monks; thus did they pour forth their love and their sorrow. And he, also, who writes these lines, mingles his tears with those of these religious. What will become of him? He loses, in the conclusion of this work, the dear object which has employed his thoughts, consoled his leisure, and softened his griefs, through many a year of suffering. He has become habituated, by a voluntary illusion, to live with the saint, to follow him everywhere, to seek his delight in his words, to take pride in his writings, his merits, his triumphs, as if he had been one of his children, as if he had the happiness of being reckoned amongst his disciples! And now death, pitiless death, tears away his consolation, and forces him to lay down his pen. O holy and beloved Bernard, receive my farewell, and deign to bless this book, and him who wrote it. Alas, what have I done? Was it not a rash undertaking to write the history of your life? Have I not lessened the estimation of your merit, and tarnished your glory, by trying to describe your labors? I fear it much; for it is impossible to relate all the wonders which God shows forth in His saints; and I have fallen far short of the truth. Let the Truth himself, then, deign to make up for the insufficiency of this work, and produce in the soul of its readers one of those movements of grace which God wrought of old by the word and at the mere name of St. Bernard! May it reanimate in them the love and desire of heaven, the life of virtue, the holy joys of peace and piety, and, above all, charity—celestial charity—without which life has no consolation—without which we cannot be brothers, nor children of the same father! May we obtain these heavenly favors by the intercession of St. Bernard. I implore them for all those who shall read this book, and especially for those who, in their turn, are willing to say a prayer for the unworthy writer, and for those souls which are united with him in God.

"Now, these things happened," says the chronicler, "in the same year in which the blessed Pope Eugenius, who had been one of the children of St. Bernard, passed from this light—or, rather, passed from this darkness—into the true light; under the pontificate of his successor, Anastatius IV, head of the Roman Church; the illustrious Frederick, then filling the throne of the

German empire; the most pious king, Louis VII, son of Louise le Gros, reigning happily in France; Jesus Christ, the Son of God, holding the principality of the universal Church, and the sovereign monarchy of all creatures visible and invisible; the year of the incarnation, 1153."

To Him who lives and reigns with the Father and the Holy Spirit; to the King of ages, immortal, invisible, the only God, be honor, glory, and thanksgiving, world without end. Amen.

# About the Author

FR. MARIE THÉODORE RATISBONNE, 1802-1884

Fr. Ratisbonne was one of nine children of a family of Jewish bankers in Strasbourg. He was raised in luxury and educated at the Royal College of his native city. At the age of manhood, he was considered a leader among his people, who unanimously elected him to replace Samson Libermann when the latter converted to Catholicism in 1824. The conversion of Libermann and two other of his friends led him to study the Bible and the history of the Church. For two years he pondered as the work of grace went on within him, and he was baptized in 1826. He added to his name that of "Mary" and thus became "Marie Theodore Ratisbonne."

He entered the seminary, and received Holy Orders in 1830. First teacher at the Minor Seminary and vice-rector of the cathedral of Strasbourg, he worked in his native diocese until 1840, when he became vicar and assistant director of the Confraternity of Our Lady of Victories in Paris. It was while in this city, in 1842, that his brother Alphonse, a free-thinker animated with the greatest hatred against Christianity, was miraculously converted to Catholicism at Rome.

Stimulated by his brother Marie Alphonse, in 1843 Fr. Ratisbonne founded the Congregation of Our Lady of Zion for the Christian education of Jewish boys and girls, was appointed superior general, and opened Houses. Alphonse went on to be ordained a Jesuit priest.

Pope Gregory XVI decorated Fr. Ratisbonne a Knight of St. Sylvester, complimented him for his *Life and Times of St. Bernard*, and granted his request to labour for the conversion of the Jews. Pope Pius IX gave him many marks of his affection, and Pope Leo XIII appointed him Apostolic Prothonotary. At his death he received the last Sacraments from the Archbishop of Paris, and the final blessing from Pope Leo XIII.

His chief works are: *Essai sur l'Education Morale* (1828); *Histoire de Saint-Bernard - Life and Times of St. Bernard* (1841); *Méditations de Saint-Bernard sur le Présent et Futur* (1853); *Le*

*Manuel de la Mère Chrétienne* (1860); *Questions Juives* (1868); *Nouveau Manuel des Mères Chrétienne* (1870); *Le Pape* (1870); *Miettes Evangéliques* (1872); *Réponse aux Questions d'un Israélite de Notre Temps* (1878).

# Works of St. Bernard

Bernard's sermons:

*Sermones super Cantica Canticorum (Sermons on the Song of Songs).*
*Sermones per annum (Sermons on the Liturgical Year).*
*Sermones de diversis (Sermons on Different Topics).*

Bernard's works include:

*De gradibus humilitatis et superbiae (The steps of humility and pride).* c. 1120.
*Homilies on the Gospel 'Missus est'.* c. 1120.
*Apologia ad Guillelmum Sancti Theoderici Abbatem (Apology to William of St. Thierry).* In the defence of the Cistercians against the claims of the monks of Cluny.
*De conversione ad clericos sermo seu liber (On the conversion of clerics).* c. 1122. A book addressed to the young ecclesiastics of Paris.
*Liber ad milites templi de laude novae militiae (In praise of the new knighthood).* c.1129. Addressed to Hughes de Payns, first Grand Master and Prior of Jerusalem, this is a eulogy of the Knights Templar order, and an exhortation to the knights to conduct themselves with courage in their stations.
*De diligendo Dei (On loving God).* Outlines seven stages of ascent leading to union with God.
*De gratia et libero arbitrio (On grace and free choice).* c. 1128. The dogma of grace and free will is defended according to the principles of St Augustine.
*De praecepto et dispensatione libri (Book of precepts and dispensations).* c. 1144. Answers questions about which parts of the Rule of Saint Benedict an abbot can, or cannot, dispense.
*De consideratione (Considerations).* c. 1150. Addressed to Pope Eugene III.
*Liber De vita et rebus gestis Sancti Malachiae Hiberniae Episcopi (The life and death of Saint Malachy, bishop of Ireland).*
*De moribus et officio episcoporum.* A letter to Henri Sanglier, Archbishop of Sens on the duties of bishops.

547 letters survive.

Caritas Publishing brings you spiritual
riches of the Holy Roman Catholic Tradition
at the most affordable prices possible.
caritaspublishing.com

www.ingramcontent.com/pod-product-compliance
Lightning Source LLC
Chambersburg PA
CBHW021137080526
44588CB00008B/99